URBAN DYNAMICS IN BLACK AFRICA

URBAN DYNAMICS IN BLACK AFRICA

an interdisciplinary approach

William John Hanna
The City University of New York
Judith Lynne Hanna
Fordham University

ALDINE·ATHERTON
chicago — new york

ABOUT THE AUTHORS

WILLIAM JOHN HANNA, Professor of Political Science, Lehman College and Graduate Center, The City University of New York, received his Ph.D. in Political Science from the University of California, Los Angeles. JUDITH LYNNE HANNA received her M.A. in Political Science from Michigan State University and is currently Adjunct Professor of Social Sciences, Lincoln Center Campus, Fordham University. They have done extensive field work, written and co-authored numerous journal articles, and co-authored *Students and Politics in Black Africa* and *Leadership and Politics in Urban Africa.*

All photographs by William John Hanna

First published 1971 by
Aldine · Atherton, Inc.
529 South Wabash Avenue
Chicago, Illinois 60605

Library of Congress Catalog Number 73–149840
ISBN 202–24038–X

Printed in the United States of America

Acknowledgments

Credit for bringing this study to fruition should be widely shared. James Coleman first interested us in the politics of independent Black Africa. Several research trips to Africa provided us with necessary first-hand knowledge of Africa and Africans. The African Studies Centers at the University of California, Los Angeles, and Michigan State University, the National Science Foundation, and the Ford Foundation supported these trips. Work on this manuscript has in part been supported by The American University, Washington, D.C. (under whose auspices a preliminary draft was prepared), The Research Foundation of The City University of New York, and the Comparative Administration Group of the American Society for Public Administration. Many of our ideas were sharpened by collegial discussions at the University of Ibadan and Makerere University College. William Bascom, Doris Condit, Peter Duigan, Daniel McCall, Alvin Magid, Ralph Swisher, Immanuel Wallerstein, Aristide Zolberg, and the late Hortense Powdermaker read earlier versions of the manuscript; their comments were of considerable help in preparing the final draft. Vivian Zeitz contributed to the preparation of the manuscript in a variety of ways.

It is our hope that this book may in some small way repay the people of Africa for the hospitality and friendship they have shown us here and abroad. Our dedication, therefore, is to our friends in Ibaban, Umuahia, Mbale, and elsewhere in Africa who have made it all possible.

v

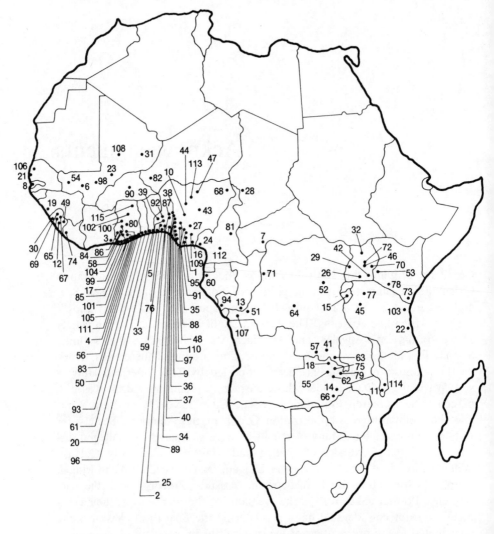

Urban Areas of Black Africa Referred to in This Study

1. Aba, Nigeria
2. Abeokuta, Nigeria
3. Abidjan, Ivory Coast
4. Accra, Ghana
5. Ado, Nigeria
6. Bamako, Mali
7. Bangui, Central African Republic
8. Bathurst, Gambia
9. Benin (City), Nigeria
10. Bida, Nigeria
11. Blantyre-Limbe, Malawi
12. Bo, Sierra Leone
13. Brazzaville, Congo
14. Broken Hill, Zambia
15. Bujumbura (Usumbura), Burundi
16. Calabar, Nigeria
17. Cape Coast, Ghana

18. Chingola, Zambia
19. Conakry, Guinea
20. Cotonou, Dahomey
21. Dakar, Senegal
22. Dar es Salaam, Tanzania
23. Djenne, Mali
24. Douala, Cameroon
25. Ede, Nigeria
    Ekuasi, Ghana (*see*
       Sekondi-Takoradi, Ghana)
26. Entebbe, Uganda
27. Enugu, Nigeria
28. Fort Lamy, Chad
29. Fort Portal, Uganda
30. Freetown, Sierra Leone
31. Goa, Mali
32. Gulu, Uganda

33. Ibadan, Nigeria
34. Ife, Nigeria
35. Ikere, Nigeria
36. Ilesha, Nigeria
37. Illa, Nigeria
38. Ilorin, Nigeria
39. Iseyin, Nigeria
40. Iwo, Nigeria
41. Jadotville, Congo (Kinshasa)
42. Jinja, Uganda
43. Jos, Nigeria
44. Kaduna, Nigeria
45. Kahama, Tanzania
46. Kampala, Uganda
47. Kano, Nigeria
48. Katsina, Nigeria
49. Kenema, Sierra Leone
50. Keta, Ghana
51. Kinshasa (Leopoldville), Congo
52. Kisangani (Stanleyville), Congo
    (Kinshasa)
53. Kisumu, Kenya
54. Kita, Mali
55. Kitwe, Zambia
56. Koforidua, Ghana
57. Kolwezi, Congo (Kinshasa)
58. Kumasi, Ghana
59. Lagos, Nigeria
60. Libreville, Gabon
61. Lome, Togo
62. Luanshya, Zambia
63. Lubumbashi (Elisabethville),
    Congo (Kinshasa)
64. Luluabourg, Congo (Kinshasa)
65. Lunsar, Sierra Leone
66. Lusaka, Zambia
67. Magburaka, Sierra Leone
68. Maiduguri, Nigeria
69. Makeni, Sierra Leone
70. Mbale, Uganda
71. Mbandaka (Coquilhatville),
    Congo (Kinshasa)
72. Mengo, Uganda
73. Mombasa, Kenya
74. Monrovia, Liberia

75. Mufulira, Zambia
76. Mushin, Nigeria
77. Mwanza, Tanzania
78. Nairobi, Kenya
79. Ndola, Zambia
80. New Juaben, Ghana
81. Ngaoundere, Cameroon
82. Niamey, Niger
    Nkontompo, Ghana (*see*
      Sekondi-Takoradi, Ghana)
83. Nsawam, Ghana
84. Nyakrom-Nkum, Ghana
85. Obuasi, Ghana
86. Oda-Swedru, Ghana
87. Ogbomosho, Nigeria
88. Onitsha, Nigeria
89. Oshogbo, Nigeria
90. Ouagadougou, Upper Volta
91. Owerri, Nigeria
92. Oyo, Nigeria
93. Palime, Togo
94. Pointe-Noire, Congo (Brazzaville)
95. Port Harcourt, Nigeria
96. Porto Novo, Dahomey
97. Sapele, Nigeria
98. Segou, Mali
99. Sekondi-Takoradi, Ghana
100. Sunyani, Ghana
10Γ. Swedru, Ghana
    Takoradi (*see* Sekondi-Takoradi,
      Ghana)
102. Tamale, Ghana
103. Tanga, Tanzania
104. Tarkwa-Abosso, Ghana
105. Tema, Ghana
106. Thies, Senegal
107. Thysville, Congo (Kinshasa)
108. Timbuctoo, Mali
109. Umuahia, Nigeria
110. Warri, Nigeria
111. Winneba, Ghana
112. Yaounde, Cameroon
113. Zaria, Nigeria
114. Zomba, Malawi
115. Zuarungu, Ghana

Contents

URBAN DYNAMICS IN BLACK AFRICA

Societal center, Kampala, Uganda

1

Introduction

Black Africa[1] initially came to the attention of most Americans in 1957, the year Britain's Gold Coast colony became the independent country of Ghana. This was the first independence achieved by a territory in Black Africa since freed Negroes declared Liberia's independence in 1847. Ghana provided momentum for the rush to nationhood, and within five years sovereignty had been transferred to more than a score of new states.

The United States first became deeply involved in African affairs as a result of the 1960 independence of Congo (Kinshasa) and the tragic events that soon befell the country. Recent developments, such as the unilateral declaration of independence (UDI) by Rhodesia's white minority government and the spate of coups d'état, civil wars, and other upheavals, have forced Americans to focus anew upon Black Africa. The challenges that these and other events have posed to social scientists have resulted during the 1960s in a considerable expansion of research on Africa in general and the urban areas of independent Black Africa (among other foci) in particular. What do we now know about African towns?

Importance of African Towns

Urban areas are of enormous political, social, economic, and cultural importance to the countries in which they are located, as well as to the international arena. Reissman's assertion applies generally to Black Africa:

1. The term Black Africa will be used herein to refer to independent countries in the area extending north to include Senegal, Chad, and Kenya, and south to include Congo (Kinshasa), Zambia, Malawi, Botswana, and Lesotho. We believe that using Black Africa as the geographic unit of analysis is a viable research strategy because of the area's marked similarities in colonial past, revolutionary change, and contemporary dynamics. In addition, there is virtually unity in race—although not all indigenous Africans are Negroid—and, at least according to some Africans, there is considerable cultural uniformity. (Arguments favoring this unit of analysis are elaborated in Hanna 1964a.)

1

"The study of the city perforce has become the study of contemporary society. The centers of decision and the triggers for social change are located in cities, and it is urban not rural societies that control the world's destiny" (1964:3). African towns, especially, contain the fuels of revolutionary change, and they are the forges of new national communities (Hanna and Hanna 1965b:1). In a sense, then, this entire study demonstrates the importance of towns in Black Africa. However, two dimensions—"importation and innovation" and "societal center"—call for special comment.

IMPORTATION AND INNOVATION

The urban areas of Black Africa are in contact politically, socially, economically, and culturally with the non-African world as well as with the rest of Africa. It is usually in the towns that the practices and perspectives of Britain, France, the Magreb, the United States, the Soviet Union, and other countries first penetrate, intermingle with indigenous counterparts, and create opportunities for change as well as crises of adjustment. The town "is a place where one generation may enter in blankets worn like togas and with torn and elongated earlobes, only to emerge in the next as Western-educated and Western-dressed civil servants" (Werlin 1963:7). This pattern was operative in the early years of European contact—most African towns are the offshoots of this contact—and it remains true in Black Africa today.

In Africa, as throughout the world, the urban area provides an environment that is generally favorable to innovation. Not only does the urban milieu appear to be essential for the development of some types of social organization (Sjoberg 1960b:15–16) and mobility (LaPiere 1965:394), but great advances in art and science are probably fostered by the kind of intensive interaction that takes place in urban areas (Kuznets 1963:115, n. 1). Lerner hypothesizes that this is the general pattern of development: "The secular evolution of a participant society appears to involve a regular sequence. . . . Urbanization comes first. . . . Cities produce the machine tools of modernization" (1958:60–61).

One visible arena for importation and innovation is the political. The idea of Western constitutional democracy was largely imported to African towns during the first half of the twentieth century with the result that it made an important contribution to the formation and direction of independence movements: the first nationalist party in Nigeria was established in Lagos; the major nationalist movements of Ghana were established in Cape Coast, Takoradi, and Accra; political groups in Congo (Kinshasa) were most deeply rooted in the towns and were led almost exclusively by townsmen (Bustin 1963:77); and the histories of virtually all other nationalist movements have been closely linked with major towns. In the post-independence period, most of the ideas for nation building, economic development, and even revolution have been born in the towns.

SOCIETAL CENTER

The towns of Africa are the epicenters of their societies—as indeed they must be if, as has been argued, the increase in societal scale that has been taking place "requires those concentrations of control centers and population we call cities" (Greer 1962:194). They are the centers of polity, society, economy, and culture, and the hubs of communication and transportation networks.[2] The towns of Africa "are not merely the focal points where the break with tradition may be seen most clearly, but also the centers in which a major restructuring of African society as a whole is taking place, a restructuring which is reaching deep into the countryside" (Gutkind 1962c:185). Thus the influences between town and countryside, although mutual, are not symmetrical. There are many dramatic statistics that can be cited to illustrate this centrality. We found, for example, that although the capital city of Ghana, Accra, has only 5 percent of the country's population, it is the residence of 45 percent of the country's men and women who have attended a university. And Hance reports that Dakar, which has only about 16 percent of Senegal's population, accounts for more than two-thirds of the country's commercial and manufacturing workers, over half the employees in transportation, administration, and other services, and approximately 95 percent of the country's electrical consumption (1970:209–210).

The urban impact upon an entire society operates in a variety of ways. To illustrate, town-dwellers often work to improve their rural home areas by supporting the construction of modern homes, schools, hospitals, and roads in them which are equivalent to those in the towns where they live. Villagers who return home from the town often introduce new perspectives and practices while criticizing some of the old ways. Political organizations formed in the towns have been exported to the countryside, as have the new symbols of citizenship and nationhood. In politics especially "the towns today give us an insight into the future. 'As the city is, so will the nation be'" (McCall 1955:160).

Of course, change also emanates from Africans who live in rural areas. In Sierra Leone, for instance, rural protests were so frequent and intense in the years following World War II that it is appropriate to talk about a peasant revolt. This revolt reached a high point of intensity in October 1950, when an estimated 5,000 rural and small town residents rioted and destroyed property worth the equivalent of approximately $2 million (Kilson 1966:60). Congo (Kinshasa) provides examples of the potential impact of rural protests upon both colonial (Weiss 1967:183–299) and independent African regimes. In general, "rural radicalism," writes Kilson, "is

---

2. "The movement to the cities," Nelson notes, "facilitates wider distribution of certain services, particularly schools and clinics" (1970:395).

such a potential source of instability in post-colonial African states that it warrants much more attention from social scientists than it has received" (Kilson, loc. cit.).

Urban Analysis

Scholars and policymakers now generally agree that there is an urgent need for analyses of urban dynamics in Black Africa. In 1956, Forde wrote of "the need for systematic study of the social conditions and trends among urbanized and industrialized African populations" (p. 13). Yet a decade later the Joint Committee on African Studies of the American Council of Learned Societies and the Social Science Research Council considered it necessary to sponsor a conference devoted to research on urban Africa in order to focus scholarly concern on this important subject matter (see Miner 1965b).

There are both scientific and policy (including humanitarian) justifications for studies of urban Africa. Scientifically, there is a knowledge gap concerning an important arena of human behavior, a "rare opportunity to study . . . cases of historical reiteration" (Reissman 1964:153) which may "shed light on the antecendent and consequences of urbanization in the West" (Hauser 1965:34), and a theoretical requirement to explore cross-cultural variation because "many propositions, once widely accepted as true, are coming to be recognized as excessively culture-bound" (Sjoberg 1960b:2). Unfortunately, previous research and analysis on urban areas in Africa and elsewhere have too often been atheoretical, noncomparative, and nonbehavioral. "Most persons who have studied African towns are provincial in the sense that they fail to take full advantage of either current developments in social science theory or the results of urban research in other parts of Africa and outside the continent" (Hanna 1966b:127).

Analyses are also needed by the African policymaker and administrator. Decisions must be based upon knowledge rather than myth or undisciplined generalization, and these decisions must be effectively implemented, so that some of the problems common to most urban areas around the world need not be repeated or magnified. There is already a large body of evidence demonstrating that failures in community development and other kinds of projects can often be traced to the planner's or administrator's ignorance of local sociopolitical structures and dynamics. For example, development of a new transportation grid without reference to the relevant patterns of social organization might cause unnecessary disruptions. A new bureaucracy formed or advised without reference to the relevant social setting and the backgrounds of prospective participants, as well as those in the community who must cooperate to ensure success, might result in low levels of efficiency or effectiveness. In general, "at a time when many communities are in the process of formation or rapid expansion, facing problems for the first time . . . it is particularly important that as much knowledge as possible be brought to bear in meeting these problems" (Coleman 1957:2).

Judging from our survey of the literature, a sufficient number of apparently valid reports and reliable data are now available to prepare a general analysis of the dynamics of African towns. "Though much of Africa remains *terra incognita* from the sociological viewpoint," Southall has written introducing a collection of studies on social change, "the results so far obtained require constant coordination if effort is not to be wasted. . . . The macroscopic picture has begun to emerge and it is already time to attempt an assessment" (1961b:1). The present study signifies our conviction that these observations now apply to the subject of urban Africa.

GENERALIZATION ABOUT URBAN AFRICA

In this study heavy reliance is placed upon general statements concerning Africa's urban dynamics. These statements are based upon a comprehensive survey of the Enlish and French literature on urban areas and urbanization in Black Africa and upon personal field observations in many urban areas of East and West Africa. The geographic scope of the localities about which information has been obtained is suggested by the map on pp. vi–vii, which identifies towns mentioned in the text or bibliography.

This approach is designed to maximize the usefulness of the analysis presented herein to an understanding of all urban areas in Black Africa or of any randomly selected one, whether or not specifically covered in the text. Obviously, comparable detailed information about every town could not be obtained. Therefore, the generalizations presented should be viewed as a series of working hypotheses.

While the emphasis here is upon general statements, it is of great importance to recognize that Black Africa's urban areas and the perspectives and practices of their inhabitants vary considerably and that the illustrations we present do not take the place of systematic tests of the working hypotheses. Because indigenous cultures and European interventions differed, the impact of contact was not uniform throughout the continent and did not lead to uniform urban processes or structures. Many observers of the African scene have emphasized this point. For example, Schwab comments that one must expect "a very wide range of variations both in the amount and the kind of disruption and in the adaptability of different social systems to the influences of urbanization" (1965:86). And Forde, while noting a number of common effects of the process of urbanization, warns that many factors have differential impacts upon the lives of town-dwellers (1956:14). Unfortunately, there are not enough sets of comparable data for extensive multivariant analyses.

THE URBAN AREA

What is an urban area?[3] One possible answer to this definitional question is to use meanings employed by indigenous peoples. Some Africans, for example, think of a town as any settlement, however small, in which a powerful and authoritative chief resides. Others think in terms of numbers of people in a relatively small area. The statistical offices of African governments have by no means settled upon a uniform specification of an urban area, although intranational uniformity is generally maintained. Because international comparability is lacking and the theoretical or policy significance of some definitions is uncertain, we take the view that criteria must be established by the researcher. It appears useful to establish at least three criteria of an urban area: population density, role density, and permanence.

The first criterion is that the population must be relatively dense within a relatively confined area. For some purposes, an arbitrary cutoff point of 2,500 inhabitants per square mile is used because many international statistics that distinguish between urban and rural areas employ it. However, it is not an adequate cutoff point if the object is to divide localities in which significantly different practices and perspectives are manifested. Although evidence demonstrating such differences is minimal, clues are available, perhaps the most impressive of which come from census data showing that the demographic characteristics of "towns" with less than approximately 10,000 population differ significantly from those with over 10,000. The 1960 census of Ghana presents such a contrast: most relatively small "towns" are characterized by an underrepresentation of working-age males, whereas most towns with populations of at least 10,000 display overrepresentation in this category. Based upon such clues, the use of "urban area" in this study is usually confined to localities with concentrated populations of 10,000 or more.

A second criterion concerns the number of social roles in which an average inhabitant is involved. In the simplest society imaginable, a person has one all-inclusive role. That is, he essentially behaves for and is sanctioned by one "audience" composed of his entire community. In urban areas, the individual usually has many more or less distinct roles (e.g., employee, father, and churchman) with distinct primary audiences (e.g., firm, family, and congregation). Of course, role overlap exists: deviant religious behavior may lead to job loss, deviant family behavior may lead to rejection by one's congregation, and so forth. With roles, as with population density, there is no obviously appropriate cutoff point to distinguish urban and nonurban areas. But as a working approximation it is useful to think

3. The terms urban area and town will be used interchangeably. When the intent is to denote a legal-geographic entity, such as a municipality or a township, this is explicitly done in the text.

of the average townsman as having at least several partially distinct roles.

A third component relates to the relative permanence of population and socioeconomic infrastructure. The purpose of this criterion is to highlight the importance of ecology and to distinguish towns from such transient communities as ships and training camps (which may fulfill the requirements of population and role density).

Using the three indicators specified above, numerous types of localities can be imagined. Although the focus of this book is upon only one of these, references are made to—and explicit and implicit contrasts are made with—the other types of localities. There are, of course, many ways by which towns themselves can be classified.[4] Although distinctions among types are sometimes made in this book, it should be emphasized that the primary effort here is directed to the identification of general processes and patterns that pertain to the large majority of Black Africa's towns, of whatever type.

URBANIZATION

The term urbanization has been used in a variety of ways in the scientific and policy literature. Variations are in terms of orientation, scope, and sphere. Orientation refers to the distinction between process over time and patterns at a point in time. In this study both orientations are employed.

Turning to scope, some scholars use the term urbanization quite broadly—as the equivalent of modernization, development, or Westernization. In this sense it subsumes several more specific processes of change. At other times, urbanization's meaning is specified so that its scope is narrow (although the substance of the narrow scope also varies, as will be indicated below). Some writers use the term urbanization in both ways (see Reissman 1964:169). The present work will employ it only in a narrow sense, retaining modernization to refer to the larger social change process.

A special aspect of the scope dimension is the occasional practice of coupling separable processes, especially "industrialization-urbanization" (see Lerner 1967). We demur on historical and conceptual grounds: these processes have not always been contemporaneous and they can easily be distinguished. Typologically, the distinction can be clarified by Table 1.1.

---

4. Harris developed a functional classification for urban areas in the United States which included the following types: manufacturing, retail, wholesale, transportation, mining, university, resort-retirement, and diversified (1943:86–99). Conferees discussing the role of cities in economic development and culture change concluded that there are at least four types of urban areas, the typology based on the attributes orthogenetic-heterogenetic and generative-parasitic (Berry 1962b:53). These types in part drive from Hoselitz's distinction between the generative city, which has a favorable impact upon economic growth, and the parasitic one, which has the opposite effect (1960:187–188). Of course, many other urban specialists have developed typologies of urban areas.

Of course, nowadays urbanization and industrialization *usually* occur together—the correlation between the rank orders of territorial urbanization and territorial industrialization among the less developed countries of the world is very high: 0.85 compared with 0.395 for the more developed countries (Sovani 1964:115)—but that does not mean that they must do so, in Africa or elsewhere. The emergence of towns in precolonial Africa and in Europe before the industrial revolution, as well as the current practice in some countries to locate industries far from urban centers, provide evidence of exceptions. The "normal" sequence is for the establishment of industry to be followed by the attraction of workers from rural areas, but it is also possible for a large urban area to develop without modern industry and then for industrial plants to be located in the area, since it is likely that a labor force will be available.

Table 1.1. Types of urbanizing/industrializing areas.

	Urbanizing Area	*Area Not Urbanizing*
Industrializing Area	modernizing area	industrializing rural area
Area Not Industrializing	preindustrial urbanizing area	preindustrial rural area

Commentators also employ the term urbanization to refer to a variety of specific spheres. In this study population urbanization concerns the process of territorial population concentration, both in terms of urban-rural ratios and, to use Tisdale's words, "the multiplication of points of concentration and the increase in size of individual concentrations" (1941–1942: 311). Personal urbanization concerns the changes that take place in an individual's perspectives and practices as a result of migration to and life in urban areas. The product is urbanism as a way of life.) Ecological urbanization concerns environmental products and processes; economic urbanization concerns market products and processes; social urbanization concerns social organizational products and processes; and political urbanization concerns products and processes in the political arena. Sections of this book focus upon each of the spheres of urbanization noted above. Thus, in a sense, urban dynamics are the processes and products of urbanization within various spheres of human behavior.

THEORETICAL PERSPECTIVE

Our objective in this book is to synthesize the relevant available knowledge on African towns and townsmen in mid-twentieth century. We have not attempted to construct a formal theoretical model of the many relationships that are identified,[5] although a theoretical perspective has guided us.

Chapter 2 is concerned primarily with the effects of external intervention and socioeconomic modernization upon the birth and development of Africa's new towns and the rapid expansion of its old ones. Chapter 3 explores urbanization at the level of the individual, especially his decision to migrate to town and remain there. Chapter 4 considers the impact of migration and town life upon these Africans, suggesting that severe problems might be created without the apparently functional living conditions and ethnic relationship that develop. Chapter 5 details the urban conditions that exist throughout Africa as well as their costs and benefits. Chapter 6 explores urban ethnicity, giving special attention to the bases for the remarkable staying power of this phenomenon. Chapter 7 describes the nonethnic perspectives and practices which appear to be becoming increasingly important throughout urban Africa, and it suggests how ethnic and nonethnic factors interact. Chapter 8 shows how contemporary political conflict in urban Africa is based upon both ethnic and nonethnic ties. Chapter 9 points out how these ethnic and nonethnic ties serve as the bases of a system of political integration unique to polyethnic communities. And Chapter 10 presents at a more abstract level a summarizing commentary on these and related patterns of change. The diagram on page 10 indicates some of the primary relationships referred to. (To indicate all the relationships involved, bidirectional arrows would have to be drawn between almost all the possible diads.)

Because of the considerable number of descriptions and statistical materials presented in this book, it is possible to lose track of the theoretical perspective. We think it important, however, to bear in mind theoretical linkages that establish the relevance of each chapter and section. For example, the urban conditions we describe are important to the social scientist because of their functional linkages with in-migrants and townsmen, the climate they provide for sustained ethnicity and eventually the emer-

5. Few formal models of urban-related change phenomena have been constructed. Perhaps the most important work in this area is reported in Forrester's *Urban Dynamics* (1969). His complex simulation incorporates variables and parameters related to such factors as birth rate, in- and out-migration, underemployment, housing construction and obsolescence, population density, family size, personnel needed for new, mature, and declining businesses, taxes levied, and taxes needed. The results of his work clearly demonstrate the utility of viewing the urban system as "a complex interlocking network of positive- and negative-feedback loops" (1969:121). To fully understand the urban areas of Black Africa or, indeed, any part of the world, dynamic models informed by systematic field research will probably have to be developed.

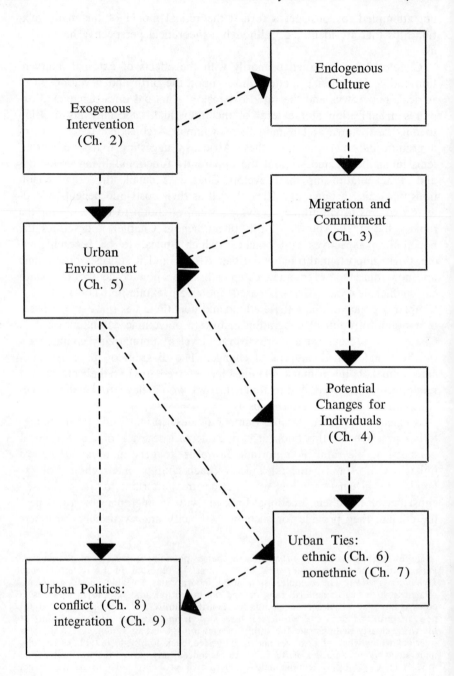

gence of class, and the environmental setting they constitute for contemporary urban politics.[6] We therefore urge our readers to think about the forest when they read about the trees.

6. Urban conditions are also of concern to the policymaker, who must understand the linkages if effective remedial action is to be taken.

Urban sprawl, Abeokuta, Nigeria

2

Patterns of Urban Growth

There were relatively few towns in Black Africa before its colonization by Europeans, although the often-heard statement that there were no towns in old Africa is far from true. The lack of urban growth was due to a complex set of factors. Some of the more important factors were the generally sparse population, the low level of technological development, and the many indigenous social organizations which did not require urban centers.

Precolonial urban development in Black Africa extended from Senegal through the western and central Sudan to the Lake Chad area, the Kongo Kingdom, and thence to the Indian Ocean. One of the highest degrees of precolonial urban development was among the Yoruba people of what is now southwestern Nigeria. Mid-nineteeth century estimates of Yoruba town size, made by early European visitors, placed the populations of Abeokuta and Ibadan at approximately 100,000, and fourteen other towns at 20,000 or more (Mabogunie 1968:91). The social systems of these premodern towns were in some respects similar to their modern counterparts. Schwab, for example, reports that Oshogbo had a semiautonomous legal system, institutionalized exchanges of agricultural surpluses for goods and services, and social differentiation based upon occupation, skill, and/or political position (1965:96).

Elsewhere, the Bini, who are distantly related to the Yoruba, developed the city of Benin, which, to an early European visitor, had many characteristics in common with Amsterdam of the same period. There are early reports by Arabs and (later) Europeans of such West African towns as Djenne, Kano, Segou, Gao, and Timbuctoo. Miner, who studied Timbuctoo in 1940, concluded that it had developed into a city independent of Europe's industrial revolution, capitalist economy, or democratic ethos (1965a:285). In central Africa, the capitals of such kingdoms as Kongo and Lunda were unquestionably towns. The ruins of Zimbabwe, in what is now Rhodesia, indicate the development of stone buildings of advanced construction and design, irrigation dams, a specialized division of labor, and trade across the Indian Ocean. Thus Thomas's remark about West Africa

13

has widespread, although not universal, applicability in Black Africa as a whole: "The historical and cultural tradition for urbanization, in at least a limited form, has existed for centuries" (1965:25).

The New Towns

The new urban phenomenon in Black Africa is of a different order. Greenberg correctly argues that postintervention urbanization differs quantitatively and qualitatively from its earlier counterpart, citing such contrasts as the size and number of the new towns as well as the new or radically changed functions they perform (1965:50).

It has only been since the coming of the Europeans—and especially since the scramble for African territory that followed the 1884–1885 Congress of Berlin—that new towns began to emerge and many old towns radically changed. The most visible cause of this emergence was economic, since many of the new towns were (and remain today) industrial-mining complexes linked to a European economy or entrepôts between the European metropole and African hinterlands. Thus, as McCall points out, the typical new town "did not grow out of the needs of, and in service to its own hinterland" (1955:152).

The single external event that probably most influenced the growth of African towns was World War II. Needs for strategic resources, bases, and local industries were created, and employment opportunities increased significantly. Urban in-migration was highly correlated with the industrial requirements of the imperial country. (See Commission for Technical Co-Operation in Africa South of the Sahara, Inter-African Labour Institute 1961:14.) The war's end had an especially profound impact upon urban growth. African soldiers who returned from overseas had developed consumption patterns that could most fully be satisfied in towns (the impact of these patterns was magnified because they were to some extent diffused to other Africans), and many European soldiers decided to seek their fortunes in an Africa that had become more visible to them because of wartime contacts and assignments.

The dramatic growth of urban Africa following World War II is illustrated by population changes over time. A case in point is Bamako; the total population and French population are shown in Figures 2.1 and 2.2. (Patterns of urban growth will be examined in greater detail later in this chapter.)

Modernization and Urban Geography

There is a clear relationship between (a) the spread of commerce, industry, mining, and services, and (b) the establishment and/or expansion of towns. The relationship exists whether or not a town's history predates

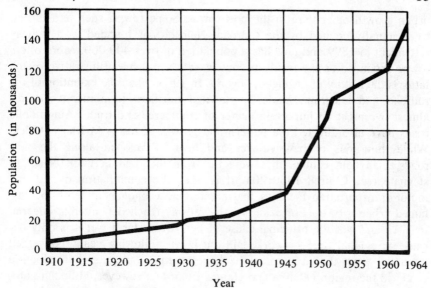

Figure 2.1. The Total Population of Bamako, 1910–1964. (Adapted from Villien-Rossi 1966:315.)

European intervention, because there has been a qualitative change in the before-and-after characters of most older towns.

COMMERCE

The first new African towns were located at ports, their function being the transshipment of goods and the safe housing of expatriate and indigenous traders (as well as those persons who facilitated their work). Among the better known port towns are Abidjan, Accra, Conakry, Dakar, Dar es Salaam, Douala, Freetown, Lagos, Libreville, Mombasa, Monrovia, and Port Harcourt. Indeed, of the Black African countries that have coastal land, only Congo (Brazzaville), Congo (Kinshasa), and Kenya do not have their major town on a coast. Furthermore, many of the noncoastal towns are inland ports, including Bamako, Brazzaville, Kinshasa, and Niamey. After pointing out the historical importance of African gold, ivory, and slave trade, as well as the strategic geographical importance of coastal cities in relation to territorial transportation networks, Hance writes: "When one notes the high proportion of the total money economy of tropical Africa that is accounted for by the export-import economy it is not so surprising that ports have so frequently become the leading cities in a country" (1960:135).

Construction of African railroads began just before the turn of the century, and by the middle 1930s most trunk lines had been completed. Almost all lines link prime export-producing areas with ports. Trackage is relatively short, e.g., 379 miles in Cameroon and 304 miles in Togo. The completion of railroads, added to stimuli from the outside world (especially during wartime), was responsible for the spread of commerce, and thus for urban growth other than in the port towns. Some towns, such as Nairobi, were actually created by the railroad. Nairobi was founded as a railway settlement in 1899 and now has a population of over 400,000. More often, towns expanded as the result of contact with a rail line. Illustrative of the latter is the history of Oshogbo, Nigeria. In 1905, when the extention of the railroad and telegraph made the town a northern terminus, it became almost overnight an important center of commerce and trade. Automobile roads have also affected the pattern and growth of towns in Black Africa. While thousands of new villages and towns developed along the new roads, many old centers that were far from the road network began to stagnate (see Church 1959:20). It is often the combination of rail and motor transportation facilities that creates the economic impetus for sustained urban growth. For example, the railway reached Umuahia, Nigeria, in 1913 and was the principal cause of that town's birth, yet it is only because a regional road network, laid out in the following years, converged upon the town that it became the largest cattle trading and distribution center in the region (Hanna and Hanna 1965:4). However, although automobile roads provide essential access and therefore make some trade and travel possible, their impact should not be overestimated. One can even question the use of the term road for some African routeways, where pedestrians have been known to overtake vehicles.

INDUSTRY AND MINES

Although many towns were founded in Africa and elsewhere before the local introduction of industry, sustained and rapid urban growth is usually

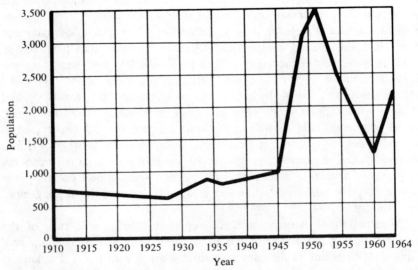

Figure 2.2. The French Population of Bamako, 1910–1964. (Adapted from Villien-Rossi 1966:326.)

linked with industrialization, including mining (see Chapter 1.) Wood and Galle are among those who argue that heavy industrialization is one of the main supportive processes of urbanization (1965:1). Industrialization in Black Africa was delayed both by relatively limited intercontinental contacts between Africa and Europe during the latter's industrial revolution and by the continental division of labor which crystallized after the intensification of contacts. Africa produced primary surpluses and developed the limited industry required for processing some primary products for export (e.g., extracting oil from groundnuts and palm nuts, sawing logs into boards, and smelting ore into ingots). Zambia provides a good example of urban development linked to resource exploitation: Chingola grew up around the Nchanga copper mine, Kitwe is at the site of the Nkana mine, Luanshya stems from the Roan Antelope copper mine, and Broken Hill is at the Broken Hill mine, to name only some of the prominent Zambian town-mine complexes.

Required labor for industries and mines was initially difficult to obtain because members of many African societies were relatively unresponsive to financial inducements. The Europeans' frequent solution was to impose a head tax upon Africans, the money for which often had to be obtained by migrating to an industrial or mining site, which was usually a nascent town. Those unable to pay the tax were sometimes forced to contribute an appropriate amount of work. According to Mitchell, early settlers in central Africa had the attitude that "the best way to make [an African] work was not to pamper him, but to tax him so that he would learn the dignity of labour" (1962c:200).

The creation of towns in response to industrial and mining requirements has not ceased with the transfer of sovereignty to African states. There are a number of projects, usually joint ventures of the state and a foreign government or private corporation, that form the basis of new towns. An example of this was the plan of the Ghanaian State Meat Products Corporation, in cooperation with the West German Ministry for Economic Development, to build a new $2.5 million township at Zuarungu in the northern region in order to staff and service a new meat products industry (see Fraternité-Matin 1966).

NONECONOMIC URBAN SERVICES

Although commerce and industry have had profound impacts upon urban growth in Black Africa, such activities as administration, education, and entertainment have also been important. These services are performed both for expatriates and for indigenes. Herskovits notes that many towns in Africa are so organized that they are compatible with the style of life to which Europeans were accustomed in their former homes (1962:263), and Berry refers to the towns as "rural service centers" offering crop-collection facilities, trade, water, sanitation, and schools (1962b:59). In either case, the services need staffing and their availability in towns attracts potential users.

The largest city in a territory usually contains the area's seat of government, whether it be a national capital or county headquarters. The government was somtimes sited in a previously established town, providing a catalyst for urban growth (see Denis 1958:77). For example, the British used the traditional Ashanti town of Kumasi as their main administrative center in northern Ghana. As a result, this town not only survived but also expanded and was given new functions. The other pattern is for a government station to be established first and a town to emerge as a result of the implantation. Examples include Entebbe, Kaduna, Lusaka, and Zomba. Such towns are usually located in areas that satisfy such expatriate needs as pleasant surroundings, short distances from commercial centers, and environments conducive to relatively good health. Whether a town preceded or followed the installation of an administrative center, administrative towns have grown rapidly. Hance points out that an important cause of the growth of some African towns has been "the increasing importance of the governmental force, Parkinson's Law being just as applicable to tropical Africa as to Europe or America" (1960:136).

Europeans established schools in Africa primarily to train the personnel needed to support European administrative and economic projects and to convert Africans to Christianity. Because European interests were best served in the nascent towns, they also became the sites of most schools, especially at the postprimary level. (With the dispersion of schools resulting from Africa's educational explosion, many primary schools are now located in rural areas, but postprimary schools are still predominately in urban areas.) The result of this pattern of school location is that Africans were drawn to towns and then acculturated to town life. Wallerstein writes of "the education system which, at the post-primary level, concentrated students in a few central institutions . . . and, at the university level, in Europe. For the prospective urban elite this 'migration' was very often longer in duration than that of a laborer, and more psychologically uprooting" (1965:151). The immediate and residual urban ties are, in a somewhat different way, also noted by Lux, who writes about the dual educational impact: direct because young people were attracted to towns and acquainted with urban life, and indirect because of the urban cash nexus in which their political earnings involve them (1958:828).

Even the young people educated in Africa's rural areas are most likely to migrate to towns. A survey in the Ashanti region of Ghana revealed that 95 percent of the boys who completed their primary educations left their home areas to work in mines and towns, and in Malawi another survey discovered a high correlation between years of education and percentage of cohorts who emigrate (Read 1955:74). Apparently, the perspectives obtained in school create aspirations that can best be realized in urban areas. (These dynamics will be further explored in Chapters 3 and 4.)

Quantitative Urban Growth

Concern with the pattern of an area's urbanization focuses attention upon three population statistics: the proportion living in urban areas, the total in urban areas, and the total in individual towns. The first statistic is a function of both the rural and urban population size. The second and third statistics are independent of total territorial populations. Thus Denis concludes from his study of urban areas in central Africa "that there is no correspondence between regional population density and urban development" (1958:48), citing as evidence that Rwanda and Burundi had a combined density of 75 inhabitants per square kilometer but were without a town of 20,000 or more population, whereas the Katanga in Congo (Kinshasa), with scarcely two inhabitants per square kilometer, includes such populous towns as Lubumbashi, Jadotville, and Kolwezi.

NATIONAL LEVEL

The population of the United States was 70 percent urban in 1960; i.e., about 130 million Americans lived in towns. Comparative figures from Black Africa are highly unreliable because of inaccurate census taking. (During colonial rule, many inhabitants disappeared at census time to avoid taxation or forced labor. Since independence, the political implications of population counts—e.g., the distribution of power and wealth—have introduced additional sources of unreliability. Nigeria, for example, was unable to conduct a successful census twice in the 1960s; in fact these failures contributed directly to the recent military coups d'état and the secession.) However, it is clear that less than 20 percent of the population of Black Africa—i.e., perhaps less than 30 million—lives in urban areas.

Useful comparative urban statistics on Africa have been compiled by the United Nations; they are relatively complete for urban areas with populations of 20,000 or more. (In the United States, approximately 51 percent of the population lives in such urban areas, and this accounts for 73 percent of the total urban population.) Table 2.1 presents the reported figures for 22 countries.

The percentage of Africans living in urban areas is rapidly increasing. Dramatic evidence is displayed by using a relatively early year as the base for comparison. Thus between 1900 and 1960, the number of Africans living in towns with populations of 100,000 or more increased from under one million to over ten million. In the United States during the same period the rise was only about two and one half times. (Although this comparison can be misleading because of the urban nature of American society, it emphasizes the rapid development of African towns in the twentieth century.) Some representative rates of growth in Africa are presented in Figure 2.3. Of course, the increases do not disguise the fact that, as Davis and Hertz put it, "the present towns and cities are still urban islands in a sea of rurality" (1954–1955:22).

Another aspect of the national-level analysis of urbanization patterns is the development of a "primate town"—i.e., the emergence of a town that has a considerably larger population than any other urban area in the country and that is predominant in the country's political, social, economic, and cultural spheres. Berry hypothesizes that there is a negative

Table 2.1. *Percentage of total population in urban areas. (Adapted from United Nations, Economic Commission for Africa 1965b:50-51; United Nations, Department of Economic and Social Affairs, Statistical Office 1966a:128–130, 140–142; and Hance 1970:228.)*

Country	Census Year	In Towns of 20,000 or More (percent)	In Towns of 100,000 or More (percent)
West Africa			
Senegal	1960	21.6	12.0
Ghana	1960	11.6	10.8
Nigeria	1952–53	11.4	8.9
Gambia	1958	7.7	0.0
Ivory Coast	1967	17.0	12.7
Dahomey	1965	11.3	5.1
Togo	1966	8.9	7.7
Guinea	1960	> 5.0	5.0
Upper Volta	1966	4.0	2.2
Mali	1965	6.2	3.6
Central Africa			
Congo (Brazzaville)	1950	>16.5	16.5
Congo (Kinshasa)	1959	9.1	5.9
Cameroon	1963–64	9.3	3.7
Central African Republic	1950	> 8.2	8.2
Burundi	1960	2.1	0.0
Chad	1962–63	6.2	3.2
Zambia	1960	16.8	6.9
East Africa			
Zanzibar and Pemba	1958	19.4	0.0
Kenya	1962	5.9	5.2
Somalia	1962	> 5.9	5.9
Tanganyika	1967	4.7	2.3
Uganda	1959	2.4	1.6

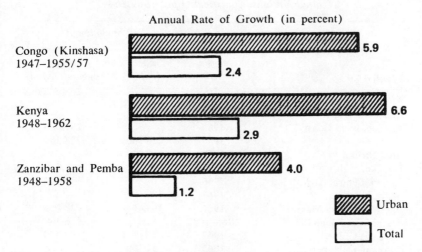

Figure 2.3. Urban and National Population Rates of Growth. (Adapted from United Nations Economic Commission for Africa 1965b:52.)

correlation between degree of urban primacy and both socioeconomic development and territorial size (1962a:12). East Africa provides two excellent examples of primacy: Dar es Salaam in Tanzania has a population of approximately 275,000, but the next largest towns are Tanga with about 40,000 and Mwanza with about 20,000; Kampala-Mengo in Uganda has approximately 120,000 inhabitants compared with next-ranking Jinja (approx. 20,000). East Africa also provides an exception: Kenya includes the towns of Nairobi (approx. 480,000) and Mombasa (approx. 200,000), although it should be noted that no other Kenyan town has a population of over 40,000. (On the costs and benefits of primacy, see Hauser 1963: 204–205.)

TOWN LEVEL

To portray the pattern of urbanization it is also necessary to focus on the absolute size and growth rate of individual towns. There are relatively few large cities in Black Africa: about 52 urban areas have populations of 100,000 or more. (The unreliability and noncomparability of demographic statistics make precise statements hazardous. For example, some countries report "city proper" populations, whereas others rely upon the "urban agglomeration.") The most urbanized country, Nigeria, has 24 of these urban areas (see Table 2.2). In comparison, Europe has about 300 urban areas with populations of 100,000 or more, Asia has about 350, and North America has about 214 (179 in the United States). However, the emergence of large cities is taking place more rapidly in Black Africa than in any other major world area.

Table 2.2. Urban areas with populations of 100,000 or more. (Adapted from United Nations, Statistical Office 1969:164–166.)

| | | Population | |
Urban Area	census year	within city limits	in entire urban agglomeration
Aba, Nigeria	1963	131,003	
Abeokuta, Nigeria	1963	187,292	
Abidjan, Ivory Coast	1964		282,000
Accra, Ghana	1968	615,800	758,300
Ado, Nigeria	1963	157,519	
Bamako, Mali	1967		175,000
Bangui, Central African Rep.	1966		150,000
Benin, Nigeria	1963	100,694	
Blantyre-Limbe, Malawi	1966	104,461	
Brazzaville, Congo (B)	1961–1962		136,200
Conakry, Guinea	1967		197,200
Cotonou, Dahomey	1965	111,100	
Dakar, Senegal	1961	374,700	374,700
Dar es Salaam, Tanzania	1967	272,821	
Douala, Cameroon	1965		200,000
Ede, Nigeria	1963	134,550	
Enugu, Nigeria	1963	138,457	
Fort Lamy, Chad	1964		100,000
Freetown, Sierra Leone	1968	163,000	
Ibadan, Nigeria	1963	627,379	
Ife, Nigeria	1963	130,050	
Ikere, Nigeria	1963	107,216	
Illa, Nigeria	1963	114,688	
Ilesha, Nigeria	1963	165,822	
Ilorin, Nigeria	1963	208,546	
Iwo, Nigeria	1963	158,583	
Jadotville, Congo (K)	1966	102,187	
Kaduna, Nigeria	1963	149,910	
Kampala, Uganda	1959	46,735	123,332
Kano, Nigeria	1963	295,432	
Kinshasa, Congo (K)	1967	901,520	
Kisangani, Congo (K)	1966	149,887	
Kitwe, Zambia	1966		146,000
Kumasi, Ghana	1968	281,600	340,200
Lagos, Nigeria	1963	665,246	
Lome, Togo	1968	90,600	134,800
Lubumbashi, Congo (K)	1966	233,145	
Luluabourg, Congo (K)	1966	140,897	
Lusaka, Zambia	1966		152,000
Maiduguri, Nigeria	1963	139,965	
Mombasa, Kenya	1968		234,000
Mushin, Nigeria	1963	145,976	
Nairobi, Kenya	1968		479,000
Ndola, Zambia	1966		108,000

Table 2.2. (Continued)

Urban Area	census year	Population within city limits	in entire urban agglomeration
Ogbomosho, Nigeria	1963	319,881	
Onitsha, Nigeria	1963	163,032	
Oshogbo, Nigeria	1963	208,966	
Oyo, Nigeria	1963	112,349	
Port Harcourt, Nigeria	1963	179,563	
Sekondi-Takoradi, Ghana	1968	128,200	209,400
Yaounde, Cameroon	1965	101,000	
Zaria, Nigeria	1963	106,170	

A report on the growth of a typical town illustrates these patterns. Douala, now the largest town in Cameroon, is located in the tropical rain forest along the Gulf of Guinea in the vicinity of what once was a cluster of villages. It was established in 1858 by missionaries, and its growth was catalyzed by traders in the years that followed. Gouellain argues that Douala owes its existence entirely to the fact that the estuary of the river became the center of a considerable trade in colonial products (1961:269). The town began to grow rapidly after the turn of the century, as a result of the health and sanitation programs of German administrators, and had a population of approximately 10,000 at the outset of World War I. (Cameroon was a German colony from 1884 to 1916.) When the Germans abandoned Douala during the war, these programs were terminated and the rapid growth of the town was interrupted. However, Cameroon was put under French trusteeship and new programs to improve the living conditions of Douala were instituted (LeVine 1964:49–58). Since the 1920s, the population of Douala has risen sharply and steadily, probably as the result of commercial expansion (Gouellian 1961:270). There were only 20,000 residents in the town in 1926, but current estimates place the population at near 200.000.

The growth patterns of Douala, as well as those of Dakar, Lagos, and Kinshasa, are shown in Figure 2.4. To provide additional perspective, Etherington's projections for Nairobi, as modified by recent population estimates, are presented in Figure 2.5. An equivalent projection has been developed at the national level for Ghana. Caldwell foresees that in the last 40 years of the twentieth century the urban population of Ghana is likely to increase tenfold while the rural population will only double. If so, there will be more townsmen than rural-dwellers by 1990 (1967:190).

Even if Africa's urban population surpasses its rural populace in number, it is important to note that the rate of urban population growth is certain to decline in many areas. There are at least two explanations for a flatten-

24 *Urban Dynamics in Black Africa*

ing of the growth curve (see Thomas 1970:4–7). First, there are simply not enough people in most African countries to support a continuing rapid urban growth rate. Abidjan, for example, grew from a town of 10,000 in 1929 to a major urban center now estimated at 400,000. If this rate were to continue during the next 40 years, Abidjan would have a population of 16 million—yet the entire Ivory Coast has a population of only 4 million and with its present rate of growth it will not reach 16 million by the time Abidjan would be projected to do so. In other words, the population curves of Abidjan and Ivory Coast would cross—an obvious absurdity.

Second, many of the historical causes of rapid urban growth are not likely to be repeated in the decades to come. For example, the founding and building of commercial, industrial, mining, and service infrastructures need not continue (and could not be sustained) at the pace of the recent past because of what has already been accomplished. In sum, the relative urban-rural shift is likely to decline in the decades to come. But the decline will probably not be accompanied by a lessening of the importance of

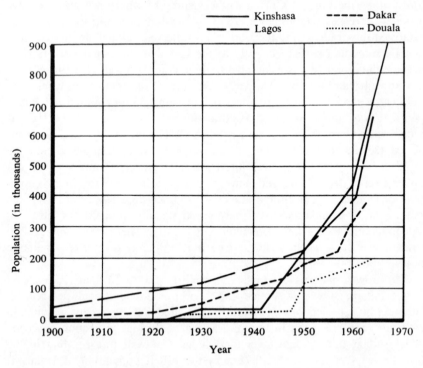

Figure 2.4. The Urban Population Explosion in Black Africa. [Adapted from Afrique occidentale française 1958:6 (Dakar); Economist Intelligence Unit Limited 1966:3 (Dakar and Douala); Le Vine 1964:52 (Douala); Mabogunje 1961:88, 93 (Lagos); Denis 1958:91–97 (Kinshasa); United Nations Department of Economic and Social Affairs, Statistical Office 1966a:140, 141 (all towns), and 1969:164–166.]

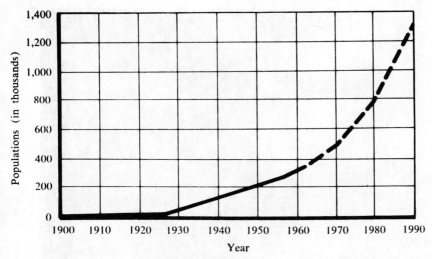

Figure 2.5. The Actual and Projected Growth of Nairobi. (Adapted from Etherington 1965:70.)

urban areas, because the absolute proportion of Africans living in urban areas will undoubtedly continue to increase.

In the following chapter we further explore why Africans are moving to towns. Succeeding chapters examine the impact of migration and urban life upon individual Africans and the societies of which they are a part.

Open air entertainment, Umnahia, Nigeria

3

Urban Migration
and Commitment

There are basically two ways an urban population can increase: naturally, as the result of a higher urban birth-to-death rate, and by net migration, when in-migration[1] exceeds out-migration. (Annexation and the qualitative change of a locality from rural to urban are two other ways.) Studies of the causes of urban growth in Black Africa indicate that net migration is probably still the predominant factor. There are, however, many African towns in which natural growth has already become the primary cause of population expansion, and the trend is clearly in this direction because the rural population supply is undergoing a relative decline, and there is an increasing number of women of childbearing age in towns. Denis's report on the trends for Kinshasa's causes of growth, presented in Figure 3.1, illustrates a general pattern.

Importance of Causes

An examination of the causes of in-migration and continued urban residence helps to provide an understanding of African townsmen's practices and perspectives, as well as the prevailing social forces in localities and their nation-states. To illustrate the former, we will show below that a principal cause of in-migration is the quest for economic betterment. This means that persons in prime wage-earning categories are most likely to migrate. And, indeed, the evidence clearly shows that the typical African town has a disproportionate number of men in the 20-45 age category. The imbalance means, in turn, that the social controls normally imposed by

1. "In-migration" refers to movement into an urban area.

27

elders and members of one's family will often not be operative. This leads
to the prediction that "deviant behavior" is more common in towns than
in rural areas, and to some extent the evidence supports this. (There are,
of course, other supportive explanations of urban deviance, e.g., many new
town-dwellers have tasted opposition to authority elsewhere.) However,
it is significant that deviance in towns is not extreme. Murder, rape, and
lesser acts of deviance do not prevail in urban Africa. This leads the analyst
to ask why and as a result to focus on new urban social controls and urban
conditions that minimize the disjunction between rural and urban life.

Knowledge of the causes of in-migration and continued urban residence
also facilitates an understanding of the larger political, social, economic,
and cultural systems of which the urban areas are a part. Greer displays
concern with a similar extrapolation by asking: "What is happening to a
society that makes possible, if not mandatory, this concentration of population?" (1962:33) In other words, the urban area can be a "dependent variable" in the sense that it is a product of the larger forces of a country's
polity, society, economy, and culture.

The relationship between urban areas and larger sociopolitical environments can also be viewed in terms of the impact of in-migration and town
life. The disruption of family life is one example of a "negative" impact.
However, in-migration and town life also have "positive" effects. Perhaps
the most important of these is their contribution to panethnic integra-

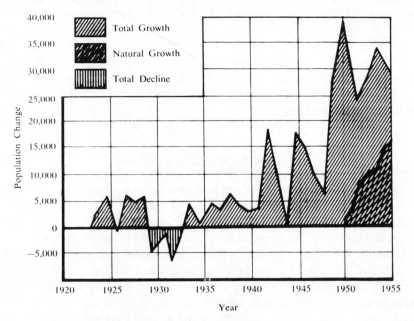

*Figure 3.1. Annual Population Changes in Kinshasa. (Adapted from Denis
1958:92.)*

tion—substituting for other forms of social revolution (Germani 1965:74–75)—since they serve to bring rural inhabitants from all parts of a country into contact with the centers of their new society. Scaff puts it this way: "The towns, and especially the national Capital, bring together the people of different tribal and language backgrounds and help to produce the more cosmopolitan relations necessary to support a modern nation" (1965:14). A "positive" economic function is also operative in that labor supply and management demand are brought into closer harmony by virtue of migration; thus migration patterns are indicators of the state of supply and demand. Balandier is among those who argue that the colonial economic system was not initially able to absorb those Africans disrupted from their traditional way of economic life, and that urban migration was the individual's attempt to cope with the maladjustment (1955c:40). Of course, such migration was for some rural-dwellers made possible only by the physical and psychological security established by Pax Britannica and its other colonial equivalents.

Types of Migration

There are various types of migration that can usefully be distinguished in attempting to delineate causes and effects. Here we differentiate (relying upon ideal types) between temporary and permanent migration, spontaneous and controlled migration, and directional and nondirectional migration. Since each differentiation is mutually exclusive, the combinations produce eight migration types (e. g., one of them would be temporary-spontaneous-directional). This typology is meant to be suggestive of the variety that exists.

TEMPORARY AND PERMANENT

Until fairly recently, the preponderant majority of migrants were temporary (although their temporary stay might last several years). This could largely be explained by the manifest and latent support for the migrant labor system which was given by many concerned: male African workers preferred the system because urban wages did not compensate for their wives' work in the subsistence economic sector (which a permanent move would sacrifice), urban welfare systems were not as well developed as those in the rural home areas, and a long-term urban commitment was not required; the employers were able to avoid the costs of housing, schooling, and otherwise providing for the worker's family; and the territory's government avoided the potential threat of a large and politicized urban population, as well as the responsibility for welfare in times of depression and unemployment (Byl 1966:171). For the poorly paid unskilled worker, temporary labor migration is efficient from the point of view of his village, which can maintain much of its traditional framework, and from the point of view of the individual, who can maximize the income of his household as a consuming unit (cf. Berg 1965:173–174).

As wages and demands for urban skills have increased, and welfare systems have improved, temporary labor migration has become less useful. Consequently, immigration (i.e., relatively permanent migration) is becoming more common in contemporary Africa. To illustate, the average monthly employee turnover rates of the East African Tobacco Company declined from 7.5 percent in 1954 to 3.8 percent in 1957 and to 0.7 percent in 1960. Equivalent reports come from all parts of Black Africa.

SPONTANEOUS AND CONTROLLED

It is useful to distinguish between spontaneous and controlled migration, although a particular act of migration may have elements of both. Most colonial regimes were opposed to spontaneous movement because it in-increased the difficulty of administering indigenous people, collecting taxes, and recruiting labor. This explains why many regimes attempted to control migration—often with success; coercion or encouragement would be used to increase migration, coercion or discouragement to decrease it. The effectiveness of one type of migration control is indicated by a United Nations report which refers to "the pressure of labour-recruiting agents, administrators and chiefs, which has been in the past, and still sometimes remains, an important factor in movement in the cities" (UNESCO 1957: 146). Indeed, recruiters still operate in various parts of Black Africa, although the obligatory nature of their appeals is minimal. The Syndicat Interprofessional pour l'Acheminement de la Main-d'Oeuvre, at least until recently, transported volunteer workers from Upper Volta to Ivory Coast and fed them until they obtained employment; after six months, their employer became responsible for providing a job or repatriation.

Although there were significant differences among the migration policies of the colonial regimes (see below), three policy stages were common to most African territories that are now independent states. In the first stage, European administrators encouraged in-migration through taxation and other devices to supply labor for subordinate jobs in nascent towns (then usually small administrative or trading centers). The second policy stage, encompassing most of the first half of the twentieth century, began when colonial administrators and businessmen came to believe that additional in-migration would "overcrowd" the towns; controls were introduced involving a variety of restrictive measures or inducements. The final pre-independence policy toward in-migration was to lift many restrictions in response to nationalist pressures and, later, African regimes of internal self-government.

Contrasts in the policies of colonial powers were greatest during the second stage. Migrations into the towns of French and British West Africa and into Dar es Salaam were relatively uncontrolled. By contrast, the administrators of British East and Central African territories maintained relatively complete control, viewing most of those in the towns as temporary residents. European control, but with the view that urban migrants should be stabilized in town, was found in the (Belgian) Congo, where the advantages of a permanent labor force were recognized. Herskovits refers to the preindependence contrast between the relative freedom of West Africans and the restrictions placed upon Africans in most of the other parts of the continent as "an essential point which differentiates the character of the migratory movements" in these areas (1962:276). (Greater population control is associated with extensive European settlement and industrial development.)

Beginning with the third stage of colonial policy toward in-migration, and then with the attainment of African independence, controlled in-migration to towns diminished while spontaneous movement has become predominant. One reason for the change is that Africans have become increasingly attracted to opportunities in urban areas: the highest paying jobs, best schools, liveliest dance bands, and an increasing number of relatives are in the towns. (The importance of relatives for potential African migrants parallels the situation confronting Europeans in a previous era with regard to immigration to America: rural inhabitants often follow their relatives to town so that an increase in townsmen leads to an increase in temporary and premanent in-migration.) Another reason is that independent African governments have hesitated on political, if not ideological, grounds to introduce controls against in-migration or to coerce citizens to move. It has been only in the last few years that African governments have turned their attention to the disruptive effects of uncontrolled in-migration and to the most politically feasible means of intervention. Such a return to colonial concerns parallels what Abernethy found in the field of education: "Once in power Nigerian leaders began to display something of the mentality of their former rulers. They could not dismiss as easily as before the British concern over the dangerous effects of rapid educational expansion because they were responsible as never before for the consequences of their own actions" (1965:520). Despite the increasing concern, it is still true today that when an African goes to town or decides to remain there, it is usually spontanous in the sense of being a personal or family choice.

DIRECTIONAL AND NONDIRECTIONAL

Because the causes of migration to urban areas are not randomly distributed among areas and peoples, a clear geographic pattern of migration emerges. Prothero reports that the most patterned migratory movements in Black Africa are in the western part of the continent. These are north to south movements, the main countries of origin being Mali, Upper Volta, and Niger, as well as the northern parts of Ghana and Nigeria. The destinations of these migrants include rural plantations (rural to rural migrations are not investigated in this book), the mining towns of Sierra Leone and Liberia, and such economically active towns as Abidjan, Accra, Dakar, Ibadan, Kano, Kumasi, and Lagos (1964a:204–206). The patterns of migration in eastern Africa are less well developed. In general, of course, there is a flow from poor to rich areas; this means from such areas as Malawi and western Tanzania to the mining towns of Katanga and the Copperbelt, and to the Witwatersrand of the Republic of South Africa. Figure 3.2 portrays the major movements of migrant labor in Africa.

The direction of an African rural-to-urban migrant is also determined by specific perceived opportunities. Jobs are sometimes contracted for before departure, especially when a recruiting agent is involved. Even when the migrant has no job at departure time, the distributions of his relatives may determine the specific direction. Thus, with equal economic development and job openings in several towns, an African is likely to go to the area where free room and board will be available and job contacts will be provided.

There is evidence to suggest that some embarking African migrants select paths of movement rather than specific urban destinations. This means that the first urban area that provides the opportunity for acceptable work, room, and board is likely to become the migrant's residence. Such a pattern indicates that differential opportunities, such as wage differences and number of resident relatives, are not always fully evaluated. Other Africans leave home with neither a specific destination nor direction in mind; however, these migrants appear to make up a small proportion of the total number.

Revolution of Values

Migration in Africa is not a new phoenomenon. Over the centuries, entire peoples migrated to more productive areas, and individual sojourns of various duration have been made to visit relatives, attend funerals, and so forth. The basic contrasts between precolonial and contemporary migration are that in the former fewer individuals (as opposed to entire peoples) were probably involved and rural-to-rural migration was proportionately greater.

In contemporary Black Africa, the basic spontaneous cause of in-migration has been the "revolution of values" brought about by the European presence, which introduced a new set of values and established an infrastructure (e.g., modern schools and industries) providing Africans with opportunities to obtain what was newly valued (e.g., education and wage-earning employment). This revolution has not involved a substitution of

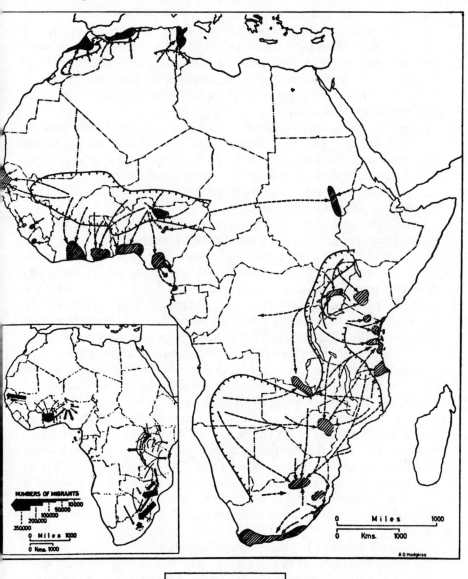

Figure 3.2. Major Movements of Migrant Labor in Africa.
(Adapted from Prothero 1964b:27.)

one value system for another, but only the addition or exchange or modi-fication of a relatively large number of specific values. Nor has it involved uniform change throughout Black Africa; local cultures and conditions obviously influence responses, as do the types of outside interventions and the personalities of individuals. For our purposes, the revolution has meant that *many* Africans incorporated new values that encouraged an urban presence—a rarity in old Africa.

Several stages can be distinguished in Africa's value revolution. Because European influence has been greatest, our description of stages focuses upon it. However, various other influences have been operative in the area termed independent Black Africa. The most important of these has been the Arab-Muslim impact, especially in Chad, Gambia, Guinea, Mali, Niger, Nigeria, Senegal, and Upper Volta.

During the first stage of the value revolution, individuals were the predominant agents of change. They included Europeans acting as general social and specific functional elites, and those Africans who had been in-ducted into the new Western culture. At least until the emergence of nationalist movements, many Africans believed that Europeans were all-powerful, and some thought they were all-knowing demigods with virtu-ally a divine right to rule. This was partly because Europeans were powerful, skilled, and so forth; it was also due in part to some Africans' transference of deference from their traditional leaders to Europeans.

Many Europeans were happy to encourage the demigod image; indeed, it can be argued that Africa attracted some Europeans because of the opportunity to be demigods surrounded by "primitive" indigenes. The expatriates soon became social elites who were imitated by Africans at-tempting to share some of the power, knowledge, and life style. (Europeans have also been functional elites in a variety of spheres, including public administration and industrial technology.) The selective questioning of European values and social elite roles has only developed over time and as yet has not affected a number of Africans. Such concepts as "the African personality" and *négritude* are relatively unfamiliar to many rank-and-file Africans.

Secondary agents of the value revolution, and thus of in-migration, have been those Africans who first came into intensive contact with European culture and were able to transmit it to others, or at least to make an attrac-tive representation of the content or benefits of that culture. These men range from members of the new African elite to returned soldiers to villagers who lived some time in a town.

The second stage of the value revolution is reached when the motivation to migrate is incorporated within the relevant sociocultural systems and therefore operates through the society's mechanisms of social control. Among the Mossi, for example, migration which initially began in response to European taxation has become institutionalized. "Labor migration has become so institutionalized among the Mossi that its characteristics are familiar to everyone, and there is a consensus as to why, how, and when certain persons should migrate" (Skinner 1965:66). And for the men of the West Niger Region of Upper Volta, going to Ghana has become a tradition. According to Rouch, all men expect to go there at least once in a lifetime (1956:194).

Concrete institutions perform increasingly important functions during the second stage of the value revolution. For example, schools in the most remote villages propagate new ("European") values. (Indeed, many teachers in Africa—and elsewhere—are propagandists more than educators in the sense that critical analyses of values are rare even at the secondary and postsecondary school levels.) In rural Ghana, Caldwell has shown, the level of educational attainment is highly correlated with the desire to migrate. Among men above the age of 20 who have no formal education, only 1 out of 17 who have never migrated are planning to do so; but fully one third of their secondary school educated cohorts are planning to migrate (see Table 3.1).

The media contacts of urban Africans have further contributed to the value revolution. As Figure 3.3 shows, approximately half the respondents in sample surveys of four African urban areas listened to the radio daily and one out of three read a newspaper every day. (Data are not available on the qualitative aspects of media exposure.)

As a result of the various change agents, many Africans now aspire, to borrow the phrase of Doob, "to become more civilized" (1960). The truly civilized man is perhaps rare on any continent, but the indicators of what many Africans consider to be civilized can be specified. They include using modern transportation (minimally a bicycle), telling time by modern methods (clocks and watches), obtaining a modern education (to provide at least functional literacy), and the like. Weissmann writes: "Growing masses of people everywhere are seeking the better life that modern sci-

Table 3.2. The effect of education upon men's migration plans.
(Adapted from Caldwell 1969:62.)

	Education			
Plans	*none (percent)*	*limited primary school (percent)*	*primary or middle school (percent)*	*secondary school (percent)*
Never migrated and have no plans to do so	94	89	81	68
Never migrated but plan to do so	6	11	19	32

ence and technology have made possible, industrialization and higher levels of living made probable, and which universal education and mass communication media helped to make an aspiration common to all mankind. In our time the city offers conditions for the fulfillment of these aspirations" (1965:65–66).

Weissmann's assertion is substantiated by date collected under the supervision of Free (1964:25,32). According to this researcher, 69 percent of his sample of Nigerians (urban and rural residents) expressed the personal aspiration of "improved or decent standard of living for self or family," "sufficient money to live better or to live decently," or "relief from poverty." This was the highest ranking aspiration, followed in order by welfare for their children (61 percent) and good health (47 percent).

New values affect patterns of migration in many ways. Our foci are (a) the quest for economic betterment, (b) the relative attraction of town life, and (c) the sojourn as status—all related to the value revolution. They are presented in what is probably the descending order of importance, judging from the few relevant research reports which are available (see Table 3.2 for comparative statistics based on studies of Brazzaville, Luluabourg, and urban and rural Ghana). We do not separately discuss the familial motive (e.g., a young man migrating to town to apprentice under his uncle) because it can be categorized in another way (e.g., apprenticeship for employment). It is worth noting, however, that having family members in town increases the rate of immigration. (The term *chain migration* has been used by demographers to indicate that an urban link is important to

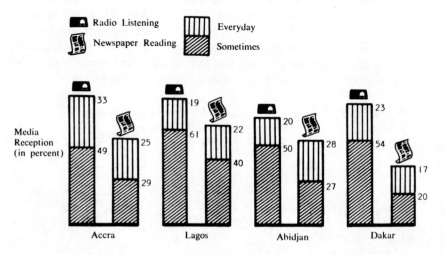

Figure 3.3. The Media Reception in Four African Towns. (Adapted from USIA 1961:13, 16.)

Table 3.3. Migration motives. (Adapted from Balandier 1952:26–27,
Lux 1958:692, and Caldwell 1969:89.)

Motive	Brazza-ville (percent)	Luluabourg from rural areas (percent)	from other towns (percent)	Ghana rural residents** (percent)	urban residents** (percent)
Economic (including employment requirements)	69	73	57	82	75
Relative attraction of town life	13	9	25	14	19
Status as sojourn	13	*	*	3	6
Other	5	18	18	0	1

*Included in "Other" for this column.
**Multiple responses were permitted. For comparability, the familial
motive was dropped and percentages were arbitrarily relativised to 100.

prospective migrants.) In rural Ghana, for example, having a household
member in town had a considerable affect upon the plans of men who had
not formerly migrated. Nine percent of those without household links to
a town were planning to migrate, but 20 percent of those with five or more
such links had plans to go to town[2] (Caldwell 1969:81).

It is important to emphasize that the decision to migrate to or remain in
town is based upon images of options, e.g., that in-migration will increase
wealth. This consideration is relevant in two ways. First, some townsmen
might materially be better off living in rural areas because regular meals
and comfortable sleeping space are usually available. In 1954, for example,
a Kenyan government committee established to study African wages concluded that unskilled married workers were far better off, according to
objective European criteria, in rural rather than urban areas. But whatever
the objective situation, the town has much relative *subjective* appeal. Banton argues that the migrant "prefers urban squalor to the more humdrum
life of the village" (1965:146). A similar view has been expressed by
Silvert, who reported in a 1965 lecture at Michigan State University that
in Latin America most migrants to urban areas think they are better off
than before their move regardless of the objective conditions that obtain.

Second, the image of urban areas may be more favorable than the
reality, since returnees must describe their experiences in positive terms

2. The intermediate percentages are as follows: one household townsman, 10 percent; two household townsmen, 16 percent; three household townsmen, 19 percent.

or be charged with failure. In West Africa, the countries along the Gulf of Guinea—especially the Ivory Coast and Ghana—became Eldorados where people went to find adventure and accumulate wealth (Commission for Technical Co-Operation in Africa South of the Sahara, Inter-African Labour Institute 1961:323), yet these adventures often result in un- or underemployment and residence in urban slums.

Thirty-seven percent of Caldwell's respondents in urban Ghana, when asked whether town life was "just like you thought it would be," did not think so. The explanations of approximately two thirds of the respondents in this subset were negative, e.g., unexpectedly overcrowded, few jobs, high cost of living (1969:121). Even so, most town-dwellers view their plight as temporary, since the obvious availability of money makes it appear likely that sooner or later they will succeed. (In Chapters 4 and 5, this situation will be examined in detail.)

Economic Betterment

One of the most widely reported findings from research on in-migration in Africa is that informants say the economic motive was predominant in their decision to come to a town. Leslie found that in Dar es Salaam "the primary object of the average immigrant African is to get cash" (1963: 104); migrants come to Ghana, according to Rouch, "to make money and take it home" (1956:140); the principal reasons for labor migration in Malawi, Mitchell reports, "were overwhelmingly economic" (1959a:22); and Balandier states that among those who migrate to Brazzaville, "economic motives are primary" (1952:26).

NEED FOR MONEY

Early research led to the conclusion that most Africans were "target workers"—that they came to town temporarily to make a specific amount of money or to achieve some other specific goal. That money accumulated, the migrant would return home. (This finding may have been biased by wishful thinking, for one of its implications is that the employer can keep wages low on the grounds that the higher the wages the sooner the employee departs—taking with him whatever skills he has acquired.) The realization that the target worker concept was not fully applicable to early wage labor or the contemporary scene has been demonstrated by Byl (1966) and others. Individual labor supply curves are in reality affected by a variety of factors; their patterns are slowly approaching Western-applicable forms as goals generalize and time of urban residence lengthens.

Some of the voluntary financial needs of Africans are new, such as investment capital, school fees, donations to the church, Western clothes, bicycles, and (for the elite) automobiles. A young man who was interviewed in Freetown probably had these in mind in stressing that "the foremost reason for coming to the towns was that the money was so easily obtained there and that so many fine things could be bought with it" (Banton 1957:57). Some voluntary needs represent modifications of old ones. For example, the socially specified subsistence level has been appreciably raised because of contacts with new (and prestigious) ways of life. The monetization of old requirements has also taken place in some areas; an example is bride-price, a practice common in many societies of Black Africa, designed to enhance family stability while compensating the bride's relatives for the loss of a productive worker. Other needs such as taxes have been imposed from outside. It is interesting to note in this regard that some Africans left their rural homes to obtain money for taxes, while others left to avoid paying taxes or to be taxed at lower urban rates.

Veblen's concept of conspicious consumption is useful for understanding the sometimes apparently exaggerated needs of townsmen. Some Africans "spend their incomes on articles which clearly demonstrate their 'European' way of life. First and foremost is the expenditure on clothing" (Mitchell 1956a:228). In remote villages under a tropical sun, one occasionally sees women dressed in heavy nineteenth-century styled European gowns which their relatives first saw on Europeans a half century or more ago. (Ironically, Europeans in the same area may be dressed in less formal and more modern clothes.) Prestige is sometimes based upon the ostentatious display of wealth, such as a large house, a watch that may not be read, and expensive clothes. "To make a big splash, to show that he has beaten the odds, has pitted his wits against the world and won, how better than to buy clothes, fine clothes, bright, unusual clothes, and wear them through the streets?" (Leslie 1963:110). These display objects, and the money to purchase them, often can be obtained only in a town. Items that can be purchased in the village are, by reason of their availability, often less prestigious.

RELATIVE RURAL DEPRIVATION

Agriculture is Africa's primary resource. Indeed, about seven out of ten working Africans are on the land, while another two are in such related rural activities as fishing and forestry; the remaining one in ten works in an urban area. Unfortunately, "in almost all countries, incomes in agriculture are lower than in other sectors of the economy" (Sovani 1964:119). The countryside is relatively underdeveloped because capital is concentrated in towns and manufacturing industries, and many young adults leave rural areas during their prime years of productivity and innovation.

Land productivity is closely linked to the probability of out-migration. Read's study of migration in six Malawi localities, for example, revealed a significant positive correlation between rural resource deprivation and out-migration (1942:617). Evidence from various parts of Black Africa supports the proposition that migration intensity reflects the degree of rural-urban disparity (cf. Prothero 1964a:204–206). A correlate is that the introduction of a cash crop tends to reduce out-migration and—temporarily—to stabilize the rural population. However, the crop may soon become a cause of disruption if new settlers move into the now-attractive area in significant numbers (cf. Colson 1960:63).

Rural overpopulation is a problem in some areas because mortality rates have dropped sharply, due to the introduction of public health practices, medicines, and sanitary controls. They have not, however, been accompanied either by a drop in fertility or by a sufficient increase in agricultural production. The "excess" population, sometimes faced with a nearly hopeless situation at home and a chance for improvement in relatively wealthy urban areas, is naturally motivated to migrate. It should be pointed out that such overpopulaton can exist in areas of varying population density, the crucial factor being how large a population the land can support given the existing resources.

Within a family, excess population may also be a factor contributing to out-migration. Among rural male Ghanaian respondents, the number of siblings (total and male only) was positively correlated with out-migration. For example, 63 percent of the males without a brother had never migrated and 13 percent were absent from their rural homes on a long-term basis. Comparable figures for males with four or more brothers were 49 percent and 28 percent. Part but obviously not all of the explanation for these differences is related to responsibility as head or prospective head of household (Caldwell 1969:72).

Because of the apparent relationship between out-migration and deprivation, it was expected that the economic level of a family would be negatively correlated with the out-migration rate. At least based upon the evidence available from Ghana, this appears not to be true. Of the respondents who had never migrated and had no plans to do so, 16 percent were classified above average economically. This figure contrasts with the 24 percent for long-term absentees from the rural areas (determined reputationally) and the 31 percent for those who had never migrated but were planning to leave the rural area for an extended period of time (ibid.:82). The relationship can be explained in at least two ways. First, families that are economically well-off are in a better position to send their children to school, and it is the better educated people who tend to migrate to town. Second, rural economic well-being is in part related to the number of family residents in towns, because the townsmen often send money home. But is is also rural residents with relatives in town who are most likely to migrate because of the room, board, and other benefits they can at least temporarily take advantage of (ibid.:83).

Migration from rural areas is not invariably a satisfactory solution, because the urban areas then become heavily populated while those who remain in the countryside tend to be the women, children, and old men—all relatively dependent people. (Although women generally do a great deal of the agricultural work, and in some societies most of it, they are often dependent on men for clearing the fields before planting.) The current pattern, in other words, is to relieve absolute rural overpopulation by draining off the most productive people. Unfortunately, "old people do not make an agricultural revolution" (Vennetier 1963:271)—yet such a revolution is necessary because production from the land must meet not only rural subsistence requirements, but also those generated by the increasing number of nonagriculturally productive townsmen.[3]

ECONOMIC GAIN IN TOWNS

In-migration continues at an ever-quickening pace. At the economic level, the explanation is that many Africans are behaving rationally by coming to towns. Berg, writing about West Africa, argues that the migrant labor system "has a secure foundation in the economic environment" (1965: 181); and the East African Royal Commission reported that "in the existing situation the migrant labour system appears to be the only one through which a considerable section of the African population can meet its needs" (1955:154). This is not to imply that all urban migrants find highly productive work, or even find employment. But for the average migrant, his move appears to represent a personal economic gain, slight though it may be.

The African in town usually has more cash to spend, although much of it must be spent for items that are free or nominally priced in the countryside. For example, a study of the Amba people of Uganda indicated that the real income of an average family living in the countryside was 512 shillings, compared with the 527 shillings earned by the average unskilled urban laborer (Winter 1955:38). However, to this near equality should be added the income the migrant's family may be making from his farm in the countryside; sometimes, it is only the seasonal presence of heavy labor—by the migrant himself or by cooperative work parties in his absence—that is necessary to keep a farm producing at its customary level. On the other hand, withdrawal of the most productive labor force has in some areas led to a virtual collapse of a local rural economy, from lack of either manpower or motivation.

Attraction of Town Life

The attraction of town life has been a subject of prose and poetry in the United States, Africa, and elsewhere. "We cannot all live in cities," wrote

---

3. The impact of rural out-migration upon tribal cohesion appears to depend upon a number of factors, e.g., whether those in town send a substantial amount of their earnings home (see Watson 1958).

Horace Greeley, "yet nearly all seem determined to do so." American troops sang of Paris during World War I and now there are Africans who sing of Niamey, Kumasi, and other towns of Black Africa. A well-known saying of French-speaking Africans living near northern Ghana is: *"Qui n'a pas été à Koumassi, n'ira pas au Paradis"*—He who has not been to Kumasi will not go to Paradise! Doucy and Feldheim assert that, in Africa, "the tentacular lure of the town appears to crown all other considerations" (1956:679). In this section we explain, in terms of two kinds of personal satisfactions, why African towns excite imaginations and emotions.

EXCITEMENT AND MODERNITY

Excitement and the benefits of modernity are readily available in urban areas. There is entertainment in the form of motion picture houses, television, sporting events, and hotel bars. Merchandise is available in great quantity and variety. Even the streets have an extraordinary vitality.[4] Reflecting all this is one visitor's reaction to a small town, as reported by Little: "I became a sort of idiot as we moved along, for I stood to gaze at whatever English-made articles I have ever seen before, for example, cycles, motorcycles, and cars. I took a very keen interest in gazing at two-storey buildings, I admired people moving in them, and I often asked my brother whether they would not fall from there" (1951:26). Southall and Gutkind report that in the two subdivisions of Kampala-Mengo which they studied, the daily life of the residents is far from boring; excitement and unusual events are quite common (1957:103). Sometimes the excitement is self-made. The authors note that disputes, often ending in a fight, are a common diversion for the people in Kisenyi. Within seconds, outbreaks of violence usually attract a large number of bystanders who react with what appears to be pleasurable excitement (1951:24).

FREEDOM

There is, for many Africans, freedom in towns. "Make I go Freetown make I go free" say many Sierra Leoneans (Banton 1957:57). Life in rural areas is often restricted by traditional obligations, customary law, and exigencies of the land. Among the reasons that have been given for leaving rural

---

4. Rural Ghanaian respondents were asked what three or four things "make town life pleasant" (Caldwell 1969:93). In the categories relevant to excitement and modernity were the following (multiple responses were permitted):

entertainment in general	46%
better shopping and marketing	41
better transport and culture	30
water supply	29
electricity supply	25
cinemas	23
exciting and faster life	20
medical and health facilities	19
bars, clubs, dances, women	14
educational facilities	6

homes are oppression and extortion by traditional or warrant chiefs, demand for communal labor, customary punishment for "woman damage," financial exploitation by one's own family, the menace of sorcery, and loss of dignity. (It should be emphasized that there are many obligations operative in rural areas, only some of which a migrant might wish to avoid by going to town.) Of course, there are some people who would be psychologically or physically maladjusted in most social systems, but leave rural homes which provide them with fewer options for deviancy—including creativity and delinquency. From this perspective, the towns serve as safety valves in the same way it has been hypothesized that America performed this function for Europe, the West performed it for the eastern United States, and some urban neighborhoods—perhaps Haight-Ashbury—do today. "The social disruption which inevitably accompanies extensive culture changes," writes Linton, "always brings to the fore numerous individuals who find the innovations congenial and are ready to exploit them. . . . Such persons are very frequently misfits in their societies, handicapped by atypical personalities" (1952:75). They are likely to migrate to urban areas seeking to exploit the opportunities for achievement which exist there.

In the town, there are more alternatives and innovative opportunities. The migrant or immigrant may choose among several jobs, some of which might not be condoned in the village society. "The city," writes Miner, "provides a social milieu in which economic success may be achieved with less regard for activities which are not primarily economic in nature" (1965a:293). One may also more freely choose associates, including those from other families, tribes, or even races. There is a greater choice of women, as Banton reports based upon his Freetown research: "There were plenty of women and everyone looked after himself" (1957:57). And there are fewer restrictions upon how an immigrant spends his money, whether it be upon necessities, cigarettes, or the cinema.

The feeling of freedom is expressed in this quotation from Watson's Zambia study: "A trip to the Copperbelt is an experience that a young woman never forgets. For at least once in her life she is free from the everlasting duties of fetching water and stamping meal, and acquires the outward appearances of European women, if not their leisure" (1958:40). One of the more colorful descriptions of town attractiveness was written by the novelist Ekwensi: "L-A-G-O-S. Lagos! The magic name. She had heard of Lagos where the girls were glossy, worked in offices like the men, danced, smoked, wore high-heeled shoes and narrow slacks, and were 'free' and 'fast' with their favours" (1961:167). Many African novels are concerned with town life, and they make important contributions to our understanding of urban practices and perspectives.

A special aspect of town freedom is greater opportunity for accelerated upward social and political mobility. Societies in rural Africa also provide opportunities, but these tend to be based on an older, relatively traditional system of values and status in which heredity, age, and/or sex are of special importance. Furthermore, downward mobility is often more frequent than upward because populations are increasing but the number of high status positions in rural societies is relatively stable (see Lenski 1966:289–291). Alternative channels of mobility are especially sought by young people, who in most rural African societies must defer to elders until they themselves reach an advanced age. To achieve ambitions early in life, many youths must migrate to town.

Sojourn as Status

In a variety of ways, urban experience is related to rural status. Three relationships are noted below: increased prestige derived from an urban sojourn, the experience as an initiation rite, and a decline in status which may result from some migration practices.

PRESTIGE ACCORDED TOWN EXPERIENCE

In most African societies it is highly prestigious to have been to a major urban area. When rural Ghanaian residents were asked whether "village people see the people who live in big towns as more important and show them more respect," a total of 78 percent answered affirmatively. Similarly, there was a 75 percent affirmative response among townsmen to the question, "When people who have come from the villages to work in [a large urban area] go back to their home villages, do people there see them more important and show them more respect?" (Caldwell 1969:143).

Success in town is especially valued. Gugler correctly observes that "the man who has won success in town plays a role very similar to that of a man prominent in the traditional context. . . . He has attained rural status through urban achievement" (1965:9). Leslie writes about the young man who returns home on leave loaded down with his new clothes, a bicycle, a watch, stockings, records, and a phonograph. "Everyone, elders and youngsters, comes to welcome the conquering hero. . . . His stay-at-home contemporaries listen with barely concealed envy" (1963:24). The Ghanaian data indicate that approximately nine out of ten townsmen visiting their rural home bring presents and about eight out of ten bring money (Caldwell 1969:162). Some returnees may soon exhaust their resources, but it is the urban experience plus the initial impact they make upon returning which usually matters. Mercier observes that in French-speaking West Africa the prestige of having been in Kumasi lives on even after earnings brought back from town are dissipated (1954a:155). The other side of this relationship is that it may be difficult to return home without gifts and other evidence of gain. Plotnicov tells of the Jos resident who is afraid to return to his rural home because the villagers, if disappointed with what he brings, might try to poison him (1964:185).

SOJOURN AS INITIATION

In some African societies, a trip to town is now an initiation rite often replacing a traditional practice. The most common initiation involved is induction into manhood. A study of migrant labor in Nyasaland (now Malawi), for example, speculated that migration was a functional equivalent of the war raid in proving oneself a man (Malawi [Nyasaland] 1935:21). Similarly, there are overtones of initiation in Africans' courage-proving trips from the former French colonies to Ghana (Rouch 1956: 194). Perhaps even more important is the informal initiation into the sophisticated, cosmopolitan "modern" world that is provided by a stay in town. Respondents in both the urban and rural surveys conducted in Ghana by Caldwell, in explaining why it was good for boys or men (and in a separate question, girls or women) to spend time in a town, most frequently gave responses that were categorized "to obtain knowledge and ideas, to become sophisticated" (1969:104, 106).

Prestige and the symbolic achievement of adult status are both related to the advantages a "townsman" has with the women of his home village. Hodgkin comments that many "a youth cannot expect to win a girl's favours unless he can show the brand of the town upon him" (1957b:71). Similarly, Schapera writes about the Botswana girls' strong preference for the well-dressed men who return from abroad bearing gifts and telling fascinating stories (1956:206).

SOJOURN AS DEPRIVATION

Migration to an urban area does not invariably bring prestige to the traveler. The relationship between prestige and migration is a function of the specific culture involved. The Mossi of Upper Volta display an interesting variant—children born outside the tribe's traditional homeland are considered Tarboussi ("born in the bush") rather than real Mossi. A general belief is that no clear-thinking Mossi could permanently live away from his homeland (Skinner 1960:381). It is also possible for the frequency of migration to surpass sociocultural limits. Gulliver reports that among the Ngoni and Ndendeuli of southern Tanzania, "the relative few who have migrated a large number of times are often rather pitied because they have been unable to settle down at home. They are felt to be possessed of an odd kind of 'wanderlust' or perhaps by certain inauspicious or even malevolent influences at home" (1955:31). These cases, it should be emphasized, illustrate exceptions to the general pattern.

Rural Ties

Assertions of the attractiveness of towns must be qualified by the knowledge that many Africans never reside in them, those who do usually visit their home villages regularly, and most town-dwellers sooner or later return home permanently. For example, Caldwell found that in rural Ghana 36 percent of the males and 48 percent of the females had never migrated to a town and had no hope or intention to do so, and that another 9 percent and 7 percent, respectively, had decided permanently to return to their rural homes after having lived in town (1969:41).

Townsmen are faced with many decisions, but without some of the security and control of home and tradition. This is an ordeal that obviously not all Africans can—or want to—survive, although those who do usually develop a new sense of security and a new ability to innovate. Gulliver notes that some men "prefer the rural atmosphere and placidity of the estates and farms and dislike, even fear, the rush and bustle and believed anonymity of town life on the Copper Belt" (1960:162). Hoyt, seeing the problem for some as economic versus personal satisfaction, suggests that "the attractions of new goods and services do not completely outweigh the objections to regimented production, loss of leisure, [and] closer contact with outsiders as officials or task-masters" (1956:12). For example, most Ngoni of Tanzania, "whilst agreeing on the economic causes of migration, also say readily and voluntarily that were it not for such necessity they would not go away and that they much prefer to stay at home" (Gulliver 1955:30). Of course, those whose home village is close to a town can combine seemingly opposed economic and personal satisfactions by commuting. Suburbia represents an equivalent American solution.

Most African townsmen retain links with their rural home and continue to take the opinions of rural relatives and friends into consideration. A study of selected rural compounds in eastern Nigeria reports that 89 percent of the absentees had visited their home at least once in the preceding three-year period, and that 76 percent had visited at least once in the preceding 12 months (Gugler 1962:7). Residents of the two Nairobi neighborhoods studied by Ross report extensive contacts with their rural home areas. Most respondents visited their homes for several weeks during the year, 81 percent had visitors from home, about half received food from home during the year, and 81 percent sent money home, as many as 44 percent of them at least once a month (1969:70–71). It should be noted that there is a material reason for maintaining such links. Systems of freehold are rare and therefore rural land cannot easily be converted into cash; the permanent severance of ties with one's rural home might well mean the loss of a valuable asset, land. (Fifty-nine percent of Ross's respondents owned farms outside Nairobi.) Thus, the personal urbanization of most townsmen is far from complete, for old ties and ways remain strong.

Whatever their pattern of migration, most Africans want to return to their traditional home sooner or later—at least to die there because of the religious significance of the relationship between land and ancestors. Schwab found that among the settlers of Oshogbo, "perhaps the only common characteristic" was their desire to return home someday (1952:16). Fully 80 percent of the urban respondents interviewed in Caldwell's study either owned a house in their rural village, are building one, or at least are planning to do so (1969:167). However, it is Plotnicov's opinion that the desire to return home is sometimes more symbolic than real; indeed, he reports that several elder Jos residents left town to retire in their village but changed their minds and returned (1964:56).

Multiple Causation

Because economic factors are so frequently mentioned by African migrants and long term townsmen in explaining their respective decisions, there is a temptation to dismiss other factors as irrelevant. However, a careful examination of patterns of migration indicates that there are many factors—those mentioned above and others—that influence migration to towns and continued residence there. Gutkind argues that "it is manifestly impossible to single out any one single reason which motivates the migration of people from one habitat to another" (1962c:172) and van der Kolff writes, "Practically any case of exodus shows that the motives are complex, so that economical, social, juridical, political, and cultural incentives may simultaneously be in the picture" (1952:267–268).

For the potential in-migrant or the townsman considering whether to remain in town, there is usually a noneconomic operative factor that contributes to his final action. "The last straw, so to speak—may well lie in some [noneconomic] factor . . . [which] does not in any way diminish the real importance of the basic motivation" (Gulliver 1955:28). Thus economic factors are probably necessary, but not sufficient and the *rate* of labor migration is probably determined by economic conditions, whereas *incidence* probably depends upon social and psychological conditions (Mitchell 1958:17).

A further clue to the intricacies of multiple causation is provided by an examination of migration patterns in and near towns. If economic factors were predominant, one would expect relatively uniform migration rates within various groups. Bettison, however, has shown that in the Blantyre area sons are considerably more likely to work away from the proximate town than are husbands. This contrast is true for residents in the suburbs and in nearby rural areas (1958:34). One possible explanation for these different rates is that the sons seek freedom from their immediate families.

Unfortunately, neither the Bettison study nor any other which has been completed provides reliable and valid weights to the various factors which might contribute to the decision to migrate to or remain in town. Therefore, we can conclude that multiple causation appears certain, but the importance of each cause is yet to be confidently determined.

Security forces, Mbale, Uganda

4

Impact of Migration
and Town Life upon
the Individual

Many African town-dwellers have had to cope with potential disjunctions: between their current environments and the rural environments into which they were initially socialized. Such disjunctions usually exist for first generation migrants. They also exist for many so-called second and third generation townsmen for at least two reasons. One is the common practice in many parts of Africa of sending children to the family's rural home for upbringing. The urban cost of living is high, and some parents think the urban environment is corrupting. The second reason is that the early upbringing of some town-dwelling children does not provide a satisfactory preparation for town life because it is largely conducted by relatively traditional rural-oriented women whose urban experiences are sharply restricted.

Of course, the problems of adjusting to town life are not equally severe for all Africans, and their solutions are varied. Adjustment does not usually involve a "detribalization" or complete change of practices and perspectives because contemporary urban and rural ways of life are both blends of the traditional and the modern. Usually, townsmen discard some traditional ways, incorporate some aspects of modernity, and develop compatible combinations of the two so that cultural differences are minimized. Some completely reject rural ways in reaction to a past which is perceived as being "primitive." Others reject urbanity either by returning to the village or by creating a highly circumscribed world in an ethnic ghetto. The latter option has been taken by, among others, Muslimized Fulbe of Munsar, especially by avoiding certain community-involving occupations (Butcher 1964), and—of comparative interest—the "Red" Xhosa in East London, South Africa (Mayer 1961).

To illustrate the potential impact of migration and town life upon many individual Africans, the following four sections of this chapter examine selected differences between urban and rural Africa. These differences (which tend to be stated in terms of polar opposites to emphasize potential disjunctions, although the real urban/rural differences are often considerably less extreme) are in social control, family composition, status, and personal aspiration. A final section suggests the potential impact of these differences.

Disjunction in Social Controls

By means of social controls, "a person is conditioned and limited in his actions by the groups, community, and society of which he is a member" (Wolff 1964:650). Conditioning implies socialization: learning, habituating, and internalizing social norms so that the expectations of relevant other people are anticipated. Limiting refers to those coercive actions of other people, operative when expectations are not anticipated and met, which are designed to enforce conformity to the norms of the group (or community or society), or of the group's dominant minority. For the group, the function of social controls is to maximize solidarity and order; for the individual, they maximize predictability and security. Of course, social controls are only partially effective in any group or on any individual; all men deviate from at least some social norms.

RURAL CONTROLS

Social controls can conveniently be described in terms of their content, origins, and agents of enforcement. The content of social controls in rural Africa tends to encourage placing collective interests first, acting toward other people according to their relationship to the individual or his group (e.g., nepotism may be the norm), evaluating people according to their ascribed qualities (e.g., age might bring high prestige regardless of ability), and having relationships with others which are broad in scope (e.g., a personal relationship might encompass expectations concerning political, economic, and affectionate behavior). The origin of most social control content is in tradition, often within a body of religious beliefs; as a result, change is relatively slow. Agents of social control in rural Africa fall into three categories: the individual, since group norms are usually learned, formed by habit, or internalized after a lifetime of relatively homogeneous socialization; those who engage in special activities, such as magicians and practitioners of witchcraft; and the primary group or association which comprises the multifunctional network that is pervasive in the individual's social, political, cultural, and economic affairs. Individuals and groups combine as agents. As the Ottenbergs write, "Social control and behavior are clearly linked to an individual's sense of reciprocity with the groups to which he belongs. This is certainly more important in Africa than any sense of obligation to laws in the abstract" (1960:57).

It is obviously impossible to survey the multiple aspects of the traditional social controls of the more than one thousand ethnic groups represented in urban Black Africa. However, a brief illustration will suggest some contrasts and similarities between the social controls operating upon a rural African and upon his town-dwelling confrere (cf. discussion, p. 53). The Nyakyusa of southern Tanganyika, as reported by Wilson (1936: 75–98), employ three social control agents of religious origin—the ancestor cult, witchcraft, and magic—each with its own sphere. The ancestor cult is primarily concerned with sanctions for moral behavior among members of the same kin group, witchcraft is especially concerned with customary behavior between members of a local group or chiefdom, and magic (which uses special "tribal" medicines) punishes the transgressors who are in neither the same kin group nor the same chiefdom. It should be noted that witchcraft accusations usually take place between persons who are competing with each other, but who are prevented by the prevailing group norms from openly expressing their mutual hostility. The accusations provide opportunities for bringing the hostility into the open and attacking the competitor (Mitchell 1965b:198). The question now arises, what are the adjustment problems of a town-dwelling Nyakyusa who has been socialized in a rural area to respond to these three religious control agents? After discussing urban controls and adjustment difficulties in general, we shall attempt to answer this question.

URBAN CONTROLS

Because the residents of a typical African town represent many ethnic groups, there is no single set of standards shared by a large majority of the townsmen; instead, there are many distinct or partially overlapping sets. In the more modern business and residential sectors of town, modern Western perspectives and practices are prevalent. But elsewhere, varying traditional norms mingle in kaleidoscopic melange with social controls from the modern sector.

The content of urban social controls tends to encourage individual interests, universal standards (e.g., everyone has to pass the same test), performance evaluation (i.e., what one does rather than who one is), and relationships with other people based on specialized interests (e.g., politics with politicians and economic transactions with businessmen—although politicians often develop economic interests and businessmen exert pressure on politicians to protect vested interests). The origins of urban controls are in tradition, legislation by modern authorities, and the economic market. (If the content originates in either of the latter two, change can be relatively rapid.) The agents of control are the individual to the extent that socialization has taken place, primary and secondary groups for that content which they support, specialized structures such as the police and courts, and the competition of the modern market economy.

There are several reasons why it is relatively difficult for African town residents to anticipate and meet the expectations of a wide variety of other townsmen. Besides urban-rural differences in the content of norms, these include the rapidity of change, the fragmentation of families, contemporaneous urban and rural ties, urban heterogeneity, and norm conflicts.

The first difficulty stems from the fact that the socialization to norms that has taken place over a lifetime in the in-migrant's rural home cannot suddenly be revolutionized so that a new set of norms appropriate for modern urban life can most effectively guide his behavior when he arrives in the urban area. Usually, a lengthy relearning process is necessary. Yet the migrant does not arrive in town by stages; sometimes within an hour he may journey from a rural area little touched by Westernization to a modern town.

A second difficulty concerns the agents of socialization and reinforcement. The cohesive extended family of rural areas almost always fragments when some members move to town; nuclear families also may be divided. (The principal exceptions exist in modernizing old towns, such as Ibadan.) As a result, man's most important agent of socialization and reinforcement is impaired. A special aspect of this difficulty is the occasional repudiation of parents by first generation town-dwelling youths because the former are peasants; often this rejection takes place before new urban norms have become operative, leaving the young people only partially socialized to either rural or urban life.

Third, adult African town-dwellers usually retain close ties with friends and relatives in their rural homes, regularly visit them, and plan eventually to return home permanently. (This is often true even for those townsmen who have rejected their parents.) Furthermore, wives often serve as change deterrents reinforcing traditional rural ties. A married migrant who leaves his wife in the rural area, but returns to her periodically, oscillates between two cultural milieux and therefore may not be able to immerse himself easily in urban ways. Even when the wife comes to live with him in town, she tends more than the man to preserve indigenous customs and reject those of the town. This, of course, restricts the husband's urban involvement. There are, however, an increasing number of young women who attend school and become teachers, nurses, secretaries, and occupants of other positions that require participation in the modern world.

A fourth barrier to the African townsman's ability to anticipate and meet the expectations of a wide variety of other townsmen is that, as noted above, no single set of norms is prevalent. An Ibo living in Lagos may have to work for a Yoruba man, buy cloth from a Lebanese, purchase meat from a Hausa man, and so forth. Although the four persons in this example undoubtedly share many norms by virtue of their common residence in Lagos, significant differences also exist.

Finally, conflicting norms may create difficulties. Because the town-dweller has probably been brought up to know many rural-traditional norms as well as several sets of urban-modern norms (the latter may have been acquired through primary school education, by means of informal urban-to-rural diffusion, or as the result of having spent a period of time in town), he can often draw upon two or more sets of norms at one time and place. There will undoubtedly be decisions that can be made in accordance with one set of norms or another but not all, because the norms are not mutually compatible. Such conflicts, although they can impair the townsman's ability to anticipate and meet others' expectations, are not invariably perceived (and therefore not troubling to the townsman). And even when the conflict is perceived, the townsman can sometimes restructure it.

The difficulties noted above would appear to cause a relatively heavy burden to be placed upon the formal specialized agents of social control. But such agents are "underdeveloped," state authority is frail, and unpunished transgressions are probably common. The juvenile delinquent and the criminal, for instance, are "manifestations of the breakdown of inherited social controls. They are symptoms of the deteriorating influence in the urban environment of such social institutions as the family and the church, of the waning grip of the mores, of the inadequacy, as yet, of the emergent new controls represented by such substitute institutions as the school, the court, the prison and the reformatory" (Hauser 1957:80). Note, however, that deviance itself becomes difficult to determine because of the situational and subcultural basis of behavior and norms. For example, fornication may be deviant in rural areas but "normal" in the town, at least in some situations.

Returning to the example of the Nyakyusa, an important consequence of a tribesman's migration to a multiethnic town such as Dar es Salaam is that the influence of his traditional religion and its derivative social controls will probably decline. (On the other hand, reports from several African towns indicate that some traditional religious practices and beliefs are vigorously adhered to, sometimes in secret.) One reason is that a full complement of the dead (ancestors) and the living (magicians, practitioners of witchcraft, and others) may not be present, nor may appropriate land and medicines (leaves, roots, etc.) be available. Thus religious practices may not occur and religious perspectives may not be reinforced. In addition, it is relatively easy for a Nyakyusa town-dweller not adhering faithfully to his religious tradition to avoid having other members of his kin group or tribe know about a transgression.

There are also cross-pressures that conflict with the Nyakyusa migrant's traditions. For example, it is often useful to practice Christianity at least nominally in order to obtain a job, to enter a denominational school, or to achieve a higher social status. Leslie reports that, although less than 2 percent of his Dar es Salaam respondents admitted practicing a religion other than Islam or Christianity, "if the truth were told the great majority would be classed as 'irreligious'" (1963:210). A second example of cross-pressures is related to the Nyakyusa practice of interpreting misfortune in terms of witchcraft. Although the townsman may initially do this, it is soon likely to be found unsatisfactory. One reason is that there are numerous strangers in urban areas toward whom hostility and opposition may openly be expressed, thus eliminating the need for witchcraft accusations. Furthermore, even when hostility is expressed in these terms, the urban administrative and judicial systems do not countenance witchcraft beliefs, nor do they direct retributive action based upon them. Therefore, the individual is encouraged to think within a new reality frame, to rely upon new explanations for his misfortunes—and therefore new social controls, including self-responsibility—in order to cope more effectively with his new urban environment.

Table 4.1. Explanations of misfortune. (Adapted from
Hammond-Tooke 1970:29.)

	Residence	
Explanation	rural (percent)	urban (percent)
Mystical	73	45
Nonmystical	27	55
	100	100
N	107	99

Recent research by Hammond-Tooke (1970), although conducted outside independent Black Africa, provides some relevant quantitative evidence concerning the apparent shift away from magico-religious social controls. Respondents in two Xhosa-speaking communities in South Africa, one relatively rural and the other urban, were asked whether they had ever suffered a misfortune and, if so, if it were caused mystically. (Mystical causes included witchcraft, sorcery, ancestors, and river people.) Table 4.1 shows that there was a significant contrast between the sets of responses: rural residents were far more likely than their urban counterparts to mention mystical causes. The generality of this finding is obviously uncertain (cf. Marwick 1958), especially because of the unknown effect of white control, but it at least suggests the kind of evidence necessary to demonstrate more conclusively that rural and urban residents experience a disjunction in social controls.

Familial Disjunction

Most demographic surveys conducted in Africa reveal that there is a disproportionate number of young adults in urban areas, especially in the relatively new towns. Men in their twenties and thirties are significantly overrepresented; women from their midteens through midtwenties are overrepresented to a lesser extent. Figures 4.1 and 4.2 show the age skews by sex in three Ghanaian towns.

Sex and age disproportions are generally least important in the old towns of Africa, because demographic stabilization took place prior to the arrival of Europeans. (See for example Mabojunje 1968:138, where data compiled from the 1952 Nigerian census show that only in the large towns of the Eastern Region are men significantly overrepresented.) In such towns, fragmentation of the family is most characteristic of twentieth-century African migrants.

There is variation not only in selective sex and age migration among cities, but also among ethnic groups and socioeconomic strata within cities. Vivid evidence of interethnic variation is reported from Pointe-Noire: Figure 4.3 shows varying male/female ratios among the town's principal ethnic and locality groups; Figure 4.4 shows varying proportions of children (under 15 years of age), adults (15–50), and old people (over 50

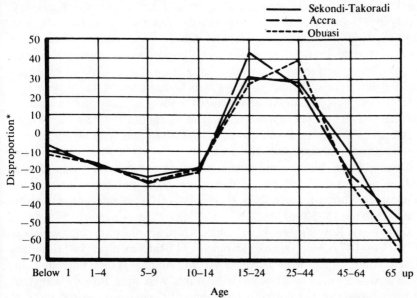

Figure 4.1. The Distribution of Urban Age Disproportion: Male (*Percent for Ghana divided into percent for town minus 1.00 times 1.00.) (Adapted from Ghana 1964a:8, 9.)

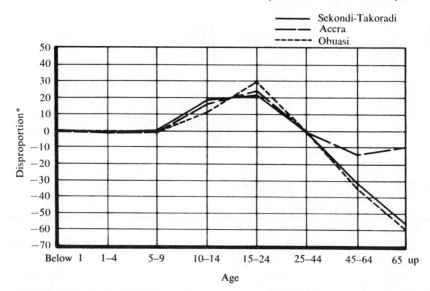

Figure 4.2. The Distribution of Urban Age Disproportion: Female. (*Percent for Ghana divided into percent for town minus 1.00 times 100.) (Adapted from Ghana 1964a:8, 9.)

years of age). As can be seen, migrants from Chad and members of the Bateke ethnic group are represented by more than six males out of every ten Pointe-Noire residents, whereas at the other extreme the Vili and migrants from Cabinda, Nigeria, and Ghana have more females than males. The modal ratio is approximately 50 males to 45 females. Evidence of variation by socioeconomic strata comes from Ross's study of two Nairobi neighborhoods. Among married men in his samples, there were significant positive correlations between (a) both education and income of the man and (b) the man's wife's residing in Nairobi (1969:63).

Age distributions in Pointe-Noire display the same type of ethnic and locality variation. Over half the residents from the distant countries of Dahomey, Togo, Nigeria, and Ghana are children under 15 years of age, and an additional 10 percent of those from the. latter two countries are over 50. By contrast, more than 70 percent of the migrants from nearby Chad are in the 15–50 age bracket.

Data from Rouch's study of Ghana further illustrate the variation (1956:146–147). More Kotokoli women (51) than men per 100 members of this ethnic group were living in Accra. Among Hausa migrants, the division was 59 men to 41 women. Migrants who were Fulani, Wangara, or from Liberia or the northern territories of Ghana were in the ratio of about one woman to two men. The Mossi and Busanga had approximately one woman to four or five men. And the Zambara had only 65 women per 1,000 resident members of the ethnic group. For some groups, it is possible

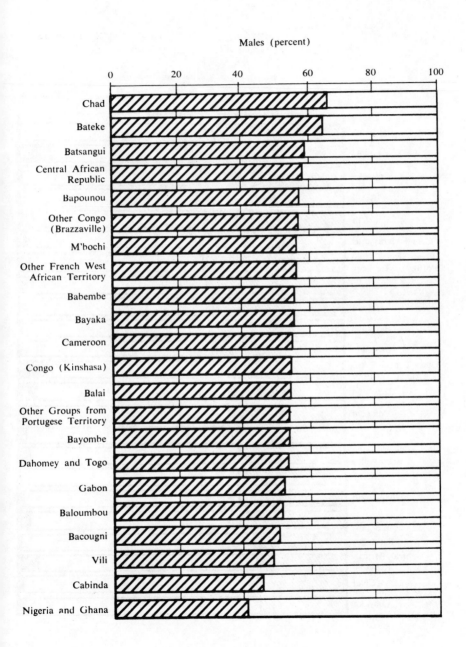

Figure 4.3. Sex Ratios of Pointe-Noire Ethnic and Locality Groups.

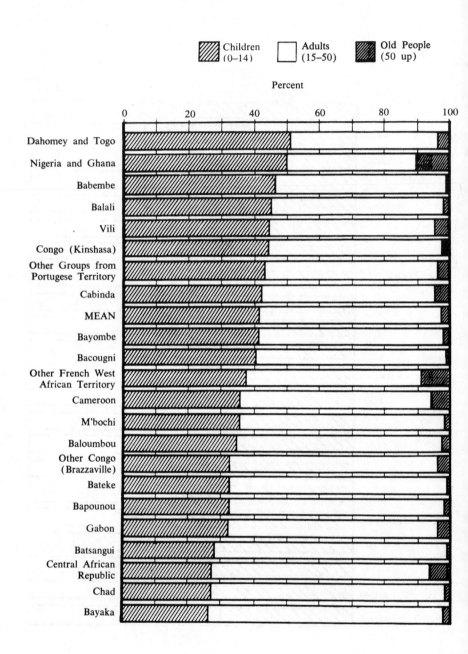

Figure 4.4. Age Ratios of Pointe-Noire Ethnic and Locality Groups.

to give a partial explanation of their urban sex ratio. Hausa men, for example, traditionally travel with their wives. An explanation for the relatively high proportion of Kotokoli women in town is that many of them come to Accra to practice prostitution. Zambara male migrants, on the other hand, who have a warrior-derived tradition of not encumbering their journeys with women, prefer to find female companionship in the village or town where they are living at the time.

Some of the reasons for the general demographic patterns that have been shown are apparent from an examination of the causes of migration. For one, most school and job opportunities are open only to young people, especially men. Watson describes a common situation: "The young and more adaptable men are out at unskilled work in industry while the older men remain at home to maintain the fields with the aid of the women. This arrangement appears to suit both the indigenous social system and the labour markets. The social and economic pressure towards earning money by working abroad is greater on young than old men" (1958:70). The attitude of this Nyakyusa women is typical in many areas: "Men go away to earn money. We cannot earn money, so why should we go?" (quoted in Gulliver 1957:47). Young adults are also more susceptible to innovation and less rooted in the social network and traditions of a family home. Indeed, they especially may want to escape from restrictions of the home.

Other explanations for the demographic skews can be indicated. Some colonial administrations, especially those in British Central and East Africa, discouraged family settlement in the towns. The elders of some tribes, adhering to traditional norms or responding to fears of urban life, discouraged the migration of females to the towns. And the male migrants themselves did not always want their families in town. Evidence on the latter point is fragmentary in Black Africa, but van der Horst reports that in the Republic of South Africa approximately two out of three heads of black African families do not want their wives or growing children to be in town. Wives are not wanted primarily because they are needed to look after the man's rural home, whereas the most frequently given reasons for not having children in town are that "it is not home" and that "there are too many bad influences" (1964:103–105).

Urban out-migration is also a factor contributing to the demographic pattern. Town-dwellers who reach their middle forties or fifties often return to the countryside because they feel that they have worked enough or because they have been forced to by the difficulty older men having in holding unskilled, physically demanding jobs.

IMPACT OF DEMOGRAPHIC PATTERNS

The demographic skews that have been described obviously signify temporary family separation which, in combination with a variety of other changes taking place in urban Black Africa, may have significant effects.

According to a United Nations report, it is within the family that the effects or urban migration are most evident. Family members are separated and scattered throughout a country (and sometimes beyond its borders) and as a result parental authority and established marital conventions are weakened. The report concludes that these changes have tended to become institutionalized in towns, impeding the emergence of stable urban societies (United Nations, Committee on Information from Non-Self Governing Territories 1958:47–49).

Two aspects of familial change should be elaborated. One is the traditional concept of marriage. In most societies of old Africa, marriage was not just a union or contract between two persons: it often amounted to what was virtually a permanent formal agreement between two extended families, and as such had important social, economic, political, and religious ramifications. Consequently, marriages were arranged with great care and their dissolution (common in some matrilineal societies) usually occurred only for relatively important reasons after family mediation failed. The abnormal urban demographic pattern has meant that heterosexual relationships are determined more by the two immediate participants than was formerly the case. (Some changes along this line have also occurred in rural areas.) This individualization of the marital decision stems not only from the geographic dispersion of families but also from fundamental changes in the operative values of urban residents. As an example, the roles of some women have been transformed by advanced education and entry into modern occupationals (e.g., nursing and teaching).

A second aspect of familial change is that the early socialization processes of some children have been altered. As in the United States, the child of a broken African home may in large part be socialized by peers, creating intergenerational cleavages and the possibility of being introduced to the delinquent world as a functional alternative to family satisfactions. Weinberg, in his discussion of delinquency in Ghana, argues that "a cultural lag exists between the needs of some youths and the lack of institutions to channelize their needs; this discrepancy places these youths in a marginal position and impels them to satisfy their needs through deviant conduct with their peers, in the process of adapting to the urban community" 1965:94). In Bamako, however, where the demographic distributions have normalized, the rate of juvenile delinquency is low (Meillassoux 1965: 130).

Busia argues that the extended family traditionally has joint responsibility for bringing up children, and that the breakdown of this responsibility was the primary cause of urban juvenile delinquency (1950). However, even when the tradition of joint responsibility is maintained, its impact upon the juvenile may be different in towns than in the traditional milieu: a shift of responsibility from one relative to another within the village context usually does not mean a significant geographic change or interaction with new faces in new places, but in town the shift may be to a new neighborhood of stangers.

The impact of family environment upon juvenile behavior is empirically demonstrated by Weinberg, who compared the residential arrangements of samples of male delinquents and nondelinquents in Accra. As Figure 4.5 shows, nondelinquents were considerably more likely to be living with both parents, whereas at the other extreme delinquents were far more likely to be living with a distant relative or nonrelative or on their own.

Although family separation has had some impact upon the concept of marriage and the socialization of children, change has been evolutionary and many continuities remain between old and new structures and functions. Two interrelated reasons for these continuities are the extended family structure which remains operative in many African towns, and the resilience of urban-rural ties.

A husband and wife are not necessarily dependent only upon each other, since their respective siblings and lineage members may play important supportive roles. Children, according to the practice of many societies, belong to the lineage and not to the parents. Thus a child will have many "mothers" and "fathers," and the impact of the "broken home" is reduced.

Ties between urban and rural residents who are members of the same extended family, or even the same clan or tribe, usually are not broken.

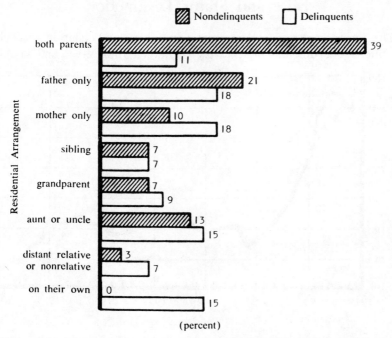

Figure 4.5. Residential Arrangements of Male Juvenile Delinquents and Nondelinquents in Accra. (Adapted from Weinberg 1965:90.)

Visiting often takes place and a dual responsibility exists: the townsman for his rural relatives and those in the rural home for their town relative. Where proximity permits, these ties are sufficiently strong that the impact of actual family separation is minimized.

DEMOGRAPHIC CHANGES

Evidence from various towns in Black Africa indicates that the abnormality of age and sex ratios is lessening, due in part to the Africanization and normalization of urban life, and to the more permissive stance toward non-employee in-migration on the part of African governments. The following proportional changes can be detected: a decrease in men (thus an increase in women) and increases in the very young and old age groups. A typical pattern of sex ratio change over time is shown in Figure 4.6. A shift in the urban age distribution toward a more normal structure is examplified by data protrayed in Figure 4.7.

There has also been a normalization of the European demographic structure. A comparison of figures from 1946 and 1955 censuses in Dakar indicates that the male/female sex ratio dropped from 1.71 to 1.00 and that the infant population increased noticeably. The details are shown in Table 4.2.

Elite and Status Disjunction

The determinants of status in general and elite membership in particular are often quite different in relatively traditional rural areas and in rela-

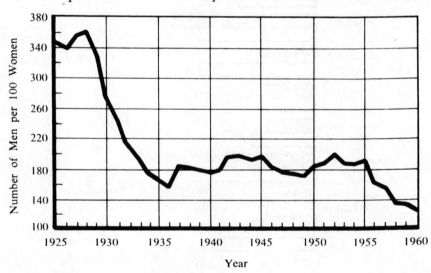

Figure 4.6. Sex Ratio Change in Kinshasa. (Adapted from Denis 1956:43 and Raymaekers 1963:4–5.)

Table 4.2. *European population ratios in Dakar, 1946 and 1955. (Adapted from* Afrique occidentale française *1958: Appendix, p. 3)*

age group	| Census of 1946 men	women	total	per- cent	m/f	| Census of 1955 men	women	total	per- cent	m/f
0–9 years	1,197	1,069	2,266	19.3	112	3,735	3,447	7,182	25.4	108
10–19	807	796	1,603	13.7	101	1,693	1,715	3,408	12.1	99
20–29	1,847	458	2,305	19.7	403	2,217	2,760	4,977	17.6	80
30–39	1,982	1,097	3,079	26.3	181	3,076	2,728	5,804	20.5	113
40–49	1,052	602	1,654	14.1	175	2,234	2,708	4,942	17.5	82
50–59	370	215	585	5.0	172	943	553	1,496	5.3	171
60 and up	130	94	224	1.9	138	224	223	447	1.6	100
Totals	7,385	4,331	11,716	100.0	171	14,122	14,134	28,256	100.0	100

tively modern towns. For the individual African, migration to a town and the broader societal patterns of urbanization usually lead to shifts in the relative importance of the two status systems.

RURAL STRATIFICATION

Although social systems in rural Africa display great variation in their bases of stratification, it is possible to indicate general tendencies. A person's status tends (relative to urban areas) to be determined in the first instance by ascriptive qualities, e.g., family, sex, and age. Positions of leadership are frequently inherited by virtue of being the member of a high status kin group; within kin groups, age is often the principal deter-

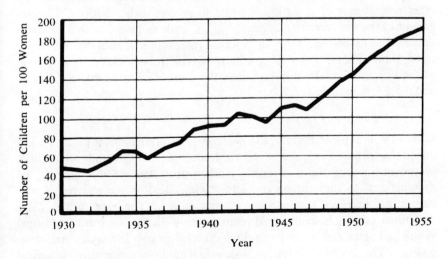

Figure 4.7. Number of Children per 100 Women in Kinshasa. (Adapted from Denis *1958:226.)*

minant of status. "In Africa," Ki-Zerbo generalizes, "the hierarchy of power, of consideration and of prestige, was in direct rapport with the hierarchy of age. . . . The council of elders in traditional Africa was the supreme political master of the city or the tribe" (1962:268–269). Wisdom and therefore the right to participate in decisionmaking are often believed to be determined by the experience of age; only over time can one gain the necessary knowledge of the soil, magic, customs, and rituals.

Having noted these general characteristics, qualifications are in order. The Ottenbergs point out that "most African societies are flexible enough to allow for particular skills in leadership, such as oratorical talent or the ability to bring about the settlement of disputes, so that individuals who would otherwise have an inferior position within a society or kin group may sometimes find a political role for themselves. Achievement for individuals in the political field is thus possible" (1960:47). Among a number of African peoples, for instance, war chiefs were young men. And in some societies, even slaves were able to achieve positions as key advisors. Wealth (number of wives, cattle, yams, and nowadays money and what it can buy) may also be an influencing factor; indeed, in some ethnic groups (e.g., the Ibo of southeastern Nigeria) it is one of the prime indicators of a man's ability and therefore of his right to high status.

Ascriptive recruitment to elite status in rural areas has been modified by the impact of modernity. Coleman is generally correct in observing that "the new classes emerging from the Western impact . . . have not only moved into the upper strata in territorial stratification systems; they have also displaced the upper strata in traditional societies" (1960:283). Conversely, some traditional rulers have obtained a modern education and other new objects of valuation in order to protect their positions. The degree of change in recruitment qualifications tends to be a function of traditional patterns and the form of colonial rule imposed; thus the indirectly ruled Hausa-Fulani states of northern Nigeria have yielded more slowly to the impact of modernity than have the more directly ruled, egalitarian, and more loosely stratified Ibo.

URBAN STRATIFICATION

Within the urban community, the position of elders has been partly undermined by changed requirements (a traditional background offers little precedent for confronting specifically urban problems and may actually be dysfunctional to some urban problem-solving) and by the striving of ambitious counterelites sympathetic to new norms. The new urban elites sometimes emerge from those Africans who are disaffected from traditional values and elites and at the same time attracted to new life styles and viewpoints. "The social disruption which inevitably accompanies extensive culture change," writes Linton, "always brings to the fore numerous individuals who find the innovations congenial and are ready to exploit them. . . . If the innovations are accepted, [they] . . . become a new elite" (1952:75). Epstein has observed this pattern in Zambian mining towns: "As the urban communities took root, new problems arose out of urban living, of which the Elders were often unaware and which they were not equipped to handle. Gradually there emerged the Welfare Societies, new groups with new leaders, whose vision was no longer confined within the framework of an ancient social order, and who were themselves actively interested in what a new order offered" (1958:132).

Several general characteristics of the emergent urban elites have been implied; here they will be briefly specified. One is that the urban elites are relatively young, often in their twenties and thirties. Thus the conflict between generations, found in Africa as elsewhere, is echoed in the disjunction between rural and urban elites.

Second, urban elites tend to be employed in occupations that developed as the result of European intervention and influence in Africa. They are school teachers, medical doctors, government administrators, cash crop farmers, and so forth. In Onitsha, for example, the occupational composition of the 1958 executive committee of the local branch of a major national political party included five professional men, ten educators, nine businessmen, four junior functionaries, seven petty traders, and one housewife (Sklar 1963:488).

Third, the urban elites tend to obtain their high position on the basis of achievement in addition to (or rather than) ascription. In other words, relevant performance usually is a more important determinant of success in towns than in rural areas. However, the frequent charges of tribalism and nepotism printed in African publications and voiced by African leaders are indications that selection based upon ascription remains operative. Furthermore, a coethnic political base is a virtual necessity for urban political elites. The quest for such a base makes ascriptive appeals likely.

Fourth, urban elites are characterized by greater specialization than their rural counterparts. In the towns there are educational leaders, key businessmen, leading politicians, and so forth. Furthermore, there is a developmental pattern toward increasing specialization. Forde argues this point concerning the political sphere: "In early phases of Westernization, political leadership was commonly expected from any and all of the few educated Africans, but in the more developed areas professional politicians had now emerged" (1956:44).

SOME CONSEQUENCES OF DISJUNCTION

Stated in the extreme, two value systems and two elite groups coexist in most African towns and, in juxtaposition, they create a potential for interelite conflict and intrapersonal stress. Elite conflict arises because those who value the traditional-rural ways and are highly valued in terms of them come into conflict with those equivalently linked with modern-urban values. (In some areas the traditional-rural elite attempted to maintain its status by trying to impede the urbanization processes.) Before independence, the conflict between elite groups was sometimes heightened because traditional elites, buttressed by a colonial administration, tried to undercut nationalist-oriented urban elites. This conflict is now taking place in Rhodesia.

Traditionally oriented elites need not conflict directly with their modern counterparts because other options are open. One possibility is that they become "realists" by adjusting to inevitable changes. Another alternative is for the traditional-rural elite to coopt potential counterelites by giving them positions in, and hence committing them to, the established elite. Examples of resistance, adjustment, and cooptation abound in the history of the towns of Black Africa. Indeed, the extreme case of interelite conflict is rarely found because in contemporary urban Africa "traditionalists" have been influenced by modernity and "modernists" have usually retained at least some of the traditional practices and perspectives of their ethnic groups.

Intrapersonal stress occurs either (a) because the migrant may leave a situation in which he is under traditional-rural elites and within a status system dominated by traditional values and go into an urban community influenced by new elites with modern-urban values, or (b) because the townsman operates within the sphere of two elites, one oriented more toward traditional values and the other modernist in inclination. The necessary adjustments are potentially stressful, not only because of changes in the bases of stratification but also because status by achievement is less predictable and therefore less stabilizing than status by ascription. Achievement is inherently less secure, both for the candidate leader and for those who must decide whom to follow. "There is no doubt," writes LaPiere, "that in a relatively open system of stratification personal insecurity is rather general throughout the society. Rather than automatically receiving social support in accordance with a traditional system, the individual is responsible for his own personal welfare; and what he gets from society is more or less in proportion to what he contributes to it" (1965: 382).

Characteristically, however, interpersonal stress can be avoided or moderated. As will be elaborated below, particular situations are often not conflict producing; syncretistic combinations of value systems arise; mechanisms of personality defense can be employed; and ethnic continuity (perhaps the most important means of adjustment) is widely prevalent in African towns.

Aspirational Disjunction

Of considerable importance in urban social and political life is the in-ability of most African townsmen to attain the heights of their aspirations in the "revolution of rising expectations." Aspirations are probably more realistic in rural areas because the distribution of values is more tradition-ally determined, the most dissatisfied villagers have emigrated, and superior alternatives are less visible. In the new towns, however, people are being resocialized, especially to aspire to a higher standard of living. Yet the conditions of life in these towns clearly do not meet the ideals held by most townsmen.

Many townsmen now want to possess the symbols and substance of "civilization," but the opportunity to do so is limited. "For the greater part of the African population of Dar es Salaam," Leslie concludes, "there can be little prospect of advancement. Those who can look forward to an im-proving status, pay and standard of living are mainly the educated. . . . But the educated are few" (1963:130). Although writing about another part of the world, Soares's comment appears to apply with equal force to Black Africa: "Feelings of relative reward are replaced by feelings of relative deprivation as urban living makes socio-economic inequality more visible. The rewarding comparison with a rural life fades into the past, and gives way to a damaging comparison with higher standards of living" (1964: 192).

At the first level of analysis, the primary barrier to aspirational fulfill-ment is the lack of financial capital (and its corollary of underdeveloped infrastructure). But at another level, two additional barriers must be con-sidered. One is the virtually unbounded aspirations and perpetual frustra-tions of relative normlessness. Durkheim argues that when the integrating and regulating norms of a society are upset, aspirations are unbound and therefore impossible to fulfill (1952:252–254). Once some benefits of modernity are obtained, additional benefits are likely to become important. For example, the man who has a bicycle and a primary school education will likely aspire to have an automobile and a secondary school education. Thus in the extreme, the wide gap between aspirations and realizations persists. (The long term problem is suggested by available international growth statistics which show that of all the "developing" countries, only Israel is catching up, in terms of per capita gross national product, with the United States and the United Kingdom. The growth rates in Africa are, with few exceptions, less than a third of that required to close the gap with the advanced industrial states by the year 2040 [see Lamers 1967:30–33].)

The other barrier to aspirational fulfillment is unequal distribution of resources. Inequality in Africa has racial overtones and originated during the colonial administration when European per capita income was much higher than that of the African. Since self-government, many privileged elite positions have been transferred from Europeans to Africans, and in most countries a new African privileged stratum with vested interests has developed. The average African, on the other hand, has experienced relatively little material improvement. Currently, the elite-mass gap is great. Another cause of unequal resource distribution operates in those countries where, even after several years of independence, commerce and industry are dominated by Europeans, Asians, or Levantines. Unless these groups are displaced by Africans or the economy's growth curve turns sharply upward, aspiring indigenous businessmen are likely to be frustrated in their ambitions by the barrier of a largely alien middle class.

Apparently, one result of these conditions has been an increasing sense of absolute and relative deprivation, not dissimilar to the feelings that developed during the period of colonial rule and contributed to its termination. The sense of deprivation has been heightened in Black Africa because "urban political and social ideologies are sensitizing the norms whereby people evaluate 'social injustice,' thus increasing the intensity of resentment and hostility" (Tangri 1962:208). Thus, it would appear that a great potential for social disorganization and anomic political outburst exists in the towns.

Impact of Disjunctions

Because of the disjunctions that have been noted, as well as others like them, the culture shock of a shift from rural to urban life—as well as the "future shock" of continuing urban change[1]—may lead to increased personal anxiety and stress. (Other possible responses include conflict management and withdrawal.) The degrees of anxiety and stress are, of course, conditioned by the causes of migration, the migrant's cultural background, characteristics of the particular urban milieu, and the migrant's personal resiliency.

Sociocultural change of any intensity is likely to be stressful, and the greater the change the more stress there is. The reason is that old ways are found to be inadequate and new ones must be learned. Mead argues that, when some of an individual's old responses are thought to be irrelevant or inappropriate, he may come to fear that his entire traditional way of life

---

1. "The future is arriving so swiftly that, for all practical purposes, we are superimposing a new, alien culture, with new values, esthetics, politics, sexual roles, on top of the old one" (Toffler 1970:20). The author uses the term *future shock* in a discussion of changes taking place in New York City, but it may also apply to the residents of some urban areas in Africa.

will disintegrate. Even when an individual willingly seeks to adjust to change, he is likely to experience considerable strain (1955:271). A cumulative process may be operative upon migrants and immigrants because the anxiety generated by confronting a new sociocultural situation may further impair their ability to respond flexibly to that situation.

There is little evidence about the relationship between (a) anxiety and stress and (b) years of urban residence. However, Imoagene has interviewed 91 rural migrants in Sapele; the cross-tabulation of his date on the length of stay and adjustment (the latter is based upon an arbitrary scale), reported in Figure 4.8, suggests that no significant relationship exists. (The figures might be interpreted to show that adjustment may increase slowly over time and that change may not be linear, but his small sample size makes even such conclusions hazardous at best.)

ADJUSTMENT PROBLEMS

Reports of adjustment problems come from virtually all parts of Africa. Herskovits has noted that the discontinuities between contemporary urban life and traditional ways confront even those people who are members of ethnic groups whose pre-European heritage includes preindustrial urban experiences (1962:266–267). The following conclusions from studies conducted in Ghana and Congo (Kinshasa) are typical of the research reports supporting the hypothesis that new (and sometimes old) townsmen have serious adjustment problems. Busia concludes that Sekondi-Takoradi's

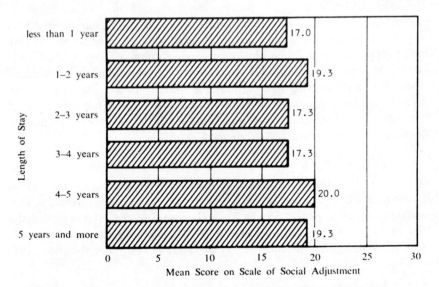

Figure 4.8. Relationship Between Length of Stay in Sapele and Social Adjustment. (Adapted from Okediji 1966:504.)

large size, overcrowded conditions, and ethnic diversity have created a milieu to which most residents have not yet successfully adjusted (1950: 106). Similarly, Clement reports that the Kisangani immigrant has a "feeling of isolation . . . accompanied by a sense of insecurity, due to the relaxation of traditional social supports and controls and further accentuated by the daily need to grapple with divers problems in an unfamiliar social setting" (1956:485–486). Fortes and Mayer (1966) conclude, on the basis of research among the rural Tallensi of northern Ghana in the 1930s and 1960s, that psychosis appears to have increased over time and that members of the tribe who have been to the alien and largely urban environment of southern Ghana manifest a greater psychotic tendency than do those tribal members without such experience. There is also evidence (from outside Black Africa) suggesting that urban life affects Africans physiologically; according to Scotch, the blood pressure of Zulus is higher in Durban, South Africa, than in the rural reserves (1960:1001–1002).

POLITICAL RELEVANCE

Adjustment problems are of more than theoretical interest. If the townsman's attempt to cope with them fails, the resulting anxiety and stress may be managed by means of aggression against society or self. [It should not be forgotten that alternative means of coping are conflict resolution (e.g., role segmentation) and withdrawal (e.g., returning to one's rural home).] If and when the aggressive responses become collective, they may crystallize into a variety of social movements, including nonviolent agitation, nativism, revolution, and extremist support of an authoritarian leader or regime. "The anomic urban person is remarkably amenable to authoritarian appeals, for once he has lost the comforting security of traditional order, he strives to regain his stability with frantic intensity" (McCord 1965:39). Such striving was partially the basis of nationalism and in part it also explains contemporary events in many parts of Africa. Because of the centrality of African towns, the kinds of social movements mentioned above can be territorially quite significant.

QUALIFICATIONS

The image that urban Africans are disorganized by disjunctions can be challenged on a number of procedural and substantive grounds. Procedurally, a large proportion of research reporting the relatively stressful life of urban Africans is unscientific in that the subjects are townsmen studied at one point in time.[2] We know, for example, that the modal tra-

2. A satisfactory scientific study of the impact of urban life would require before-and-after studies of townsmen and those who had not migrated to town.

ditional milieu in Africa contained fairly widespread and constant anxiety and insecurity (Lambo 1956:1388–1393) and that the differences in manifestations of psychiatric disorder displayed in one comparison between African urban and rural areas were in general not significant (Leighton et al. 1963: passim). Similarly, the increased stress of urban Africa cannot be proven by the high positive correlation of urbanization and admissions to mental hospitals. Clearly, the latter is a recent phenomenon; there were alternative structures to handle this social control function in most traditional Africans societies. (For a parallel discussion based upon American evidence, see Goldhamer and Marshall 1963:passim.) Furthermore, as McClosky and Schaar point out, the effects of such new processes as rapid communication media, modern education, and economic development may counteract the normal anomie-producing factors (1965:18).

The potential of anxiety and stress does not necessarily lead to their manifestation in severe and debilitating form. From a sociological point of view, the apparently conflicting elements of traditional-rural and modern-urban Africa do not in fact always conflict: few Africans are forced to bridge the disjunctions of "extreme" urbanity and "extreme" rurality, and for those who do have to bridge these extremes, operative differences in time and space may exist so that the conflict is avoided. "While there may be a wide gap between the least sophisticated villager and the most sophisticated urbanite, there is certainly no indication that migrants necessarily pass from one pole to the other" (Abu-Lughod 1961:32).

There are a number of reasons for this. First, as a town grows it almost necessarily becomes more diversified, enabling the town-dweller to chose his environment more selectively and therefore—if preferred—avoid extreme challenges of change. Second, some rural cultures were traditionally similar to and/or compatible with some urban cultures (especially those found in small towns), and many others have become so. Considerable evidence suggests that rural areas are incorporating more and more elements of the new urban life styles and world views. This urbanization of rural Africa has been caused by two types of change agents: expatriates such as missionaries and Africans who left the village and either returned or keep in communication with people in their rural home. (Caldwell 1969:41 reports that 58 percent of his rural population sample had significant urban experiences.) Third, there is some evidence from Africa and considerable evidence from other developing areas that migration takes place in a steplike fashion, i.e., from rural area to small town and then to large city. Fourth, many Africans migrate to urban areas near their rural homes so that the former bases of security and control are maintained. And fifth, most migrants to urban areas have previously been exposed to urban influences, either on short visits to towns or as the result of the urban influences reaching out into the countryside (Nelson 1969: 11–14).

From the perspective of the individual, anxiety and stress can be minimized in a number of ways. Before migrating to a town, anticipatory socialization can be an important mechanism for adjustment. Although it has not been well studied in Africa,[3] reports from other areas are suggestive, for example, Goldrich's conclusion based upon Latin American research that "a large proportion of [students' peasant families] were oriented toward urban, 'national' life during the students' childhood and probably helped to prepare them for migration and the opportunities available in the city" (1964:333). When in the town, "migrants are shaping the culture of the city," Abu-Lughod asserts, "as much as they are adjusting to it" (1961: 23). Syncretistic patterns are also found. An interesting variant stems from the aspiration some Africans have to participate symbolically in the modern social stratification system when they cannot participate in it substantively. To illustrate, Mitchell shows that urban residents of Zomba used to participate in a dance called *mbeni,* which was a pantomime of European social structure as perceived by the Africans. "The appeal of the

3. Probably the most extensive research on problems of adjusting to urban life and the political consequences of adjustment has been conducted in Latin America. As in Africa, initial reports indicated that migrants faced considerable adjustment problems and that these were conducive to political activism. More recently, however, this position has been effectively criticized. For example, Cornelius concludes that urban in-migration "does not necessarily result in severe frustration . . . and disorganization; and that even where these conditions are present, they do not necessarily lead to political alienation. Nor does alienation necessarily lead to political radicalization or disruptive behavior" (1971:103). In the table below, we have summarized Cornelius's reviews of empirical studies of the consequences of urban in-migration (1971:104–105):

	Findings			
	posi-tive	nega-tive	incon-clusive	not studied
Felt deprivation, frustration of socio-economic expectations	3	27	9	26
Personal and/or social disorganization, maladjustment, anomie, insecurity, primary group breakdown	12	25	2	26
Alienation, non-supportive legitimacy orientations	10	7	1	47
Increased politicization and/or demand/creation	5	18	4	38
Mass "availability," atomization of social relations, felt need for reintegration	1	10	0	54
Political radicalization, support for or participation in disruptive political activity (as a modal pattern of behavior)	2	20	6	37

mbeni dance," he argues, "seems to have been the vicarious participation of the Africans in social relationships from which they were normally excluded" (1956c:12). Probably the most important means of adjustment is the bond of ethnicity, which is extensively discussed in Chapter 6.

From the admittedly fragmentary evidence available, the conclusion must be reached that urban Africa is not wrought with anxiety, stress, and conflict. Comhaire-Sylvain and Comhaire note that, considering the way in which urbanization occurred in Africa, a high degree of social disorganization and maladjustment might be expected. They conclude, however, that the extent of adjustment to urban life has been astonishing (1960:42). A similar conclusion was reached on the basis of interviews conducted in conjunction with the Harvard Project on the Social and Cultural Aspects of Development. "We have found no evidence that more exposure . . . means more psychic stress," Inkeles reports (1970:22). The following chapters help to explain why.

Poverty area school house, Accra, Ghana

5

Urban Conditions

The American or European visitor to Africa discovers many similarities as well as differences between the towns he sees and those in his home country. At least in such major cities as Dakar, Kinshasa, and Mombasa, there are well-planned sections with many modern buildings, good hospitals, and well-dressed educated men carrying out the business of the day. It is in these modern sections that most Europeans and members of the new African elite live and work. The rank-and-file Africans who enter are typically temporary visitors, perhaps entering to work in subordinate positions and then returning home at day's end.

When the visitor ventures beyond the small modern sections, he sees numerous poverty pockets that may appear like his home country's slums. In these densely populated neighborhoods, where most African townsmen live, the same "ills" are individually agglutinated and geographically concentrated: unemployment and illiteracy rates are high, housing is poor, and ill health is common. In many sections, "the extensive confused mass of housing" makes it difficult to locate people, number houses, deliver mail, organize the collection of data for purposes of administration, build an effective sewage disposal system, or collect refuse (see Mabogunje 1967: 55).

In those urban areas where living conditions are closely regulated within the towns' legal boundaries, such poverty pockets develop on the periphery. The participants in a conference on urban problems in East and Central Africa concluded that it is very difficult to regulate behavior in these periurban areas. The result is a "septic fringe" which exists in part because many Africans choose to be free from urban regulations, including those which preclude ramshackle and unsanitary dwellings (Apthorpe 1958b:201).

The coexisting wealthy entrepreneurs and jobless men living below the poverty line, highrise buildings and shacks of thatch, Ph. D.'s and illiterates, and modern hospitals and surface sewage systems are manifestations of pervasive uneven change in the manifold sectors of human life. They are caused by rapid population and labor force growth accompanied by slow economic growth.

The annual rate of population growth in Black Africa is approximately 2.5 percent; the West African region ranks first with 2.8 percent, followed by East Africa at 2.1 percent and Middle Africa at 1.7 percent. Economists have discovered that in a developing country the labor force tends to grow about 50 percent more rapidly than does the population. This means that the labor force in Black Africa is increasing at a rate of approximately 3.75 percent per annum. The increases in gross national products of most African states do not exceed 5 percent per annum and many are considerably less; since employment has been found at most to expand at one half the rate of the gross national product, there are often less than 2.5 percent more jobs each year. The disparity between the labor force increase of 3.75 percent and the employment opportunity increase of at most 2.5 percent creates critical problems of un- and underemployment and urban poverty generally—including poor housing, illiteracy, and disease (see Harbison 1965).

Many researchers have reached equivalent or supportive conclusions. A United Nations report, for instance, states; "In a country with a low per capita level of income and a severe shortage of capital, rapid natural growth of population tends to add to the difficulty of saving and investing enough to [raise output]; for in such circumstances, a large part of the new capital formed each year is preempted for the working equipment, education, housing, health service and so forth required merely to maintain the existing level of capital assets per person" (United Nations, Department of Economic and Social Affairs 1955:15; see also Kamarck 1967: 23–27).

The relative impact of uneven change upon urban Africa is clear from examining urban and rural population increases: the annual rate of population increase in the towns of Africa is approximately 5.0 percent compared with the rural rate of 2.0 percent. This means that the heavy burden of uneven change is imposed upon the towns. Increasing the gross national product does not, unfortunately, offer an immediate solution because it will increase the influx of Africans into the urban wage labor force.

Urban conditions in Black Africa can usefully be described in terms of employment, housing, education and health. These are the critical problem areas, not only in the view of urban experts, but also according to the opinions of many African townsmen, as confirmed by a sample survey which asked respondents to name their "biggest problem" (see Table 5.1). These conditions provide the foci of the present chapter.

Several preliminary cautions must be invoked because of the methodological difficulties of cross-cultural descriptions. First, there is a lacuna of scientific studies dealing with the "pathology" of African urban areas.

Table 5.1. *"What is the biggest problem for you and your family?"* (*Adapted from USIA 1961:6*).

Problem	Accra	Lagos	Abidjan	Dakar
Economic	48%	61%	56%	58%
money	(42%)	(53%)	(41%)	(37%)
employment (acquisition and success)	(6)	(8)	(15)	(21)
Marriage and family	9	9	16	20
Education and education of children	13	12	13	13
Housing	15	3	10	10
Health	5	3	7	16
Long life, peace, and prosperity	—	—	3	12
Religious aims	—	—	—	5
Other problems	2	4	4	3
No problems	3	5	*	*
No opinion	9	7	*	2
	104%†	104%†	109%†	139%†

*Fraction of 1%.
†Totals add to more than 100% since some respondents gave more than one answer.

Second, biased perspectives are likely to be operative in the outsider who observes some of the slumlike conditions that exist in African towns. Too often, the observer's ideal is the healthy and virtuous bucolic life or the model "Western" town, and his points of comparison are invariably those unfavorable to realistic town living, especially in Africa. It is easy to forget that cities everywhere have problems.

Finally, caution must be taken in terms of the relative and absolute evaluation of living conditions. Clinard argues that a country's modal living standards should be used to judge whether or not an area in that country is a slum, pointing out that slum housing found in New York City or Chicago contains facilities that would be regarded as adequate or even good in many parts of the world (1966:4). It is our view that urban conditions are absolute (number of people per toilet, etc.), but that deprivation is relative (see Hanna 1966:86–88).

Employment

African town-dwellers and newly arrived migrants are faced with the problem of maintaining or obtaining employment. In rural areas, it is often possible to subsist through cultivation, herding, and fishing, drawing upon the resources of local vegetation, animal life, and streams—without recourse to money. (Of course, such "extras" as giving a monetary donation

Table 5.2. Occupations of employed persons in Kumasi. (Adapted from Ghana, Census Office 1964b:86.) *

Occupation	Male (total)	(per-cent)	Female (total)	(per-cent)
Professional, technical, and related workers	2,806	4.9	1,087	3.6
Architects, engineers, and surveyors (mainly surveyors)	174		0	
Nurses and midwives	119		523	
Professional medical workers and medical technicians	381		47	
Teachers	930		416	
Clergy and related members of religious orders	241		33	
Draftsmen and science and engineering technicians	618		39	
Other	343		29	
Administrative, executive, and managerial workers	1,444	2.5	45	0.1
Administrators,	317		13	
Directors, managers, and working proprietors (mining, manufacturing, construction, etc.)	339		2	
Other	788		30	
Clerical workers	3,996	7.0	315	1.0
Sales workers	9,048	15.9	18,680	61.3
Working proprietors (wholesale)	490		15	
Working proprietors (retail), and street and news vendors (mainly petty traders)	6,721		17,522	
Working proprietors (retail and whole-sale combined, mainly fish mongers)	208		953	
Other	1,629		190	
Farmers, fishermen, hunters, loggers, and related workers	4,265	7.5	3,617	11.9
Farmers and farm managers	2,635		3,562	
Farm workers and agricultural laborers	1,135		45	
Fishermen and related workers	5		0	
Loggers, hunters, and other forestry workers	490		10	
Miners, quarrymen, and related workers	34	0.1	0	0.0
Workers in transport and communication occupations	4,951	8.7	138	0.5
Drivers (road transport)	3,946		8	
Other	1,005		130	

*For discussion of Table, see p. 80.

Table 5.2. (Continued)

Occupation	Male (total)	(percent)	Female (total)	(percent)
Craftsmen, production process workers, and laborers	25,105	44.2	4,513	14.8
Spinners, weavers, knitters, dyers, and related workers	325		68	
Tailors, cutters, furriers, and related workers	2,961		3,200	
Cutters, lasters, sewers (leather, except gloves and garments), and related workers	730		5	
Furnacemen, rollers, drawers, moulders, and related metal-making and -treating workers	427		0	
Precision instrument makers, watch repairers, jewellers, and related workers	854		11	
Toolmakers, machinists, plumbers, welders, platers, and related workers	3,488		7	
Electricians and related electrical and electronics workers	1,093		4	
Carpenters, joiners, cabinetmakers, coopers, and related workers	3,040		9	
Painters and paperhangers	745		4	
Bricklayers, plasterers, and construction workers	1,705		12	
Potters, kilnmen, glass and clay formers, and related workers	35		121	
Millers, bakers, brewmasters, and related food and beverage workers	907		895	
Stationary engine and excavating and lifting equipment operators and replated workers	133		3	
Longshoremen, freight handlers, and drivers' mates	1,573		6	
Laborers (both light and heavy physical work)	6,813		123	
Other	276		47	
Service, sport, and recreation workers	5,140	9.1	2,081	6.8
Fire fighters, policemen, guards, and related workers	2,257		21	
Housekeepers, cooks, maids, and related workers	1,419		1,249	
Other	1,464		811	
Total	56,789	99.9	30,476	100.0

at a religious ceremony, obtaining a Western education, and receiving modern medical help usually require resources beyond the subsistence level.) But in the towns, there is a monetary price on most necessities. Money must be obtained either by the individual or his patron, yet it is difficult for many Africans to earn a reasonable living because they lack "urban" skills.

Table 5.3.   *Representative occupations ranked by income. (Adapted from Blair 1965:75.)*

Occupations	Estimated Annual Income Range (converted to U.S. dollars)	
	minimum†	*maximum*
High officials, major importers, etc.	$8,400	—
Professionals, large wholesale traders, etc.	2,800	$8,400
Civil servants, teachers, etc.	1,960	2,800
Landlords, contractors, large retail traders, lesser chiefs, etc.	1,680	5,600
Skilled workers, small cash crop farmers, etc.	672	1,680
Unskilled workers, petty traders, etc.	168	336
Casual migrant workers	56	168
Peasants who have some share in the land	14	56
Landless and unemployed	0	14

†Plus or minus two standard deviations.

OCCUPATIONS AND EARNINGS

In most African towns, there are heavy employer demands for skilled workers, but a glut of semiskilled and unskilled labor. Jobs that are obtained vary as much as one might expect in an average town. The occupational breakdown of Kumasi, illustrating the diversity and distribution of jobs in what is probably not an atypical middle-sized town,[1] is shown in Table 5.2. It should be noted that many occupations which would appear to call for special skills are actually performed by semiskilled workers.

The categories in an occupational list should, to be most meaningful, be related to earnings. Some Africans make very good livings—the equivalent of $8,000 or more officially plus additional side payment earnings—but semiskilled or unskilled laborers and petty traders usually make the equivalent of less than one dollar per day. Table 5.3 presents estimates for Africa generally.

1. The distribution of occupations is, of course, related to the size of an urban area. With the exception of special-function towns, an increase in size would probably be accompanied by an increase in the percentage of the work force employed as professionals and administrators. In Western Nigeria, for instance, five population categories of towns ranging from 5,000–10,000 to 80,000 and over had the following percentages of males in administrative and professional work: 1.5, 1.6, 2.8, 3.1, and 4.1 (Mabogunje 1968:126).

Urban wages are, on the average, high by rural standards, but they are low when aspirations, needs, and urban prices are taken into account. Where there is minimum wage legislation, as in Kenya, the basis of the statutory minimum has usually been the requirements of a single male adult worker with a very small margin above physical subsistence. Powdermaker's report of her Luanshya research states: "Although the Africans knew their standard of living was improving and was decidedly higher than in rural and in other industrial areas, a deep bitterness underlay their complaints about wages" (1962:91). Much of the bitterness could be attributed to the effect of Europeans as a higher-paid comparison reference group.

UNEMPLOYMENT AND UNDEREMPLOYMENT

Although most African townsmen are employed, a significant minority is unemployed. In addition, underemployment appears to be widespread. Both unemployment and underemployment are difficult to measure in Africa. The East Africa Royal Commission, for example, could write that "taking the East Africa economy as a whole there is no evidence of unemployment as that is commonly understood" (1955:147). However, the Commission added that Africans resident in urban areas had to support friends and relatives who came to town looking for work but were unable to find it, and that concealed unemployment and underemployment were common. It concluded that their extent "cannot be measured on the basis of the available data but there is general agreement that it is considerable."

Perhaps the primary difficulty in measurement stems from the close link between rural and urban areas. Often, the un- or underemployed person returns to his farm where he subsists and therefore is not counted as un- or underemployed by labor statisticians. A United Nations report states, "Unemployment in the accepted sense is still not significant in East Africa, since the vast majority still have family holdings in the tribal areas and have a place to go to" (United Nations, General Assembly, Committee on Information from Non-Self-Governing Territories 1961:21). Obviously, it is necessary to turn from the "accepted sense" to indicators more meaningful in African towns.

The unemployed are those, mostly in the modern sector of the economy, who are not earning wages though willing, able, and eligible to do so. Three types of underemployment can be conceptualized: (a) partial, meaning that the actual amount of labor time worked is less than the amount of time the worker (or labor force) is able to supply; (b) disguised, which refers to low-intensity work which can be intensified without major capital investment or reinstitutionalization; and (c) potential, when there is a substitutability of capital and labor (cf. Hsieh 1952). It should be noted that partial underemployment is a quantitative concept whereas disguised and potential underemployment have qualitative aspects.

Since the quantity and the quality of un- and underemployment can be viewed in terms of the worker's aspiration, the worker's ability, and the employer's need, a complex typology emerges (see Hanna in press: passim). Other variables could, of course, be introduced. For instance, some urban residents are only seasonally employed due to the agricultural cycle, whereas others are permanently dependent upon nonagricultural employment.

There are many insightful and colorful descriptions of employment difficulties. As an example, Busia's report of the Sekondi-Takoradi social survey states that there were mothers "with tears in their eyes" who told about the struggle to educate their children and the disappointment of having to continue support after their schooling was completed because a job was not to be found; and there were young people who revealed "how humiliated they felt at having to write so many applications" with no favorable reply (1950:63).

Of course, un- and underemployment often have ramifications that extend beyond the tears of job seekers' mothers. Ferman has suggested some potential effects upon the family: "A reduction in purchasing power may be felt by all members of a family and frustrate certain needs and wants. It may mean a realignment of family responsibilities as the worker's spouse or children enter the labor market. There may be changes in the frequency and kind of contact with kin outside the immediate household. Unemployment may also affect the prestige of family members in the eyes of the community and reduce the opportunities for certain kinds of social participation" (n. d.:505).

Prevalent un- and underemployment may pervert the job market. An article in the Nigerian *Weekly News* reflects a pervasive problem. Entitled "Plight of the Jobless," it rhetorically asks whether a good education, skills in typing and shorthand, or other achievements are the qualifications for employment, concluding that the boss ("Oga") has another qualification in mind: "Look here, my friend, na £10 Oga de take" (Onwuegbuchu 1963:7). Even payment may not be enough, an *Eastern States Express* editorial suggests. Entitled "Beware of Fraudulent 'Employers,'" it contains the following warning: "We therefore take this opportunity to warn all job seekers not to increase their sorrows by throwing their money into the drain when they give their last pennies to fraudulent employers who have no jobs to offer them" (1964:2).

Fragmentary reports on unemployment begin to suggest the dimensions of the problem. Although Ghana is one of the more highly developed countries economically, unemployment among males resident in towns frequently exceeds 10 percent. The figures from four Ghanaian urban areas, shown in Figure 5.1, are suggestive. Since unemployment in Ghana as a whole is only 5.8 percent among males and 2.2 percent among females, the figures for urban areas suggest that a process of concentration has

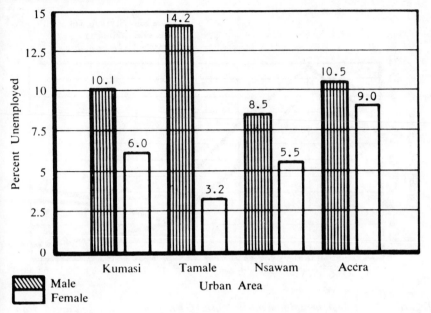

Figure 5.1. Urban Unemployment in Ghana. (Adapted from Ghana 1964c:71, 74, 76, 79.)

taken place. (Counting in towns may also be more accurate.) Unfortunately, the problem of un- and underemployment appears not to be nearing solution. Data compiled by the International Labor Organization indicates that the percentage of Africans in wage-earning employment is declining in many countries, and the results of an annual economic survey conducted by the Kenyan government reveal a decline in the numbers of people in paid employment in every occupational category except public service (Gutkind 1968:361).

A CRITICAL EMPLOYMENT CATEGORY: YOUTH

The 15 to 25 years-old age category is most critically affected by un- and underemployment. Statistics from a sampling of Ghanaians, as portrayed in Figures 5.2 and 5.3, show the age distribution of the unemployed by sex. Among un- and underemployed youths, perhaps the most critical subcategory is composed of those who have obtained a functional modern education. These are of two types: the well-educated and the dropouts.

The well-educated underemployed youths are generally in positions (a) that do not provide satisfactory opportunities for the exercise of their intellect and/or (b) that are subordinate to positions held by less educated older people. These employment "malfunctions" are due to an economy not expanding with sufficient rapidity to absorb new graduates at appropriate levels and to a pattern of recruitment in which job-related merit

Urban Dynamics in Black Africa

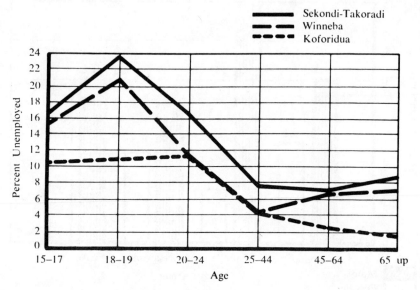

Figure 5.2. Male Unemployment in Three Ghanaian Towns. (Adapted from Ghana 1964c:68, 70, 74.)

does not always take precedence over oldtime nationalist activity, contemporary political loyalty, or family connections.

The second type is created by the failure to provide school dropouts with productive jobs that can absorb their interests and energies. Lacking

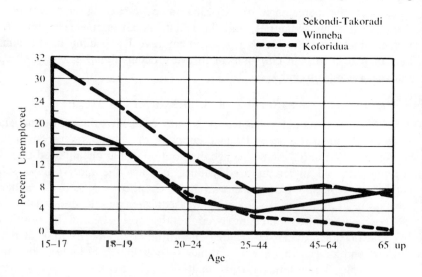

Figure 5.3. Female Unemployment in Three Ghanaian Towns. (Adapted from Ghana 1964c:68, 70, 74.)

the financial and/or intellectual ability to continue their education, yet with aspirations sparked by contacts with modernity, the school dropouts are dissatisfied with the limited opportunities open to them in a slowly expanding economy. Nevertheless, they strive to remain in the towns rather than return to the farms and villages. In Nigeria, Diejomaoh notes that "education is regarded as the means of emancipation from manual work, especially the traditional-type agriculture. Accordingly, primary school-leavers or secondary modern school graduates usually turn their backs on the countryside. When jobs are unavailable in the cities, the young people are reluctant to go back to the rural areas, partly because to return jobless is to admit failure, and partly because desirable types of jobs are not available in the rural areas" (1965:92).

The strong preference of young Africans to work in urban areas has been documented by Clignet and Foster. They show that 54 percent of the secondary school students sampled in the Ivory Coast expressed the desire to work in Abidjan or Bouake, although only 21 percent lived in these towns at the time the study was conducted. Furthermore, only 15 percent of the students expressed a desire to work in a village, although many of their homes were in such a community. "The preference for urban employment," they argue, "reflects a real conflict between community needs, as defined by government policy, and individual needs and aspirations. Students' preferences reflect a realistic appreciation of the greater opportunities and more congenial environment offered by the city" (1966:161).

The young man who has obtained at least a modest education is expected to return interest on the family's financial investment in his education (school tuition usually begins at the primary level). Often, such return can be earned in town, where wage employment is available. (The individual who cannot pay back his family's investment may be ashamed to return home, or even prevented from doing so.) Furthermore, even if a school-leaver is willing to engage in cash-crop farming to earn money, he frequently encounters such formidable obstacles as overcrowded or infertile lands, restrictive traditional land tenure systems, lack of capital loan facilities, and rudimentary transport and market systems. As a result, the youth usually remains in town. Some governments have taken steps toward ameliorating this situation by setting up farm settlement schemes that are in fact subsidized youth training programs. They are often patterned after the Israeli kibbutz and are designed to become self-supporting.

PARASITES AND POLITICIANS

The only alternatives open to many unemployed urban Africans who do not want to (or cannot) return to their rural homes are parasitical or (for a small minority) political. They can become dependent upon their families or ethnic associations, thus lowering the standard of living among the other members. Or they can become dependent upon the community at large, either through welfare agencies, where available, or by resorting to crime.

Some unemployed townsmen are drawn into party politics, engaging in such activities as selling membership cards, controlling crowds at rallies, and using violent methods to subdue opposition. Because some education is useful for many of these activities, party headquarters are often frequented by school-leavers. The earning power of these marginal politicians is usually not high, but they do achieve some sense of accomplishment, participation, and self-esteem.

For a small number of un- or underemployed Africans, another type of outlet is "nonparty politics": anomic unorganized outbursts and similar activities. An editorial in the periodical *West Africa* made these comments on the employment problem in Nigeria: "Potentially the greatest danger point is unemployment. There is no doubt that unemployment, or underemployment, could be a serious threat to political and, in consequence, economic stability. Industrialization, often held out by politicians as a panacea, has, predictably, failed to provide a solution. . . . The real problem is in the towns" (West Africa 1966b:265).

EMPLOYMENT EQUILIBRIUM

The most obvious means of bringing the number and quality of employment opportunities into equilibrium with the number and quality of jobseekers is to increase the rate of economic development so that opportunities increase more rapidly than seekers. This requires rapid industrial and/or agricultural development aided by outside skills and resources. (In the long term, population control will probably also be crucial.) Other means include controlling educational opportunities and curricula, as Tanzania is trying to do with its self-help program.

The employment problem is compounded by the practice in many African countries of subsidizing capital investment by means of allowances, tax reductions, and similar financial strategies. Yet it may be that cheap, inefficient labor is less costly to industry, and that labor-intensive methods have an overall positive effect upon the economies of the new African states. Sometimes, as Edgren points out, an investor is unaware of the advantages of employing labor-intensive methods as opposed to capital-intensive ones; alternatively, he may know about the advantages of labor-intensive methods but encounter insurmountable difficulties establishing them (1965a:178).[2] The economic analysis of the costs and

2. "Although a number of African governments have given emphasis to and experimented with extensive labor utilization," writes Gutkind, "the results have generally not been successful" (1968:359). He reports that in Kenya the Minister of Works, Communication, and Power concluded in the early 1960s that building roads with hand labor was more than twice as expensive as building them with the use of machines.

benefits of capital-versus labor-intensive methods is complex, but it is clear that opportunities for the latter have not systematically been explored and that this omission has contributed to the employment problem.

Housing

As in many areas throughout the world, the urban explosion in Black Africa has led to a serious overcrowding of poor housing facilities. Land is often densely packed with small housing units divided by narrow, rambling alleyways, and many houses are filled to capacity and beyond. Of course, the housing problem in Black Africa exists primarily for Africans living in the poverty pockets; quarters in the modern sections of towns are separated from those of most Africans and "they differ totally in urban arrangement and residence quality" (Denis 1958:277).

QUALITATIVE PROBLEM

Home construction in urban Africa varies considerably; custom, available material and capital, squatter law enforcement, and commitment to the town are among the determinants. Some African houses are indistinguishable from those in the better neighborhoods of an American town. During research tours in Africa, we established residences of several months in a number ot towns. Most of the houses we lived in were spacious and provided the usual modern amenities—running water, electricity, indoor toilets, modern furniture, and in some cases a telephone. However, such houses are usually available only to members of the expatriate elite and the new African elite.

At the other extreme are houses located in poverty pockets. A Sekondi-Takoradi house described by Busia had 16 rooms with a total of 52 occupants. There were rooms for bathing and one latrine. The occupants had to cook their food in an open yard because three rooms meant to be kitchens had been converted for sleeping. One room measuring approximately seven by ten feet was occupied by a man, his two wives and three children, and all their possessions (1950:10). These crowded conditions, which are still found today, mean that a room is used only for sleeping and the town becomes one's living room.

The construction of some houses located on Kampala's dense periphery is illustrative. Roofs may be made of corrugated iron, kerosene tins, grass thatch, papyrus thatch, or matting. Walls are usually constructed from mud and wattle, although concrete, brick, corrugated iron, kerosene tins, and wood are also found. Mud walls vary according to their finish, ranging from the cracked raw state to a hard finish which includes cement and looks like a plastered brick wall. The floors of most houses are hard earth, although some are made of cement. Windows are now common, but

ventilation is usually poor. Of course, not all urban Africans have the benefit of such marginal indoor living. In some large towns, street sleepers can
be found. They may volunteer to watch a shop or home at night in return
for the use of its threshold for occasional sleeping and perhaps a small sum
of money. (Such "verandah boys" were an influential force in the nationalist movements of West Africa.) Railroad yards and piers are also popular
locations for the homeless. Unfortunately, "street sleeping permits no
family life, no privacy, no relief from heat, no escape from cold or rain, and
no decent means for disposing of human waste" (Abrams 1964:4).

QUANTITATIVE EVIDENCE

Reports from every part of Black Africa emphasize the severity of the
housing problem. Over half of Dakar's population has neither electricity
nor water and a third live in houses with mud and straw walls and roofs.
A comparison of Accra surveys in 1948 and 1960 shows that the average
number of persons in a single house increased from 14.2 to 18.4. Four fifths
of the houses in Fort Lamy are constructed entirely of traditional materials. In Dar es Salaam, the average number of inhabitants per 16- by 20-
foot room is eight.

Because African families are relatively large and their dwelling units
are small, the average number of Africans housed per room is high. (A
common type of traditional African residential hut has only one room, but
polygamous and other relatively complex or large families occupy more
than one hut.) As indicated by Figure 5.4, in the three countries for which
statistics are available, urban density per room ranged a decade ago from 1.4
to 3.0; this compares with the United States figure of 0.6.

Estimates of the housing needs of Black Africa provide further insights
to the area's current problems. A United Nations commission which
studied the number of additional dwellings required in the urban areas of
Africa during the period 1960–1975 came to the conclusions shown in
Table 5.4. Clearly, the problem will get worse before it gets better.

*Table 5.4. Additional dwellings required in urban Africa. (Adapted from
United Nations, Department of Economic and Social Affairs, 1958: passim.)*

	Average Annual Requirements			Total Requirements
Requirement	1960–65	1965–70	1970–75	1960–75
Dwellings needed to house population increase	400,000	500,000	700,000	8,000,000
Dwellings needed to replace obsolescent housing stock	100,000	100,000	100,000	1,500,000
Dwellings needed to remedy existing housing shortages	100,000	100,000	100,000	1,500,000
Total	600,000	700,000	900,000	11,000,000

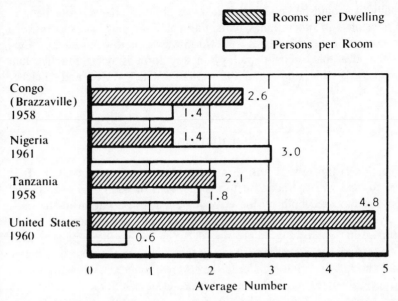

Figure 5.4. Urban Housing. (Adapted from United Nations Department of Economic and Social Affairs 1958:passim.)

BARRIERS TO IMPROVEMENT

The basic cause of the urban housing problem is a lack of funds; this in turn leads to (a) an insufficient number of houses and (b) rental or purchase prices too high for the average worker to afford (in many towns, houses cannot be purchased over time). No African country, whatever its political or administrative orientations, can afford to build enough houses for its urban residents. (The few very rich mining centers, such as the Katanga in Congo [Kinshasa], the Copperbelt in Zambia, and the Williamson Diamonds Town in Tanzania, are possible exceptions.) Furthermore, faced with the decision to allocate scarce resources to either social or productive investment, they have for the most part opted for the latter—e.g., power plants, factories, tractors, and fertilizers. The exceptions to this allocation decision resulted from a determined effort to develop a stable labor force on the part of European entrepreneurs who had sufficient resources for both social and productive investment. Thus in Lubumbashi there was a program that enabled Africans to build their own houses with materials furnished at cost.

Two additional barriers to a solution of the housing problem should be mentioned. Urban redevelopment usually requires the reorganization of social networks, a change that has often been resisted by Africans because of the important and intricate nature of their extended family systems as well as friendship relationships. The solution of moving families to new homes in suburban areas where land is available must additionally overcome the difficulty of transporting workers to their places of employment.

Finally, it should be emphasized that the physical change from poor to good housing—all other things remaining equal—is not likely to make a major change in the life styles and world views of town-dwellers. "Certainly the idea that social pathology in any form is decreased by slum clearance finds little support in the available data" (Fried and Gleicher 1961:304).

Education

Education is the central link in most Africans' aspirational chain. It is aspired to, and when obtained it forms the basis of additional aspirations. This is substantiated both by the large allotment to education in the budgets of African states (it is the highest category in most, sometimes reaching 50 percent) and by the clamor for education among the populace. "For millions of Africans, education is the key that will open the door to a better life and the higher living standards they were promised as the reward of the struggle for national liberation" (Cowan et al. 1965:v).

Throughout the history of Black Africa, an ever greater number of parents sent their children to school or went themselves. Some were forced; some wanted to imitate the ways of Europeans in order to identify psychologically with them; but most were fascinated by the secrets of European power and wisdom or were opportunists who realized that a European education was the key to new power, wisdom, wealth, and prestige (Hanna 1964a:4–5).

Some parents view education in strict economic terms—as an investment that will be repaid with profit after the graduate obtains a job. Education is also a status criterion. Powdermaker reports that Africans in Luanshya were "quick to recognize this new stratification. Although there was no reason why they could not communicate with each other in their vernacular language, a man who did not speak English felt inferior when he was talking to an English-speaking African" (1962:274).

The demand for education is especially high in urban areas for at least three reasons. First, it is likely that aspirations are higher there because young town-dwellers have more contacts with modernity than do their rural counterparts. Second, employment opportunities in the towns are visibly better for the educated man, whereas in the village or on the farm the opportunity difference is generally less apparent. Third, the educational systems of urban areas have been overburdened because of the generally heavy migration to towns as well as the special target migration of youths seeking an education in a town school.

The need for education is especially high in urban areas because of the personnel requirements of a modern infrastructure. The modernization of Africa calls for technical skills to construct buildings, run machines, man

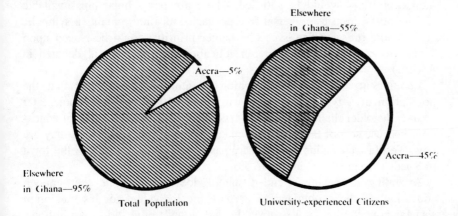

Total Population   University-experienced Citizens

Figure 5.5. The Concentration of University-Experienced Citizens: Ghana and Accra. (Adapted from Ghana 1964a:38, 49.)

bureaucratic posts, conduct scientific experiments, and so forth. Indeed, the major capital asset of an economically developed country, Kuznets has argued, is the body of knowledge it has amassed and its people's capacity and training to use the knowledge effectively (1954).[3]

Suggestively, in Black Africa there is a positive correlation between the size of a town, on the one hand, and literacy, school attendance, and educational achievement, on the other. Data on the relationship between town size and literacy in 1952 in Nigeria are provided in Mabogunje (1968:130). Large towns in the Northern Region, for example, had a literacy rate of 6.6 percent, whereas the smallest towns in the Region displayed a rate of only 1 percent. Drawing upon population and educational statistics from Accra and the rest of Ghana, a dramatic illustration of the relationship between town size and the residence of university-educated citizens is portrayed in Figure 5.5.

EDUCATIONAL DEPRIVATION

With rising aspirations, the population explosion, and the requirements of modernity (economic, political, etc.), the qualified teachers and appropriate school facilities necessary to meet the demands for education are not available. Overseas loans and grants plus such projects as the Peace Corps have filled only a small part of the gap. Even if teachers and facilities were available, many children would not have the funds to enter school or to continue their education to the level where societal needs and

3. Nonmanual education is almost the exclusive province of formal institutions of education, whereas manual craft education—the development of technical skills—takes place both in educational institutions and in apprenticeship systems. For descriptions of apprenticeship systems, see Lloyd 1953a, Callaway 1964, and Peil 1970.

their aspirations would be satisfied. There are few scholarships available and in most countries universal free primary education remains a symbolic goal for the future. (The issue of whether priority should be placed upon some education for all or in-depth education for some is still debated in Africa.)

Looking at educational deprivation quantitatively, one finds that the population of a typical African town is over 50 percent unschooled. Of course, the older the townsman, the less likely he is to have a formal education, because school facilities were much worse in times past then they are now. To illustrate school attendance, past and present, data from the town of Swedru are presented in Figure 5.6.

Attending or having attended school does not indicate that enough education has been obtained to prepare the individual for his maximum societal contribution or to satisy the individual's educational aspirations. We do not have quantitative evidence on the gap between educational aspiration and realization (although its existence is widely recognized), but the nature of actual educational achievement can be illustrated. In Swedru, about three out of ten residents who formerly attended school did not advance beyond the primary level, and nine out of ten did not advance beyond the middle school level. The details are shown in Table 5.5.

QUASI-SCHOOLS

The great demand for education in African towns, combined with the lack of educational opportunities, has led to the establishment of many illegal and/or irrelevant schools. This situation was quite serious in the towns of Congo (Kinshasa) because of a breakdown in educational administration. Unofficial "pamba" schools were set up to give young people a feeling of educational accomplishment although the substance of education in these schools was of dubious value and the schools' entrepreneurs were usually concerned with money rather than education. Raymaekers reports that many adults with only the rudiments of an education set up "schools" of their own. These entrepreneurs may be thrown-outs from training colleges or schools for medical assistants or drop-outs from academic schools. Their "schools" receive the overflow from the regular town schools, mostly unemployed young people with limited abilities (1963b:339).

One of the more popular schools of questionable utility is the commercial institute. Here youths become marginally skilled, as typists for example, but upon graduation they often remain un- or underemployed because the attitudes and concepts necessary to perform a clerk's job satisfactorily have not been learned along with whatever typing skills are obtained.

INVESTMENT AND AFRICANIZATION

Investment in education is a political decision that has consequences for employment, social mobility, life styles, and world views. These in turn

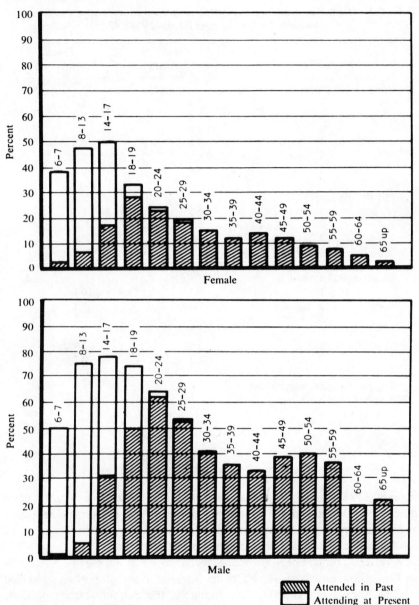

Figure 5.6. School Attendance by Age and Sex, Past and Present: Swedru.
(Adapted from Ghana 1964a:17.)

have an effect upon the political process. Abernethy and Coombe suggest that the continuing expansion of education may lead to the rise of counter-elites or social rebels who, by catalyzing old conflicts or instigating new ones, will impair progress toward meaningful territorial unity. Thus education can be a stimulant of revolution under colonial *and* independence

Table 5.5. *Highest educational level attained among those who attended school:*
Swedru. (Adapted from Ghana 1964a:47.)

Highest Level	Male (percent)	Female (percent)
Primary, all grades	22.1	38.1
1	1.4	5.4
2	2.4	4.4
3	3.0	5.6
4	5.0	6.3
5	4.7	5.6
6	5.6	10.8
Middle, all grades	65.2	53.9
1	6.5	5.9
2	5.9	7.6
3	5.3	6.6
4	47.5	33.8
Secondary, all grades	6.1	3.2
1	0.1	0.1
2	0.6	0.3
3	0.4	0.3
4	1.0	0.5
5	2.9	1.3
6	1.1	0.7
Teacher training, commercial, technical, Arabic, and university	6.6	4.8
	100.0	100.0
N	(2,635)	(1,026)

regimes (1965:288). On the positive side (from the government's point of view), schools provide a convenient setting for the dissemination of government propaganda and thus can be a force for the development of a politically desirable ideology and a sense of community.

A related political decision is the degree to which jobs will be Africanized, i.e., how rapidly there will be an increase in the proportion of skilled jobs performed by Africans. Unfortunately, the current scarcity of skills among Africans (due to educational deprivation) dictates either that expatriates must be retained or that some jobs will be performed less skillfully. This dilemma has led an anonymous observer, apparently a national of the Ivory Coast, to write: "The training and improvement of African manpower in the budding industries of our young states poses a constantly more acute problem. . . . We have stated that this Africanization seems to us indispensable, [but we do not want] bargain-counter Africanization!

... We would like to see our African brothers assemble cars, build houses, manufacture articles, soap, etc. But for that they must know how to work, must be trained" (Fraternité-Matin 1966:79). Thus investment in education must be coordinated with some degree of Africanization in order to achieve the best "fit." If the former is excessive, the political demands of the educated will be a source of unrest. But if Africanization is the more rapid, some jobs will be poorly manned and overall development will, at least in the short run, be impaired.

Health

Health conditions and facilities are generally good throughout some towns, and they are good in the modern sections of more. Nutritious food and clean water are available, a modern sewage system operates, and medical care is first rate. Hospitals such as University Teaching Hospital in Ibadan and Mulago Hospital in Kampala rank relatively high by world standards. However, these conditions and facilities are exceptions to the general pattern.

Various statistics indicate the current state of health in Africa, perhaps the most impressive of which relate to life expectancy. As Figure 5.7 shows,

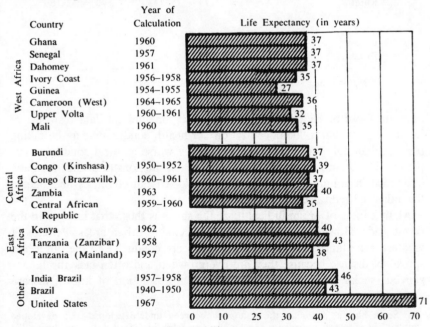

Figure 5.7. Life Expectancy at Birth. (Adapted from United Nations, Economic Commission for Africa 1965b: 65–66; and United Nations, Statistical Office 1968: 428–432.)

African children have (except in a few countries) an average life expectancy of only 30 to 40 years. This expectancy is even less than that in India and Brazil, to name two representative countries from other underdeveloped continents, and it is about half the life expectancy in the United States.[4]

It is difficult to contrast health conditions in urban and rural areas using life expectancy data because of limitations in collection and the confounding influence of frequent migrations and returns. However, some infant mortality rates specific to urban and rural areas are now available (see Table 5.6) and these reveal a sharp contrast between the two milieu. Clearly, the life chances of infants born in towns are considerably greater

Table 5.6. Infant mortality rates.* (*Adapted from United Nations,*
Statistical Office 1969:428, 432.)

Area	Year			
	1964	1965	1966	1967
Chad				
Urban	134			
Rural	162			
Sierra Leone, Western Region				
Urban	121	105	114	142
Rural	173	153	170	160
Canada				
Urban	23	22		21
Rural	27	25		25

*Deaths under one year of age per 1,000 live births.

than are those of their rural age-mates. The longitudinal data from Sierra Leone suggest that a "homogenization" of health conditions may be taking place: urban conditions appear to be getting worse as rural conditions improve. The comparative data from Canada demonstrate the dramatic difference in conditions between two Black African countries and one in the industrialized west.

Many causes of urban ill health are the same as those that operate in the countryside. However, some factors are specific to urban areas. Perhaps of greatest importance is that poverty pockets are conducive to the onset and spread of disease because they are overcrowded and often lack the homogeneous social controls to deal with both the isolation of known disease

4. Some but far from all the difference between underdeveloped and developed country life expectancy statistics can be accounted for by infant mortality during the first year of life. For example, in Chad life expectancy at birth is 32 years and by one year of age it rises to 37 years. For Togo, the figures are 36 and 40. By contrast, the figures for the United States are 71 and 72.

carriers and the disposal of waste by collective action (these activities are common in rural areas).

Analyses in this section cover four debilitating conditions prevalent in urban Africa: malnutrition, contaminated water, poor sanitation, and insufficient medical services. None is unique to towns, although each may create greater problems in towns. It should be noted that several health problems are minimized in towns. For example, maternal and child health are improved for some Africans because necessary facilities are available. Also such diseases as malaria, hookworm infestation, and endemic goiter appear to be less prevalent.

MALNUTRITION

Evidence concerning malnutrition in urban Africa is mixed, due both to urban differences and to the lack of systematic research. For example, the medical officers of Sewa Haji Hospital in Dar es Salaam reported that they had found no clinical signs of widespread malnutrition in town; the only instances discovered were among those living in rural areas (Leslie 1963: 114). On the other hand, Oram concludes that "many Africans in the towns suffer from malnutrition. . . . The migrants are often worse fed than others" (1965:26). It appears that malnutrition remains a problem in many urban areas, although improvement has occurred in some, and that variation within and between countries is considerable.

Malnutrition in towns results from the combination of rural conditions and urban circumstances. The nutritional patterns in rural Africa, often seriously deficient due to poor education or environment, may be transferred to the town by habit and custom. In addition, town life may contribute to malnutrition in the following ways. (1) Convenience and availability of foods encourage a poor dietetic balance. (2) Relatively few women come to town and thus they are not available to cook for men. On their own, many men without facilities or experience for preparing food often take what appears to them to be the easy way out, which often happens to be a malnutritious diet. (3) When wives are brought to the town, they are sometimes not available to cook because they take jobs. A further complication here is that the working mother usually weans her children early, and often does not or cannot supply appropriate nutrient substitutes. (4) The wages of urban dwellers are not always sufficiently high to allow a healthy diet, especially considering the many attractions of town life which call for the expenditure of money (e.g., new clothing) and are often preferred. (5) Buying food tends to be alien in some cultures, since it is available free to the home producer; this has led some Africans to resist buying even though nutritious foods are otherwise unobtainable. (6) Sometimes the quantity of food is nutritious, but the arrangement or number of meals contributes to malnutrition. Men will leave the house early and not return until late at night, going without food in the interim.

INSUFFICIENT OR CONTAMINATED WATER

The 1965 water shortage on the East Coast of the United States dramatically brought to the attention of urban Americans that this necessity of life cannot be taken for granted. In Black Africa, insufficient and/or dirty water are frequent dangers. Urban water shortages are often caused by expansion which outruns the extension or supply of water services. And poor drainage is a key factor in contamination.

Reports from many towns echo the following two from Malawi and Sierra Leone: "The rapid development of Blantyre/Limbe in the past ten years has created a serious water situation. . . . From 1954 to 1958, the average demand of water more than doubled" (United Nations, General Assembly, Committee on Information from Non-Self-Governing Territories 1961:44). In 1957 the Medical Officer of Makeni reported that the need for a supply of good drinking water presented a major problem in Makeni. Although every effort had been made to obtain pure water from private shallow wells (which were the town's main water source), it was judged impossible to get good drinkable water from them, regardless of their appearance (Sierra Leone 1957:3). The improvement of water systems over the past decade has just kept ahead of the urban population explosion. As a result, water service throughout Africa has improved but not nearly to the extent needed to provide all users with sufficient uncontaminated water.

INADEQUATE WASTE DISPOSAL

Water contamination can often be traced to poor systems of waste disposal. "One of the most troublesome aspects of slum life," writes Abrams, "continues to be the simple disposal of human excrement, which may be discharged into a ditch shared by dozens of families or left to decompose between shacks" (1964:5). There are still some African towns in which sewage systems and personal habits are such that some disposal relies upon surface drainage. This system, never satisfactory, creates an especially serious health problem when heavy rains cause flooding. Lagos apparently provides an example of the effect of inadequate waste disposal upon health. There, the stools of 4,759 school children were examined and 85 percent were found to be infected with parasites, the most common being roundworm and hookworm. Dysentery and diarrhea account for about 10 percent of all deaths in the town (Abrams 1964:5).

Fortunately, most major towns now have reticulated sewerage or other acceptable methods, such as septic and conservancy tanks, and bucket and pit latrines. In Lagos, approximately 13,000 "night soil" buckets collected by some 400 workers are needed to dispose of only part of the human excrement. The urban population explosion makes the maintenance of adequate sewage systems almost impossible.

INADEQUATE MEDICAL SERVICES

Residents of African urban areas tend to have relatively better medical services than do their rural counterparts, but in absolute terms there is a tremendous lack of these services. This report from Central Africa is typical: "The number of patients admitted to hospitals grows larger every year, and there is some pressure on hospital bed accommodation. The extra beds being made available are not sufficient to keep pace with the inpatients although the time spent in hospital has been considerably reduced" (United Nations, General Assembly, Committee on Information from Non-Self-Governing Territories 1961:35). And from Northern Nigeria: "The one hospital in Katsina serves the entire province. The next one is about one hundred miles away. . . . The two doctors serve a city of about sixty thousand, with a surrounding population at least as large as that of the town itself. . . . Medical care is severely restricted, but the hospital services are restricted even more severly because of the unstable water supply" (1970:140–141).

Statistics specific to urban areas are generally not available, but the United Nations has compiled national figures. A selection of these clearly demonstrates the degree of medical service inadequacy, especially when they are compared with statistics gathered for countries on other continents (see Figure 5.8).

BARRIERS TO BETTER HEALTH

Insufficient capital and trained personnel are the principal barriers to satisfactory solutions of the critical health problems of urban Africa. Two additional factors, present in some areas, are (a) the politicization of medical doctors and other health specialists, and (b) cultural barriers to change. Concerning the former, in many African towns several of the small number of doctors and specialists have given up full-time practices for active politics. Although their talents may be well spent in politics, the countries of Black Africa cannot afford even this small drain upon their investment in specialized education and health resources. As for the cultural barriers, anthropologists have found that some peoples resist going to hospitals, consulting doctors, taking modern medicines, and so forth. To improve health conditions, this resistance must be broken down; in addition, some Africans must develop new food habits, change their personal hygiene, alter their clothing, introduce shoes and other footwear, have new drinking and water facilities, and generally accept new habits of well-being and sanitation. Most faith healers, cure-all drugs, and practitioners of magic will have to be replaced by their usually more effective modern equivalents.

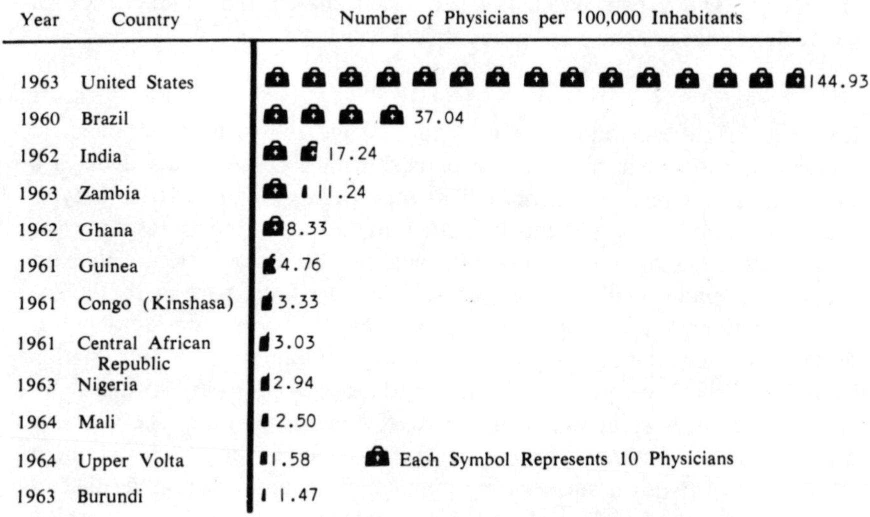

Year	Country	Number of Physicians per 100,000 Inhabitants
1963	United States	🛄 🛄 🛄 🛄 🛄 🛄 🛄 🛄 🛄 🛄 🛄 🛄 🛄 🛄 🛄 144.93
1960	Brazil	🛄 🛄 🛄 🛄 37.04
1962	India	🛄 🛄 17.24
1963	Zambia	🛄 ▌ 11.24
1962	Ghana	🛄 8.33
1961	Guinea	▌ 4.76
1961	Congo (Kinshasa)	▌ 3.33
1961	Central African Republic	▌ 3.03
1963	Nigeria	▌ 2.94
1964	Mali	▌ 2.50
1964	Upper Volta	▌ 1.58 🛄 Each Symbol Represents 10 Physicians
1963	Burundi	▌ 1.47

Figure 5.8. Medical Services. (Adapted from United Nations, Department of Economic and Social Affairs, Statistical Office 1966b: 665–667.)

Poverty Pockets

The poverty pockets of urban Africa can usefully be viewed as "semirural enclaves" into which many of the conditions existing in rural Africa are imported. Many Africans living in rural areas are underemployed or virtually unemployed, as are a significant portion of those who migrate to towns. (Sovani writes: "Can the towns and cities remain dry islands of full employment and very high labor productivity in a sea of rural unemployment and underemployment?" [1964:117–118].) The houses found in rural Black Africa are often made of mud and thatch, perhaps with a zinc or tin roof, as are many houses in the towns. The rural African has few "modern" skills, and in nine cases out of ten he is illiterate. This situation differs only slightly from that found in the poverty pockets of African towns. And health conditions in the African countryside are relatively poor; here again, the situation is not unlike that found in sections of urban Africa. In other words, many "bad" conditions are not primarily caused by urbanization but only relocated (and sometimes magnified) by this process. Urbanization also makes the conditions more visible because it concentrates the deprived in a few densely populated areas.

COSTS

Hawley has argued that, like any major societal change, heavy rural-to-urban migration involves social costs (1964:75). In a sense, rank-and-file Africans

living in poverty pockets are "displaced persons" suffering from the dislocations of the modernization process. Unfortunately, "the cities," as Reissman
puts it, "are the unprepared recipients of a stream of population from the
land" (1964:219).

Returning to previous illustrations, individual costs appear to include a
tendency for many children living in poverty areas to be undernourished
and poorly educated. As for adults faced with unpredictability regarding
the satisfaction of their basic needs as well as those of their children, they
may psychically withdraw or employ other mechanisms of defense, limiting their ability to overcome the deprived condition.

The existence of displaced persons in urban areas is, from one point of
view, quite costly to the modernizing nation state. Public resources are allocated without apparent productive return to maintain the "DP's" in their
marginal life and to prevent them from rioting against, stealing from, or
otherwise negatively affecting those citizens more integrated into the new
way of life. Police and firemen are assigned to the poverty pockets, a few
hospitals and schools are built, and attempts are made to improve some of
the housing and related facilities. Yet to the extent that employment is not
available to those in the poverty pockets, the cost of marginal maintenance
is considered to be without significant compensation. In sum, the argument is that contemporary urbanization may have a poor cost-benefit ratio.

BENEFITS

These poverty pockets, however, do provide some benefits.[5] The fact that
relatively few African urban leaders or townsmen appear to be distressed
by their existence may be an indication that they offer some advantages.[6]
(The benefits to some members of the elite include a reservoir of cheap
labor.) Indeed, many Africans who live in the poverty pockets do not move
out when they are able to. Hauser's observation that large numbers of immigrants from agricultural areas are ill-fitted to cope with the problems of
town life (1963:208) suggests that a less than "fully" urban section of
town may provide an environment to which they more easily adapt.

New values and ways of life usually cannot be assimilated totally or
rapidly without considerable disruption of the personality system. Poverty
pockets provide settings for relatively slow and selective acculturation and
assimilation, forming the basis for the synthesis of a new society, neither
modern Western nor traditional African but a selective fusion of the two.

---

5. The analysis of the benefits of poverty pockets does not imply they should continue to exist indefinitely, or that they are an absolute good. As Shannon points out,
the awareness of cultural differences should not lead to the uncritical acceptance of
any culture (1957:181). Rather, our objective is to indicate the relationship between
the urban conditions that prevail in contemporary Africa and the needs that are manifested by the inhabitants of poverty pockets (and by others) in the new states.

6. One exception was the rat-catalyzed distress in Nairobi, which in 1970 led to the
burning of many shanty-town hovels.

The corollary of such acculturation is greater predictability. The less change from known ways, the more predictable life becomes. Further, the more predictable life is, the less stressful it is likely to be. Ferman suggests, for example, that "far from placing new pressures on the worker, unemployment may actually provide a relief from certain pressures and permit a more predictable existence through . . . aid" (n.d.:509). In urban Black Africa, such aid usually comes from families or ethnic associations. The ethnic networks of urban Africa will be described and analyzed in the following chapter; it should be noted here, however, that they are highly organized and provide town-dwellers with many psychic and social satisfactions of kinds that do not represent dramatic breaks with former rural patterns. There is, however, a danger in the syncretistic halfway house. The means may become an end if upward mobility is thwarted or if second generation town-dwellers become socialized to and satisfied with living in such an enclave.

Many Africans seek adventure in the new towns, and it may be that there are more opportunities for such adventure in the poverty pockets than in the modern sections of towns, at least given the typical migrant's perspectives. What Seeley has perhaps romantically written about American slums may apply to some of their African counterparts: "No society I have lived in before or since, seemed to me to present to so many of its members as many possibilities and actualities of fulfillment of a number at least of basic human demands: for an outlet for aggressiveness, for adventure, for a sense of effectiveness, for deep feelings of belonging without undue sacrifice of uniqueness or identity, for sex satisfaction, for strong if not fierce loyalties, for a sense of independence from the pervasive, omnicompetent, omniscient authority-in-general" (1959:10). However, one must here, too, question enclave life as an end, since it is clearly not the socially and economically most productive arrangement possible, given an economy which, in the future, may expand more rapidly relative to urban growth than it does now.

The primary motive for migrating to urban Africa appears to be economic improvement. Minimizing the cost of living in town is apparently the best way to achieve this goal as well as to survive. The conditions of poverty pockets, such as low rents, represent manifestations of cost minimization, unless government subsidies of housing and other services are to be obtained and not costed. (Such subsidization is obviously impossible given the marginal economies that exist in the countries of Black Africa. Furthermore, to the governments of most African states, investment should involve more than consumption.) "Squatting offers immediate relief from the burden of rent and the threat of eviction, and a long-run prospect of a modicum of comfort and respectability," since some "shantytowns evolve over ten or fifteen years into acceptable working-class neighborhoods" (Nelson 1970:403). Thus from the point of view of the individual, as well as of the state, poverty pockets may in some circumstances be economically rational. (Even unemployment contributes something to the smooth operation of the urban social system, for those free from the constraints of employment can establish a 24-hour, word-of-mouth communications network equivalent to that which operates in rural areas.) However, as the economies of new African states expand in secondary and tertiary sectors, the economic rationality of poverty pockets may disappear.

CHANGE

It appears that change is built into the present set of urban conditions given the motives of migration and continued urban residence. As new values are assimilated, individuals are better able to incorporate additional ones. If the sociocultural system of poverty pockets becomes too static, the adventurers will press for new experiences in the town. As economizing succeeds, funds will be channeled into such high-value budget items as modern education for children.

It should be noted, however, that the dispersion of new values and success in economic activity depend upon general economic expansion. If the economic system does not expand sufficiently to satisfy the new demands of those who live in poverty pockets—put differently, if the pockets offer fewer and fewer benefits to these Africans—then the resulting disjunction is likely to lead to increased pressure upon the political decisionmakers.

Traditional dancing, Umuahia, Nigeria

6

Urban Ethnicity

Ethnic group membership powerfully influences the perspectives and practices of the residents of African towns.[1] "We Europeans and those Africans," "we Banyoro and those Baganda," "we Yoruba and those Hausa"—such conceptualizations take place in many social, political, and economic situations, and they help to maintain and structure the boundaries of culture and interaction. Despite the changes that have taken place since European colonization, "the boundaries between ethnic groups have been able to retain, *or resume,* great significance" (Mercier 1961:62). Indeed, the perceived distinctions among ethnic groups are often as sharp as or sharper than the distinction most Americans make between Negroes and whites (see United States, National Advisory Commission on Civil Disorder, 1968: passim). Thus ethnicity may be considered Africa's equivalent of the "American dilemma" (Myrdal 1944). It affects where one lives, with whom one associates, for whom one votes, at what occupation one works, and so forth. For these reasons, it is sometimes analytically advantageous to view the typical African town as a cluster of partly overlapping ethnic enclaves, each with a somewhat distinct set of perspectives and practices. Although the enclaves may be geographic realities, it is of greater importance that they are behavioral realities. Schematically, this conceptualization is shown in Figure 6.1.

Of course, most societies are composed of more or less distinct ethnic groups. The relative crystallization and intensity of ethnicity in African towns can be traced to at least two situations that contrast with the pattern typically found in more industrialized societies: the heritage of townsmen has traditionally been an important element in their self-images, and there are relatively few countervailing ties and identities.

Most townsmen's ties and identities are closest with an ethnic group

---

1. This statement is almost true by definition since the members of an ethnic group constitute a culture-bearing unit.

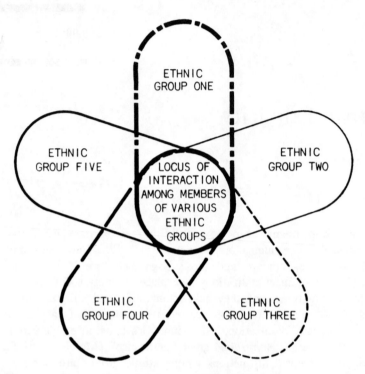

Figure 6.1. A Schema of Ethnic Enclaves.

that includes people outside the urban area: Europeans, Asians, Middle Easterners, and Arabs with those in or from their home countries (as well, perhaps, as with home classes or castes) and Africans with those in or from their home rural areas. Ask the typical African town-dweller the location of his home and he will tell you his traditional family home; the Asian or Middle Easterner will name a country such as Lebanon or India; and the European will say England, France, or Belgium. In town, these ties and identities are reinforced because most residents are to some extent "encapsulated" within their own ethnic network, which serves as a partial barrier between them and the wider urban social system. Striking cultural differences among many groups further hamper the development of an interethnic sense of community.

Turning to countervailing influences, Mitchell writes: "From the socio-logical point of view, I would choose the relative lack of counterbalancing cleavages across the component ethnic groups as one of the significant features of the plural society. The cultural and ethnic differences are by themselves of no account" (1960b:28). Illustrations of counterbalancing cleavages which are relatively weak in urban Africa are transethnic occupational groupings and sports clubs. Gluckman identifies the key factor from an alternative perspective: "The more a man's ties require that his opponents in one set of relations are his allies in another, the greater is likely to be the peace in the feud" (1959:26). Such a shifting of alliances would occur if, for instance, coethnics were actively involved in different occupations and/or sports clubs.

The intensity of a townsman's sense of ethnic identity is often greater in the urban setting than in his previous area of residence. It might even be argued that this identity normally does not exist in most areas from which townsmen came because it is a product of interactions among peoples of different cultures (cf. Mitchell 1962:2). Rouch concluded on the basis of his research in Ghana that, far from being "detribalized," many African immigrants were "supertribalized." Rather than weaken their tribal pride and cohesion, the town and modern life increase them (Rouch 1956:164). Of course, intercultural contacts can and often do take place in rural areas, one example being the historical Ibo migration into rural southern Idoma. In- and outgroup feelings of the members of these two groups clearly illustrate that, although intragroup cohesion is often reinforced by town life, other causes exist.

Attainment of self-government and the transfer of sovereignty have tended to further increase the degree of ethnic consciousness in Africa. There is a widespread fear that power in the hands of members of another ethnic group will lead to the deprivation of one's own group. The fears are probably based partly upon actual incidents of favoritism and partly upon scapegoating to relieve feelings of inadequacy. This situation may spiral if Lloyd is correct that, in the African context, "the greater the fear of one group the greater is the emphasis on their own culture" (1962a:81).

A study illustrative of interethnic perspectives and the impact of self-government was conducted by a preindependence commission "appointed to enquire into the fears of [Nigerian] minorities and the means of allaying them." The commission reported that one or several minorities in each region of Nigeria expressed fears and articulated grievances against the majority ethnic group, and that the minorities expected their problems to become more critical when expatriate administration ended (United Kingdom Colonial Office 1958:87). Recent tragic events in Nigeria suggest the prescience of their expectations.

The importance of ethnic boundaries in the lives of those who reside in African towns does not mean that individuals should be viewed solely as Englishmen, Pakistani, Banyoro, Yoruba, and so forth. On the contrary, the residents are at least in some respects interdependent townsmen participating jointly in urban social, political, and economic systems. Concerning Dakar, Crowder writes: "This maintenance of tribal cohesion is a difficult task in this city of French creation, where a new community of

Dakarois is rapidly coming into existence" (1962:83). However, because ethnicity is more important to African town-dwellers than to most of those who live in Euro-American cities or (in a sense) African rural areas, we devote this chapter to the phenomenon.

Levels of Ethnic Membership

There are essentially three levels, or categories, of ethnic membership in urban Africa. One of these differentiates broad continental ("racial") groups: Europeans, Middle Easterners or Asians (predominantly in West and East Africa, respectively), and Africans. The second differentiates the Africans indigenous to the area in which the town is located from "stranger" Africans who have migrated to it from some distance away. Third, ethnicity distinguishes various tribal, clan, and/or locality groups. In Nigeria the latter would involve distinctions between Yorubas and Ibos, for example, and then more specifically Onitsha and Owerri Ibo tribal groupings, or Ubakala and Olokoro clansmen, or even Nsirimo and Laguru villagers.

There is disagreement among scholars as to the appropriateness of including continental groups in a discussion of ethnicity. Although we believe that in general racial and cultural characteristics display considerable independent variability, significant association has been demonstrated in the African context. Indeed, the term ethnic group—the membership basis of our term ethnicity—"denotes a special group which, within a larger cultural and social system, claims or is accorded a special status in terms of a complex of traits . . . which it exhibits or is believed to exhibit. Such traits are diverse, and there is much variety in the complexes that they form. Prominent among them are those drawn from the religious and linguistic characteristics of the social group, the distinctive skin-pigmentation of its members, their national or geographic origins or those of their forebears" (Tumin 1962:243).[2]

The level of ethnic identity an individual invokes depends upon a variety of situational factors. These include the relevant referential subsystem (e.g., fellow townsmen or rural family members, Africans or Europeans), the kind of cultural response that is involved, and the relevant analytic subsystem (e.g., political or social). These variations are discussed more fully on pp. 133–137.

2. It is sometimes useful to distinguish between an ethnic group and an ethnic category, but, as Cohen notes, the latter often becomes the former as the result of increasing interaction and communication (1969:4). The meaning of "ethnic group" or "ethnic unit" has been a matter of considerable debate among anthropologists. See, for example, Naroll 1964. The meaning we employ is quite loose, but we think it is productive in the present context.

Continental "Racial" Groups and Relations

Europeans were the first relatively permanent residents in many of what are now the towns of Black Africa. The buildings they constructed for trade and administration often were the nascent centers which slowly grew into towns. The centers and towns attracted Africans from surrounding rural areas and Middle Easterners or Asians from their home countries or intermediate points. During the first half of this century, Africans and non-Africans alike came to the towns in increasing numbers. Although many non-Africans have departed voluntarily or have been forced to do so in anticipation of independence or in its aftermath, all major and many minor towns still have non-African minorities.

DISTRIBUTION OF POPULATION

Figure 6.2 portrays the African/non-African population distributions reported in the most recent censuses of three representative countries—Kenya, Uganda, and Ghana—and their three largest towns. It shows that the proportion of non-Africans located in towns is much higher than in the countries themselves. In Kenya, 3 out of 100 residents are non-African, whereas in Nairobi the figure is 41 out of 100. Similarly, Uganda's population is just over 1 percent non-African, but for Kampala the percentage is 49. Comparable situations are found in Tanzania and Zambia. A different pattern is shown for Ghana and its three largest towns: Only 2 out of every 1,000 residents of the country are non-Africans, and in Accra, the locality with the highest proportion of non-Africans, the figure is only 19 out of 1,000. The latter pattern was characteristic of West and most of Central Africa.

COLONIAL POLICIES AND NATIONALISM

During the period of colonial rule, administrative policies structured race relations in African towns. In simplified terms, these were the predominant patterns: British policy was designed to maintain separation between territory and metropole, and among European, Asian, and African, while slowly working toward territorial self-government in the distant future. Officially, this was a manifestation of belief in cultural equality, but in actuality it was perhaps as much an expression of the negative attitude toward non-Europeans held by many British. Formally, French colonial policy was "assimilationist," which meant that Africans were to be "civilized" (i.e., made into "proper" black Frenchmen) and then integrated as equals within the French Union. As practiced, the result was often paternalistic separation, since few Africans were allowed ("able" according to the French) to achieve the status of a Frenchman. Formal Belgian policy was similar to the French, but in practice segregation was common.

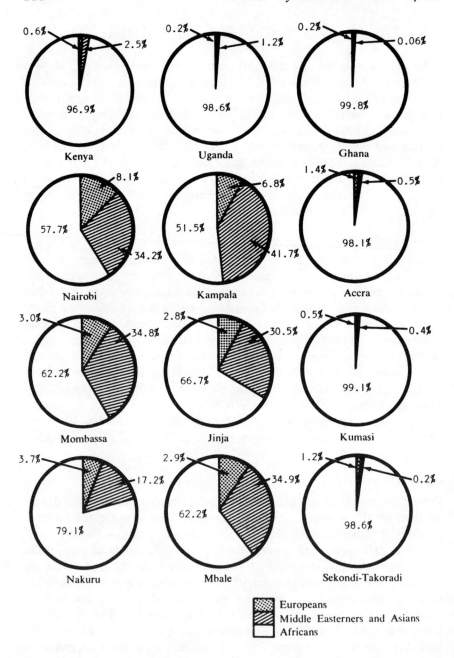

Figure 6.2. The Racial Distribution in Kenya, Uganda, and Ghana and Their Major Towns. (Adapted from Kenya 1964:66, 36–37; Uganda 1962:66, 13; and Ghana 1964a:125, 128, 133.)

The imperial powers' de facto policies of separation were all based upon interracial attitudes unfavorable to an integrated multiracial society. "The indigenous Africans, Europe's external proletariat, were looked upon as being even more licentious and improvident than Europe's internal proletariat, the unskilled worker of Manchester, Lille and Essen, and for most Victorians this was saying a great deal" (Gann 1961:28). Separation further stimulated these attitudes in a pattern of circular causation.

Interracial attitudes in urban Africa emerged from a blend of traditional racial stereotypes plus the confluence of race and class. These stereotypes (elaborated on p. 114f.) can largely be traced to the slave trade era when Europeans viewed Africans as chattels and the latter were subjected to exploitation and degradation. Interracial attitudes are confounded by the fact that Europeans were roughly the equivalent of an upper class, Asians (etc.) of a middle class, and Africans of a lower class. As with race, interclass attitudes have historically not been flattering. In urban Africa, racial and class divisions reinforced each other and made vertical mobility more difficult. Smelser observes: "The important structural feature of such an arrangement is that economic, political, and racial-ethnic memberships *coincide* with each other. Thus, any kind of conflict is likely to assume racial overtones and to arouse the more diffuse loyalties and prejudices of the warring parties" (1963:46).

Independence movements in Black Africa were led by African intellectuals whose "aspirations were frustrated because they continued to be treated as inferiors" (Hanna 1964a:13). The educated African did not receive the respect given to his European counterpart, top jobs in public and private administrations were not open to him, and his wage scale was low compared with that of the Europeans. This is why, as Banton argues, the most important categoric group to force modification of the racial stratification system has been the African intellectual elite (1961a:200). Thus nationalism was a creation of aspiring modern African intellectuals who felt that they had advanced as far as possible within a colonial regime, who wanted to advance further, and who believed that the freedom to do so could be obtained only through independence. Of course, outside influences, e.g., the United Nations, were important components of the eventually successful campaign for independence. Only in southern Africa and in a few coastal enclaves have European vested interests so far succeeded in thwarting racial majority rule.

With independence, some Africans have moved to the top and, as a corollary, Asians and Middle Easterners have been left in a somewhat ambiguous position: subordinate to the new African elite, but on some measures superordinate to the African rank-and-file. The ambiguity arises because racial boundaries prevent Asians and Middle Easterners from entering a unilinear status hierarchy.

RACE RELATIONS

Each "racial" group has its "quarter" in town, the Europeans (now joined by the new African elite) usually in modern sections with favorable locations and well-constructed houses, and the African rank-and-file in average neighborhoods or poverty pockets. If the setting is hilly, the European quarter is usually on a rise offering a breeze and a view of the surrounding countryside, whereas the African quarters are in low-lying areas. In some towns, such as those located in the former Belgian Congo, the separation among races was so extreme before independence that Africans *and* Europeans were not allowed to be in the other's residential quarter at night without a special permit. Southall writes that, in the early period of colonial rule, "It would have taken more than starry-eyed idealism to get [the racial groups] all to live together in an unsegregated fashion. De facto segregation was inevitable at this stage, undoubtedly taken for granted and desired by all" (1965a:34). Contrasting cultures, night noises and drumming, living standards, shack fires, and disease rates all contributed to the "inevitability."

With self-government, neighborhood exclusivesness has disappeared, but there is still a tendency for racial groups to live together. The histograms in Figure 6.3 illustrate the contemporary pattern: Citizens of the United Kingdom make up about one-fifth of the residents in the Harbour and New Takoradi districts of Sekondi-Takoradi, but in other districts of the town their percentage is negligible.

Most personal contacts among racial groups, especially before independence, were limited to formal or business occasions (including the most stereotypic relationship of all—that between the European housewife and her African servants). Europeans, Asians, and Africans might come together during the day to work within the walls of a single office building, interacting as their jobs required, but informal social relations would rarely cross ethnic lines. In contemporary Africa, interracial social relations are increasing, and occasionally African-European mixed couples are seen in public, especially in the towns of former French Africa. (During World War II, mixed couples could also be seen in some of the larger French African towns, but the mix was usually composed of a European and a black resident of one of France's New World colonies.) Nevertheless, such contacts are still probably the exception rather than the rule.

The informal associational life of most residents was also primarily intraracial. In the Mbale area, for instance, there was a club frequented in the main by Europeans (its name used to be "The European Club" but after independence it was changed to "The Mbale Club"); the various Asian groups have their own associations, e.g., the Indian Association, the

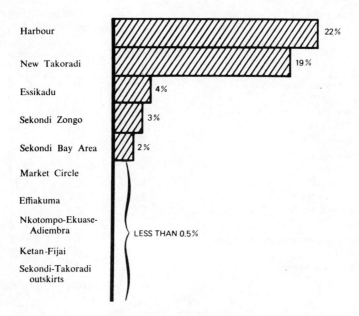

*Figure 6.3. The Percentage of Sekondi-Takoradi Neighbor-
hood Residents Who Are United Kingdom Citizens. (Adapted
from Ghana 1964c: 125–126.)*

Goan Association, and the Gymkhana; and African ethnic group coalescence is reflected by such organizations as the Bugisu Cooperative Union
and the Sebei Welfare Association.

Occupational contrasts were sharp before independence, and many
remain today. Characteristically, Europeans administered the colonial
regime and economy; Asians or Middle Easterners served as clerks or ran
small businesses; Arabs engaged in trade; and Africans provided the unskilled labor. The point is illustrated by data from the Dakar census: Table
6.1 indicates that agriculture and fishing are the exclusive province of
Africans, Lebanese are attracted to the field of commerce, and Europeans
are overrepresented in the administration and police; Figure 6.4 shows
that most Dakar residents at the managerial level were non-African,
whereas Africans made up the large majority of those at other employment
levels.

Although preindependence patterns of race relations have been modified as a result of the transfer of sovereignty, differences remain in patterns
of association, occupational distribution, and residential location. They
are in part maintained by conditions and interests beyond the immediate
control of individual racial groups and therefore cannot be changed by

Table 6.1. *Sphere of regular economic activity in Dakar: Africans,*
Europeans, and Lebanese. (Adapted from Senegal 1962:18.)

Sphere	Africans (percent)	Europeans (percent)	Lebanese (percent)
Agriculture and fishing	8	0	0
Building	8	2	0
Carpentry	5	2	1
Metal work	10	12	1
Clothing industry	5	1	1
Food industry	2	1	2
Transport	5	1	1
Commerce	8	13	73
Administration	7	31	3
Domestic work	9	1	1
Police	4	20	0
Health, religion, and education	2	6	0
Unskilled work	12	2	0
No regular sphere	15	8	17
	100	100	100
N	(61,000)	(8,000)	(1,200)

the will of any one of them. In addition, there are intragroup preferences
for compartmentalization and introversion: for example, many Asians
living in East and Central Africa want to be left alone so that they can
maintain their traditional practices and perspectives apart from those of
Africans.

PERSPECTIVES

Interracial stereotypes developed during the early part of the century have
displayed remarkable tenacity in urban Africa. Some Europeans still believe that Africans are "primitive" and essentially rural, and that Asians,
Middle Easterners, and Arabs are inferior; some members of the latter
groups denigrate Africans; and some Africans think that Asians, Middle
Easterners, or Arabs are aloof and mercenary. Some non-Europeans think
Europeans are unfriendly exploiters.

Perhaps the most mutually negative stereotypes are between the middle
groups (Asians, Arabs, and Middle Easterners) and Africans. African resentment of being "exploited" in the small retail Asian shops and tenement
dwellings parallels American Negro resentment of some white shopkeepers
in black ghettos. "Accumulated wealth is thought to have been earned
solely by the impoverishment of customers and competitors. It is a widespread article of faith that the wealth of the mercantile firms has been
extracted from the Africans and has in no way been created by the activities of the merchants" (Bauer 1954:9). From the Asian's and Middle
Easterner's perspective, a penniless beginning followed by hard work and

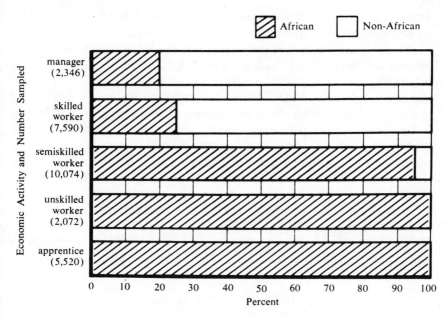

Figure 6.4. The Regular Economic Activity of Africans and Non-Africans in Dakar. (Adapted from Senegal 1962:23.)

some success is being rewarded not by admiration but by jealous hostility and official deprivation. Africanization is perceived to be an ideological guise to force him out of business rather than a constructive developmental step.

Of course, there are open-minded "moderates" in all racial groups, and their numbers are probably increasing. Unfortunately, those who fraternize with members of other groups are sometimes denigrated by their own people. A European who associates too intimately with Asians or Africans may be ostracized from "the club"; an African politician who does not occasionally incorporate an anti-Asian statement into his public pronouncements may be suspected of collaboration and have his political career damaged. As a result, racial boundaries in most African towns remain relatively strong, although some recent changes have been significant.

DIRECTIONS OF CHANGE

The changes in race relations initiated by self-government and independence will continue until new patterns are crystallized. Europeans will be accorded less and less ascriptive deference, but their achievements and failures are likely to be recognized, especially as their structural positions are increasingly in the form of advisor. Personal relationships will be based upon the dual bases of ethnic and functional ties, the latter facilitated because patterns of expatriate self-selection to African posts will preclude most "segregationists" from coming.

It is an almost universal conviction that the beginning of the end has arrived for the small non-African (usually Asian or Middle Eastern) retail merchants and that these "outsiders" will soon be relegated to second-class citizenship (cf. Winder 1962:310) or forced to leave if they do not have African citizenship. Some have turned their attention to manufacture, entertainment, and agricultural credit, but recent sweeping national-izations in Tanzania and business restrictions (or license terminations) in Kenya illustrate a likely trend. The reason for such changes is that neither European protection nor a firm legal umbrella still exists, while at the same time scapegoating and legitimate African aspirations are both rapidly in-creasing. A seminar report of the East African Institute of Social and Cultural Affairs expressed a commonly held position in most of Black Africa: Members of minority groups will have to live in an explicitly African society, and their cultures will not be given a special place (1966: 131).

African Ethnicity

In an Africa increasingly dominated by Africans, attachments to and relations among ethnic groups based upon ties of common kinship and/or rural home area have assumed great importance in the social, economic, and political affairs of most towns. This is reflected in a widespread con-cern for the problem. Most African leaders and the mass media make efforts to condemn "tribalism" and "clannishness," and special conferences have been arranged to discuss the problem. Two newspaper headlines articulate the widely held opinion: "No Unity While Tribalism Lives"; "Our Tribalistic Instincts Stink to High Heaven" (quoted in Hanna 1964a: 22). The editor of a Nigerian newspaper summarized the situation in his country as follows: "Europeans talk about the weather; *Nigerians talk about tribe*" (Enahoro 1966:3). And in introducing the sixteenth confer-ence of the Rhodes-Livingstone Institute, which was entirely devoted to the subject of the "multitribal society," Mayer asserted: "Today it has be-come obvious that multi-tribalism is a focal problem, perhaps even *the* problem, in some of the African states from which the colonial powers have departed" (1962a:vi).

The African population in a typical town is composed of the members of many ethnic groups from within the country plus citizens of several nearby states.[3] Kisumu can serve as a case in point; its 23,526 African

___

3. Subdivisions also exist among the Europeans, Middle Easterners, and Asians liv-ing in African towns. The orientations of European "oldtimers" and "newcomers" differ sharply, often causing two social groups to form. And all expatriates tend to group according to country of origin and/or religion. However, our analyses here focus upon African subdivisions because of their predominant population proportions in virtually all the towns of Black Africa.

residents include members of at least 25 ethnic groups and citizens from Burundi, Ethiopia, Malawi, Rhodesia, Somali, Sudan, Tanzania, Uganda, Zambia, and other African countries. The ethnic totals are shown in Table 6.2.

Table 6.2. The ethnic composition of Kisumu municipality. (Adapted from Kenya, Ministry of Economic Planning and Development; Statistics Division 1965:97.)

Ethnic Group	N
Elgeyo	13
Embu	22
Gabbra	1
Hawiyah	2
Iteso	189
Kamba	224
Kikuyu	498
Kipsigis	123
Kisii	144
Kuria	43
Luhya	4,120
Luo	7,553
Masai	18
Meru	11
Mijikenda	15
Nandi	152
Ogaden	6
Pokomo Riverine	2
Sabaot	4
Sakuye	4
Swahili Shirazi	62
Taita	36
Tharaka	4
Tugen	3
Turkana	5
Ethiopia	17
Rhodesia, Zambia, and Malawi	17
Burundi	1
Somali	43
Sudan	70
Tanzania	477
Uganda	405
Other African countries	9
Unknown	26
Total African population	14,119
Asian	8,355
Arab	371
European	598
Other	83
Total municipal population	23,526

Over a period of time, the heterogeneity of African towns tends to increase. As the following section demonstrates, the ratio of strangers to indigenes has grown significantly. It should be noted here that the composition of the stranger component has itself come to include the representatives of more ethnic groups. In Dakar, for example, the Sereres, Peuls, and Casamancais ' (the latter is a regional grouping of several tribes) were virtually unrepresented in the town according to 1926 and 1931 censuses although they constitute, respectively, 14 percent, 11 percent, and 17 percent of Senegal's population. However, the 1955 census reported that the three groups constituted 5 percent, 5 percent, and 2 percent of the town's population, and recent unofficial statistics place their percentages even higher.

INDIGENES AND STRANGERS

Although most African towns began their growth as the result of European contact and therefore do not have "native oldtimers," the towns were sited on land occupied or claimed by one or a few ethnic groups. In the early stages of urban growth, Africans drawn to a town usually came from its surrounding area and could justly be called "indigenes." Soon afterward, however, people from more distant areas began to migrate to the towns in ever-increasing numbers; these were the African "strangers." Illustrative of stranger-indigene proportions in urban Africa are those in Table 6.3 which report the birthplaces of the residents of fourteen Ghanaian towns using the classifications "this locality," "another locality in the same region," "another region in Ghana," "another country in Africa," and "another country outside Africa." Approximately four out of ten townsmen are "locality" indigenes, and slightly more than one tenth of the townsmen came from outside the country.

Over a period of time, the proportion of strangers in most African towns continues to increase. Figure 6.5 shows the extent to which strangers have "swamped" indigenes in Grand Quartier de New-Bell, Douala. Because the rate of increase for New-Bell strangers has been significantly greater than the rate for indigenes, strangers constitute about two thirds of the locality's population according to the latest census, despite the fact that they were only one eighth of the population in 1916.

Because of cultural differences (for instance, interethnic sanctions are difficult to apply and a common language may not exist) and the frequent conflict of interest between landowners and merchants, relations between strangers and indigenes are often marked by hostility. Henderson's analyses of social and cultural patterns in Onitsha and Calabar led him to conclude that when indigenes reside in their home city, "their particularistic relationship to an entrenched collectivity regarding themselves as 'rightful owners' of that city inevitably tends to be foremost in their minds, but this particularism may diminish when they reside in other cities" (1966:

Table 6.3. *Manifest stranger-indigene proportions in selected Ghanaian towns. (Adapted from Ghana, Census Office 1962:18–24.)*

	Town-Dweller's Birthplace				
		another locality,	another region	Outside Ghana	
	this locality	same region	in Ghana	African country	other country
Town	(percent)	(percent)	(percent)	(percent)	(percent)
Sekondi-Takoradi	31.1	35.3	17.9	14.3	1.4
Cape Coast	64.8	16.0	14.0	4.8	0.4
Swedru	40.5	31.6	18.4	9.3	0.2
Nyakrom-Nkum	65.2	22.6	4.3	7.9	0.0
Tarkwa-Abosso	21.7	41.2	21.4	15.3	0.4
Accra	48.3	2.9	31.6	15.5	1.7
Tema	23.6	16.1	45.4	13.0	1.9
Nsawam	37.8	22.6	22.8	16.6	0.2
New Juaben	43.8	24.3	21.4	10.4	0.1
Oda-Swedru	59.5	12.2	17.7	10.5	0.1
Keta	54.3	29.2	7.2	9.3	0.0
Obuasi	30.4	21.3	36.7	10.6	1.0
Kumasi	39.0	19.1	29.5	11.6	0.8
Sunyani	38.0	16.0	34.5	11.3	0.2

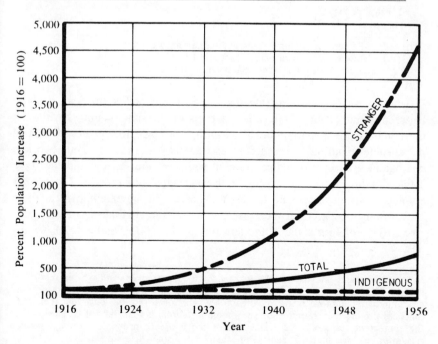

Figure 6.5. *The Total Indigenous and Stranger Population Growth in New-Bell, Douala. (Adapted from Gouellian 1961:257.)*

387). For such reasons, Kuper asserts that the indigene-stranger division is the dominant emerging cleavage in urban Africa today (1965:16).

Among the clearest divisions between strangers and indigenes are those involving freed Africans resettled on a coast and those indigenous to the local area. Two prominent examples of this pattern involve the Americo-Liberians of Liberia and the Creoles of Sierra Leone. In both cases the resettled group began with considerable advantages over the surrounding indigenes in education and other fields. However, whereas the Americo-Liberians have maintained many of their advantages, the Creoles had until the recent military coup d'etat lost much of their control to "natives." A noted Creole writer, the Rev. E. N. Jones, observed that many of his coethnics find it almost impossible to adjust to the now-equal status of those Sierra Leonians who were recently servants and manual laborers. When thinking of Protectorate people, some Creoles have in mind the situation which existed 50 or more years ago (quoted in Banton 1957:109).

Table 6.4. Contrasts in achievement imagery among four Nigerian ethnic groups. (Adapted from Levine 1966:56.)

	Ibo	South Yoruba	North Yoruba	Hausa
Ibo	43%	*	#	#
South Yoruba	*	35%	*	*
North Yoruba	#	*	27%	*
Hausa	#	#	*	17%

% = Percent of coethnic respondents manifesting achievement imagery
# = Interethnic contrast significant at 0.1 level
* = Interethnic contrast not significant at 0.1 level

Tensions in Nigeria illustrate the intensity of conflict that can develop between ethnic groups from different parts of the same country. Although the conflicts are in part political as groups struggle for territorial control or self-determination, cultural contrasts are also significant. Thus two key combatant groups in the Nigerian civil war were the Hausas and the Ibos; Table 6.4 illustrates one aspect of these groups' differences: The former emphasizes achievement norms least, whereas the latter emphasizes them most.[4] Some observers of the Nigerian scene have attributed to the aggressive striving of Ibos some of the tension that led to the outbreak of hostilities.

4. Achievement imagery was determined by a content analysis of written reports of dreams. The author "did not . . . assume that all the reports constituted genuine descriptions of nightdreams or daydreams that had occurred, but only that they were fantasies produced in response to an ambiguous stimulus that did not dictate or bias the content of the story. . . . The request for a dream probably allows a greater relaxation of the subject's censorship than . . . other techniques. . . ." (Levine 1966:52). Actual scoring of dream content relied upon a slight modification of the McClelland-Atkinson system.

Strangers and indigenes do not constitute two monolithic opposing groups. In most African towns, strangers are made up of representatives from several ethnic groups (usually differentiated at the tribal or territorial level), and the same is true of the indigenes (at the clan or tribal level). Often, the members of each stranger and indigenous group restrict their informal contacts to coethnics, live in ethnic residential clusters, and have their own ethnic associations. Thus strangers and indigenes are both fragmented and only on rare occasions act as unified groups. An illustration of this pattern among strangers is provided by Rouch from his research in Ghana. He notes that the migrants who come from outside the country have only one thing in common: that they are strangers. They may not speak the same language or come from the same country. As a result, one finds alliances and conflicts within the stranger category (1956:158).

It should be noted that the operating definitions of stranger and indigene change as a function of the relevant reference group in a particular situation. Ibos from Owerri are strangers in Aba, but they become redefined as indigenes when relationships between Ibos and Yorubas are in question. The concept of stranger itself evolves over time. At the beginning of the colonial era it usually referred to those who did not have local land rights, but in recent years it has sometimes been changed to indicate only noncitizens.

RURAL-URBAN GROUP DIFFERENCES

Among the variety of differences between the urban ethnic group and its rural counterpart, three will be noted here: structure, identity, and function. The first directs attention to the changing character of the extended family and its urban substitutes; identity is concerned with the individual's self-identification and the way others can identify him, and function involves what the alternative structures do.

The extended family is probably the most important structure in the lives of a majority of rural-dwelling Africans. Next in importance come the clan and tribe, which overarch and interrelate with family subdivions. Urbanization has had a profound effect upon the extended family structure, modifying it in significant ways. Litwak's conceptualization is relevant here: "The 'modified extended' family differs from the 'classical extended' family in that is does not demand geographical propinquity, occupational involvement, or nepotism, nor does it have an hierarchical authority structure. On the other hand, it differs from the isolated nuclear family structure in that it does provide significant and continuing aid to the nuclear family" (1960b:10).

Because not all relevant traditional statuses are represented in town, pseudo or ritual kinship is sometimes resorted to as a way "of maintaining a family atmosphere under circumstances looked at as undesirable and temporary" (Comhaire 1956a:50). However, perhaps the most important structural development in urban areas is the emergence of associations that organizationally cohere and sociopolitically represent members of the same ethnic group. They are not common in rural areas precisely because the functions performed are subsumed within traditional structures, especially the classical extended family.

The primary bases of ethnic identity (thus loyalty) in rural Africa are also the extended family, the clan, and/or the tribe. Some Africans who live in towns retain their primary rurally derived identities, but for most a modification takes place. The result is a syncretistic phenomenon, combining a heritage from rural "tribalism" with the requisites of urban living. Wallerstein suggests that ethnic group membership in urban areas is established by urban social relationships rather than traditional criteria. Ethnicity to him means loyalty to an urban-based ethnic group (1960: 133). Thus common home territory (e.g., Malawi) and even common neighborhood (e.g., Brazzaville's Poto Poto) may become bases of quasi-ethnicity in the sense that some cultural similarities and mutual identification develop (see Balandier 1955c:118). Often, identities based upon rural locality and tribe (or clan) are merged or at least mutually reinforcing. In the Copperbelt, according to Harries-Jones, "the 'bond of common home place' and the 'more general categorical similarity of tribal interest' are merged so far as organization of urban activities are concerned" (1969:340).

For the rural-to-urban African migrant, an expansion of identity often takes place. "The urban recognition of common kinship fades almost imperceptibly into that of common ethnic origin between those of the same tribe. There is a tendency to extend the concept of brotherhood metaphorically to all fellow tribesmen" (Southall 1961b:35). A striking example of this phenomenon can be found in Western Nigeria. The use of the term *Yoruba* to refer to the predominant tribe in that area is largely the result of nineteenth-century missionary influences—especially standardization of the previously heterogeneous Yoruba language. It is widely recognized that the concept of "being a Nigerian" is new, but it also appears that "being a Yoruba" is also a relatively new concept (Hodgkin 1957a:42). On the Copperbelt, Africans usually categorize members of tribes not from their home area (where greater discrimination is cutomary) into three or four major groups, such as Bemba, Ngoni, and Lozi. There is also a tendency to place all persons from a given territory into one group; thus all Africans from Malawi (formerly Nyasaland) are called "Nyasa." Failure to differentiate among such Malawi groups as the Henga, the Tonga, and the Tumbuks, Epstein comments, "makes it evident that we are not dealing with some situation of 'resurgent tribalism' or persistence of loyalties and values stemming from a traditional social order" (1958:236).

Two important determinants of the extent to which identity expands are culture (many variations may be involved) and the number of coethnics in a town (large groups tend to subdivide, whereas small ones are often unable to compete on an equal basis and therefore attempt to amalgamate or ally with others). Parkin reports that in Kampala East, the most viable ethnic associations derive from uncentralized tribes with localized, polysegmentary lineage structures. When the immigrants from a tribal group become sufficiently numerous, their urban association is likely to multiply into smaller, independent, segmentally arranged organizations (1966b:91).

Occasionally, complete ethnic redefinition takes place in urban Africa. This is made possible because one's identity is a product of the definitions of self and others. The reason for redefinition usually is related to political, social, or economic needs, e.g., attachment to a group with greater political power, a better social reputation, or greater economic advantage. Banton reports that in Freetown, because the prestige of the Temne is low, some ambitious young members of the tribe seek to pass as Aku or Mandinka by joining their ethnic associations and learning their languages (1956:360).

A third difference between urban ethnicity and its rural counterpart relates to the functional scope and relevance of the group. (See also pp. 139–143.) In rural areas the group is responsible for the distribution of virtually all important values, including wealth, power, and affection; many of the relevant kinship relationships are obligatory. In most urban areas, by contrast, many structures are involved in performing societal functions; the relevance of the ethnic group itself is more limited and may be uncertain or permissive. This conceptualization of change parallels the distinction that Mitchell has made between two uses of the term tribalism. He argues that in rural areas tribalism refers to a total system of interrelationships, but that in towns it is a category of interaction within a wider urban system (1956c: passim). Looked at from the point of view of the individual African town-dweller, change in the functional scope and relevance of ethnicity can analytically be interpreted as a shift in his response orientation, from responding to many aspects of a person or object to responding to a restricted range of them (cf. Parsons and Shils 1954:83).

The towns have many specialized structures to perform portions of what in traditional-rural areas are kinship group functions. Political parties and the government structure are concerned with governing, business and commercial houses with the economic system, and so forth. Smelser notes that changes leading to the development of specialized economic institutions have the necessary consequence of specializing family institutions within non-economic functional spheres, especially emotional gratification and socialization (1963:37).

There are, of course, many exceptions to this general pattern of contrast between rural tribalism and urban ethnicity. One example is provided by the Hausas (whose traditional home is in northern Nigeria) who live in the towns of southwestern Nigeria. As strangers, the Hausas live in communities that are highly autonomous, multipurposive, and integrated. Their "men are engaged in occupations which are functionally interdependent and which bring them into intensive interaction with each other" (Cohen 1966:33). Interdependence also extends to religion, entertainment, and companionship, so that their sector of town "is a highly enduring, on-going system of roles" (idem). The factors that have created such a multifunctional ethnic community are not easy to identify, but the Hausas' kola trade monopoly and their minority status in southwestern Nigeria are undoubtedly important. Yet even in the Hausa case, there are several significant differences between practices and perspectives in their northern homes and in their stranger quarters in the South (Cohen 1969: passim).

ETHNIC CLUSTERS

In the towns of Black Africa, as elsewhere, people tend to reside, associate, and work with their "own kind." The residential tendencies are manifested in ethnic clusters, the organizational manifestation of ethnic associating is the voluntary association, and occupational patterns are expressed in an ethnic division of labor. Clustering is examined in this subsection, and succeeding ones explore associational and occupational patterns.

Ethnic residential clustering is a common phenomenon, both within dwelling units and within neighborhoods. The townsman who chooses to live with or near coethnics increases the predictability of his environment while minimizing the anxiety and stress that derive from uncertainty, and he facilitates the expression and satisfaction of affection among coethnics. Clustering is also imposed by others where segregation is the policy of authority or majority, and is encouraged within cultures with norms to provide hospitality to those who come to town for work, school, family celebrations, and other legitimate activities. Some groups refuse to accept residents of other tribes within their living areas because they feel outsiders would not recognize the authority of their leaders.

The voluntary aspect of most ethnic clustering should be emphasized, since observers of the African—and American—scenes too often point to restrictive housing and other coercive measures. Glazer and Moynihan's explanation of the ethnic composition of Great Neck, New York, applies as well to many neighborhoods in African towns. Great Neck became a Jewish community because it was attractive to Jews, not because they were barred from living in most of the other sections of the city. And as soon as the Jewish population of Great Neck was large enough to establish synagogues and temples, to support ethnic social activities, and to open such specialized businesses as delicatessens, the community became increasingly attractive to them (1963:59).

The dwelling units into which coethnics often cluster range from the multiple household compound to the rented room. (Urban housing costs and shortages help to explain the large numbers of occupants per dwelling unit.) A large house or compound may contain up to one hundred or more coethnics. In some Lagos houses, rooms are allocated to descendents of the original household's founder. As a result, a dozen separate households may exist within a compound—headed by sons, brothers, cousins, aunts, uncles, and grandparents (Marris 1960–1961:120). Rooms also may become little ethnic "cells." Rouch found that coethnic migrants to Ghana often joined together in groups of up to ten men to share one room (1956:152).

Another type of ethnic residential clustering takes place at the neighborhood level. Urban ethnicity is often expressed by the formation of ethnic enclaves and semiautonomous networks of interaction coterminous with them; this pattern is more predominant in towns where there are no administrative controls over place of residence (cf. Gutkind 1962c:180). Many neighborhood clusters are based primarily upon identities derived from tribal ties, but others are formed on bases as narrow as the clan or as broad as between strangers and indigenes. There is, for example, a *zongo* (foreigners' quarter) in virtually every Ghanaian town. McElrath has demonstrated that the most important determinant of neighborhood residence in the 314 subareas of Accra is migrant status, although ethnic group membership and social rank also have significant influence (1968: 43).[5]

Douala provides a useful example of tendencies towards ethnic clustering. Table 6.5 indicates the ethnic composition of the town as a whole, of each of the four sectors, and of the quarters within each sector. Some of the more obvious clustering includes the tendency for members of the Douala ethnic group and their relatives to live either in the Urban Sector or in the Bonaberi Sector, avoiding New-Bell and Bassa. The Basa-Bakoko make up three fourths of the residents in Babylone quarter and constitute a majority in T.S.F. and Nkongmondo quarters. The Bakoundou-Moungo concentrate in the Deido and Akwa-Ville quarters. And those from outside Cameroon make up approximately one out of three residents of the Lagos Senegalais and Banyangui quarters.

The opportunity for coethnics to live in the same neighborhood does not always exist. This has been especially true in towns where settlement patterns were controlled by Europeans and occupancy was on a first come, first served basis. In Zambia, men with families in town were usually placed on a waiting list for married housing and took the first vacancy. This system effectively prevented ethnic clustering (Mitchell 1956b:4). Under such conditions, many families chose to live outside the formal

5. Suttles's study of Chicago's Near West Side, a neighborhood largely populated by Italians, Mexicans, Puerto Ricans, and Negroes, revealed a pattern commonly found in Black Africa: "The boundaries of the neighborhood itself form the outermost perimeter for restricting social relations. . . . Within each neighborhood, each ethnic section is an additional boundary which sharply restricts movement. Adults cross ethnic boundaries to shop or go to work, while children do so in running errands or attending school. Free time and recreation, however, should be spent within one's own ethnic section" (1968:225–226).

Table 6.5. Ethnic residential clusters in Douala. (Adapted from Cameroun, Direction des Affaires Economiques, Service de la Statistique Générale 1956:passim.)

Area	Ethnic Group (percent)										Totals (percent)		
	Douala and relatives	Basa-Bakoko	Bakoundou-Moungo	Yaoundé	M'Bam et Sanaga	Maka	Bamiléké	Bamoun	Other groups	From outside Cameroun	Quarter	Sector	Douala
Douala	21.4	16.4	3.2	9.6	7.2	1.1	26.2	1.5	7.0	6.3			100.0 (113,212)
Urban Sector	52.6	14.3	8.6	2.3	11.4	0.8	4.4	0.9	1.0	3.7		100.0 (36,983)	
Bonanjo Quarter	75.6	8.3	4.2	3.2	2.9	1.0	1.2	0.2	1.0	2.5	100.0 (6,383)		
Akwa-Nord Quarter	64.2	15.1	2.4	7.3	9.4	0.3	0.6	0.3	0.2	0.2	100.0 (1,621)		
Deido Quarter	71.1	1.8	10.8	0.1	5.1	0.1	2.8	0.1	0.8	7.4	100.1 (6,325)		
Akwa-Ville Quarter	40.1	19.6	9.7	2.3	15.6	1.0	6.1	1.3	1.0	3.3	100.0 (22,654)		
New-Bell Sector	1.0	6.7	0.0	3.6	5.2	1.2	41.5	2.2	9.9	8.7		100.0 (61,890)	
T.S.F. Quarter	0.5	56.9	0.0	14.1	6.9	0.1	11.1	3.0	6.3	1.1	100.0 (5,232)		
Ndjongmebi Quarter	0.3	23.6	0.0	13.2	2.4	0.1	54.6	0.5	3.7	1.6	100.0 (4,668)		

Mbambvondo-Bamileke Quarter	0.9	2.8	0.0	13.9	6.9	0.3	57.2	1.7	5.4	10.9	100.0 (4,013)
Haoussa Quarter	0.2	1.7	0.0	13.2	2.3	0.8	69.4	0.6	3.5	8.0	100.0 (6,000)
Lagos Senegalais Quarter	2.4	6.0	0.0	4.3	4.2	3.9	28.5	6.0	12.7	32.0	100.0 (2,603)
Congo Quarter	0.2	2.8	0.0	5.2	2.0	4.0	48.6	4.8	19.5	12.9	100.0 (4,021)
Banyangui Quarter	4.8	6.9	0.0	5.6	7.7	0.5	16.5	3.3	20.6	34.1	100.0 (4,887)
Nkololoun II Quarter	0.1	6.1	0.0	14.6	7.9	0.5	58.6	0.6	10.6	1.0	100.0 (4,301)
Nkongmondo Quarter	1.3	53.0	0.0	7.4	11.1	1.5	5.7	0.6	16.2	3.2	100.0 (6,489)
Nkololoun I Quarter	0.1	1.1	0.0	28.5	2.4	2.3	53.5	0.3	10.6	1.2	100.0 (4,881)
Nkolmitag-Kassalafam-Sebendjoungo Quarter	0.7	6.7	0.0	26.8	4.4	2.2	50.4	0.1	0.0	0.6	100.0 (6,378)
New-Bell Bamileke Quarter	1.1	2.9	0.0	10.3	4.1	0.2	53.7	6.7	7.4	13.6	100.0 (6,983)
Babylone Quarter	0.0	75.9	0.0	10.9	3.1	0.0	9.3	0.0	0.6	0.2	100.0 (1,434)
Bonaberi Sector	46.4	9.2	5.2	6.1	3.9	0.4	22.2	0.6	2.6	3.4	100.0 (8,759)
Bassa Sector	2.0	36.5	1.8	20.7	6.5	3.8	6.8	0.4	20.8	0.7	100.0 (5,580)

town boundaries in unauthorized compounds where they could select neighbors more freely. (The Zambian situation is discussed in Bettison 1961:280.) Now that African leaders make residential policies for the towns, there has been considerable pressure to ease housing regulations. Immigrants' preference for living in ethnic clusters have considerably greater impact than before independence.

Counterforces to ethnic clustering include urban growth, restratification, and some townsmen's preferences for isolation. Urban growth tends to disrupt ethnic clustering because the residents of an overcrowded ethnic enclave tend to scatter in their attempt to find better housing. In Ibadan, for instance, stranger coethnics were separately settled in the first decades of the century under the auspices of the British colonial government and the Ibadan local authorities. But as the town grew and new groups arrived, neighborhood mixing began (see Okonjo 1967:99).

Concerning restratification, Forde comments: "In the early stages of settlement new populations with substantial ethnic homogeneity often developed an esprit de corps of which constructive use could be made in administration, social welfare, etc. But with growing differentiation of occupation, incomes and education in all too frequent conditions of unsatisfactory housing, social cohesion appeared to be poorly maintained" (1956:42). Gable reports that during the early history of Lunsar ethnic neighborhood clustering was common, but that there is now no significant clustering on the basis of occupation, class, or ethnic group (1963:209). The composition of single dwelling units appears to have been similarly affected, for his study revealed that only 22 percent of the houses he sampled were occupied by members of only one ethnic group.

With respect to preference for isolation, some migrants come to town to escape from the ties of family and custom. Speaking about his relatives, one of Balandier's respondents in Brazzaville said: "If I should live with them, they would ruin my life" (1955c:121). As for those already in town, some want to avoid being burdened with family "parasites." Based upon research conducted in Kisangani, Clement reports that " 'family sponging,' in any aspect, is beginning to arouse bitterness among the *evolues,* when it prevents them from saving or devoting a portion of their pay to the satisfaction of their various needs in the spheres of leisure, culture, housing, etc." (1956:373). Indeed, the demands placed upon salaried African town-dwellers constitute one of their most critical personal problems. Thus the preference for isolation may lead a migrant not to settle with coethnics or a town-dweller not to accept coethnics in his home.

ETHNIC ASSOCIATIONS

Most Africans associate disproportionately with coethnics as opposed to members of other ethnic groups. In the two neighborhoods of Nairobi studied by Ross, for example, 83 percent of the respondents indicated that their closest friend was a member of their own tribe (1969:78). And in

Kisangani (then Stanleyville), Pons found that 77 percent of the marriages that took place in the town or in other employment centers were between members of the same tribe (1969:96). The most obvious explanation of the tendency for coethnics to associate with each other is that people with similar practices and perspectives are usually attracted. It is true of Americans in Paris, Chinese in San Francisco, and Italians in Chicago. Another explanation for coethnic associating is related to the probability of meeting members of various ethnic groups. Southall even suggests that "casual friendships may be between kin because they are liable to meet and become acquainted, rather than because non-kin are unacceptable" (1961a: 220). This probability is generated in part by the tendency toward ethnic residential clustering. (Since clustering is partly caused by the tendency of townsmen to associate with coethnics, the relationship is circular and mutually reinforcing.) However, what Parenti reports about the United States is also true of the urban areas of Black Africa: "Residential segregation is not a necessary prerequisite for the maintenance of an ethnic subsocietal structure; *a group can maintain ethnic social cohesion and identity, while lacking an ecological basis*" (1967:721). In Luanshya, for example, Harries-Jones has shown that a townsman's contacts with "homeboys" (people from the same rural locality) are really based upon two different networks and for two different purposes. The homeboys who live in the townsman's urban neighborhood provide the basis of urban political, social, and economic activities, e.g., the development of credit relations, but are typically local ties of relatively short duration. The homeboys comprising the other network, typically near kin, are scattered throughout a territory (although some may be urban neighbors) and serve as links in a communicative system between rural homeland and urban area (1969: 303–304).

The organizational manifestation of ethnic associating is the voluntary association. In most African towns there is a large number of such associations, and most ethnic groups are commonly represented in towns by them. Some of the associations are formally identified as ethnically exclusive; in Umuahia, for instance, clan-based organizations included the Ohuhu Youth Organization and the Ibeku Clan Union. Other associations appear not to be exclusive but in fact are so; Ross reports that in Nairobi there are at least 46 congregations of the African independent church, and many of these have members almost all of whom are coethnics (1969:182).[6]

There is often considerable social and economic pressure to join. Lloyd

6. West and East Africa have often been contrasted in terms of ethnic voluntary associational development, the former being ahead in numbers of organizations and members. Our own research in Umuahia and Mbale indicates that the difference may not be great if functionally equivalent organizations such as cooperative unions and socioreligious groups are counted. It may also be that the West African trend is toward a decline in the ratio of ethnic to nonethnic associations with an opposite trend in East Africa. In Nairobi, for instance, Ross reports that the number of ethnic welfare associations is growing rapidly.

reports that in some parts of Nigeria, "Every man is expected to belong to [his] ethnic association and to attend a reasonable number of meetings; a refusal to join not only deprives a man of any benefits from the association but would also make him unpopular in his home town" (1962b:140). Business demands may also lead to the organization of coethnics. Cohen's study of the Hausa living in southwestern Nigeria indicates that they had to organize in order to protect their kola trade monopoly. "The monopolizing tribal community is forced to organize for political action in order to deal effectively with increasing external pressure, to co-ordinate the co-operation of its members in the common cause, and to mobilize the support of communities from the same tribe in neighboring towns. In this way a closely knit network of well-organized Hausa communities developed . . ." (1966:19). And ethnic associations may be encouraged by politicians interested in developing a reliable basis of support among coethnics (see below, pp. 170–178).

Ethnic associations are not universally joined or even present in a town. Cohen found that a number of Hausa migrants living in southwestern Nigeria "live in small, scattered, loosely knit worker gangs, without forming or joining organizations" (1965:19) and Hamilton's exploratory research in Accra led her to conclude that a majority of that city's residents are not affiliated with voluntary associations, ethnic or otherwise (1966: 111). However, of those associations in Accra for which ethnic composition is reported, the membership of 67 percent was made up of at least 90 percent from one ethnic group (calculated from ibid. :90).

There appear to be at least four general factors that inhibit the development of ethnic associations: insufficient candidate members in town, lack of time in town to organize in the new environment, a traditional sociopolitical system which is centralized (Parkin reports that such centralized groups as the Nyoro, Toro, Soga, and Ganda have no viable ethnic associations in Kampala East [1966:91–95]), and residence by coethnics in towns close to their ethnic group's traditional land, so that the traditional structure satisfies urban organizational needs (as in the case of some Yoruba groups in Lagos). Regarding the last factor, Henderson writes: "It is clearly difficult to create and develop effective new forms of 'tribal' organization in the presence of one's own urban-based tribal community when that community has preserved the prerogatives of its traditional roles. . . ." (1966:389–390). In terms of individual behavior, another possible factor is the socioeconomic status of potential association members. Data from research in the United States suggest that joining and status are positively correlated, a pattern reflected in the scattered evidence available from urban Africa.

Although the ethnic association may perform many of the same functions of the tribal structure—e.g., integration, socialization, and control (of course, associations vary in function)—there are several significant differences between the two. One difference, noted above, is that the boundaries of membership may differ. Some ethnic associations recruit territorially, whereas tribal membership implies meeting customary anthropological criteria. Confusing the two structures is common, and one printed misperception has been subjected to sharp review by Njisane, who charged the author with a serious misconceptualization by referring to "tribal associations" in places where the substantive concern was regional, town, or clan organizations. He thinks that the concept "tribal" has outlived scientific utility and has become emotive, provocative, and obscuring. Njisane concludes by arguing that the spread of nontribal associations is a product of the urban immigrant's increasing needs (1965:15). Of course, there are many variations in the bases and structures of ethnic associational recruitment. Cohen reports that home traditions are relatively unimportant determinants of the character of community participation among Hausas resident in southwestern Nigeria (1966:19), but according to Nzimiro the Ibo State Union in Nigeria "is an urban replica of the structure of Ibo society in rural areas" (1965:25).

A second difference between the new ethnic association and the old tribal structure is that the former is consciously organized, whereas the latter is largely the product of traditional ways. This is similar to the contrast between enacted and customary law. Third, ethnic associations are voluntary, whereas tribal structures are ascriptively encompassing. An active minority develops to organize and lead the association, whereas the average member may be only nominally linked with it. The tribal structure, on the other hand, is a basic element in most Africans' lives.

Fourth, a particular ethnic association may not represent the entire ethnic group. The larger the number of coethnics in any town, the more likely the formation of occupation- and interest-oriented associations. Broom and Kitsuse point out that the ethnic communities enduring after the early periods of immigration are likely to include coethnics in varying stages of individual urbanization. As a result, there is a tendency for plural societies to develop in which the institutions of each ethnic group mirror the larger urban society (1960:117). The tribal structure, in contrast, is invariably multifunctional and generally representative. A fifth difference is in the qualities required for effective leadership. Traditional social systems rely more heavily upon elders, because it has been believed that only over time could one become familiar with the depth and scope of a society's traditions. The leaders of urban ethnic associations, by contrast, should be able to cope with the demands of modernity. This requirement leads to the selection of younger men because it is they who are most likely to have had the relevant preparation: at least some modern schooling.

ETHNIC DIVISION OF LABOR

Members of African ethnic groups are not randomly distributed in the various urban occupations. To the contrary, there is a marked ethnic division of labor in many towns. It is especially clear for the less prestigious occupations, such as night soil collection and prostitution. The division is produced by preferences deriving from particular group cultures, differential opportunities caused by the unequal spread of Western education and other modern means of upward occupational mobility, the efforts of various ethnic groups to maintain their predominance in certain economic areas, and the trust and efficiency that is made possible by collaborating coethnics. (An example of the latter is Hausa predominance in the Nigerian cattle and kola trade. Cohen concludes that under "pre-industrial conditions, the technical problems can be efficiently, and hence economically, overcome when men from one tribe control all or most of the stages of the trade in specific commodities" [1969:20].) Once established, ethnic divisions of labor become institutionalized and free competition may be progressively restricted (cf. Shibutani and Kwan 1964:235). Protection of the resulting vested interests often forces ethnic groups to organize politically.

In order to illustrate the discussion of ethnic division of labor, its manifestation in Dakar is presented in Table 6.6. It shows, *inter alia,* the following differential selection patterns: One out of four Lebous is in agriculture or fishing work, almost one out of four Peuls is in domestic work, more than half the Naures are in commercial pursuits, and two out of five Cap-Verdiens are in building. Clearly, no ethnic group and occupation have an exclusive relationship, but strong tendencies are apparent.

There are at least two important consequences of such an ethnic division of labor: cultural coalescence and status based conflict. Turning to the former, such a division reinforces ties among coethnics because people sharing economic interests tend to interact and to cooperate with each other. Thus an economic component is added to the original ties. As for status based conflict, it stems from the fact that occupation is a prime determinant of status in the new towns. Groups that have many members in white-collar jobs obviously rank higher than those with many members at the blue-collar level. As lower status groups become aware of their rank, attempts may be made to change the division of labor. Conflict among ethnic groups is often based upon such attempts.

Variations in Ethnicity

Ethnic perspectives and practices vary according to the personality characteristics of individual townsmen, the sociocultural characteristics of ethnic groups, the situations in which townsmen find themselves, and the structural positions of the relevant townsman. At the level of the individual, there is a wide variety of personality factors that may determine which perspectives are held and practices performed. These are difficult to specify because, for example, the same personality need may lead to such

Table 6.6. The sphere of regular economic activity in Dakar: African ethnic
groups. (*Adapted from Senegal 1962:18.*)

Occupation	Ethnic Group (percent)									
	Ouolofs	*Lebous*	*Sereres*	*Casamancais and Soussous*	*Toucouleurs*	*Peuls*	*Mandingues, Bambaras, and Sarakoles*	*Maures*	*Cap-Verdiens*	*Others*
Agriculture and fishing	7	26	9	9	5	7	4	2	1	2
Building	9	12	8	9	4	3	6	2	40	2
Carpentry	7	6	5	4	2	2	5	1	8	2
Metal work	11	12	7	11	6	4	13	2	11	10
Clothing industry	7	2	3	7	4	3	2	1	6	2
Food industry	2	1	1	0	1	1	0	10	0	0
Transport	6	6	6	4	4	4	5	1	2	2
Commerce	8	2	6	4	7	11	5	52	3	14
Administration	9	8	7	7	5	3	7	1	6	22
Domestic work	4	2	15	10	19	23	10	4	3	8
Police	2	1	2	12	3	5	8	0	0	17
Health, religion, and education	2	1	2	2	2	2	3	1	1	4
Unskilled work	8	3	17	5	22	18	16	9	1	5
No regular sphere	18	18	12	16	16	14	16	14	18	10
	100	100	100	100	100	100	100	100	100	100

contrasting behavior as rigid retention of traditional ways or their total
rejection. Presumably, healthy personalities are not found at either of these
extremes, since they prefer selective retention or rejection on the basis of
realistic needs.

Perhaps the most important bases of group variance in the quality and
quantity of ethnicity are the traditional perspectives and practices that migrants and immigrants bring with them from their home tribe or clan. One
useful way of examining traditions, suggested by Linton (1952:86–87), is
to distinguish sociocultural systems according to whether they are more or
less integrated. It appears that well-integrated systems are likely to
undergo significant dislocations as a result of rapid change, whereas the
more loosely integrated systems tend to be more receptive to change.[7]

7. Another approach is Apter's distinction between instrumental and consummatory
traditional systems (1960). The former innovate easily by legitimizing change in

Another variable is related to a group's opportunity structure in town. Pons describes two insular groups in Kisangani, the Lokele and the Topoke. The former was quite successful in town and apparently tended "to reject association with other tribes partly on account of their success." The Topoke, on the other hand, was composed of recent migrants considered by others to be "backward"; they were relatively insular "partly because most other tribes tended to reject them" (1969:98).

It is not the purpose of this section, however, to analyze individual personalities or group characteristics for clues to the relationship between them and the perspectives and practices of their members when living in town. Rather, we shall simply note two major factors operative within an urban system that are likely to affect the quality and quantity of ethnicity: the individual's relevant situation and his structural position. Both are related to the general social science proposition that human behavior depends upon the individual's definition of the situation.

SITUATIONAL VARIATION

The world of the average urban African can be viewed in terms of referential, cultural, and analytic subsystems. Those important for him in a particular situation depend upon such factors as where he is physically located, with whom he is associated, and what he is doing. (These are, in turn, influenced by such environmental factors as war and economic development. In a booming economy, for example, a townsman may be less likely to exhibit certain manifestations of ethnicity because he can independently obtain and hold a job. With a depression, he might have to rely upon the welfare of coethnics.)

There are several operative referential subsystems, as illustrated by the townsman who works in the modern section of town, lives in a poverty pocket, and visits his rural home regularly, perhaps during Easter and Christmas vacations. Thus when living in an environment that provides strong reinforcements for customary perspectives and practices, it is likely that custom will prevail regardless of the extent to which the visitor is at other times involved in the modern world of the town. Mitchell is one of several members of the British school of social anthropology who have pointed out that the immigrant's urban environment is likely to change his practices and perspectives but that these changes may not persist if the

---

terms of tradition; achievement norms tend to predominate. The latter are hostile to innovation, while using religion as a pervasive cognitive guide; change tends to take place only as the result of major social upheaval. It can be hypothesized that Africans coming from instrumental systems are more likely to respond effectively to the urban environment, drawing upon elements of custom selectively. Those who come from consummatory systems, on the other hand, would appear more likely to be extreme in their response to town living, either breaking sharply with former perspectives and practices or adhering compulsively to them.

immigrant returns to his traditional home (1962a:128–129). To support this argument Mitchell refers to evidence that town-dwellers who return home usually have little difficulty adjusting to the rural environment, and they resist changes as rigidly as those who have never left the area. Of course, the frequency and length of visits home are important factors. Those who cannot adjust to rural living do not visit often, and when they do it is for a short period of time. Other qualifications should also be introduced, such as the townsman's educational background and occupation. Presumably, these and other conditional factors would influence adjustment.

Within each referential arena, variation takes place as a result of the particular audiences involved. Thus an African's clan may be important in his confrontation with a member of another clan within the same tribal grouping, but it is relatively unimportant when a stranger African is the object of concern. Similarly, Africans of various ethnic groups tend to unite when a confrontation between an African and a European occurs. Banton found such a behavioral pattern in Freetown: "The immigrant . . . is involved in a series of oppositions, African versus European, tribesman versus Creole, Temne versus, say, Mende. The identity he adopts at any moment depends upon how he defines the situation in which he is involved" (1965:145). An example of the relevance of the referential audience is provided by the Rivers State controversy in Port Harcourt. The issue was whether the many tribes in the Rivers area or the many clans of Iboland would control the town. Although there is constant conflict among Rivers tribes and Ibo clans when outsiders are not involved, they both formed united fronts when pitted against each other. The all-embracing Rivers Chiefs and Peoples Congress and Ibo State Union became highly important political organizations throughout the controversy. But when the matter was resolved (temporarily), narrower identities reasserted themselves (Wolpe 1966:422). The importance of the referential audience phenomenon has led leaders of some states to symbolize an international opposition, such as neocolonialism generally or a particular territorial neighbor, as a means of unifying the population within the state.

Culture can analytically be divided into subsystems in a variety of ways. Perhaps the division most relevant for our purposes is between material and nonmaterial elements—e.g., between bicycles and beliefs. In urban Africa, as elsewhere during rapid change, it is clear that the former are significantly more changed and less ethnically determined than the latter. This difference, combined with an overemphasis (on the part of outside observers) of one of the sets of elements, explains two contradictory popular views about Africans who live in urban areas.

One view is that urban Africans are "detribalized" in the sense that they are transformed from tribally oriented villagers into modern-oriented townsmen. The Belgian colonial term *centre extracoutumier* reflected this thinking, for it referred to African sections of a town, implying an artifical and transitory area inhabited by deracinated and detribalized indigenes living under an imposed administrative and judical system. The other popular polar view is that Africans living in town are still "primitive natives" of a "dark continent" who, although cloaking themselves in some vestiges of modernity for aping or opportunistic reasons, really are tribalistic (even retribalized) rural men without realistic prospect of becoming urbane in the foreseeable future.

Visions of detribalization and the primitive satisfy the needs of the holder more than the requirements of accuracy. Reports of detribalization were probably caused by the outside observer's perception of obvious changes in material culture along with his failure to perceive a greater continuity in nonmaterial culture. It is easy to see Africans wearing European clothes, riding bicycles, and listening to the radio, but operative religious beliefs and political styles are more difficult to observe. The outsider's differential perceptions of the two cultural levels were also, as Herskovits put it, "rooted in the ethnocentrism of the industrialized societies and their emphasis on the importance of technological change" (1962:287–288).

Thus detribalization appropriately describes a subset of the practices and perspectives of African townsmen, but for a second subset less change can be observed, and for many townsmen a third subset is going through the process of retribalization. For the latter, "an ethnic group adjusts to the new realities by reorganizing its own traditional customs, or by developing new customs under traditional symbols, often using traditional norms and ideologies to enhance its distinctiveness within the contemporary situation" (Cohen 1969:1).[8] The Hausa people living in Yoruba towns of Western Nigeria, Cohen found, manipulated their own cultural tradition—fostering retribalization—in order to develop an informal political association that could be used as an organizational weapon in contemporary political struggles.

The town life of Africans can be divided into analytic subsystems (which may also be concrete subsystems). Three subsystems prominent in the lives of most town-dwellers are the economic, the political, and the social. It is important to recognize that these subsystems are not likely to display the same degree of ethnicity. The urban economic subsystem is the most modernized, the political subsystem has many elements of both modernity and tradition, and the social subsystem is the most ethnic of the three. Banton gives an important explanation for contrasts such as these: "Whereas a new role as worker in an industrial concern can be added on to a man's other roles without having many immediate effects

8. Mazrui distinguishes between tribalism and traditionalism, arguing that the "erosion of traditionality did not necessarily entail the dimunition of ethnicity" (1969:93).

upon his relations with his fellows, changes in domestic norms react upon a wide range of relationships" (1961b:116). Of course, each subsystem is linked in a number of ways with all others.

The average African townsman participates in many analytic subsystems despite differences in ethnicity among them. For example, the trade union leader is deeply involved in the modern economy analyzing industrial profits and the probability of a layoff. He is likely to be active in a political party or faction, although the particular political unit will tend to be dominated by one ethnic group and opposed by others. And he also participates in a social subsystem, probably by associating disproportionately with coethnics.

STRUCTURAL VARIATION

As a modal pattern, socioeconomic status and ethnicity are inversely related. That is, the higher one's status, the less "ethnic" are his perspectives and practices. Jacobson's study of Mbale (1967) indicates that members of a town's positional "elite" (identified on the basis of office and income) form an identifiable subsystem within the community which in many respects overrides ethnic differences and shares a set of common values and beliefs. (The fact that most of Jacobson's respondents were strangers helps to explain the relatively low intensity of their ethnicity.) In the political arena, we have identified two local subsystems, the "ethnic," in which most coethnics participate, and the "locality," in which most community influentials participate (Hanna and Hanna 1969b). Ethnic group leaders have roles in both subsystems and their ethnicity is overlaid with locality considerations, whereas rank-and-file ethnic group members participate more exclusively in the ethnic subsystem, making countervailing influences minimal.

Greer, whose research has been conducted largely in the United States, reports a highly suggestive finding: "The lower the occupational and educational level, the smaller the scale of an individual's participation. This means, not that he is uninvolved, but that the radius of his interaction is shorter. Kinfolk and the small-scale world of the neighborhood grow relatively more important as we move through the urban landscape toward the low end of the social-rank continuum" (1962:127).

This concept of scale can be used to interpret Ross's data from interviews in two Nairobi neighborhoods. As Table 6.7 shows, negative correlations significant at the .01 level were found between (a) education and income, on the one hand, and (b) same birthplace as best friend, percentage of three best friends from same birthplace, and percentage of three best friends in the same tribe; but there was no significant relationship between either education or income and whether or not the respondent's best friend was a member of the same tribe. Noting also that the birthplace correlations are all higher than the tribal correlations, it is

Table 6.7. *Socioeconomic status and ethnic friendships. (Adapted from*
Ross 1969:201.)

Friendship Relationship	Education	Income
Best friend from same birthplace	—.17*	—.16*
Percentage of three best friends from same birthplace	—.22*	—.21*
Best friend member of same tribe	—.06	—.08
Percentage of three best friends members of same tribe	—.12*	—.16*

*Significant at 0.1 level. N's in the eight cells range from 456 to 471.

possible that for these Nairobi respondents the lower the income and educational level the smaller the scale of their participation. However, the
enlarged scale of those in higher socioeconomic strata tends to go beyond
birthplace locale but *not* beyond tribe. As Ross puts it, "individuals with
higher social status . . . choose their friends from a wide group within
their own ethnic community" (1969:202).

There are several factors that confound a neat linear relationship. The
first is that higher socioeconomic status often requires interethnic contacts,
but such contacts do not necessarily lead to a lessening of ethnicity. The
outcome in part depends upon whether the contacts are perceived in positive or negative terms. If the member of another ethnic group helps the
person to get a job, the result may be a more positive valence toward nonethnic behavior. But if in a situation of job scarcity the competition for an
opening is between members of different ethnic groups, the loser (and
perhaps the winner too) may come out of the situation with a more negative valence. As van den Berghe points out, "studies of culture contact
have overemphasized 'borrowing' of cultural items as the major process of
change through contact. . . . The fact that cultures almost invariably adjust
to and react against as well as borrow from one another has . . . been under-
emphasized" (1964:15).

Second, the resources available to individuals at different status levels
vary. Thus visits to one's rural home provide an opportunity for traditional
behavior and its reinforcement; yet such trips usually require money, and
the necessary funds are not available to all townsmen. In Nairobi, Ross
found that both education and income were significantly correlated with
an index of contact with one's rural home area (1969:73). Similarly, the
practice of polygyny in an urban area requires resources not usually available to wage earners in the modern economic system; Clignet and Sween
found that among members of some ethnic groups polygyny declined and
then increased as one went up the socioeconomic ladder.   Thus means
rather than ends may explain initial change (1969:142).

A third complicating factor is that an individual can obtain status by
association *or* deference (Litwak 1960b:11). If he is of relatively high
status, he may choose to minimize ethnic ties in order to associate with

other members of the elite, or he may emphasize these ties so that his satis-factions come from deference. Note that the need to choose between these alternative means of status is more likely to arise in small towns than in large ones because, in the latter, the community is sufficiently fragmented to permit the pursuit of one without compromising the other.

Fourth, the status of a townsman within a traditional social system may influence the degree of his ethnic orientations. Lloyd, for instance, reports that in Warri increased age tended to be associated with more exclusively coethnic relationships. He attributes the correlation to the increased status an older person has in family and village associations (1962:137). This suggests that a person is attracted to the sphere that offers him the greatest status rewards.

Bases of Sustained Ethnicity in Towns

To many town-dwellers, the prevailing urban discontinuities and con-ditions of Black Africa are potentially stressful. Strangers and new situa-tions must constantly be confronted. An individual may, unpredictably, be deprived of employment, residence, and other necessities. What behavior can be expected in such a situation? (see Hanna 1965:241–242). For one, it is known that potential stress and solidarity of the group are positively associated, at least up to the point at which the former becomes so over-whelming that previous patterns of behavior break down. Thus Lanzetta concluded, on the basis of experimental research, that "as stress increases, individuals attempt to keep interpersonal tensions at a low level, substi-tuting positive, group-oriented behaviors for negative, individually-ori-ented behaviors" (1955:46). Second, it has been found that there is an association between stress and reliance by group members upon their traditional perspectives (cf. Rokeach, Toch, and Rottman 1960:passim). In urban Africa, important intervening factors in these relationships in-clude a sense of continuity, assistance, and resocialization.

SENSE OF CONTINUITY

The ethnic group provides town-dwellers with a sense of continuity by enveloping them in familiar perspectives and practices. Hoselitz observes that persisting social traditions may significantly soften the disorganizing and dislocating effects of rapid technological change and industrialization (1963:15).

Special note should be taken of the continuity that exists in behavioral regulation. Authoritative agents of urban social control do not have the manpower, resources, and perhaps respect that are necessary to insure satisfactory levels of predictability and order. Nor are transethnic norms sufficiently learned, habituated, or internalized. In this common situation, ethnic associates and associations make an important contribution. Some coethnics are quite active in regulating behavior, and negative sanctions can be severe—even more than those of a public court because the reputation of the ethnic group may be at stake. For example, the Luo association in Nairobi has been known to return all girls suspected of prostitution to their rural homes. The general point is made by Banton: "Membership in any particular tribal group often acquires prestige value so that migrants may express concern about the image of their group held by others, and seek to improve it" (1965:147).

Ethnic continuity would appear to be in conflict with the aspirations for new values and ways of life. Ross, for example, suggests the hypothesis that maintaining "strong [home] ties serves to subject individuals to severe cross-pressures. They must respond to demands, often quite contradictory, from the rural and urban environments in which they exist" (1969:68). Thus there is an apparent paradox if in fact most individuals cannot progress "forward" without a link "backward." Sjoberg among others has argued that revolutionary change requires that certain traditions be sustained or revived (1960a:passim). (Of course, it is exceedingly difficult to determine the optimal balance between rapid change and continuity.) But the paradox is more apparent than real, as we have argued above in the section on situational variation.

ASSISTANCE

Coethnics provide town-dwellers with assistance in time of need. Indeed, Southall argues that ethnic relations in a town are principally determined by mutual assistance needs and that the influence of a town-dwelling ethnic group member is based less upon his tribal status than upon his length of stay in town, his material success, and his housing facilities—all determinants of his ability to help others (1965:42).[9]

Some modern industrial states provide citizens with social security so that in time of need minimum housing, food, clothing, medical services, and psychiatric care can be obtained. The state and local governments of Black Africa are not sufficiently wealthy to perform these services. Conveniently, however, communal self-help is customary in many African societies. In the towns this self-help has often been institutionalized within ethnic associations. For instance, Busia reports that in Sekondi-Takoradi members are assisted during litigation, illness or bereavement, unemployment, and other times of need (1950:75). Funds for such services are usually accumulated by charging membership dues and receiving donations from wealthy coethnics, but other methods are also employed. In

9. This subsection is primarily concerned with the social welfare type of coethnic assistance because it appears to be so widespread and important. It should be noted, however, that political assistance for collective advantage in the urban political arena has also been found to serve as the basis of sustained ethnicity. Thus, as noted above, the Hausa living in the Yoruba towns of Western Nigeria have become "retribalized" in order to fight the political battles necessary to maintain control of their traditional trading commodities.

Kampala, for example, members of the Watutsi Welfare Association present exhibitions of traditional dances before European, Asian, and African audiences, charging admission for the performances.

An individual may be assisted upon his initial arrival in town or later on when trouble arises. It is common practice in many ethnic groups for prospective migrants to contact relatives in town to secure lodging before departure so that they have a base of operations while job hunting. Fully 85 percent of the respondents in a Nairobi sample indicated that they had stayed with relatives upon first arriving in the town. The responses of rural respondents in Ghana reveal that among prospective migrants approximately two thirds plan to stay with a relative or fellow villager when they first arrive in town, and slightly over half the urban respondents reported that they had stayed with such a person when they first arrived (Caldwell 1969:130). The smaller urban figure may be an artifact of the fewer number of relatives (etc.) in town when the now town-dwellers arrived sometime in the past, and or/or hopes of an easy time upon arrival.[10] Relatives are also relied upon when an individual is unemployed (e.g., for food), threatened (e.g., for protection), and so forth. "However much [the migrant] may be bewildered by the strangeness of life in town he is never alone, nor is he dependent on his own strength and confidence to anything like the same extent as the man who has only the support of his wife" (Leslie 1963:60). A side benefit of hospitality is that interurban travel is facilitated because a fellow ethnic group member can be counted on for free room and board in most of the towns of a country, given the ethnic scatter that results from intense urban migration.

Townsmen are often helped in getting employment by coethnics. In Ghana, according to Caldwell's urban survey data, 80 percent of the responding townsmen help relatives from their village find jobs (1969:132). This is done in two ways: transmission of insider knowledge and hiring directly. Thus in Ibadan, according to Okonjo, a payment must be made under the table to get most jobs or to take screening tests. "If the wrong persons are approached it is possible to spend £30 on trying to obtain a job without success. It is here that the experience of the members of the community who have lived in Ibadan longest is of importance." They know who to contact, how much to pay, and so forth (1967:103). Direct hiring assistance is especially relevant to those ethnic groups with members well placed in business or government circles. Even though the business might not be highly successful or large, a delivery boy is needed and perhaps a salesman too. If so, it may be "easier" and safer to employ a coethnic. Credit for investment also tends to remain within the boundaries of family or friendship groups because the investor prefers to deal with those with whom he shares norms and upon whom social pressures can be

10. Okonjo reports that the hosts of new Ibo migrants in Ibadan often intervene to such an extent that they "prove irksome to the migrant, [leading] to the newly employed seeking rooms of his own as soon as possible" (1967:104).

exerted (Breton 1966:4). In the United States, the economic strength of such groups as the Jews, Armenians, and Greeks can in part be traced to strong family ties, entry into family businesses, transmittal of skills, and ethnic patronage. The poor economic status of most Negroes, on the other hand, might be related in part to a lack of coalescence in these ways (cf. Glazer and Moynihan 1963:passim).

The desire and obligation to assist coethnics may slowly erode, especially among the more "modernized" members of a family. Perhaps their principal objection is the inability to accumulate wealth owing to the escalation of demands by poor coethnics as earnings rise. However, although there is a tendency for those Africans who are more deeply involved in urban life to criticize the obligation to assist coethnics, it is rare that a request for help is turned down (United Nations Secretary General 1958:42).

RESOCIALIZATION

Coethnics can help new arrivals adjust to, and become integrated in, the urban environment. Banton argues that "the immigrant is absorbed into the urban system, not by a process of individual change in line with the melting-pot conception of assimilation, but through his membership in a local group of people drawn from his own tribe" (1965:147). Thus ethnic associations "blend apparently divergent aims and interest. On the one hand, they emphasize tribal duties and obligations; on the other, they urge the adoption of a modern outlook and they establish new social practices." In other words, "they build for a migrant a cultural bridge" (Little 1965:87).

Coethnics can contribute to resocialization in a variety of ways. They pass on town lore, provide political education and guidance, indicate where certain necessities are located, offer adult education classes which teach the rudiments of the local lingua franca, give technical training, instill discipline, and so forth. Two means of resocialization deserve special note: the ethnic association as a societal model and the ethnic group as a basis of differentiation.

Many ethnic associations are partially representative models of the larger urban system in which they are located. Sometimes the titles given to members are the same as titles used in the larger system—e.g., "mayor" and "councillor." In this vein, Parkin hypothesizes that one latent function of associations is to provide a miniature hierarchical set of positions for socializing migrants from egalitarian societies who are unfamiliar with urban status systems" (1966b:93).

The ethnic group also provides town-dwellers with a means of vertical social differentiation. "Except in a small village," Shibutani and Kwan remind us, "one cannot possibly treat each individual he encounters as a unique human being, for he has neither the time nor the opportunity to acquire all the pertinent details. In such contexts as these, ethnic categories assume importance" (1965:39). This generalization was shown to apply to Black Africa by Mitchell in his monograph *The Kalela Dance*. In it he argues that categorization by ethnic group makes it easier for an African townsman to determine what behavior would be most relevant toward any other townsman (1956c:22).

The impact of the ethnic group's resocialization function potentially goes far beyond the urban area because of the constant flow of individuals, ideas, and money between town and countryside. "The main channels through which the wealth of civilization flows into most of the rural areas today," writes Wilson, "are the personal obligations which bind the African labourer in town to assist his people in the country" (1942:38). Ethnic rivalries often increase the outflow of money to rural areas, for each group wants his home to be more modern than nearby ethnic areas. Less measurable but more important is the dissemination of styles and viewpoints. In many rural areas returnees enhance their prestige in the village by manifesting urbane practices and perspectives.

Gugler argues that in the former Eastern Nigeria, the main concern of ethnic associations was with the affairs of their rural home areas (1965:6). The name *improvement union* when used for a group's ethnic association often refers to improvement of the home rather than to the well-being of townsmen or the town itself. (Many decisions concerning village affairs are made by town-dwellers rather than village residents; the former may be called home to advise or control during holidays or local crises.) Thus the association helps to build roads, schools, libraries, hospitals, dispensaries, and maternity clinics, to advise or control local policymakers, and so forth. Of course, such improvements have direct and indirect benefits for the town-dwelling coethnic: they moderate family parasitism by tending to equalize urban and rural satisfactions, improve "resort" facilities because many Africans spend vacations in their home rural areas, and improve "retirement community" conditions because most Africans living in urban areas plan to return to the countryside after their working days are over. An effect of a different order is that contacts with coethnics in the townsman's rural home serve to reinforce traditional practices and perspectives in town.

In the preceding paragraphs we have emphasized the resocializing function of coethnics. It is important to recognize, however, that beyond a certain point the involvement of a townsman with his coethnics might impede resocialization. Continuity, under these conditions, may predominate over change. A similar situation is found in some ethnic ghettos located in the United States where subcultures have in part been cut off from the mainstream of the American society. Perhaps one requisite of maintained resocialization is an open society in which members of all ethnic groups have opportunities for upward mobility so that new life styles and world views can be communicated to coethnics willing to listen and still able to aspire within the mainstream.

Elite wedding, Kampala, Uganda

7

Nonethnic Perspectives
and Practices

The presence of nonethnic perspectives and practices provides an important indicator of an individual's relationship to modern urban society and of the nature of the society itself. For the individual, these patterns usually represent new involvements, sometimes reflecting alienation from former alternatives. At the societal level, these patterns indicate the direction of change and the inherent character of formative institutions.

Syncretism

Although we examine ethnic and nonethnic behaviors sequentially, contemporary societies in urban Africa are characterized by syncretistic combinations of ethnic and nonethnic perspectives and practices. Ward and Rustow are correct in writing that "no society is wholly modern; all represent a mixture of modern and traditional elements" (1964:444).

There are basically two kinds of syncretistic "mixes." One is fusion, the combination of tradition and modernity in specific elements of culture or patterns of interpersonal interaction. The second kind of syncretism is characterized by parallel cultural elements or interactional patterns. Parallel interactional structures are often the privilege of the affluent, because "the new 'affluence,' often cited as a conductor of greater assimilation, may actually provide minorities with the financial and psychological wherewithal for building even more elaborate parallel sub-societal structures" (Parenti 1967:721).

Thus ethnic and nonethnic behaviors need not be antagonistic or mutually exclusive. "It has often been thought," Ward and Rustow write, "that these elements stood in basic opposition to each other, and that there was implicit in the social process some force which would ultimately lead to the purgation of traditional 'survivals,' leaving as a residue the purely 'modern' society" (1964:444–445). However, as they demonstrate in

Japan, "the role of traditional attitudes and instrutions in the modernization process has often been symbiotic rather than antagonistic" (ibid:445).
Similarly, Mayer forcefully argues against the notion of mutually exclusive
sets of practices or perspectives. "Active involvement in within-town
social-systems," he writes, "is no index of non-involvement in extra-town
systems" (1962b:581).

Further insight into the pervasiveness of syncretism is provided by evidence from a number of the "more developed" countries which suggests
that, in modified form, some elements of ethnicity continue to influence
behavior. Aldous surveyed data from such cities as Detroit, London, San
Francisco, Los Angeles, and New Haven, concluding that kinship remains
a viable interpersonal tie (1962:6–12). Glazer and Moynihan observed
that, among the Jews and Catholics of New York City, the extent of the
differences in the perspectives of the two groups has not significantly declined over time (1963:299). And in Los Angeles, Greer found that the
extended family remained important, judging by the fact that one third of
the respondents in his sample visited uncles, cousins, and equivalent relatives at least once a month (1962:90). Thus it is reasonable to expect that
in Africa, despite the development of nonethnic perspectives and practices, ethnicity will remain operative for an indefinite period of time.

Nonethnic Clusters and Associations

In Chapter 6, the ethnic structures that buffer the potential stresses of
urban life were analyzed. Functionally equivalent nonethnic structures
coexist with them, some dating to the earliest period of a town's history,
but more of them the result of recent changes taking place in urban areas.
Among the many nonethnic structures that help a town-dweller cope with
urban life, two of the more important are residential clusters and associations.

RESIDENTIAL CLUSTERS

Most town-dwellers in Black Africa live in neighborhoods that display at
least some characteristics of ethnic clustering. However, there are a few
towns in which ethnic clustering has never existed beyond the level of the
dwelling unit. As pointed out, this has for the most part been the result of
European administrative policies, often taken over by independent governments, rather than the preferences of African townsmen. Where dwelling units are controlled by a central administration, they too have been
ethnically mixed because assignments were often on a "first come, first
served" basis.

Significant to the observer of urban African affairs is the slow but steady
shift from residential clustering based upon ethnic identifications to clus-

tering based upon other factors, especially wealth and education. One of the reasons for this shift is the departure of Europeans from elite residential neighborhoods. In Lusaka, as elsewhere, "the *de facto* racial segregation of the past has now given way to social segregation by income group" (Collins 1969:23). An important correlate of the shift is that, in more ethnically heterogeneous residential areas, friendship patterns are likely to be more heterogeneous. This often leads to a lessening of other relationships based upon ethnic group membership and an increase in those based upon other qualifications.

Nonethnic clustering is most characteristic of upper and middle class townsmen. Pons's research in Kisangani, for instance, indicates that the higher a home owner is on the occupational ladder, the less likely he is to have immediate neighbors of the same ethnic group. His data are reported in Figure 7.1.

The emotional strength of nonethnic interests is demonstrated when residents resist having coethnic neighbors. A study of the Nakawa housing estate in Kampala showed that ethnic solidarity between resident and potential in-migrant "diminishes when the issue revolves around entry into a small neighborhood group, where membership according to criteria of income, occupation and education is mutually recognized" (Parkin 1963a: 6). The overlap of ethnic group and social "class" doubles such resistance,

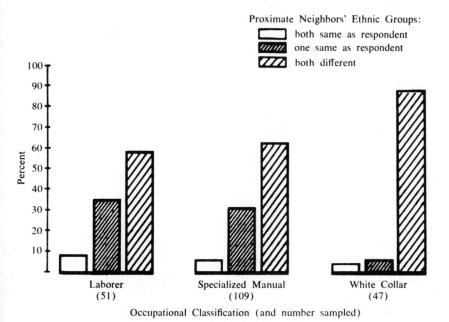

Figure 7.1. Ethnicity and Occupation as Factors in Residential Clustering. (Adapted from Pons 1956a:665.)

just as a similar pattern in the United States does with regard to white and nonwhite neighborhoods.

ASSOCIATIONS

Although ethnicity powerfully influences a townsman's choice of associates, other factors are clearly operative. Socioeconomic class, neighborhood,[1] place of employment, political faction, and religion are among the more important conducive commonalities. There are, as a result, many nonethnic associations in the towns of Black Africa, including sports clubs, old boys' associations (for graduates of a particular secondary school or college), women's associations, religious groups, political parties, labor unions, associations of the unemployed, and in some areas *bondoi* (for residents who have the same Christian name). In some African towns, nonethnic associations may equal or outnumber their ethnic counterparts, although data on this point are not generally available. In Bamako, according to Meillassoux, only 30 of 149 associations registered in 1963 were based on out-of-town origin and some of these were not ethnically homogeneous (1968:61). However, Mali represents a special case because of the government's negative stance on regionalism and ethnicity, reflected in both the constitution and an article of the criminal law. "Not knowing the exact terms of the law, people are only aware that regionalism is treated with suspicion and accordingly act with care. They often neglect to register their associations for fear of falling under some possible prohibition" (ibid:70).

With relevance to the apparent shift to nonethnic associations, it has been argued that modern industrial society is an associational society composed of an intricate network of organizations designed to foster such special interests as the professional, the welfare, the political, the religious, and so forth. In Oshogbo, for example, one "development closely linked to the greater economic and political diversity of [the town] is the emergence of associational structures which were not characteristic of traditional life, and [which] stress identity of interest rather than common descent" (Schwab 1965:102). Of course, in a polyethnic urban area, common descent is usually one basis of shared interest.

It is sometimes difficult to classify an association on the basis of an ethnic-nonethnic dichotomy because membership may be open but actual recruitment may be based upon ethnically oriented self-selection. Thus of the 27 associations for which Hamilton collected ethnic membership data, ten had from 90 to 99 percent of their membership from a single ethnic

1. Only 22 percent of the respondents in Ross's Nairobi samples reported that their best friends lived in the same neighborhood that they did (1969:76). But Pons found on Avenue 21 of Kisangani that "neighbours and near-neighbours constantly interacted in a variety of small-group situations irrespective of their tribal affiliations" (1969:167).

group (1966:90). These associations were obviously "open," but self-selection led to virtual homogeneity.

Another complication in the classification of associations is that those with obviously nonethnic recruitment may be highly ethnic in their dynamics (just as interethnic relationships may provide a key dynamic in African countries). Based upon a study of Lubumbashi (then Elisabethville), Caprasse reports that local leaders, when competing for political posts, are not adverse to making family, tribal, and ethnic appeals. Ethnic bonds may also determine the side one takes in personal conflicts (1959: 79). Thus it is useful to view some nonethnic associations as federations of ethnic subassociations.

Both nonethnic and ethnic associations are products of change as well as instruments of further change. They are usually led by more educated segments of a town's population. The functions of these two types of associations are often similar, especially with regard to adaptation, integration, and the representation of special interests. As Moore has noted, they can replace multifunctional structures (e.g., the extended family or age grade) that form the bases of traditional village life (1963:347). For example, Gutkind found that associations of unemployed townsmen have begun to arise in those situations where mutual aid based upon ethnic ties ("traditional mutual aid") has begun to break down. "It appears that only when they are conscious of their exposed social and economic position do they become aware of the existence of large numbers of other men whose situation does not differ greatly from their own" (1968:374). One of the main reasons the exposure and realization come slowly is that "the unemployed use their ethnicity . . . as an instrument of competition for employment" (ibid:378).

An important difference between the ethnic and nonethnic associations relates to the membership's degree of urban acculturation and assimilation. Clement's observations in Kisangani apply in many other urban areas: "The [nonethnic] associations having the broadest geographical and ethnic representation are those which draw the largest proportion of their members from among the evolués. They are conducive to the elimination of tribal and regional attitudes of mind" (1956:491). Of course, it is difficult to determine whether the association influences attitudes, attitudes influence choice of associations, or both; the latter is probably most common in Africa as elsewhere.

Based upon degree of urban acculturation and assimilation, a developmental sequence of association can be hypothesized. Southall has conceptualized three stages in the history of associations in African towns. During the first, most migrants' ties to the town are too tenuous to provide a basis for the development of lasting voluntary associations, founded on either ethnic or nonethnic identities. However, ethnic ties are used for ad hoc efforts to facilitate adaptation and integration. In the second stage, ethnic associations are formed on a more or less permanent basis, but non-ethnic town involvement does not yet extend to the point where other bases of association become important—with the exception of religious groups for many townsmen and a variety of associations for some members of the new "middle class." The final stage, into which many African towns have already moved, marks the widespread development of multiple interests, ethnic and nonethnic, and the concomitant emergence of relatively permanent nonethnic as well as ethnic associations.

The Labor Union:
A Nonethnic Association

To provide further insights into processes of change and the characteristics of nonethnic associations (including their relationships with government), it is useful to examine in depth a nonethnic association. The labor union has been selected for this purpose because of its growing economic, political, and social importance in the towns of Black Africa.

TYPES OF LABOR UNIONS

According to the customary Western definition, a labor union is a continuous association of wage earners with the purpose of maintaining or improving the conditions of their working lives. This meaning, unfortunately, appears to be culture bound. A more useful approach is to begin with the structure (labor unions) and then explore functions (see Hanna in press).

The term labor union should, from a structural point of view, be used to refer to any organization that calls itself a labor union. An examination of labor unions would then lead to the development of a set of ideal types, according to their functions. The "consumptionist" labor union is an organization conforming to the Western definition (above), with the possible exception that some goals outside the working life sphere might be pursued. The "productionist" union is part of the firm's hierarchy (in Africa the "firm" is often the government) and has as its primary purpose the increase of production. Sékou Touré, for instance, argues that a union leader's first obligation is to represent the state. The "intercalary" union is primarily concerned with mediating and communicating between employer and employee, firm and household. An example of this type would be the company unions organized by the United Africa Company. Of course, most labor unions do not conform completely to any one of the above three types. Galenson points out: "Every trade union movement looks two ways. . . . On the one hand, a union represents the interests of its members as consumers. . . . But it is less well understood that unions are integral parts of the productive mechanism" (1959:12–13). Productive activities include delivering labor at the agreed-upon rate and maintaining discipline in the relevant industry.

The existence of all types of labor unions in urban Africa reflects the diverse ideologies and interests of governing elites. Preference for a state-managed economy usually leads to the development of productionist unions, whereas those regimes favoring a mixed economy combining free and state enterprises tend to permit labor unions to exercise greater freedom and thus to develop along consumptionist lines (see Lofchie and Rosberg 1966:35). Elite self-confidence is more likely to lead to a permissive approach toward labor union activity than is a pervading concern for self-survival.

The trend in urban Africa appears to be toward unions that have productionist orientations. A number of the labor unions in Black Africa have been incorporated, one way or another, into the state or party institutional framework. "The labor movement, if not completely subordinate to the party, is at least pliable and responsive to party pressures" (Berg and Butler 1964:366). Independence itself had an important effect upon union orientations and activities. When governments were run by Europeans, those African-dominated trade unions permitted to exist by colonial regimes were striving not only for better working conditions but also for freedom and independence. Now that Africans are in power at the state and local levels, labor union oppositionalism is viewed as unpatriotic and antinationalistic. Since many unions cannot legitimately function in their customary Western role for these political reasons, one alternative is for them to become productionist and therefore to contribute to the national interest. Friedland writes: "Post independence sees ever increasing involvement of government in the regulation of industrial relations and, frequently, in internal union affairs. Part of the reason for this is in the concern of the government with increasing production" (1963:49–50).

Governments intervene to increase production because of the desperate economic situation that exists in most African countries. Capital accumulation is slow, requiring labor-intensive methods of development. Many countries depend upon a single crop to meet foreign exchange requirements, so that a strike affecting this activity can be severely damaging. "The hard decisions on wage policy and related matters seem to require swift action by government, without obstruction by trade unions which defend the narrowly-conceived self-interest of wage earners" (Berg 1964:37).

Supporting government intervention is the ideology that individuals and organizations must subordinate themselves to the requirements of social reconstruction and economic development. This is what the former Prime Minister of Senegal, Mamadou Dia, referred to as "the temporary identification of the state and the nation" (quoted in Hapgood 1962:8). In many

French-speaking countries, state and union are organizationally fused because officers of the former are employed in the latter. Hapgood sees the fusion virtually complete: "By class, by personal interest, and by political circumstance, the union leaders are responsible to the Government rather than to their membership" (1962:8).

This is not to suggest that unions are necessarily puppet organizations. Under colonial and independent regimes, strikes have been a significant weapon of labor grievance. Freetown was the site of a strike by harbor workers as early as 1874, and major labor stoppages occurred in Copperbelt towns in 1935 and 1940. Events in Luanshya led strikers to storm the mine compound office and police to fire on them. Six lives were lost and 22 persons wounded (Epstein 1958:29). A 1949 strike at the Enugu coal mine also triggered violent police action, resulting in 21 dead and 51 injured. There are many other examples of strikes during colonial rule.

Independence did not terminate the strike activities of labor unions, even though the economic development and nation-building goals of government and union were seemingly similar or identical. In 1961, for instance, a strike by rail and harbor workers in Sekondi-Takoradi resulted in the declaration of a state of emergency, clashes between police and strikers, and the arrest of key leaders of the Ghanaian opposition. Industrial disturbances have also occurred in towns of other countries with mobilization regimes, e.g., Guinea (1961) and Tanzania (1963), although in these cases the disturbances were followed by purges within union ranks. Berg and Butler argue that "in all instances the unions are allowed some expression of opinion. . . . But it is only on party sufferance that they are given a role to play, and they are constrained to be 'reasonable' and 'responsible' organizations which emphasize productivity and hard work" (1964:370). Thus this nonethnic association, as well as most others, has some independence of action, initially by virtue of the individual needs of members, and secondarily because the government deems it wise to provide some independence so that frustrations do not build to unmanageable degrees. This makes it possible for labor unions to channel protest in ways that are least disruptive to the state. "The handling of local grievances can indeed be called a 'productionist activity'" (Fisher 1961:956). Nevertheless, many grievances are not "constructively" channeled, as we will indicate in the following chapter.

LABOR UNION STRENGTH

Observers of the African scene have made widely divergent assessments of the strength of labor unions in Black Africa. Part of the divergence arises because African economies contain modern, mixed (e.g., tradition-based cash crops), and subsistence sectors. Some view union strength in absolute terms, and others judge it relative to the modern sector only. Disagreement is also caused by the ambiguity that exists concerning membership; e.g., should one count as members those who think of themselves as such but do not pay dues? We suggest that, in general, labor unions in Africa are absolutely weak compared with unions in some other parts of the world, but relatively strong within the African institutional network in the spheres of their concerns.

The strength of unions stems from their dominant position in urban (largely modern) infrastructures and the relatively frail authority of governing elites. A small union can paralyze the economic system, since several score men may work at the heart of the rail system, the harbor, or the telecommunications network. Because "ruling elites have difficulty in legitimizing their power, the unions become an important vehicle for control or alternatively a threat to survival" (Davies 1966:10). Yet the small size of their memberships and the underdevelopment of their organizations combine to militate against a major and continuous political role.

The specific types and strengths of labor unions vary from country to country in Black Africa, depending upon the internal development of the organizations and the external environment of the economy, the polity, and the social structure in which they operate (cf. Cole 1953:34). The economy is relevant to strength because, as development takes place, the labor force increases and stabilizes while relative unemployment probably decreases. This gives labor unions a larger base of strength. Stability is obviously a function of migrancy. "Migrant labour has no interest in joining trade unions: The workers consider regular payment of union dues a waste of money, because they expect to be going back soon to the reserves or to move on to another district. They are also scared of taking part in strikes for fear of losing their precarious job" (Group of Kampala Students 1960:152). Politically, most governments "are wary of encouraging the growth of bodies which might easily become major challengers to their supremacy . . . [and] fear the effect on foreign investment if unions, sufficiently well-organized, prove too powerful to resist in campaigns for higher wages" (Davies 1966:226–227).

There are, of course, many other factors that have influenced union strength; they have generally handicapped the emergence of unions as an important political force. (1) Workers are at the same time ethnic group members; for many of them the needs imposed by town living are satisfied by ethnic clusters and associations, making unions appear to be superfluous. (2) Sometimes unions are formed for the advancement of the organization's leadership rather than for the improvement of working conditions. Epstein reports that the sense of unity developed among unionized Luanshya mine workers was eroded by an emergent gap between the union's leadership and its rank-and-file (1958:passim). The leaders were fluent in English (thus able to communicate with Europeans), better educated, and in relatively high paying jobs. They developed higher standards of living and conspicuously consumed in ways that could not be matched by the rank-and file. "Such leaders are more able to interact socially with Europeans, and in some cases are suspected of having moved into the 'enemy camp.' . . . They are afraid of strikes, it is said, because they are afraid to lose their jobs" (1958:134). (3) Widespread illiteracy makes it difficult to communicate some issues to potential members and prevents union members from fully participating in the life of the organization. Hapgood writes: "It seems likely that most wage-earners do not see in the trade union (which is, after all, a foreign import) a useful channel for their needs and ambitions" (1962:8).

NONECONOMIC FUNCTIONS OF LABOR UNIONS

The noneconomic functions of nonethnic associations are increasingly important to African townsmen. One of the most important functions performed by labor unions is socialization to the new ways of urban life. For example, unions contribute to the development of attitudes concerning the acceptance of industrial employment conditions and the entrusting of one's interests to the labor market (see Parsons and Smelser 1957:148). In a number of countries unions have active literacy programs which "have the advantage of selectivity, of reaching those who have already made a personal commitment to participation in economic development by abandoning the traditional subsistence economy" (Zack 1964:16). There are also numerous training programs, as in the case of the Kenya Federation of Labor which teaches members such skills as construction and the operation of consumer cooperatives. At the political level, labor unions provide town-dwellers with the opportunity to participate in small-scale political systems with relatively modern rules of conduct. Zack calls unions one of the most important institutions "open to untrained and uneducated individuals where they can learn about and experience democracy" (1964:23). Of course, labor unions are not necessarily democratic. The latter possibility leads to a consideration of the relationship between the politics of organizations and the politics of the state of which they are part. It may be that the tendency toward oligarchy in the former is what facilitates broker-type politics in the latter, as has occurred in the United States.

A second important noneconomic function performed by labor unions is providing psychological, social, and economic security to townsmen. "The informal social group in the workshop, which is the basis for unionism, gives the new recruit to industry an emotional sense of security and of belonging. Membership in an industrial primary group . . . may serve as a substitute for membership in the extended family, tribe, or peasant village" (Knowles 1960:307). The Fish Sellers' Union in the Ghanaian towns of Nkontompo, Ekuasi, and Sekondi provides an interesting example (see Busia 1950:25). This union's main activities concern what might be called burial insurance: when a member dies, those remaining each contribute a small fixed sum to cover such costs as cash gifts to relatives of the deceased and beverages for the mourners. Of course, most unions have a wider range of mutual aid activities. To these should be added the symbolic importance of labor unions. Powdermaker refers to the African Mine Workers' Union of Luanshya as a "a symbol for security and authority, not only for its members, but also for most Africans on the Copperbelt" (1962: 112). Thus the union may serve as a basis for social cohesion beyond that provided by common ethnic background.

Third, labor unions provide opportunities for leadership training and for the exercise of leadership by those whose mobility is otherwise blocked. Leadership training is especially relevant for the regime in power; candidates for high offices can be tested in voluntary associations where wrong decisions may not be very costly. An alternative channel of upward mobility is especially needed by townsmen who in some ways are outsiders. In Port Harcourt, for example, unions provided opportunities for ambitious non-Ibos who were denied access to local and regional party offices (Wolpe 1966:434).

Emergence of Class

There are a number of indications that one of the major changes taking place in the towns of Black Africa is the emergence of nascent socioeconomic classes and the dynamic relationships that such a structural pattern implies. "We may perhaps speak of [ethnicity] and 'class' as pervasive concepts in the sense that they pervade and operate within all the various sets of relations which make up the urban system" (Epstein 1958:240).

More than ten years ago, research in Zambian towns led Mitchell and Epstein to conclude that the increasing differentiation taking place among African townsmen, using such criteria as wealth, skill, education, and living standards, might possible lead to the development of classes similar to those in the west. (1959:36). Similarly, McCall, whose research in Africa has primarily been in the West, observes that, with urban stabilization and urban-rural differentiation, objective and subjective factors (e.g., wealth, education, status identity) create new urban divisions, including a nascent class structure (1955:157).

There are some who object to the application of the class concept to Africa. Sékou Touré, the president of Guinea, writes: "Actually, Africa has no bourgeoisie; its population is 85 percent peasant; it lacks national financial capital; nor does it know 'social classes' or the struggles born of their contradictions" (quoted in Hodgkin 1964:249). Objections to the concept of class stem largely from the Marxist corollary that if they exist, there will be contradiction and conflict—a development no member of a governing elite would encourage. This point is suggested by Mali's Madeira Keita. "We obviously cannot assert that [Black] African society is a classless society," he writes. "We do say that the differentiation of classes in African does not imply a diversification of interests and still less an opposition of interests" (1960:34).[2]

We shall not present a theoretical discussion of the various conceptualization of class. For our purposes, Lasswell and Kaplan's broad definition provides a useful working approximation: "A class is a major aggregate of persons engaging in practices giving them a similar relation to the shaping and distribution (and enjoyment) of one or more specified values" (1950: 62). In this sense, "differentiation" has occurred and continues to take place throughout Black Africa. Indeed, virtually all societies differentiate, and the resulting divisions usually influence social, economic, and political perspectives and practices. However, "the new divisions within society have not in any way produced hard categories; there is little evidence that 'class consciousness' has been developed sufficiently among either the peasants or the wage-earners for them to put a class-loyalty before tribalism, regionalism or nationalism. But the areas for tension are there" (Davies 1966:132).

The lack of "hard" class categories is demonstrated by the fact that there is still considerable vertical mobility in urban Africa and the new upper classes remain permeable. Although it helps to have wealthy and educated parents, the son of a poor farmer can still reach high positions in most African towns. The principal reason for the persistence of a relatively open stratification system is the set of vertical channels provided by ethnic ties. A man can always help his poor "brother." (Intergenerational continuities are discussed on pp. 159–160).

Rapid development of class consciousness has been impeded by these vertical ethnic ties, plus a common belief (similar to that current in the United States) that anyone can reach the top (in Nigeria, the destruction of this myth was a cause of civil war) and "a cultivated feeling of class-lessness [which] may indeed be necessary to ensure government stability in the present situation of marked contrasts in wealth and privilege" (B. Lloyd 1966:163).

In the subsections that follow we examine (a) aspects of material differentiation in urban Africa, (b) indicators of coalescence within the differentiated aggregates, and (c) four of the most clearly delineated aggregates (quasiclasses): the governing elite, the modernists, the businessmen, and the wage-earners.

MATERIAL DIFFERENTIATION: HAVES AND HAVE-NOTS

An important element in the examination of emergent class structures in African towns is the distribution of resources (including things valued). The analyst must ask, "Who gets what?" In Chapter 5, four basic urban conditions were examined: un- and underemployment, poor housing, lack

2. For a discussion of social stratification in Africa, see Tuden and Plotnicov 1970.

of education, and ill health. It should be reemphasized here that each of the four conditions was marked by a significant gap between segments of the population. (1) Some townsmen have well-paying jobs but many others are un- or underemployed; (2) some live in modern houses with all the modern conveniences, but others reside in poverty pockets; (3) literacy in towns in increasing dramatically, and there are now towns with several thousand university-trained residents, but many town-dwellers remain illiterate, and access to schools is far from automatic; and (4) there are some urban residents who live under excellent health conditions and have the best medical facilities, but the majority must cope with inadequate services. Thus a gap between the haves and the have-nots exists and is quite visible.

Since independence, the trend in most African countries has been toward an overall increase of resources but an unequal distribution of them. At least prior to the recent spate of coups d'etat, the well-off have improved their lot whereas the rank-and-file have been more or less standing still. Evidence of the increasing gap between haves and have-nots in some countries depends upon the determination of real wage trends. The *Quarterly Economic Review* for Congo (Kinshasa) reports that, based upon 1960–1967 data, the real income of military personnel and white collar civil servants in Kinshasa kept well ahead of inflation, whereas the real income of workers in nongovernmental productive enterprises declined significantly (1967:15). The overall decline in the index of the standard of living in Kinshasa is shown in Figure 7.2.

ASSOCIATIONAL AND GENERATIONAL HOMOGENEITY

Two important indicators of the changing social structure of African towns are the horizontal patters of association and the continuities between generations of the same family. Preliminary studies have been conducted in both these areas.

Clement's research in Kisangani indicates the relationship in that town between social status and patterns of association. Congolese in the "socio-professional class" were asked to name their neighbors, friends, and wives' friends. Then, categorizing these people according to class yielded the distribution shown in Figure 7.3 Clement concluded that, for his respondents, class appeared to be the predominant influence determining in broad categories the kinds of people who socialized with each other (1956: 442). Unfortunately, the ethnic membership data needed for multivariant analysis are not provided. Plotnicov's impressions from research in Jos support a double role hypothesis: the modern elite were found to display "a distinct preference for social interaction with persons following the same style of life," but "they take pride in their tribal histories and traditions, cite achievements of their countrymen, and participate actively in their tribal unions" 1964a:71).

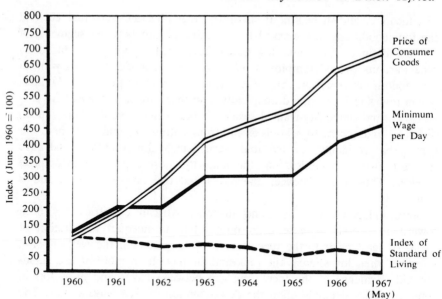

Figure 7.2. Indices of Declining Average Real Income in Kinshasa. (*Adapted from Economist Intelligence Unit 1967:15.*)

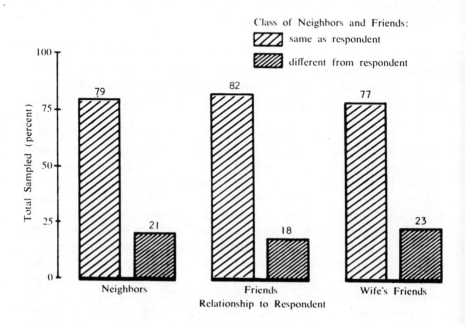

Figure 7.3. Neighbors and Friends According to Class Categorization. (*Adapted from Clement 1956:442.*)

Jacobson's study of Mbale provides further evidence of role duality among urban "elites." Dividing his respondents into three occupational ranks (claimed income was used as the key indicator), he found that friendship choices were significantly structured by specific rank (1967: 155). Table 7.1 specifies the relationships found. However, the impact of ethnicity is still significant, as Table 7.2 indicates.

Table 7.1. The influence of occupational rank upon the friendship choices of African elites in Mbale. (Adapted from Jacobson 1967:155.)

	Respondent's Occupational Rank		
Friends with Occupational Rank Same as Respondent	*High (e.g., senior administrators and professions; income above £1000) (percent)*	*High-Medium (e.g., technical and executive personnel; income between £1000–£700) (percent)*	*Medium (e.g., technical and executive personnel; income betwen £700–£350) (percent)*
Actual	68	61	52
Expected*	44	35	22

*Generated by assumption of randomness.

Turning to generational homogeneity, it appears that occupational status and educational achievement display marked continuities between generations of the same family. B. Lloyd goes so far as to argue that "the well-educated and wealthy elite is tending to become a predominantly hereditary group" (1966b:57). Studies of students provide the best available evidence of generational homogeneity. Clignet and Foster show that in the Ivory Coast sons and daughters of managerial and clerical workers have the best chance to enter secondary school, whereas those from farmer and fisherman families have the least (proportionate to their numbers in the country's total population). The details are shown in Figure 7.4. Among students at the University of Ibadan, Hanna found that 39 percent were from such higher occupation status backgrounds as the professions, whereas only 3 percent of all Nigerian males were so classified (1964b:421).

Table 7.2. Friendships of Mbale African "elite" sample: choices by members of three ethnic groups within the central government occupational locus. (Adapted from Jacobson 1967:155.)

	Ethnic Group (percent)		
Friends in Same Ethnic Group as Respondent	*Ganda*	*Teso*	*West*
Actual	44	43	40
Expected*	28	19	10

*Generated by assumption of randomness.

And Fraenkel's study of Monrovia shows that the fathers of one fourth of the boys and one half of the girls sampled in grades seven, eight, and nine were in professional or clerical professions, although the proportion of males in Monrovia holding such occupations is estimated to be considerably smaller (see Figure 7.5).

The level of parental attainment is not the only relevant boost, for more distant relatives or neighbors may also help. The Monrovia students' chances of completing their education and finding good jobs depended in large part, according to Fraenkel, upon contacts with influential patrons; typically, these contacts are based upon family or neighborhood ties (1964:219).

QUASI-CLASSES

Before independence, three primary urban classes could be identified. Dominant European businessman and administrators constituted an "imported oligarchy"; African (plus Asian and Middle Eastern) professionals, civil servants, businessmen, and those in similar ranking occupations constituted the middle class; and African blue collar workers and those in other low income categories constituted the lower class. Nationalism can usefully be viewed as an African middle class movement to oust the upper class imported oligarchy from its dominant positions. Hodgkin argues that nationalism "clearly expresses the dissatisfaction of an emerging African middle class with a situation in which many of the recognized functions

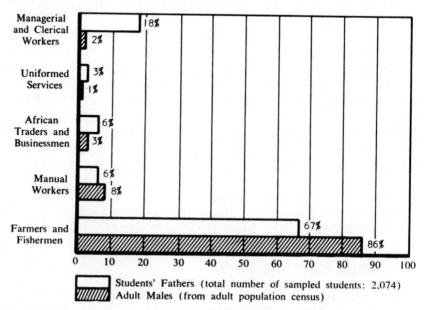

Students' Fathers (total number of sampled students: 2,074)
Adult Males (from adult population census)

Figure 7.4. Occupations of the Fathers of Secondary School Students and Adult Males in the Ivory Coast. (Adapted from Clignet and Foster 1966:57.)

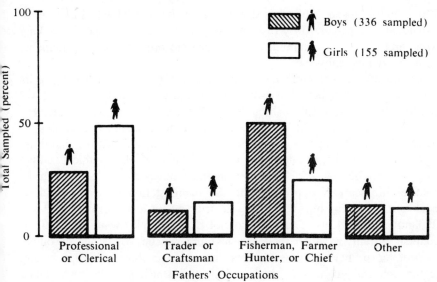

Figure 7.5. Occupations of Fathers of Schoolchildren in Monrovia. (Adapted from Fraenkel 1964:218.)

and rewards of a middle class—in the commercial, professional, administrative, and ecclesiastical fields—are in the hands of 'strangers'" (1956: 88). With independence, some members of the old African middle class, joined by prominent members of the traditional elite, moved into leading positions in the political, economic, prestige, and other hierarchies.

There are now at least four influential population aggregates—perhaps they should be labeled quasi-classes—which can be identified. These are the governing elite, the modernists, the businessmen, and the wage-earners. Membership in these quasi-classes is not mutually exclusive, and the likelihood is that in most towns some individuals are contemporaneously in several. However, the characteristics of quasi-class members and the nature of their mutual identifications and vested interests argue for conceptualizing them as semiautonomous units. The relationships among quasiclasses are schematically presented in Figure 7.6.

Governing Elite. By governing elite, we refer to those participants in the urban social system who play important descisionmaking roles in the allocation of values. The most inclusive specification of the governing elite includes decisionmaking and implementing members of the civil and military service. (Information on real wages in Kinshasa, reported above, suggests the advantages that accrue to those who are well placed in the local administration and the police force.) Many are "modernists" (see below), although there are still towns in Africa where traditional leaders remain quite strong (e.g., see the description of the Emir of Katsina in Dihoff 1970: 66–89). Research in a number of African towns (see Hanna and Hanna

1969a and Simpson 1968) has demonstrated that a relatively small set of individuals are perceived by residents as playing important decisionmaking roles, and that these community influentials are often the key participants in an interethnic subsystem.

The governing elite sometimes displays vested interests which indicate its emergence as an upper class—or Africa's equivalent of the "new class" (Djilas 1957). Although written about Nigeria, the following statement in a Nigerian journal of opinion applies to a number of countries in Black Africa: "There is . . . evidence of a growing solidarity of interests, especially economic, among the top members of the political class" (Nigerian Opinion 1965a:2). From another perspective, "contemporary political life scarcely appears to be the manifestation of a structure of established classes, but rather the instrument of *one* formative class" (Balandier 1965:139). The elite do not, for example, want to create a political system in which they can involuntarily be voted out of office. Two of the primary reasons for this are their sometimes disdainful view of the political judgment of rank-and-file townsmen, and the high stakes of power.

The governing elite's disdain is in part a product of the gap between their styles of life and world views and those of the rank-and-file. The political consequence of the disdain is that, as Lipset hypothesizes, many of those in the upper strata come to believe that it is neither governmentally possible nor morally right to permit those in lower strata to exercise political influence (1959:66). This view is similar to the one Europeans long held about all Africans, a not surprising equivalence given the many

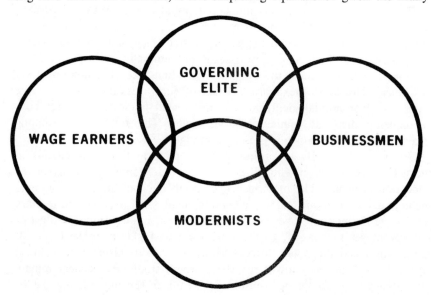

Figure 7.6. A Schema of Influential Quasiclasses in Urban Africa.

parallels between the preindependence European position and the current position of many African leaders.

The governing elite also have tremendous stakes in their positions of power. Vested interests are likely to be intense in towns where the difference between being "in" and "out" is great. The "ins" have the satisfactions and perquisites of power; out of power, they might lose all this. "At the moment," a Nigerian editorialist wrote in 1965, "the concern of the politicians for the very rewarding spoils of office—power, pomp and property— is impressing people more than their hastening of economic development" (Anonymous 1965b:1).

Modernists. Members of the modernist quasi-class, who in some towns number in the thousands, are well educated, relatively wealthy, and, perhaps most importantly, modern in their style of life and world view. Jacobson focuses upon this quasiclass in his Mbale research, concluding that they had a common culture and intensively interacted with each other to the extent that many ethnic differences were overridden. Such a pattern, we believe, is most likely to be produced by a sample such as his: a set of positionally identified high-ranking individuals who are geographically mobile strangers living in a relatively small town without large numbers of coethnics present. It is nevertheless true, as Smythe and Smythe concluded on the basis of their study of Nigerian elites (most of whom were urban residents), that "interest in issues, places and ideas beyond the awareness of the masses draws them together and gives them common ground for understanding and fellowship. . . . The organization of urban life tends to provide some unity; the elite work in similar surroundings, associate with each other, attend the same social affairs, go to the same recreational clubs, share the same schedule" (1960:93–94). Similarly, Plotnicov reports that "the modern African elite in Jos are few enough in number for most to know one another personally. . . . They interact more frequently with one another both by choice and through structural determinants such as occupational activities. Thus they share both a sense of identity and a common social network" (1970:280–281).

Mayer's research among the rural-born Xhosa migrants in East London, South Africa, reveals a distinction that may well develop in many of the towns of Black Africa. He found two relatively distinct sets of Xhosa, each with its own culture and network of interaction. One, the "school people," have been socialized by missions and schools. Their ideals incorporate literacy, Christianity, and other "Western" ways. The other, called the "red people" because of the characteristically smeared red ochre, are conservative traditionalists who have retained many of their old life styles and world views. "The smarter and more educated people in the town locations evidently do not want a 'raw' tribesman as their associate. . . . If [the red migrant] tries to mingle with [school people], he may meet with rebuffs or insults" (1961:284). This research has not, unfortunately, been replicated in the towns of Black Africa. It is our impression, however, that a distinction as sharp as between the school and red people has not emerged in many towns, and because of the strength of ethnicity is not likely to in the near future.

Businessmen. In the typical African town, there are a score or more relatively wealthy businessmen. Lloyd concludes from his research in Iwo, Shaki, and Ado that "traders, whether they are produce buyers, wholesale or retail shopkeepers, butchers or lorry owners—and most of them combine two or more of these occupations—are the wealthiest men in these towns" (1953b:328). Although members of ethnic groups, businessmen tend to develop common perspectives and practices leading to their emergence as a quasi-class. "Many continue to live in their family compounds and their elegant two storey houses rise above the thatch roofs of their relatives" (ibid.:329). Meillassoux describes the merchants of Bamako as follows: "Taken together, these African merchants form a bourgeoisie of African stock and culture, working in an almost exclusively African milieu, providing an African market with African goods or in response to African demand" (1965:137).

Most urban businessmen are not well educated, especially those advanced in age. This fact and the prevalence in some cultures of a dislike for those who follow the *enrichissez-vous* maxim (Shils 1958:passim) help to account for the failure of businessmen to be accorded high respect in some areas (cf. McCall 1956:69; Smith 1955:101). However, there are many exceptions to this pattern. Katzin's study of Onitsha businessmen found that the leading traders are among those local residents held in highest esteem by public officials and rank-and-file citizens. These traders' pictures and activity reports often appear in local newspapers, their positions include many of the important offices of local governments, religious organizations, and ethnic associations, and their presence is sought at the most exclusive functions (1964:197).

Because of the close link between wealth and power in urban Africa, some businessmen are active in the political arena and some politicians have developed significant interests in business. "If they had little interest in their local government," writes Lloyd in remarking about a phenomenon with broader application than the three towns he studied, "it is often because their local authority rarely seemed to discuss anything worth while; such things as the cocoa trade and taxation are arranged at much higher levels" (1953b:334). Thus many businessmen are politically active through other than formal governmental channels (see discussion of bifurcation in Hanna 1968b). Our study of two urban-centered African communities revealed that big business was the most frequent principal occupation of those identified as political influentials (Hanna and Hanna 1965b: 10–11). A majority of these influential businessmen were not active in formal local government, but they were active in governance through informal channels.

Wage-Earners. Those who earn relatively high wages in regular nonprofessional employment and whose interests are often represented by consumptionist or intercalary labor unions comprise the wage-earning quasi-class. The bases of this quasi-class are developing as a result of changes in the occupational structure combined with attenuating ethnic identifications. With reference to employment, from one third to two thirds of the adult males in many towns are engaged in occupations that did not exist before the imposition of colonial rule. For example, a sample of adults in central Lagos revealed that 18 percent were clerical workers and 29 percent were skilled manual workers (Marris 1961:162). Concerning Congo (Kinshasa) as a whole, Bustin notes the increase in the Congolese labor force from 292,000 in 1925 to 1,183,000 in 1955 and concludes that the growth of the proletariat was the country's most significant social phenomenon in the preindependence period (1963:80).

Wage-earners sometimes form one of the most privileged aggregates in African towns. Fanon argues that "the workers are in fact the most favoured section of the population, and represent the most confortably off fraction of the people" (quoted in Davies 1966:11). "No matter how badly off the industrial worker in a newly developing economy may be," writes Galenson, "he is almost invariably in a favored position compared with his cousin back on the farm. . . . [This] induces the individuals who are fortunate enough to occupy the jobs to seek means of protecting this newly emerged type of property right" (1959:3–4). Thus they are a privileged minority, not an underprivileged majority. As indicated in the previous section, labor union members have the potential of a strategic hold upon the economic infrastructure and manifest the resulting vested interest by pressuring the government for further advantages while limiting access to their ranks so that their competitive postion will not be endangered. Gutkind's observation holds true in many urban areas: "the trade unions view the large pool of unemployed as a constant threat to their bargaining position" (1968:381–382).

Political demonstration, Umuahia, Nigeria

8

Bases of
Political Conflict

Politics in urban Africa are prominent in the lives of many townsmen, profoundly influencing their economic and social affairs. The character of urban politics is often reminiscent of American boss and machine politics at the turn of the century. The impact of urban politics sometimes extends beyond the locality to the country in which it is located, and occasionally even to intra-African affairs and international relations. Mercier has argued that "urban centers deserve attention, above all, because of the role they play in the development of a radically new type of political life" (1959: 58).[1]

Taking the loci of political inputs, decisions, and outputs into consideration, there are many different types of urban politics. For example, the input may be from rural areas, national leaders may make the decision (although the national decisionmaking unit may happen to be located in an urban area), and the output may be back into rural areas. Obviously, then, not all urban-related types are of equal concern to the observer of urban politics. Of primary relevance in this study are politics involving urban inputs, decisions, and outputs; they form the core of analysis in this and the following chapters. However, other types should be kept in mind because of the different structures of politics they imply.

---

1. Ross submitted 18 political participation items drawn from his study of two Nairobi neighborhoods to factor analysis and found that there were apparently two relatively distinct participation styles, one characteristic of activities during the nationalist period (e.g., attending rallies and paying party dues) and the other of activities that have become common in the contemporary independence period (e.g., following events through mass media and attending legislative sessions) (1969:117–118). Perhaps it can be argued that the "radically new type of political life" to which Mercier referred is what Ross has identified as the independence style of political participation; those who exhibit this style are relatively young, well educated, and wealthy (Ross 1969:122).

Scope and Intensity

Many factors have contributed to the broad scope and high intensity of politics in urban Africa. Some of the most important of these, none of which is by itself unique to Black Africa, are briefly mentioned below.

One caveat must, however, be stated. Initial research on the relationship between urbanization and political participation revealed a high correlation between these two variables when countries were used as the units of analysis. Early theoretical statements and supportive data (e.g., Deutsch 1961 and Lerner 1958) were followed by the world survey of Russett et al., which established a simple correlation between population urbanization and voting in national elections of .38 (1964:270). More recently, however, Nie et al. demonstrated that an ecological fallacy was involved in the intercountry correlations. Using data from the United States, the United Kingdom, Italy, Germany, Mexico, and India, they found no significant correlation between the two variables at the intranation level using individuals as the units of analysis (1969:365). The evidence they present suggests that economic development leads to urbanization and to social structural change (class structure and secondary group structure), but it is only the latter, through the change in attitude distributions, that leads to increased political participation. If this set of relationships exists in independent Black Africa, we would have to conclude that the apparent great scope and high intensity of urban African politics is attributable to the universally great scope and high intensity of all African politics, which is more visible in urban areas due to the concentration of numbers of participant-prone people. Unfortunately, the necessary research (with appropriate cross-cultural indicators) has not yet been carried out.

(1) Self-government removed the common antagonist and turned competition inward as rivals pursued the power that had been gained. As Apter has colorfully put it, "Power is left to the nationalists like gold dumped in the streets, and many are bruised in the hectic scramble to gather it up again" (1962:156). Mazrui relates the scramble to the retribalization of politics, noting "the resurgence of ethnic loyalties in situations of rivalry in the arena of resource allocation and domestic power politics" (1969: 89). Along the same line, Okot has written:

> Someone said
> Independence falls like a bull buffalo
> And the hunters
> Rush to it with drawn knives,
> Sharp shining knives
> For carving the carcass.

And if your chest
Is small, bony and weak
They push you off,
And if your knife is blunt
You get the dung on your elbow
But come home empty-handed
And the dogs bark at you! (1966:188–189)

(2) Some politicians struggle to retain or obtain power because of characteristic charismatic self-images, the disdainful view they often have of their opposition and the rank-and-file, and the great difference between "ins" and "outs" in terms of access to goods and services. (See above, pp. 162–163.)

(3) Many politicians view their mandate strictly in terms of satisfying their own constituencies or retaining their political bases, eschewing broader considerations. In Warri, for example, Lloyd reports that councilmen are expected to work only for the interests of their constituents (1956: 109). Perhaps such an outlook is based on the myth that if each player of the political game tries to maximize his position the community's satisfactions will be optimized (cf. Pye 1962:3).

(4) Relationships in changing communities are, of course, not perceived as fixed. As a result, many issues are not resolved and political participants have relatively ambiguous self-images and conflicting aspirations for change. The stakes of politics so based are greater than with the politics of adjustment among competing vested interests. Shibutani and Kwan observe that "the more spectacular clashes between ethnic groups generally occur in periods of transition, when the degree of institutionalization of stratified systems is low" (1965:342).

(5) Politics are intense partly because some alternative behavioral spheres are not highly developed. Thus the low level of industrialization means that the number of unemployed politically recruitable men is high and the number of upwardly mobile strivers who can leave politics for industry is low. What Holden found in an American setting does not exist in many African urban areas: "The fluidity of the economic structure diminished their necessity to focus clearly or vigorously on politics as a major source of direct material return. In effect, then, there was a 'trickle-up' process which created slack in the political system" (1966:178).

(6) The local economic structures of many African towns are controlled by politicians as much as or more than by business interests. Mechanisms of political control include patronage, licensing, and letting contracts. In such towns political intensity is heightened because of the economic stakes involved (cf. Coleman 1957:7).

(7) The underdeveloped condition of formal institutions of urban gov-

ernment probably also contributes to the intensification of politics per se. (Although there is some evidence to suggest that urban governments stemming from the French tradition of greater centralization and executive dominance are more efficient than those of the English tradition, which featured decentralization and legislative dominance, both can properly be described as underdeveloped.) The appointed staff and elected legislators serving in some towns are not highly trained or deeply imbued with the public interest of the urban community at large (see pp. 194–196).

As the leaders of several African countries have noted after civilian rule was overturned, there are many drawbacks stemming from politics broad in scope and high in intensity. Perhaps the disadvantages can be summarized by noting that political victory may become more important than socioeconomic development. It should be recognized, however, that political primacy does carry with it some serendipity. Conflict over control of a town, for example, tends to focus attention upon the institutions of the town and thus resocializes those whose perspectives were formerly limited by the boundaries of ethnic group or neighborhood. Coleman argues that an increase in community disputes is an indication that interest in the local community is continuing or even reawakening (1957:4); for the African case, we should add that it is also an indication of an initial awakening interest.

Polyethnic Politics

The patterns of political conflict in African towns are highly complex and constantly in flux. However, two basic patterns emerge; they derive from the vertical divisions of polyethnicity and the horizontal divisions of a nascent class structure. The former result from the enclosure of many ethnic groups within the boundaries of one political system. Horizontal divisions are produced by uneven or multidirectional change and social mobility (see Hanna 1964a:8–9). In addition, there are factions and nonethnic associations that represent more specific or more general ethnic or nonethnic interests.[2]

Since self-government was attained, the predominant channel of political solidarities and conflicts in urban Africa has been the polyethnic structure; leaders as well as rank-and-file citizens tend to relate to the community's political system through a screen of ethnicity. The basic ethnic

2. Nelson (1969:25) writes: "Political socialization appears to be much more important in determining migrants' political behavior than are assumed widespread psychological characteristics of anomie and frustration. The migrants' political behavior . . . flows from the political attitudes and patterns of behavior migrants bring with them from the country . . . and from an active process of political socialization through situations and agents to which they are exposed in the city."

alignments may conveniently be classified into three categories: one indigenous group versus another, indigenes versus stranger Africans, and Africans versus non-Africans. (In a few areas, nationals of different countries interact like ethnic groups.) The first two are common to most towns, whereas independence plus the diminished role of non-Africans have limited the areas where relationships between Africans and non-Africans are significant factors in local politics.

In the political arena, responses of African townsmen are clearly oriented to coethnics. Residents of two Nairobi neighborhoods were asked to name the members of the national cabinet. The first name that came to mind was significantly more frequently a coethnic than the proportion of coethnics in the cabinet would produce by chance (Ross 1969:197). And sampled adults in Umuhia and Mbale were far more likely to name a coethnic as a town influential and a personal political advisor than a member of all other ethnic groups combined (Hanna and Hanna 1969:197).

In towns where a multiple party system exists, party and ethnic affiliations are highly correlated. "When the political system itself is based on ethnic differences," writes Americanist Pomper, "political and ethnic differences simply reinforce one another, making reconciliation less likely. The voters' identification with their separate ethnic groups is strengthened, while their attachment to integrating, common groups is weakened. An increase in community incohesion is a likely result" (1966:96). In one party or "nonpartisan" environments, the correlation is parallel: membership in factions is related to ethnic group membership. And "under certain circumstances in the contemporary situation in African societies, ethnic loyalties and ethnic customs are used to articulate, in an informal way, a political organization which cannot be formally institutionalized" (Cohen 1969:24–25).

Competitive elections are often characterized by appeals to ethnic sentiment. This pattern characterizes contemporary urban Africa just as it has urban America. Writing from research experience in the United States, Dahl comments: "Any political leader who could help members of an ethnic group to overcome the handicaps and humiliations associated with their identity, who could increase the power, prestige, and income of an ethnic or religious out-group, automatically had an effective strategy for earning support and loyalty" (1961:33).

Politicians in most African towns strive to establish a base in their home ethnic group. Some leaders encourage the development of ethnic identifications and associations because of the presumed reliability and easy mobilization of such support. For example, some of the leaders Parkin studied in Kampala "encouraged tribal association, having become partly dependent on an ethnic clientele for economic and political purposes" (1969: 181). Another reason for establishing an ethnic base is that "ethnic groups are in an advantageous strategic position, for it is difficult and costly for any state to suppress the customs of a group. . . . And it is these very customs that can readily serve as instruments for the development of an informal political organization" (Cohen 1969:3). Rank-and-file African citizens, for their part, have often been found to respond most readily to ethnic appeals, which in terms of salience are the equivalent of combined party and religious appeals (and intense ethnic appeals) in the United States.

Reports from most African towns contain evidence of polyethnic politics. Summarizing the comparative study of five elections in Africa, Mackenzie concludes that "it is very difficult to approach local electors except by a campaign which enlists the support of local magnates, hammers at local issues, and repeats very simple slogans about tribal loyalty and the wicked ways of strangers. If tribalism is the enemy, elections are partly responsible for encouraging it" (1960:484). Along the same line, Lloyd reports that in Warri, since policy differences between competing parties are not perceived by the voter, only tribal issues are able to arouse election interest (1956:110). This explains why few Africans are elected from a constituency that does not contain a significant proportion of voters linked to them ethnically. Of course, the link is not as strong in heterogeneous towns as it is in rural areas; nevertheless, towns contain ethnic residential clusters which are important factors in candidate selection and election.

There are many other reports of polyethnic politics. For example, in Ibadan, according to Sklar, ethnic rivalry between two Yoruba subgroups, the Ibadan and the Ijebu, is one of the important bases of local political conflict (1963:285). Drawing upon his experience as Municipal African Affairs Officer in Nairobi, Askwith reports: "To anyone who has worked and lived among Africans in such towns it is very clear that the old tribal animosities are still very close to the surface, and little is required to bring them to light" (1950b:292). In Maiduguri after 1958 each of the major ethnic groups was represented by a different party: Kanuri by the Bornu Youth Movement, Hausa by the Northern Elements Progressive Union, Yoruba by the Action Group, and Ibo by the National Council of Nigeria and the Camerouns (Sklar 1963:341–342).

A principal organizational weapon of ethnic politics is the ethnic association. It may control political party branches (or be controlled by them), select nominees for elections (or legitimize their selection), spearhead campaigns, and so forth. A critic of associational involvement in politics gave the following portrayal in a Nigerian newspaper commentary: "Some tribal unions and cultural organizations have, of recent, meddled a lot in party politics. Some have become sycophants while others are more or less political hirelings. . . . [Some] are dictating to a party the candidate of their choice. . . . [All] are busy canvassing for one party or the other" (Udoh 1964:2).

ISSUES

The primary conflict among competing ethnic groups appears to be over control of the town. There are three, usually overlapping, arenas of this conflict: ownership, economic opportunities, and prestige.

Town control involves "ownership" where the urban boundaries are at or near the division between the traditional land of two indigenous ethnic groups. Ownership is of great importance because with it may come the disproportionate distribution of economic advantages, government posts, or, what may be of even greater importance, symbolic superiority over a rival. Warri is a case where the "town ownership" issue most acutely intensified ethnic rivalry. Since neither the Itsekiri or Urhobo has any other settlement of such size or importance, each considers Warri its capital (Lloyd 1956:106). The issue of town ownership came vividly to the forefront of the 1959 election for Warri's representative to the Federal House of Representatives. At that time, a member of the Itsekiris wrote of the opposition's attempt "to prevent Itsekiris from exercising their civic rights in their own home" (quoted in Post 1963:413). A similar battle over ownership took place in Mbale between the Bagisu and the Bakedi (Hanna and Hanna 1965:17–18). The area where the town is located was probably unoccupied before the coming of Europeans, but it lay between the traditional land of the two groups. Conflict over ownership became so heated and politically sensitive that the town was given special federal status, and the divisional headquarters of the peoples from both groups were until recently located there.

Economic opportunities are closely linked with polyethnic conflicts. Indeed, Sklar argues that tribalism often "becomes a mask for class privilege" and that, in many areas, "tribalism should be viewed as a dependent variable rather than a primordial political force in the new nation" (1967:6). There is scattered evidence from a number of towns that jobs and contracts are often awarded according to merit within ethnic groups, whereas favoritism is a stronger determinant among ethnic groups. It was said that, before the Nigerian civil war, employees of the two major industries of Umuahia were predominantly from the politically powerful Ohuhu Clan. Lloyd reports that residents of Warri believed control of local government determined which ethnic group would be awarded the use of publicly owned shops and market stalls. A rumored campaign issue in that town was that the winning group would restrict stall leases to its own members, assuring a local trade monopoly (1956:100). Of course, there may be institutional barriers to extreme favoritism. In Enugu, for example, the Municipal Council had little power over the allocation of plots and none for taxation; market stalls were allocated by raffle. Only rates, fees, licenses, and the engagement of local staff were under the Council's control.

Nevertheless, ethnic favoritism is a common fear among Enugu townsmen (Sklar 1963:213–214).

Prestige is another important factor, because the evaluation of an individual is influenced by the evaluation of his group. In Warri one of the issues is one of prestige, because members of any tribe may live in the town and there is no legal discrimination (Lloyd 1956:106). In Mbale, representatives of the two major indigenous ethnic groups vied at celebrations for prestigious seating positions and speaking order. And the Ibeku people of Umuahia were able to change the name of the town to Umuahia-Ibeku but were very bitterly opposed in this effort by other ethnic groups in the area (Hanna and Hanna 1965:16). Holden argues that an essential feature of conflict among ethnic groups—including racial groups—is respect demanded and offered. Politics "serves the ethnic minorities *symbolically* by providing them with a vehicle to assert a sense of their own worth" (1966:178–179). If the assertion is met with condescension, the "subordinate" group often responds with a "politics of respect" designed to force the "superordinate" group to show respect.

CONSEQUENCES

Polyethnic political conflicts have, considered from the perspective of a government's performance, positive and negative consequences. The most important disadvantages concern conflicts of interest at the official and rank-and-file levels. Ethnic ties can create an especially dangerous situation for government officials since they call into question the impartiality of the government itself. Fallers has argued that ethnicity can be "a constant threat to the civil service norm of disinterestedness. The wide extension of kinship bonds means that a chief [or any other official] is frequently put into the position of having to choose between his obligations to favor particular kinsmen and his official duty to act disinterestedly" (1955:301). Although such conflicts are minimized by mediators, selective perception, and situational relevance, they remain factors to be taken into account.

Even if a government official's ethnic ties do not conflict with his loyalties to the larger community, town-dwellers may imagine such a conflict. Consequently, members of each "out" ethnic group become fearful of being exploited and suppressed by the "in" group. This weakens the effectiveness of government, for its actions are resisted on the grounds that they are likely to be designed for exploitation or suppression. Awa reports that the opposition party often impedes the operations of local government and the party in power tends to penalize the opposition, even to the extent of violating the law, e.g., by illegally excluding them from committee memberships (1959:12). Because of government fragility and socioeconomic underdevelopment, such resistance is especially harmful to the future of African urban areas. Shils thinks that the intensification of dissensuality in a polyethnic society encourages a government to attempt to achieve consensus through coercion (1960:270).

A second disadvantage is that ethnic political loyalty may stand in opposition to the civility of rank-and-file townsmen. This is especially true during periods of interethnic conflict when "there tends to be a sharper definition of group boundaries and greater consciousness of kind. . . . there is a bipolarization of the participants into the good and the evil" (Shibutani and Kwan 1965:383–384). Examples exist in the towns of Congo (Kinshasa), Kenya, Nigeria, and elsewhere.

There are several possible advantages that derive from the polyethnic structure of politics predominant in urban areas; two of them will be noted here. First, the identities of many Africans are enlarged by their modified, politicized ethnicity. Formerly bound by lineage or clan, the African in an urban area becomes part of a larger group than he has ever been a member of before. Indeed, the concept of "tribe" did not exist for many Africans before migrating to town, their conceptualizations having previously been in terms of smaller entities. Ethnic identity may in turn be a step toward community identity, for conflict among ethnic groups in order to control a town makes the individual considerably more aware of the town as an entity than he otherwise might have been. Of course, it is possible that if ethnic ties did not exist, the migrant would be free to identify directly with the urban community or even the new state. It is more likely, however, that self-images would remain rooted in smaller units such as the lineage or the neighborhood block.

Second, rivalries among ethnic groups sometimes satisfy aggressive needs and therefore lessen attacks upon the fragile local government structures. Thus a mayor who is a member of the Bakongo ethnic group may be attacked qua Mukongo rather than as the occupant of a government position that is structurally and/or functionally weak. Wallerstein points out the differential impact of attacks upon ethnic occupants and nonethnic positions. Interethnic scapegoating shifts the target from governing party to ethnic group and from officeholder to group member; thus the system is implicitly accepted while the particular actors are explicitly rejected (1960:137). This phenomenon had earlier been noted by Gluckman: "In certain types of society, when subordinates turn against a leader . . . they may only turn against him personally, without necessarily revolting against the authority of the office he occupies. They aim to turn him out of that office and to install another in it. This is rebellion, not revolution" (1959: 28). Unfortunately, the more able and public-minded administrators and legislators are sometimes driven from local government because they do not wish to stand such abuse. This is one of the causes of the bifurcation between authority and influence that characterizes many African towns (Hanna 1968b).

ILLUSTRATIVE CASE: UMUAHIA-IBEKU

Events in Umuahia-Ibeku exemplify primary conflict between two indigenous groups and secondary conflict between one indigenous group and
a majority of the resident strangers. Five clans of the same tribe surround
Umuhia-Ibeku and each contributes to its population. However, the
most intense conflict in the locality pitted the two largest proximate clans
against each other (Hanna and Hanna 1965:passim). One of these clans,
the Ohuhu, has relatively unproductive land and, as a result, has shown
considerable initiative striving for alternative methods of satisfaction; the
new (i.e., after European contact) politics have been at the forefront of
their endeavors. A rival put it this way: "Their area was not fertile, so that
they had to struggle. They got into politics before we did; they
studied politics in school." Some men from the clan joined the nationalist
movement early and rose to prominence when power was transferred from
the British. The first three representatives from the locality were from the
Ohuhu and one of its members attained a high position in the central
government.

   The second large proximate clan, the Ibeku, owns land that is very fertile. Until recently, members of the clan appeared to have been satisfied
working the land; they did not actively engage in the new politics when
it was first introduced. "We feed copiously," said one member. "My people
became lazy and did not go to school." The Ibeku did have one significant
advantage over the Ohuhu: traditional ownership of the land where early
British administrators sited the town.

   Politics in Umuahia-Ibeku have been dominated by the conflict between
the influence of the Ohuhu and the land ownership of the Ibeku. Each has
envied the other's advantage and has striven to maintain or attain dominance in local and state affairs. For example, contests over the office of
mayor of the town council have often been between an Ohuhu candidate
(supported by fellow clansmen and allies drawn from resident strangers
and other local tribes) and one from the Ibeku (similarly supported).
Stranger groups have at different times supported each of the rivals,
probably in an attempt to maintain a balance of power. The office has
changed hands several times, since power is in close balance between the
major rivals.

   Political contests over local representation to the central government
are similarly fought. In the 1950s, when representative government was
first permitted, the area encompassing the town and its periphery was a
multiple member district. The prominence of the Ohuhu was reflected by
the fact that it produced two of the constituency's three representatives.
In 1961 the single member district system was introduced and, of necessity, constituency lines were redrawn. The result was that only one seat
was available for the two Ohuhu incumbents—one of whom was promi-

nent in the central government. In order not to deprive an incumbent of a seat in the new legislature, the influential members of the Ohuhu Clan decided that the prominent incumbent would stand for election in his home area and the other incumbent would contest in the constituency that included the town proper and the home land of the Ibeku clan.

By the early 1960s, the Ibeku people had clearly recognized the importance of power and influence in the new political system. Against the will of the area's monopolizing political party, the Ibeku advanced one of its own members as an independent candidate for election in the constituency. Thus the battle was joined: an Ohuhu man trying to remain in power by running for the legislature from what was basically an Ibeku constituency, and an Ibeku man contesting as native son against outside power. The election had a further implication in that it was a contest for voters between their new political loyalties (the Ohuhu man was standing as a member of the monopolizing political party) and their ethnic loyalties (the Ibeku man campaigned for ethnic self-determination). Although the monopolizing party brought many· dignitaries into the constituency, the end result of this heated campaign was a resounding electoral victory for the representative of the Ibeku Clan. Ethnicity (and self-determination) predominated.

Elections are battles, not wars. During the four-year period beginning with the election just described and ending with the first Nigerian military coup d'état, members of the Ohuhu Clan dominated the central government and party politics. Using these advantages, they took revenge upon the rebels of the "wrong-voting" constituency: patronage was withdrawn from those who campaigned for the rebel candidate and the water pipes recently laid in some Ibeku villages were disconnected. However, recent events in Nigeria dramatically changed influence hierarchies. A prominent officer in the first military regime was an Ibeku, whereas some formerly influential Ohuhu were detained and many were deprived of power. The water pipes were restored. The second military coup d'etat in Nigeria and the attempted secession of what was the Eastern Region may have established a new balance between the two clans.

ILLUSTRATIVE CASE: KUMASI

Further insight into the pattern of polyethnic politics in contemporary urban Black Africa is provided by an examination of election results in Kumasi, Ghana. They illustrate conflict between indigenes and strangers (see Austin and Tordoff 1960:138–142). Kumasi is located in the northern part of the country, and for centuries, as center of the Ashanti empire, it has been an economic and political counterweight to such urban areas in the south as Accra and Cape Coast. Economically, it is a major center of transport, commerce, and trade. Politically, Kumasi was the center of opposition to Kwame Nkrumah's nationalist and independence regimes—

so that there were times when few leaders of the predominant Convention People's Party (CPP) would chance a public appearance in the town (Apter 1963a:341).

The municipal election of 1958 and the by-election of 1959 pitted the CPP, perceived by some as the party of the south, against the United Party (UP), which was generally regarded as northern oriented and oppositional. In both cases competition was spirited and the outcome was close. To identify the relationship between voting and ethnic ties, it is necessary to examine voting patterns in relatively small—and therefore more homogeneous—areas.

There were three Kumasi wards (II, V, and XVI) that voted for the UP in both elections. What are the characteristics of these consistently oppositional wards? Ward II primarily contains poor Ashanti people living in rundown compounds and working in shanty stores. The main street and connecting alleyways form a tough area where clashes between CPP and opposition supporters were frequent and violent during previous political campaigns. Ward V, where the Ashanti regional headquarters of both the CPP and UP were located, is inhabited predominantly by upper and middle class Ashanti. Ward XVI was the strongest opposition area in Kumasi. Predominantly Muslim, this ward is the home of the Ashanti followers of the Koran (*asante nkramo*). Muslim attitudes toward the CPP can be traced to the ban of the Muslim Association Party and the deportation from Kumasi of several leading Kumasi Muslims. Thus anti-CPP feelings in this ward stemmed from the combination of Muslim bitterness and Ashanti separatism.

There are a number of Kumasi wards that have a record of CPP support, but the three that turned in overwhelming votes for CPP candidates are III, IV, and XVII. The striking commonality among them is that all are made up predominantly of non-Ashanti strangers, including a large number of southerners who are members of the Fanti, Ewe, and Ga groups. For example, Ward XVII includes part of two new housing estates in which, according to a population survey, there are 88 Ashanti families and 159 of other ethnic backgrounds. Thus politics in Kumasi is polyethnic, and is especially characterized by an indigene-stranger conflict. The voting patterns reported suggest that overlapping memberships (e.g., Ashanti and Muslim) may intensify partisanship.

Factions

Political factions probably exist in all but the smallest political systems, whether one-party, two-party, or multiparty. The literature on urban Africa contains many statements about the existence of factionalism. Typical is this one written about Nigeria: "Each party is shot through and through with factionalism so that the existence of one party in a local area is not necessarily a guarantee of smooth local administration" (Awa 1964: 311).

FORMATION

Some factions are formed on the basis of rivalries among leaders, with followers joining their favorite's camp. For others, joining is based upon differences in perspectives (often "modernity" versus "tradition" with overtones of class interests); coalescence in these cases may depend upon the actions of an organizer who is usually the most influential person in the incipient group (Nicholas 1965:29). Many factions have both leadership and perspective bases. Although factions need not initially emerge from *political* rivalries or differences, they "operate for the most part in the political field or with political effects in other fields (Firth 1957:292).

In Senegalese towns, according to Foltz, expected patronage from a leading individual or family is one of the most important bases of political group formation (1964:6). Locally, this unit is conventionally called a "clan," although it is not structurally similar to the clan described in anthropological literature. The bases of clan alignments vary, including common lineage and common religious belief, but most often there is an element of personal attraction to a successful and popular person plus an understanding of quid pro quo. Thus most Senegalese clans resemble the area's traditional patron-client relationships in which a wealthy nobleman fed, clothed, and housed a number of hangers-on who in return served and supported their patron.

A similar situation, also based upon a traditional pattern, is reported to prevail in Kita (Hopkins 1966:4–10; 1967:301, passim). Prestige and positions are contested by two rival factions, each essentially a patron-client network. Each faction is headed by one or several key persons and bears their names; the membership is quite similar judging from such available biographical information as ethnic group membership and age. The inner core of a faction is relatively stable, whereas the rank-and-file clients tend to move from one faction to another according to their immediate interests. Perspectives appear to have some influence upon affiliation because the two factions each trace their heritage to a political party of the days before a mobilization movement (see pp. 181–182) was established in the country.

PERFORMANCE

The most clearly identifiable Senegalese factions, according to Mercier, are those that control an urban government. The network of a key patron's influence is broadly extended by means of the strategic use of patronage jobs and financial rewards (where they exist), and by being linked with superordinate and subordinate patron-client networks based upon the traditional model of social relationships. The predominant political role of controlling factions is demonstrated by the fact that, at least among women, "the essence of political affiliation can be reduced almost entirely to the relation with the [faction] leader" (Mercier 1959:72).

In Kita, factions are not openly organized, because they are viewed disapprovingly by the mobilization regime; meetings are usually secret. Nevertheless, competition between them is vigorous and relatively equal. Official positions in the town are fairly equally divided between the factions; indeed, "position balancing" is apparently viewed in the same light that ethnic ticket balancing is in New York City.

Sklar's report of the politics of chieftaincy control in Oyo provides a more extended example of factionalism (1963:235–238). In Oyo there was an injection of regional politics into the town as well as a conflict between the factions based upon the new and the old orders. The Alafin (traditional leader) of Oyo was of the old order, lacking a Western education and the modern outlook of new elites. In contrast, some Oyo indigenes were prominent in the Action Group and other new political movements which emerged in the 1950s. A clash between the two arose over the issue of supremacy in the Oyo Divisional Council. Anti-Alafin forces attained ascendancy and voted to reduce his salary by the equivalent of almost two thousand dollars. To defend the Alafin, the Egbe Oyo Parapo was organized, and it gained the support of the majority of uneducated Oyo citizens. In response to this threat, the Divisional Council suspended the Alafin's entire salary. The conflict between the two factions reached a high point when members of the one linked with the Action Group physically attacked members of the Egbe Oyo Parapo at one of the latter's meetings. Six people were killed in the melee. Whether the disturbance was cause or excuse, the result was that the Action Group-controlled government at the regional level suspended the Alafin from office, banished him from Oyo, and then officially had him deposed. A regional commission of inquiry was held on the matter and it recommended that the Alafin be restored to his throne, but the Western Region's government chose to ignore the recommendation and reaffirmed its earlier decision.

Political Movements and Other
Nonethnic Associations

There is clear evidence derived from a number of towns in Black Africa that changes are taking place in the prevailing sociopolitical structures. New unifying influences—political, religious, and economic—are at work bringing diverse tribes together, stimulating interaction and developing awareness of mutual interests (cf. Banton 1957). The organizational impact of these developments is the formation of associations that either cut across ethnic lines or bring coethnics together for nonethnic reasons. And as Hoselitz and Moore have noted, because economic transformations alter political structures, they also alter the distribution of political influence (1963:191).

Associations based upon nonethnic ties, like their ethnic counterparts, often play significant roles in urban politics. These roles were first performed early in the modern histories of African countries. In Nigeria three decades ago, for example, an association called The Study Circle was already debating such subjects as "resolved that all sane literate males in the municipality of Lagos . . . should be granted suffrage" and "resolved that capitalism is a better institution of national economics than socialism" (quoted in Coleman 1958:216).

Throughout Black Africa, nonethnic associations have been active participants in the nationalist movements, and, since the transfer of sovereignty, they have been pressure groups representing the interests of their memberships. There are even many formally nonpolitical associations that in fact perform important political functions. Writing about some African welfare societies in Zambian towns, Mitchell comments: "It is clear that these societies had political objectives—the word 'welfare' was interpreted in the widest possible sense" (1956a:231). Of course, some associations more manifestly enter the political arena.

POLITICAL MOVEMENTS

The most political nonethnic association is the organization that was called the nationalist movement before independence and political party (or mobilization movement) after the transfer of sovereignty (Hanna 1964a:11–12, 30–32). Before independence, the combination of personal insecurity, rising aspirations, and some feeling of political efficacy contributed to the rise of nationalist movements. Personal insecurity was important because it led some African townsmen to seek precisely what a social movement such as nationalism has to offer: identification with a leader, the support of fellow members, a sense of purpose, and occasional satisfactions of concrete accomplishment. Rising aspirations are important because they contribute to the felt gap between what one has and what one wants; the gap, in turn, tends to lead either to political action or to withdrawal, depending upon other factors in the environment and an individual's psychological structure. This leads to the third factor, sense of political efficacy; only with this sense (realistic or not) is it likely that a townsman will opt for action as opposed to withdrawal.

Since independence, most nationalist movements have been converted into the political arm of the ruling elites. As such, they are designed to provide an additional channel of communication between center and locality as well as a relatively direct means of rank-and-file mobilization. Parties in most African countries are, in a sense, nonpolitical, because they are a means of obtaining consensus rather than a unit of conflict. Suggestively, there has been no change of government in Black Africa that resulted from an open election between two competing political parties. (Sierra Leone came closest, but after the election returns indicated that the opposition party had defeated the governing party, a military coup d'etat abrogated the results and terminated civilian rule.) At the local level, there have occasionally been changes of government based upon interparty conflict, but the norm is for changes to take place either from the outside or from local contests among ethnic groups or factions based upon patron-client relationships. (Parties are discussed further in Chapter 9.)

LABOR UNIONS: AN ILLUSTRATION CONTINUED

Although African labor unions are not strong in absolute terms and they are structured within many regimes in productionist terms (see Chapter 7), it is still true that as organizations they are at least potentially powerful and that their members are relatively politicized (cf. Davies 1966: 10–11). Union power stems from their "mid-elite" resources (e.g., education and wealth) and their strategic location in the economic system. "Unions tend to occupy a politically strategic position in the society; their greatest strength is in the large cities and in those sectors of the economy which are vital to modernization" (Lofchie and Rosberg 1966:31).

In spite of these resources and loci, unions have in general played a relatively limited political role. However, a few strikes have had significant political objectives or ramifications, as events in Nigeria illustrate. A general strike began in Nigeria on June 1, 1964, and lasted 13 days, during which time work was almost completely halted in the wage sector of the economy. "From the third day onwards the strike paralyzed all the urban centres, not just in the relatively advanced regions in the South such as Lagos, Ibadan and Port Harcourt" (Braundi and Lettieri 1964:606). Strike leaders directed their attention not only to industrial issues but also to the broader social and political structure of the nation. Union leader Wahab Goodluck is quoted as follows: "What is the meaning of independence for a worker? Did he fight for independence so that only the pot-bellied politician will continue to grow fatter and more secure, while he vegetates in insecurity?" (ibid.:608). Tension ran so high during the strike that on June 8 troops were ordered to strategic positions in Lagos and Kaduna; all public transportation was halted; supplies of water and power were terminated; postal services were suspended; and many schools were closed. Although the strike ended without a clear gain for the union members, the government was made aware that labor was a political power to be dealt with.

Labor unions have been politically involved in other ways. They played an important role in the opposition party of Sierra Leone, including sponsoring candidates in elections (the opposition APP controlled Freetown with union support). And they have backed coups d'état in several countries, including Dahomey and Congo (Brazzaville). However, follow-through to political control in the form of labor government has yet to occur. A major factor limiting the political role of labor unions is their failure to develop programs embracing large segments of their countries' populations. To the contrary, they have largely remained urban-oriented organizations of self-interest. Of course, some unions have no chance to expand their scope because they are under close governmental control.

Class

The dual processes of an increasing concentration of wealth in the hands of fewer and fewer citizens and the decreasing earning capacity of an expanding majority of the population, lead to the possibility of moderate or even severe political dislocations (Edgren 1965a:179–180). Shils, who has been especially sensitive to the problems engendered by the elite-mass gap, argues that it can lead to interclass alienation and thence to politicized hostility (1960:272). One of the former leading Nigerian political parties, the Action Group, included the following statement in its manifesto: "The clash of interests between . . . classes and social strata increasingly provides the motive forces of the political life of the new Nigeria. . . . Political programmes and arguments are at bottom the objectives and views of definite economic classes and groups" (quoted in Grundy 1964:388). Indeed, horizontal divisions may be potentially more disruptive in "developing," as opposed to "developed," societies because the institutions of peaceful class conflict have not yet developed or stabilized.

The potential political impact of the gaps between the haves and have-nots can be suggested by looking at the categories of un- and underemployment, poor housing, lack of skills and enlightenment, and health. The un- and underemployment problem has channeled a number of Africans into the political arena. Some workers have sought remedy through labor unions. Educated but dissatisfied youngsters have sometimes drifted into oppositional activities. Some school dropouts have moved into either such disruptive groups as gangs or marginally legitimate political party "youth wings." (The youth wing, an organizational attempt to coopt youthful aggressiveness, is usually highly militant.) The political relevance of young people's disruptive behavior is suggested by Abernethy and Coombe: Antisocial actions are communications, both to political leaders and to rank-and-file citizens, that serious problems exist. Such communications about unemployment are more visible than are the masses of quiet unemployed hangers-on, the urban-to-rural returnees, or the psychological dropouts (1965:292). Even well-educated young men find it increasingly difficult to enter the upper level of government or advance within it. The editors of *Nigerian Opinion* have commented on recent political blockages, but the relevance extends to other spheres. "This may cause considerable frustration at a moment when education, especially university education, is producing more potential aspirants to political leadership than at any previous period of [Nigeria's] history. Unless the new potential recruits to the political class find a way into the present party system, they may begin to think in terms of other parties and other systems" (Nigerian Opinion 1965b:4).

The urban explosion overwhelms the housing programs of town councils and national legislatures with the result that there are now extensive poverty pockets in most large towns in Black Africa. Several riots and other political acts have been attributed to the housing problem. In Ndola, a government report stated: "In addition to the increase in rent, another cause of the riots at Ndola main location in April was the dissatisfaction of the residents with the bad conditions under which they lived and their disapproval of the rents for these hovels being raised" ([Zambia], Northern Rhodesia 1958:2).

Somewhat less than half the African children of primary school age are actually enrolled in classes, and after completing primary school only about one young person in twenty continues on to secondary school. A small proportion of the secondary schools' graduates enter institutions of higher education. These educational bottlenecks create especially emotional conditions in the towns of Black Africa where aspirations run high yet realization depends fundamentally upon obtaining an advanced education. An occasional result is anomic political outburst. Abernethy and Coombe report that the political actions of youths are usually not rebellious or revolutionary in nature, but criminal acts aimed at specific political adversaries (1965:292). Educational bottlenecks have also led youths in some towns to participate in organized oppositional activity.

Added to the problem of educational bottlenecks is the occasional practice of distributing scholarships on ascriptive rather than achievement bases. It is sometimes to whom you are related or how much you can pay, rather than how able a scholar you are, that decides scholarship awards. A Nigerian editorial reported the concern of town-dwellers: "The general outcry has been that at least the lion share of these scholarships has always gone to applicants who have what many people call 'long legs' or 'right connections'" (*Daily Times* 1963:5). Clearly, this is the basis of class formation and class politics, as the same editorial recognized: "In the long run, the already powerful, wealthy family becomes even more powerful whilst the weak, poor family becomes poorer. And the chances of a classless society become more remote. And who suffers in the end? Of course, it is the nation." Intergenerational continuity is one aspect of the problem; another is results. Shils is correct in writing about the enormous difference between the typical life styles and world views of modern educated Africans and those without such education (1960:272). This has an important effect upon patterns of association. Based upon a study of Kinshasa, Raymaekers reports that for many years school-leavers and uneducated youth joined together in the gangs, but that "more and more with the increase in post-primary education and the social advantages which it bestows there is growing up a separation between the educated and the uneducated" (1963b:349).

The diets of, and medical services available to, the haves and have-nots vary considerably. The more affluent can draw upon an unlimited variety of nutritious foods, but poorer people are on relatively unnutritious, high starch diets. First rate medical service is available to the privileged few, whereas the have-nots often must wait in line for an entire day to obtain medical advice, from a doctor if they are lucky, but often from a less-than-well-trained medical technician. The elite have tap water and flush toilets, whereas the average urban dweller must walk to community water taps and rely upon the bucket method for waste disposal. The direct link between health deprivations and political actions has not been established, but there is reason to believe on inferential grounds that these deprivations have served both as physiological causes for minimal political participation and (when the necessary energies are available) as political catalysts or "last straws" of anomic outbursts and oppositional political activities.

Politics based upon class and other nonethnic ties remains, in most towns, subordinate to or submerged within politics based upon ethnic group membership. Ethnic salience is high, class salience is low, vested interests are widespread, and "the urban poor are particularly unlikely to choose aggressive political action to express their grievances" due to their vulnerability, lack of organization, and low level of political awareness (Nelson 1970:404). However, evidence from all regions of Black Africa suggests that, very slowly, a new politics is emerging. The new politics is not necessarily a substitute for ethnic conflicts and solidarities, since it is possible for the two types to coexist, each being manifested situationally or one within the other. But in some towns, it is clearly an important feature of contemporary political life.

How are horizontal and vertical gaps bridged? How are fragmented urban sociopolitical systems integrated? Tentative answers are suggested in the following chapter.

Key townsmen, Mbale, Uganda. (Reproduced by permission of Rand McNally.)

9

Bases of
Political Integration

Urbanization and other modernization processes "naturally [pose] intrinsic problems of social integration—of adjustment, containment and reaction" (Moore 1952:284). They are exacerbated in Africa because of the prevailing polyethnic patterns and horizontal cleavages, especially in their urban manifestations. Yet the problems must be solved by African leaders if their communities and nations are to be viable single entities.[1]

Because the term integration is employed in a variety of ways and various words refer to the subject with which we are concerned, initial clarification is appropriate. There are, according to the conceptualization herein, two spheres of integration: that of practices and that of perspectives (see Hanna and Hanna 1969c:passim). Integration of practices implies social interaction—patterns characterized by such terms as common effort, collective action, and mutual facilitation. Integration of perspectives directs attention to mutual identification and shared (or at least compatible) values.

Two provisos are in order. First, interacting practices and common perspectives are closely interrelated.[2] Second, integration is not a concrete visible entity. "People are disposed to respond in an integrative way toward certain objects or stimuli under certain conditions. Thus, integration cannot be 'seen'; it must be inferred from certain observations" (Jacob and Teune 1964:10).

Research in Africa on urban political integrative institutions has largely focused upon formal structures. The actual behavioral patterns have remained at the periphery of most scholars' work. Nevertheless, drawing

---

1. Whether African communities and nations should be viable single entities is an entirely separate issue.

2. Parsons and his associates demonstrate this in their theoretical exploration of the theory of action by using the linking concept of "expectations," which are seen, *inter alia*, as deriving from perspectives and influencing practices (cf. Parsons and Shils 1954:passim). Here however, we shall retain the differentiation.

upon some direct and more indirect evidence, it is possible to indicate the general patterns of political integration that appear to exist.

Most African towns display integrative patterns that maintain sufficient continuity that it is appropriate to term them political systems. Each system, in turn, appears to be composed of several distinct primary subsystems so intercoupled that the output of one acts as an input for the other. These subsystems are of three types: ethnic, locality, and interlevel (Hanna and Hanna 1969c:passim). Each local polity contains several ethnic subsystems, one locality subsystem, and one interlevel subsystem. (All of these are operative situationally.) A simple hierarchical schematic of the subsystems appears in Figure 9.1.

The boundaries of perspective subsystems tend to overlap those of the interactional subsystems. Ethnic subsystems manifest the highest degree of coterminousness, and indeed it was because of this that the term ethnic was chosen. The degree of coterminousness for other subsystems varies widely, depending upon a number of local characteristics. For example, the more ethnically homogeneous a town is, the greater correspondence between the boundaries of its interactional and perspective locality subsystems.

The degree of integration, it should be noted, .is not necessarily correlated with those societal patterns that facilitate "constructive" social change. For instance, a "fully integrated" society may not be the optimal arrangement. This observation is in accord with the view expressed at the 1961 Abidjan meeting of urbanization specialists, where it was pointed out that institutional flexibility and at least some social disintegration were necessary correlates of rapid social change (Commission for Technical Co-Operation in Africa South of the Sahara, Scientific Council 1961a:20). Thus ethnic subsystems, which are usually more highly integrated than

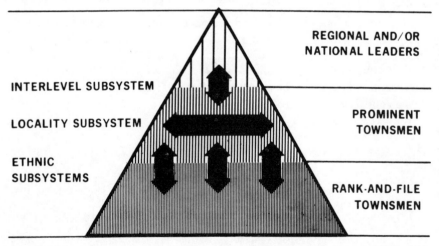

Figure 9.1. Urban Subsystems. (Adapted from Hanna and Hanna 1966a:10.)

those of the locality or interlevel, are often barriers to rapid change. On the other hand, a highly integrated interlevel subsystem may be the optimal arrangement for such change. It is clear, however, that a high degree of disintegration serves as a barrier to constructive social change within the perspective of a relatively short time span (say ten years or less). The long term payoff of disorganization may be a different matter. Shils has argued that the loosening or disruption of the extended family system might facilitate the release of ambition and the development of economizing behavior. Those who suffer from disruption's corollary, anomie, "are the painful and perhaps inevitable price which is paid for a process which liberates creativity by allowing individuality to develop" (1958:15–16).

Ethnic Subsystems

An ethnic subsystem is coterminous with an ethnic group. The term group itself implies "regular and relatively permanent relationships, that is, who act towards and in respect of each other, regularly in a specific, predictable, and expected fashion" (Nadel 1951:146). Ethnic subsystems may, of course, be internally differentiated and factionally divided.

As indicated earlier, many urban and suburban residents in Black Africa think of themselves as strangers without civil rights or responsibilities in the town. The low degrees of civility and norm homogeneity permit the manifestation of polyethnically structured practices and perspectives, and vice versa. Typical of the comments of many articulate Africans is the following: "People don't have much civil sense. They don't think of themselves as citizens of the town" (Hanna and Hanna 1963b:462). However, people do think of themselves as members of ethnic groups.

Ethnic subsystems provide a significant number of African townsmen with their most important means of articulating interests in the wider sociopolitical community, of receiving communications from the outside, and of establishing a sense of solidarity in the urban environment. Thus integration, in the first instance, takes place by means of the ethnic group.

Monrovia provides an extreme example of the predominance of ethnic subsystems in the integrative network of a racially homogeneous locality. There, "little attempt has been made to impose a unified system of urban administration. The long-established [ethnic] communities have developed their own urban traditions and their own forms of internal administration, which have set a pattern for leadership in the more recently arrived tribal groups" (Fraenkel 1964:70).

The organizational expression of ethnic political solidarity and shared political interest, whether the group is tribal, racial, or areal in origin, is its ethnic voluntary association (see Chapter 6). It is of relevance to integration that, as Busia points out, associations of stranger coethnics organizationally unite people of similar backgrounds and impose behavioral controls upon the membership in such a way that urban governance is in part decentralized from municipal governmental institutions. On the other hand, ethnic associations may inhibit their members from developing a sense of civic responsibility (1956:75).

Interlevel Subsystem

The interlevel subsystem links prominent townsmen with the power center of the larger territorial political system (country or perhaps region). A territorial center is almost invariably more powerful than any one of its urban counterparts, but considerable variation exists across Africa in the division of power. Typical of the comments heard from residents of less powerful towns is the following: "We local people in the town don't have a say. It's decided in [the capital] and then made known in the press" (Hanna and Hanna 1963b:32). On the other hand, center intervention is more selective in some other areas: "Leaders at the center come in only when something goes wrong," said one townsman. "Interference [also] depends upon the type of problem" (ibid.).

In most areas three parallel, in part overlapping, interlevel networks appear to exist, one formal, a second informal, and a third containing both formal and informal elements.

FORMAL NETWORK

Of the three networks, most is known about the formal one. It is the most visible and therefore the most easily researched. This network includes the relevant officers of territorial and local governance, e.g., territorial ministers, provincial commissioners, district officers, and town councillors. Authoritative interlevel communications flow through this channel.

Two broad patterns emerge, one based upon the concept of political decentralization and the other based upon centralization. The former especially characterized British colonial practice, whereas the latter was more typical in French and Belgian territories. An indication of the contrast is that elected local councils were established in Eastern Nigeria in 1950 and in the Gold Coast (now Ghana) the following year. With the exception of the traditional communes of Senegal, it was only in the late 1950s that French administrators took steps to develop representative local institutions. In a sense, the British were simply applying to their colonies long-standing theories and practices of their home country, whereas French colonial policies were at least in part "the uncritical extension to Africa of the 'statist' and centralist tradition of metropolitan France" (Coleman 1955:55).

These patterns of government, as reflected at the local level, have been usefully summarized by Alderfer: The British model is distinguished by "decentralization, legislative dominance, co-option through the committee system, multipurpose activity, and voluntary citizen participation" (1964: 10). By contrast, the French model incorporates "centralization, chain of command, hierarchical structure, executive domination, and legislative subordination" (ibid.:7).

Urban government within the framework of a decentralized system is established by the state and usually supported financially by grants from it, in addition to local rates determined and collected by the urban government itself. Each essential change in the structure or function of councils usually has to be approved and gazetted by the ministry of local government or an equivalent agency. For example, the gazette announcement of the establishment of the Enugu Urban District Council in 1958 included such details as number of wards and councillors, method of elections, date of the first election, size of a quorum, first order of business of a new council (election of a mayor), the standing committees, and every function that could legally be performed, e.g., maintaining markets, licensing and controlling slaughterhouses, prohibiting the use of any inflammable material in the construction or repair of any building, and regulating the digging of pits and other excavations (Eastern Nigeria 1958:B105–B109).

One observer prefers to call the French system "local administration" rather than "local government" because of the predominance of the central regime. Indicators of central control are that one third of the 90 municipal councils in French-speaking West Africa have appointed rather than elected mayors, and one third of them have been dissolved in favor of appointed caretaker committees (Brierly 1966:66). Even elected mayors in French-speaking Africa essentially play a dual role: representative of the central regime and spokesman for local constituents. An extreme indicator of centralization comes from the Ivory Coast, where most municipalities went without an election for over ten years. A statement by the Senegalese Minister of Interior clearly indicates the prevalent French-speaking African leader's position toward local government: "The Government has, in fact, preferred to retain the French administrative formula, which centralizes in the hands of a prefect the complete range of administrative powers, rather than adopt the English solution, for example, which does not contemplate this centralization" (quoted in Post 1964:98).

In contemporary Black Africa, the tendency of territorial leaders has been to retain or move in the direction of the French centralized model because of its presumed utility for forging national unity and minimizing opposition. Some French-speaking countries have, since independence, tightened control of urban governments. The communes of Guinea have been incorporated into surrounding administrative districts, and the chief executive officer, formerly elected, is now appointed. Even in Senegal, which has a centuries-long tradition of urban autonomy, the central government has moved to bring local government in line with the central regime. A number of municipal councils have been dissolved and opposition candidates for the councils have seen their prospects diminish rapidly in the past few years (see Zolberg 1966: 118–119).

An example of the tendency toward centralization in English-speaking countries is provided by Tanzania where, following reform, local control has been vested in the regional commissioners (Tordoff 1965:87). And in Kenya, the Mayor of Nairobi is reported to have complained that the Minister for Local Government "procrastinated in approving the Council's expenditure proposals and appointments; he needlessly vetoed Council projects and generally humiliated the mayor and the Council" (Werlin 1966b:182).

Military governments have encouraged the tendency toward centralization because it is compatible with traditional military structures and functions. Indeed, Napoleon, who established the French system, was essentially applying his military organizational brilliance to the civic arena's perceived needs for a new social order. Military rule is not, however, a requisite of increased centralization. It is interesting to recall in this regard that colonial regimes (even the British initially) were "highly centralized, even quasi-military, systems" (Coleman and Rosberg 1964:659); the socializing impact of these regimes upon contemporary African leaders has probably been significant.

Thus the overall pattern of change in formal center-local government relationships has been in the direction of a *return* to the more authoritarian centralized patterns which prevailed before self-government. Perhaps African leaders have concluded that decentralized grass roots democracy had been too quickly introduced and that a longer period of time must elapse before they can work effectively on African soil. (Some of the deficiencies of African local government within the decentralized model are discussed below, in the section on locality subsystems.)

INFORMAL NETWORK

The second interlevel network is informal but sometimes more influential than the first, especially in English-speaking Africa. It comprises the leading political actors of the center and the town—whether or not they are officials—who communicate with each other on important matters regardless of the propriety of such communications in terms of formal rules and regulations. Major decisions are often made within the informal network and then communicated to formal bodies for "ratification."

The extent to which this informal network is operative and predominant depends upon the nature of the entire political system of which it is part. An informal network of influence is more convenient, especially within a decentralized system, from the point of view of the center leadership. Barnard is among those who have noted that informal structures are highly effective channels of executive control (1940:passim): The leader is not bound by the regulations of the formal system; rather, he can control un-bounded by such conventions.

PARTY NETWORK

An integrative structure that has characteristics of formality and informal-ity and enlists the active support of both officials and influential clique members is the political party network. "Designed to mobilize (and there-fore possibly *not* to represent) the population at large in support of the goals of the leaders" (Hanna 1964a:30), it includes not only the "party" per se but also such ancillary organizations as youth wings and women's groups.

Although some African countries still have multiple party systems and others have nonparty military regimes, the most typical institutional ar-rangement remains the government and party at least partially distinct from one another with opposition parties either banned or restrained. One important reason for retaining distinct institutions is that leadership is pro-vided with an alternative and more flexible channel of communication and control. There are various ways in which the party can be used by leaders at the center to control urban affairs. Influencing the nomination of local candidates for election, and then the elections themselves, are mechanisms of control that appear to be commonly employed. In Western Nigeria during the 1959 federal election, for instance, the Action Group's nominating procedure was highly structured and centrally controlled; the party headquarters retained veto rights over all local decisions (Post 1963: 232). Of course, integration is usually enhanced if consensus can be reached rather than decisions imposed upon the locality; for this reason, local initiative is often encouraged. However, the nomination and thence election of a townsman opposed to the central regime is less common than opposition itself. The municipal election results of Ivory Coast are repre-sentative of many areas: candidates of the Parti Démocratique de Côte d'Ivoire were unopposed in all but two of the country's urban constitu-encies (Zolberg 1964:211).

At times, a crisis concerning the relative strength of the party and the governing administration arises. Immediately following independence it was invariably the former that predominated. In Mali, for instance, Madeira Keita's guiding principle was "dominance of the political machine over the administrative machine" (quoted in Hodgkin and Morgenthau 1964:248). However, as Wallerstein notes, "the precedence of the party has tended to be more formal than real. If invoked in a crisis situation, it cannot prevail against those who have access to the military" (1966a:211). Furthermore, there are signs that the "one party" network is in some countries turning into a "no party" regime as the assigned func-tions and manifest activities decline and mobilization itself becomes a threat to the ruling elite already overburdened by demands from the body politic.

Locality Subsystem

The third political subsystem is townwide and interethnic. Thus it is responsible for bringing together those people otherwise separated by ethnic or factional divisions. Participants in the locality subsystem come disproportionately from the upper strata of society, because their work and leisure orbits more often bring them into contact with members of ethnic groups other than their own, and because they have the education and skills that make such contacts easier to manage. Key political actors in the locality subsystem include town officials and influentials.

In those areas where the members of one ethnic group predominate, common culture and identity are locality integrative factors. But in many African towns, there are several distinct ethnic cultures that impart different perspectives and encourage different practices. Thus a key bond of community may be missing. In the predominantly Ibo town of Umuahia, for example, the index number representing the political cultural homogeneity of key political actors was only slightly less than the index number of the average ethnic group, whereas in Mbale, a town composed of many races and ethnic groups, the difference between the two index numbers was quite large (Hanna and Hanna 1969c:185).

Potential transethnic links such as occupation, neighborhood, and recreational activities are often weak, limited, or sporadic in urban Africa. Labor unions discussed earlier, are important in some towns but their participating membership is small.[3] However, increased education, income, and social and political participation will undoubtedly increase the number of shared cultural elements and therefore contribute to perspective integration. Evidence from the Umuahia and Mbale studies indicates that among key political actors there is even a remarkable similarity of perspectives between one town and the other, although the rank-and-file adults display few between-town similarities (Hanna and Hanna 1969c: 186).

FORMAL NETWORK

Most formal networks of authority operative in urban Africa were established during the period of colonial rule to serve the purposes of the regime that was then in power. Generally, local government structures (particularly those in a relatively decentralized territorial political system) have been judged failures. Consequently, they have often been informally circumvented, formally constrained, or abolished by national leaders.

Reports of ineffective local government abound. Typical is this comment

---

3. Yet in Africa, as elsewhere, "organizational affiliations and informal relations provide the chain which links different members of the [locality] together; if these affiliations are confined mostly within ethnic groups . . . and fail to tie these groups to one another, the lines of cleavage are already set" (Coleman 1957:22).

by a Nigerian official: "Most people in Nigeria feel today that there is a great deal wrong with our local government. It is not simply a question of the distribution of functions between local government and central government. It is a question more of efficiency of administration" (Adebo 1966:68–69). The reasons for the disappointing performance of many local urban governments are threefold: Local governments have been overloaded; they have not been redesigned to cope with the dynamic problems of the independence period; and they have been poorly staffed.

Turning to the first point, Jacob and Teune have observed generally what clearly applies in the African setting: The extraordinary rate of urbanization has created a mass of suddenly perceived social needs. These needs are too great and too complex for most existing local governments to satisfy or control, and new governmental units tailored specifically for urbanized man have not yet been created. This disparity menaces even the most basic living conditions, and yet the rate of urbanization does not appear to be declining (see 1964:1–2).

Second, local governments in Africa have not, with few exceptions, been redesigned to cope with the sociopolitical dynamics of the independence period. Rather, the institutional structures inherited from colonial regimes have been retained, despite the fact that these regimes—like virtually all others—articulated their own personal requirements, self-interests, and cultural biases in the institutional structures they created. Local governments were often hybrids of paternalism and imported tables of organization. Yet the sociopolitical givens upon which a meaningful set of local government institutions must be built include polyethnicity and underdevelopment. Only recently has there been an attempt on the part of some African leaders to reexamine the entire system of local government in their countries.

The third reason, poor staffing, is perhaps the most important. Comments on the staffing problem abound. "The main difficulties in local government which have arisen in Tanzania," observes Tordoff, "have been caused by weak, and sometimes dishonest, council staff and by councillors largely ignorant of their duties" (1965:87). And difficulty with the urban council in Nairobi has been attributed to the councillors' failure to understand the issues on their agenda, the procedures of the Council, and the extent to which they should depend upon administrators' advice (Werlin 1966b:193).

The staffing problem is attributable to the combination of underdevelopment and the attraction of state activities. Concerning the former, it has been pointed out that the countries of Black Africa lack personnel with sufficient training and experience to man all posts at a satisfactory level of effectiveness. Thus, governments have had to fill the gap with expatriates or inadequately prepared indigenous personnel. On the grounds of nationalist ideology and bootstrap development theory, the decision in many parts of Africa has been to opt for the latter. As for the attraction of state activities—Africa's internal "brain drain"—many talented Africans have chosen to pursue careers in the central administration or party where major decisions about the present and future of the country, or region, are being made. Furthermore, opportunities for wealth, status, and other benefits are typically perceived to be greater at the center as compared with the town. And so reports of dishonesty, inefficiency, and inability will probably continue for the foreseeable future.

Generally, data from African towns lend support to the Jacob and Teune hypothesis that a government must be reasonably effective to obtain or retain the loyalty of its citizenry, and this loyalty is in turn necessary for maintaining locality integration. Ineffectiveness leads to pressures for new means to desired ends, including external controls, and also to new patterns of loyalty. Thus many preconditions of even greater central control of urban administration are present.

INFORMAL NETWORK

The second network of the locality subsystem is informal, but probably more powerful. Composed of influential members of the constituent ethnic groups, it might be referred to as a clique or set of cliques (no negative connotation is implied by this term) with specific membership situationally determined. Concerning the distribution of power between council and cliques, one African stated a prevalent view: "A fair amount of decisions are made outside the council. Few councillors make decisions" (Hanna and Hanna 1963b:557).

Informal networks may be supported or adhered to because they are at least partially analogous to many traditional patterns of influence and patronship. In many traditional political systems, a peasant farmer would tend not to go directly to a chief or king but would communicate through a middle-level patron. Such "patrons" also form the middle core of the contemporary informal network of influence.

Another facilitating factor is that informal influential townsmen are accessible, representative and protective, and understandable. Concerning accessibility, it is often true that "the lines of communication through the formal system are tenuous and difficult to follow. . . . Those desiring to communicate are faced by the rigid apparatus of a ponderous bureaucratic system" (Boissevain 1966:29). Representativeness stems from the fact that the influence of informal decisionmakers may be terminated abruptly rather than only at election time. This dynamic characteristic encourages the decisionmakers to be more representative and protective of their group —among other things, protecting the rank-and-file member "from a powerful government which he feels has been imposed upon him and which he regards as corrupt" (ibid.). As for understandability, this quality relates to the fact that local government forms are still foreign to many Africans. There is still much truth to Clement's report of more than a decade ago about the African's "daily need to grapple with divers problems in an unfamiliar social setting whose administrative structure, because it is not easily comprehensible, he tends to regard as threatening or arbitrary" (1956:485–486). On the other hand, the informal influential townsmen is often freer to satisfy the demands of his constituency than is the official who is restrained by written rules and regulations. "In this struggle between alternative structures for fulfilling the nominally same function of providing aid and support to those who need it," writes theorist Merton, "it is clearly the machine politician who is better integrated with the groups which he serves than the impersonal, professionalized, socially distant and legally constrained [official]" (1957:75).

PARTY NETWORK

In the urban areas of Black Africa the party sometimes performs a sufficiently wide range of service activities that some town-dwellers—as well as villagers—are attracted to it as a functional alternative to the more parochial ethnic association. For example, party leaders have encouraged their organizations to perform many service activities, such as sponsoring traditional dance festivals, mediating occupational disputes, and donating money to waking ceremonies. Abrahams writes: "For the younger people [of Tanganyika] politics and entertainment are inextricably interwoven. T.A.N.U. [a party] is very powerful amongst the younger elements in the town and has produced the political masterstroke of starting a youth league with community singing five nights per week" (1961:250).

There are striking parallels between party activities in the urban areas of Africa and those of the political machine in urban America at the turn of the century. In both cases political organizations satisfy some of the needs of immigrants, including new bases of solidarity and new sources of security, in return for political support. The party does not, however, provide a permanent solution itself; other institutional mechanisms are necessary. Shils is quite correct in asserting that the veneer of nationalism may only temporarily—usually in times of crises—cover up parochial divisions (1960:283). A more stable basis of integration probably requires a more pluralistic infrastructure. (The Shils hypothesis may explain why leaders so frequently announce and/or perceive crises.)

REINTEGRATION

Recent events in Africa indicate that power and authority are being reintegrated at the local level. In some countries councils have been abrogated in favor of powerful center-appointed administrators whom influential townsmen will have to interact with rather than circumvent. Elsewhere, central control has generally been strengthened (see above), which is also likely to lead to reintegration. Furthermore, some central regimes are rediscovering the utility of ethnicity as a basis of governing. Rather than try to merge all identities into one, the alternative concept is to build upon identity blocks already available. "To effectively govern on the local government level," writes Mezu, "Africa must resurrect her traditional communalism by infusing into its well-tried and simple system, now anemic from disuse, the red blood of social revolution" (1966:150). Such a resurrection would return local areas to a form of "indirect rule" not unlike the form employed by colonial regimes in some African countries before independence. Along this line Wallerstein asserts that what were once parties "are in the process of becoming transformed into coalitions of local elites interested in obtaining a cut of the increased income of a market economy but fearful of more rapid modernization because it may threaten their newly acquired privileges" (1966b:212). This is resurrection with a difference—the goal of local elites becomes self-interest rather than social revolution.

Linkages Among Subsystems

It is implicit from the use of the terms system and subsystem that the latter are interconnected as component units of the former. In this section we note some of the interconnections and their correlates. It should be borne in mind that the integrative challenge to the system as a whole is similar to that facing the ethnic subsystem which must integrate families and lineages, the locality subsystem which must integrate prominent individuals and situational cliques, and the interlevel subsystem which must integrate leaders at the center with prominent individuals and cliques of the locality.

System integration is in part accomplished at the subsystem level; interlevel and ethnic practices and perspectives provide the vertical core for the larger system, and locality practices and perspectives provide the horizontal core. Put differently, when the three subsystems are integrated, the system will also be integrated. Conversely, disintegration òf the constituent subsystems can be equated with disintegration of the system as a whole. Among the explanations for the slowed momentum of modernization evident in many African countries, for example, are fractionalization of parties and centrifugal factors within the government.

ETHNICITY AND CIVILITY

For a variety of reasons (see Deutsch 1964:186 and Sumner 1906:12–13), ethnic group integration would appear to be inversely related to locality and interlevel integration (two manifestations of a civil culture). Thus "black power" would not appear to contribute to the integration of New York City or to the interlevel subsystem composed of Harlem leadership plus federal and/or state authorities. However, some evidence indicates that ethnic integration need not be a deterrent to the integration of other subsystems or the larger system.

Wallerstein suggests the following beneficial consequences of ethnicity: diminishing the importance of kinship roles, keeping the class structure open, and absorbing some of the hostility that otherwise might be directed toward frail authority structures (1960:137). Noel has found that in-group

pride (but not chauvinism) is positively correlated with attitudes and behavior favorable to integration. One manifestation, according to Noel, is
a greater willingness of those with in-group pride to participate in civic
politics (1966). This relates to Almond and Verba's observation that subgroups provide their members with a way to relate to the center. Because
local and parochial institutions and cultures were not entirely destroyed
during the development of a "subject culture" in England, they served (in
modified form) as networks of influence relating Britons as effective citizens to their government (1963:25). Handlin argues that the problems
facing the Negroes and Puerto Ricans of New York City "can best be
solved through the development of communal institutions, under responsible leadership that will give order and purpose to their lives" (1959:19).
And it may be that ethnic solidarity is at least sometimes correlated with
competitiveness rather than hostility. "The functional relationship of leaders to followers," Luttbeg and Zeigler observe, "is keyed to the necessity
for cohesion as a weapon in extra-group competition" (1966:655). This is
especially relevant because competition may be integrative, as Gluckman
demonstrates in his essay "The Peace in the Feud" (1959:1–26).

KEY TOWNSMEN AS INTEGRATORS

Many types of individuals contribute to the integration (or disintegration)
of African urban societies and political systems, but the most important are
those townsmen who participate in all three political subsystems and
therefore serve as essential links among the subsystems (Hanna and
Hanna 1969a). The key townsmen are "men of individual strength and of
broadening group identity, able to forge a synthesis of old and new life-
styles, capable of self-direction and aware of the realities of the situation"
(Powdermaker 1962:310). In sociological terms, such men occupy positions that are associated with a set of "linkage roles" (cf. Warren 1963:
253). Discussing these, Southall has argued that the individual who plays
many apparently contradictory roles is essential for the cohesion of complex societies, systems, and situations. Such an individual is responsible
for the intermeshing of institutions and therefore for societal integration
(1967:330 et passim). This is precisely what key townsmen do. Thus key
townsmen "make up the social bridges between otherwise distinct and
separated political sub-communities" (Berelson et al. 1954:131).

In the African setting, the linkage role has most often been discussed in
terms of a two subsystem conflict which is imposed from above and from
below. For instance, Epstein's analysis of the tribal elders in the mining
town of Luanshya indicates that these men had one set of relations in
which they represented the interests of coworkers to management, and another set of relations in which they represented the interests of management to their coworkers (1958:65). The elders' problem was to perform
successfully in both sets, not always an easy assignment. The role of the
modern African chief has also been analyzed along these lines. "It is a

role," Fallers writes, "which is played out in a matrix of diverse and often conflicting institutions. . . . On the one hand, he has a series of roles in the indigenous institutions of African society. On the other hand, he occupies roles in the imported institutions of colonial government" (1955:290). The emphasis in many analyses of the occupants of linkage roles has been upon the intense conflict that is imposed by apparently incompatible expectations. However, as Magid has shown, this need not be so, at least in the sense with which the concept of conflict has generally been employed in the literature. Mechanisms of avoiding conflict include selective perception and interpositional buffering (1965:passim).

There are several ways by which the key townsman's contribution to the integration among the three subsystems and thus to the integration of the system as a whole can be examined. We shall briefly do so in terms of three activities: passive transmission, active manipulation, and symbolic identification. There is, however, no implication of mutual exclusiveness among these categories, nor are they exhaustive.

Passive transmission, in the context of intersubsystem integration, involves communicating the perspectives of actors in one subsystem to those in the other subsystems (cf. Pye 1958a:345). Barker, discussing local integration in Senegal, notes that in order to implement development policies and manage political inputs, the central government must work through "intermediaries" who are integral members of the local political system. Thus these intermediaries are both agents of the central government and spokesmen for local interests (1966:2).

In terms of downward communication, the local key townsman is equivalent to the opinion leader which Lazarsfeld and his associates identified in Erie County as part of their conceptualization of the two-step flow of communications. These authors report that ideas are often communicated from the mass media (and center leadership) to local opinion leaders and from them to the local rank-and-file residents (1944:151). Little describes the situation in Africa: the leader has the ability "to interpret what he has learned through reading books and newspapers, through work and through travel, in terms that are meaningful to the illiterate rank and file" (1965:113). Communications also flow upward, from rank-and-file ethnics through the group's leadership to the local council, local cliques, or territorial center. This is an important flow for, as Hoselitz and Moore have indicated, agitation tends to be peaceful and orderly if access is provided to those responsible for policymaking, but blocked access increases the probability of violence and other deviant solutions (1963:45). Although the effect of specific communication content upon intersubsystem integration has not been adequately studied, it can be assumed that a wide range of content could be integrative and that, for structural reasons, a large proportion of both upward and downward communications which are transmitted by key townsmen would be integrative.

Active manipulation involves making the sociopolitical practices and perspectives of the various subsystems less divergent and contradictory. There are obviously tremendous gaps between the relatively modern inter-level and locality subsystems and the more rural and/or tradition-oriented ethnic subsystems. Yet the key townsman must participate successfully in all three. Focusing upon the cognitive dissonance of cultural duality, we assume that the "existence of dissonance in a person leads to a process of social communication by which he attempts to reduce the dissonance" (Festinger 1957:204). The key townsman's cultural duality is constantly reinforced by regular contacts with individuals in each of the principal subsystems. Perhaps in order to create consonance in the face of cultural diversity, many key townsmen appear to seek to actively manipulate the subcultures to make them mutually compatible. Such manipulative activity obviously has an important integrating affect upon the political system as a whole. Transmitting and manipulating can be viewed in terms of a general mediating activity. A variety of research has been conducted on mediation, ranging from union-management relations to the linking of immigrants to a core social unit. Of direct relevance to Africa is Eisenstadt's study of the leaders of immigrant groups in Israel. He concludes that "the elite performs a very important function as 'mediators' between the primary groups of the immigrants and the wider social structure. . . . The elites seem to influence the formation of the values and activities of the primary groups" (1952:226).

Symbolic identification makes it possible for the development of a sense of unity while remaining to some extent encapsulated within an ethnic enclave. Eisenstadt's research again has theoretical relevance for Africa. "The identification of the immigrants with the new society," he writes, "is to a large extent affected through their identification with the elites" (1952:226). Such identification is probably a critical precondition for certain types of ethnic involvement in locality affairs. In Jos, for instance, the modern elite, "as valued members of their ethnic associations . . . have been able to involve their tribal unions in Jos community affairs" (Plotnicar 1970:289).

It appears that over time there has been an increase in the number of persons who link rank-and-file ethnic group members with the interlevel and locality subsystems. This is a result of an increase in the typical townsman's roles and a decline in the authority of traditional leaders. Among the Ijebu of Ibadan, for example, "the importance of the local leader was greatest . . . when the Ijebu community was relatively little differentiated in terms of socioeconomic characteristics." Contributing to the leader's decline was the community members' perceived "need to deal with their problems and complaints direct with [an elected urban] Council" (Mabogunje 1967: 93–94).[4]

4. In Hanna and Hanna 1969c:195–197, we refer to the increase in the number of linkage role occupants as a shift from a fused to a prismatic and then to a diffracted linkage model.

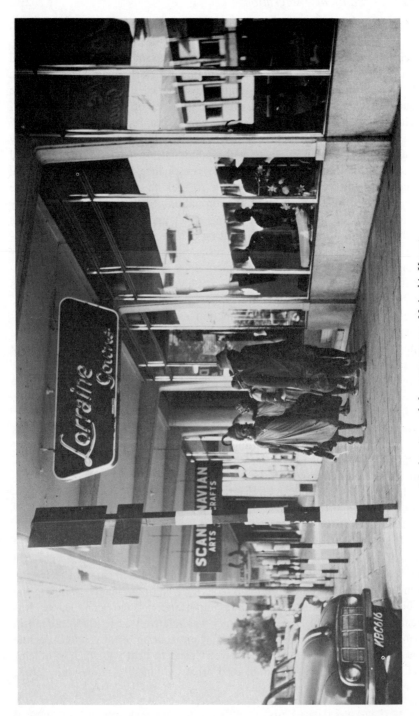

Modernity and the newcomers, Nairobi, Kenya

10

Patterns of Change

In the preceding chapters we have focused upon a series of "urban dynamics" in Black Africa. There are two larger issues that will not be explored in depth because our objectives are limited and available data are sparse, but that should be raised because of their implications and the high priority they should have in future social science research. These issues are the scope and direction of change. We assume, with Eisenstadt, that "the direction and scope of change are not random but dependent . . . on the nature of the system generating the change, on its values, norms and organizations, on the various internal forces operating within it and on the external forces to which it is especially sensitive because of its systemic properties" (1964:247).

Scope of Change

Migration and commitment, environmental developments, changes in social controls, family structures, status systems, and opportunity structures, the urbanization of ethnic ties and the emergence of nonethnic ties, the development of ethnic and nonethnic political conflicts, and the emergence of polyethnic systems of political integration—these process appear, based on the evidence presented, to be significantly interrelated. Whether urbanization is an early, late, or contemporaneous development along with other aspects of modernization, it is clearly part of a change in independent Black Africa that is broad in scope.

Additional evidence concerning the scope of change can be derived from the contrasts that exist between relatively urbanized countries (as measured by the proportion of persons in the total population residing in urban areas) and those less urbanized.[1] Table 10.1 presents such contrasts

---

1. A proper study of the scope of change requires a multivariant longitudinal approach using both countries and individuals as units of analysis.

based upon the work of Banks and Textor (1963) and Russett et al. (1964).

The 18 correlates of urbanization, taken as a whole, indicate that the scope of change is quite broad. Those countries with a high proportion of their citizens resident in urban areas tend to be characterized by industrial development, good health, good education, homogeneity, stable democracy, and efficient neutral public administration. The identification of correlates of urbanization does not, of course, carry with it an implication of cause and effect. For example, whether urbanization causes a relatively high gross national product, or a relatively high gross national product causes urbanization, or both are caused by some other factor, or whether all causes are conditional upon a specific set of factors being operative, is exceedingly difficult to determine given the data now available.

Direction of Change

The general historical pattern of events and conditions concerning urbanization and urban change, which has been reported in this study, appears to have some analytic regularity. Exogenous intervention into endogenous cultures led, as has been shown, to urban in-migration and commitment. The growth of towns created potential changes for individuals, and these in turn affected urban environmental change. Ethnic and nonethnic urban ties represented, to a significant degree, the townsman's attempt to cope with the urban situation, and it was on the basis of these ties that much of the political life of urban Africa has been built. Of course, the patterns of individual changes display considerable variation, indicating that extreme caution should be exercised in overgeneralizing about the past or extrapolating from the past to the future.

ANALYTIC REGULARITY

An overview of the urban-related changes that have occurred in Black Africa suggests that, at a more abstract level, there may be a quasicyclical pattern. The pattern appears to have four sequential components (cf. Smelser 1959:passim):

(1) The environment changes by external or internal means, or by the radical relocation of individuals.

(2) Some older social roles become the object of dissatisfaction, as do the perceived existing distributions of values. There is a gap between reality and prevailing legitimate symbols, e.g., "equality" and "plenty." Thus tension increases.

(3) The immediate responses to the dissatisfactions range from withdrawal to aggression. Examples of aggression, the most visible type of re-

Table 10.1. Correlates of urbanization.

Characteristics of Relatively Urbanized Societies	Characteristics of Relatively Unurbanized Societies
(1) Relatively high gross national product (GNP)	(1) Relatively low gross national product (GNP)
(2) Relatively low proportion of GNP from agriculture	(2) Relatively high proportion of GNP from agriculture
(3) Relatively high percentage of labor force in industry; low percentage in agriculture	(3) Relatively low percentage of labor force in industry; high percentage in agriculture
(4) Relatively high proportion of wage and salary earners among the working-age population	(4) Relatively few wage and salary earners among the working-age population
(5) Relatively long life expectancy	(5) Relatively short life expectancy
(6) Relatively few inhabitants per physician and hospital bed	(6) Relatively many inhabitants per physician and hospital bed
(7) Relatively literate population	(7) Relatively illiterate population
(8) Relatively high per capita enrollment in higher education	(8) Relatively low per capita enrollment in higher education
(9) Relatively high proportion of young people five to nineteen years of age enrolled in primary and secondary schools	(9) Relatively low proportion of young people five to nineteen years of age enrolled in primary and secondary schools
(10) Relatively high per capita postal mailings, radio sets, television sets, cinema attendance, and newspaper circulation	(10) Relatively low per capita postal mailings, radio sets, television sets, cinema attendance, and newspaper circulation
(11) Relative freedom of press	(11) Relative press restriction
(12) Relative linguistic homogeneity	(12) Relative linguistic heterogeneity
(13) Relatively constitutional political regimes	(13) Relatively aconstitutional political regimes
(14) Relative political stability	(14) Relative political instability
(15) Relatively more likely to have a political system with legitimate political competition and two or more political parties	(15) Relatively more likely to have a political system with political competition not legitimate and only one political party (or mobilization movement)
(16) Relatively little sectionalism	(16) Relatively widespread sectionalism
(17) Relatively modern bureaucracy	(17) Relatively nonmodern bureaucracy
(18) Relatively likely to have an apolitical police force	(18) Relatively likely to have a politicized police force

sponse, include destruction of property, strikes, and agitation. Aggression is often justified in terms of the legitimate symbols of the society.

(4) Gradually, the aggressions and other responses are brought into line by mechanisms of social control, whether revolutionary, evolutionary, or restorational. Thus social disruptions tend to be "followed by social reorganizations aimed to re-establish some security. . . . Most men do not like

to live indefinitely under conditions of insecurity, anxiety, uncertainty, and disorder" (Berelson and Steiner 1964:616).

Along these lines, Eisenstadt writes: "The history of modern social systems is full of cases of unsuccessful adaptation, or of lack of adaptation of existing structures to new types of problems and organizations and of the lack of ability of these institutions to assimilate, to some extent, the various movements of protest inherent in the process of modernization. . . . [Eruptions] may lead either to the transformation of the existing regime into a more flexible one . . . or to breakdowns of modernization, to the development of regressive or deformed regimes with autocratic tendencies" (1963:40).

The four-component sequential pattern appears to have occurred at two analytic levels four times: both in the histories of most towns and in the biographies of many urban in-migrants. (The time span and scope of each recurrence may vary considerably.) The initiating environmental changes have been (1) new values, (2) immersion in town life, (3) intensified intrusion of modernity, and (4) restratification. In a highly generalized fashion, the four cycles are presented in Table 10.2.

CHANGE VARIATIONS

Given the possible generalizing utility of our cyclical model, it is important to note that change in urban Africa is neither linear, teleological, nor consistent.

Table 10.2. The quasicyclical pattern of change.

Cycle	Environmental Change	Dissatisfaction	Responses to Dissatisfaction	Social Control of Responses
1	European or other new value intervention: new regimes and models	Dissatisfaction with old ways	Some dissatisfied persons immigrate	Rural solidarities, urban controls by Europeans or new African leaders
2	Immersion in town life	Adjustment problems	Potential or actual individual and social disorganization	Urban ethnicity
3	Intensified intrusion of modernity	Dissatisfaction with constraints of ethnicity	Broadening of orbits	New associations and other non-ethnic responses
4	Restratification	Dissatisfaction with blocked mobility channels, etc.	Some riots, coups, etc.	Repression or regime change

At a set of points in time, change pattern possibilities include (as illustrated in Figure 10.1 by the ethnic-nonethnic dimension), *inter alia,* (1) uniform change toward nonethnic perspectives and practices, (2) change by stages toward nonethnic perspectives and practices, (3) an increase in nonethnic perspectives and practices followed by a reassertion of ethnicity (i.e., a U-curve), and (4) continuous intensification of ethnic perspectives and practices (see Hanna 1965a:passim).

An example of reassertion will serve to make the patterns concrete in the African context. Clignet's research in Abidjan and the rural areas from which some of its residents came shows that childbearing practices do not change according to a linear model as parents move to town and ascend the socioeconomic ladder (1967:passim). Rather, the newly arrived manual laborer's wife is less likely to manifest certain traditional practices than is the wife of a longer term townsman in a white collar job. This reassertion can be attributed to such factors as the greater provisions and travel opportunities open to those in better paying occupations.

The inevitability of developmental change should constantly be questioned. The assumption that there is a sociopolitical "takeoff" stage, after which self-sustained institutional growth sets in, has been called into question by Eisenstadt among others. He notes that economic and political data reveal many instances of discontinuous change, including the dramatic cycle of modernization followed by breakdown (1965c:459).

Although the various subsystems of a society are interrelated, each may have a certain measure of autonomy so that "the tempo and character of change are not evenly distributed over the whole field" (Epstein

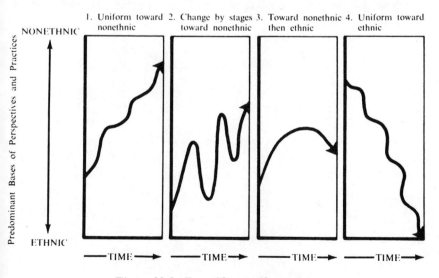

Figure 10.1. Four Change Alternatives.

1958:232). With reference to patterns of change such as those presented in Figure 10.1, it is appropriate "to view many or most of them not as competing generalizations but as appropriate to different aspects of social systems. . . . For the moment, partial theories appear to be the best that can be expected, whether in terms of the sources of changes or the directions of their course through time" (Eisenstadt 1963:44). A related point is made by Whitaker, who advocates a dysrhythmic rather than eurhythmic model of change. "Significant change in one important sphere or aspect of social activity," he writes, "may ramify in other aspects or spheres; however, such ramifications are not always consonant with the character and direction of the initial change" (1967:216). Therefore, the introduction of a modern industrial plant into an African town will not necessarily and inevitably lead to coordinate changes in other sectors of the urban system, including associational practices and political perspectives. Indeed, for some individuals a reaction formation may set in which places greater emphasis upon traditional perspectives and practices.

Future Research

Throughout this book, many simple and some conditional statements have been made about probable, prevailing urban dynamics in Black Africa. In this final chapter we have introduced the broader issues of the scope and direction of social change, about which little is yet known. The demonstrated need is additional theoretical development and empirical research so that our understanding of Africa, urban areas, and change itself will be further advanced.

Bibliography

This bibliography includes all works referred to in the text plus others that we found especially helpful in its preparation. Items with one asterisk (*) focus on a part of Africa other than independent Black Africa; those with two asterisks (**) are not primarily devoted to Africa.

Abernethy, David. 1965. "Education and politics in a developing society: The southern Nigerian experience." Unpublished doctoral dissertation, Harvard University.

Abernethy, David, and Trevor Coombe. 1965. "Education and politics in developing countries." Educational Review 35:287-302.**

Abrahams, R. G. 1961. "Kahama Township, Western Province Tanganyika." In Aidan William Southall, ed., Social change in modern Africa. London, Oxford University Press, pp. 242-253.

Abrams, Charles. 1964. Man's struggle for shelter in an urbanizing world. Cambridge, M.I.T. Press.**

Abrams, Charles, Vladimir Bodiansky, and Otto Koenigsberger. 1956. Report on housing in the Gold Coast. New York, United Nations.

209

Abu-Laban, Baha. 1967. "Social change and local politics: The case of Sidon, Lebanon." Paper read at
the Annual Meeting of the American Sociological
Association, San Francisco, 28-31 August.**

Abu-Lughod, Janet. 1961. "Migrant adjustment to city
life: The Egyptian case." American Journal of Sociology 67:22-32.**

1965. "Tale of two cities: The origins of modern
Cairo." Comparative Studies in Society and History
7:429-457.*

Acquah, Ione. 1965. "The development and functioning
of municipal government." In (Proceedings of the)
Fifth Annual Conference of the West African Institute of Social and Economic Research. University of
Ibadan, pp. 77-78.

1958. Accra survey. London, University of London
Press.

Adam, V. 1963. "Migrant labour from Ihanzu." In East
African Institute of Social Research, January Conference Proceedings, n.p.

Adams, Robert McC. 1966. The evolution of urban
society: Early Mesopotamia and prehispanic Mexico.
Chicago, Aldine Publishing Company.**

Addo, Nelson O. 1967. "Assimilation and absorption of
African immigrants in Ghana." Ghana Journal of
Sociology 3(1):17-32.

Adebo, Simeon O. 1966. "African local government since
independence." In Lincoln University, Institute of
African Government and Department of Political
Science, Proceedings of the Conference on African
Local Government Since Independence. Lincoln
University, pp. 58-72.

Africa Economic Digest. 1966. "New Township." 2(36):
876.

African Research Bulletin. 1967. "Kenya-accelerated 'Africanization' in private sector." 4(3):715.

Afrique Nouvelle. 1966. "Refugees in Africa: Their numbers and disposition." No. 981:9-10, May 26 - June 1. (Translated in Translations on Africa, No. 391:26-29.)

Afrique Occidentale Française, Haut Commissariat de la République. 1958. Recensement démographique de Dakar resultats définitifs [1955] (Demographic census of Dakar [1955] I.) Paris.

Agence de la France D'Outre-Mer. 1951. Le Sénégal: La ville de Dakar (Senegal: The city of Dakar). Paris.

Agger, Robert E., Daniel Goldrich and Bert E. Swanson. 1964. The rulers and the ruled: Political power and impotence in American communities. New York, John Wiley & Sons.**

Ahmed, Mohamud Giama. 1967. "The unemployment problem in the Somali Republic." La Tribuna (Mogadascio) 1(1):12, 1(2):21, 1(3):13, and 1(4):17 (Translated in Translations on Africa, No. 529, pp. 21-32).*

Ajayi, J. F. Ade. 1963. "Political organisations in West African towns in the nineteenth century: The Lagos example." In University of Edinburgh, Centre of African Studies, Urbanization in African social change: Proceedings of the Inaugural Seminar held in the Centre, January 5-7. Edinburgh, pp. 166-173.

Akinola, R. A. 1963. "The Ibadan region." Nigerian Geographic Journal 6(2):102-115.

1964. "The industrial structure of Ibadan." Nigerian Geographical Journal 7(2):115-130.

Akiwowo, Akinsola A. 1964. "The sociology of Nigerian tribalism." Phylon 25(2):155-163.

Akpan, N. U. 1957. "Chieftancy in Eastern Nigeria." Journal of African Administration 9:120-123.

Alderfer, Harold F. 1964. <u>Local</u> <u>government</u> <u>in</u> <u>develop-</u>
<u>ing</u> <u>countries</u>. New York, McGraw-Hill.

Alderton, E. C. 1956. "Developments in local government
in the Eastern Region of Nigeria." Journal of African
Administration 8:169-174.

Aldous, Joan. 1962. "Urbanization, the extended family,
and kinship ties in West Africa." Social Forces
12:6-12.

Alford, Robert R. 1967. "The comparative study of urban
politics." In Leo F. Schore and Henry Fagin, eds.,
<u>Urban</u> <u>research</u> <u>and</u> <u>policy</u> <u>planning</u>. (Urban Affairs
Annual Reviews, I) Beverly Hills, Sage Publications,
pp. 263-302.✻✻

Allen, C. P. S. 1959. <u>A</u> <u>report</u> <u>on</u> <u>the</u> <u>first</u> <u>direct</u>
<u>elections</u> <u>to</u> <u>the</u> <u>legislative</u> <u>councils</u> <u>of</u> <u>the</u> <u>Uganda</u>
<u>Protectorate</u>. Entebbe, Government Printer.

Almond, Gabriel. 1954. <u>The</u> <u>appeals</u> <u>of</u> <u>communism</u>.
Princeton, Princeton University Press.✻✻

Almond, Gabriel, and Sidney Verba. 1963. <u>The</u> <u>civic</u>
<u>culture</u>: <u>Political</u> <u>attitudes</u> <u>and</u> <u>democracy</u> <u>in</u> <u>five</u>
<u>nations</u>. Princeton, Princeton University Press.✻✻

Aloba, Abiodun. 1954. "Tribal unions in party politics."
West Africa 38:637.

Althabe, B. 1963. "Le chômage à Brazzaville" ("Unemployment in Brazzaville"). Cahiers Orstom Sciences
Humaines 1(4):1-41.

Aluko, S. A. 1965. "How many Nigerians? An analysis of
Nigeria's census problems." Journal of Modern
African Studies 3:371-392.

Amega, Louis-Koffi. 1964. "A sociological study of the
factors of juvenile delinquency in Congo Brazzaville."
Inter-African Labour Institute Bulletin 11:221-227.

American Universities Field Staff. 1968. <u>City</u> <u>and</u>

nation in the developing world (Selected case studies
of social change in Asia, Africa and Latin America).
New York, American Universities Field Staff.

Amin, G. S. 1966. "Asians in Kenya, a statement." In
East African Institute of Social and Cultural Af-
fairs, Racial and communal tensions in East Africa.
Nairobi, East African Publishing House, pp. 60-61.

Ampene, E. 1966. "A study in urbanization: Progress
report on Obuasi project." University of Ghana
Institute of African Studies Research Review 3(1):
42-47.

1967. "Obuasi and its miners." Ghana Journal of
Sociology 3(2):73-80.

Anderson, C. Arnold. 1963. "The impact of the educational system on technological change and modernization." In Bert F. Hoselitz and Wilbert E. Moore,
eds., Industrialization and society. The Hague,
Mouton, pp. 259-278.**

Anderson, Nels. 1962. "The urban way of life."
International Journal of Comparative Sociology
3:175-188.**

1964. (Ed.) Urbanism and urbanization. Leiden,
E. J. Brill.**

Anderson, Robert T., and Barbara Gallatin Anderson.
1964. The vanishing village: A Danish maritime community. Seattle, University of Washington Press.**

Angell, Robert C. 1942. "The social integration of
selected American cities." American Sociological
Review 47:575-592.**

1947. "The social integration of American cities of
more than 100,000 population." American Sociological
Review 12:335-342.**

1949. "Moral integration and interpersonal integration in American cities." American Sociological

Review 14:245-251.**

1951. "The moral integration of American cities."
American Journal of Sociology 57:130-139.**

Apter, David E. 1960. "The role of traditionalism in
the political modernization of Ghana and Uganda."
World Politics 13:45-68.

1962. "Some reflections on the role of a political
opposition in new nations." Comparative Studies in
Society and History 4(2):154-168.**

1963a. Ghana in transition. New York, Atheneum.

1963b. "Non-Western government and politics: Introduction." In Harry Eckstein and David E. Apter,
eds., Comparative politics. New York, Free Press of
Glencoe, pp. 647-656.**

1965. The politics of modernization. Chicago,
University of Chicago Press.**

Apthorpe, Raymond J., ed. 1958a. Present interrela-
tions in central African rural and urban life:
Eleventh conference proceedings of the Rhodes-
Livingstone Institute. Lusaka, Northern Rhodesia.

1958b. "Report of the conference on urban problems
in East and Central Africa held at Ndola, Northern
Rhodesia, in February, 1958." Journal of African
Administration 10:182-251.

Archibald, Kathleen, ed. 1966. Strategic interaction
and conflict: Original papers and discussion.
Berkeley, University of California Press.**

Arensberg, Conrad M., and Solon T. Kimball. 1965.
Culture and community. New York, Harcourt, Brace &
World.**

Arensberg, Conrad M., and Arthur H. Niehoff. 1971.
Introducing social change, 2nd ed. Chicago, Aldine·
Atherton, Inc.**

Arriaga, Eduardo E. 1970. "A new approach to the measurements of urbanization." Economic Development and Cultural Change 18(2):206-218.✲✲

Askwith, Tom. 1950a. "African housing in Nairobi." ∠ Journal of African Administration 2(3):37-39.

1950b. "Tribalism in Nairobi." Corona 2:292-295.

Atkinson, Anthony G. 1950. "African housing." African Affairs 49:228-237.

Auger, Alain. 1965. Kinkala, centre urbain secondaire (Kinkala, secondary urban center). Brazzaville, Office de Recherche Scientifique et Technologique.

Austin, Dennis, and William Tordoff. 1960. "Voting in an African town." Political Studies 8:130-146.

Awa, Eme O. 1959. "Local government in a developing country." Paper read at the Seminar on Representative Government, Ibadan, March.

1961. The voting behaviour and attitudes of Eastern Nigerians. Aba, Ofomata Press.

1964. Federal government in Nigeria. Berkeley, University of California Press.

Awe, Bolanle. 1967. "Ibadan, its early beginnings." In P. C. Lloyd, A. L. Mabogunje, and B. Awe, eds., The city of Ibadan: A symposium on its structure and development. London, Cambridge University Press, pp. 11-26.

Awolowo, Obafemi. 1947. Path to Nigerian freedom. London, Faber & Faber.

Axelrod, Morris. 1956. "Urban structure and social participation." American Sociological Review 21: 13-18.✲✲

Back, Kurt W. 1962. Slums, projects, and people: Social psychological problems of relocation in

Puerto Rico. Durham, Duke University Press.**

Baeck, L. 1956. "Leopoldville: Phénomène urbaine
africain ("Leopoldville: African urban phenomenon").
Zaire 10:613-636.

1957. Etude socio-economique du centre extra-
coutumier d'Usumbura (A socio-economic study of the
non-traditional center of Usumbura). Bruxelles,
Academie Royale des Sciences Coloniales.

1961. "An expenditure study of the Congolese evolues
of Leopoldville, Belgian Congo." In Aidan Southall,
ed., Social change in modern Africa. London, Oxford
University Press, pp. 159-181.

Baker, Robert A., J. Roger Ware, G. H. Spires, and
W. C. Osborn. 1966. "The effects of supervisory
threat on decision-making and risk-taking in a
simulated combat game." Behavioral Science 11:
167-176.**

Balandier, Georges. 1952. "Approche sociologique des
'Brazzavilles noires': Etude préliminaire" ("A
sociological approach to the Brazzaville Africans:
A preliminary study"). Africa 22:23-24.

1954. "Comparative study of economic motivations
and incentives in a traditional and in a modern
environment." International Social Science Bulletin
6:372-387.**

1955a. "Problèmes de desorganisation sociale lies à
l'urbanisation dans les pays en cours de developpe-
ment économique rapide" ("Problems of social disorganization linked to industrialization and
urbanization in countries undergoing rapid economic
development"). Information 6:1-15.

1955b. " Race relations in West and Central Africa."
In A. W. Lind, ed., Race relations in world perspective. Honolulu, Hawaii University Press, pp. 145-166.

1955c. Sociologie des Brazzaville Noires (Sociology

of Brazzaville Africans). Paris, Librairie Armand Colin.

1956a. "Sociological survey of the African town at Brazzaville." In International African Institute, Social implications of industrialization and urbanization in Africa south of the Sahara. Paris, UNESCO, pp. 106-109.

1956b. "Urbanism in West and Central Africa: The scope and aims of research." In International African Institute, Social implications of industrialization and urbanization in Africa south of the Sahara. Paris, UNESCO, pp. 495-509.

1962. "Introduction." In International Social Science Council, Social implications of technological change. Paris, Presses Universitaires de France, pp. 5-27.✶✶

1965. "Problématique des classes sociales en Afrique noire" ("Problematical issues concerning social classes in Black Africa"). Cahiers Internationaux de Sociologie 38:131-142.

1966. Ambiguous Africa: Cultures in collision. New York, Pantheon Books.

Banks, Arthur S., and Robert B. Textor. 1963. A cross-polity survey. Cambridge, M.I.T. Press.✶✶

Banks, J. A. 1962. "Social implications of technological change: Some reflections on historical and social research on the impact of technological change on the local community, the enterprise, and the family." In International Social Science Council, Social implications of technological change. Paris, pp. 61-106.✶✶

Banton, Michael P. 1954. "Tribal headmen in Freetown." Journal of African Administration 6:140-144.

1956. "Adaptation and integration in the social system of Temne immigrants in Freetown." Africa 26: 354-368.

Urban Dynamics in Black Africa

1957. <u>West</u> <u>African</u> <u>city</u>: <u>A</u> <u>study</u> <u>of</u> <u>tribal</u> <u>life</u> <u>in</u>
<u>Freetown</u>. London, Oxford University Press.

1961a. "Recent research on racial relations: Africa
south of the Sahara excluding Southern Rhodesia and
the Union of South Africa." International Social
Science Journal 13:197-214.

1961b. "The restructuring of social relationships."
In Aidan Southall, ed., <u>Social</u> <u>change</u> <u>in</u> <u>modern</u>
<u>Africa</u>. London, Oxford University Press, pp. 113-
125.

1965. "Social alignment and identity in a West
African city." In Hilda Kuper, ed., <u>Urbanization</u>
<u>and</u> <u>migration</u> <u>in</u> <u>West</u> <u>Africa</u>. Berkeley, University
of California Press, pp. 131-147.

Barbe, Raymond. 1964. <u>Les</u> <u>classes</u> <u>sociales</u> <u>en</u> <u>Afrique</u>
<u>noire</u> (<u>Social</u> <u>classes</u> <u>in</u> <u>Black</u> <u>Africa</u>). Paris,
Economie et Politique.

Barber, William J. 1961. "Disguised unemployment in
underdeveloped economies." Oxford Economic Papers
13(1):103-115.✺✺

Barker, Jonathan S. 1966. "Political integration and
elite recruitment in an arrondissement of the
Saloum Region in Senegal." Paper read at the Annual
Meeting of the African Studies Association,
Bloomington, Ind., October.

Barnard, C. I. 1940. <u>The</u> <u>functions</u> <u>of</u> <u>the</u> <u>executive</u>.
Cambridge, Harvard University Press.✺✺

Barnett, H. G. 1941-1942. "Personal conflicts and
cultural change." Social Forces 20:160-171.✺✺

Barrett, Raymond J. 1962. "The role of trade unions
in underdeveloped countries." Labor Law Journal 13:
1047-1059.✺✺

Barton, Allen H. 1962. <u>Measuring</u> <u>the</u> <u>values</u> <u>of</u> <u>indi</u>-
<u>viduals</u> (Reprint No. 354). New York, Columbia
University Bureau of Applied Social Research.✺✺

Bascom, William R. 1955. "Urbanization among the
Yoruba." American Journal of Sociology 60:446-454.

1959. "Urbanism as a traditional African pattern."
Sociological Review 7:29-43.

1962. "Some aspects of Yoruba urbanism." American
Anthropologist 64:699-709.

1963. "The urban African and his world." Cahiers
d'Etudes Africaines 4(14):164-185.

Basowitz, Harold, Harold Persky, Sheldon J. Korchin,
and Roy G. Grinker. 1955. Anxiety and stress. New
York, McGraw-Hill.**

Batson, E. 1956. "Social survey of Zanzibar Protectorate." In International African Institute, Social
implications of industrialization and urbanization
in Africa south of the Sahara. Paris, UNESCO, pp.
139-141.

Bauer, P. T. 1954. West African trade: A study of
competition, oligopoly, and monopoly in a changing
economy. Cambridge, Cambridge University Press.

Baum, Robert D. 1966. "National-local relationships
in Africa." In Lincoln University, Institute of
African Government and Department of Political
Science, Proceedings of the Conference on African
Local Government Since Independence. Pennsylvania,
Lincoln University, pp. 100-106.

Baumer, Guy. 1939. Les centres indigènes extra-
coutumiers au Congo Belge (Indigenous non-traditional
centers in the Belgian Congo). Paris, Domat
Montchrestien.

Bayne, E. A. 1954. Four ways of politics: State and
nation in Italy, Somalia, Israel, Iran. New York,
American Universities Field Staff.**

Beals, R. L. 1951. "Urbanism, urbanization, acculturation." American Anthropologist 53:1-10.**

Beckett, W. H. 1956. "Akokoaso: A survey of a Gold
Coast village." In International African Institute,
Social implications of industrialization and urbanization in Africa south of the Sahara. Paris, UNESCO,
pp. 96-99.

Behrendt, Richard F. 1962. "The emergence of new
elites and new political integration forms and their
influence on economic development." In International
Sociological Association, Transactions of the Fifth
World Congress of Sociology, II. Belgium, pp. 3-32.**

Beier, Ernst Gunter. 1951. The effect of induced
anxiety on flexibility of intellectual functioning.
Psychological Monographs 65 (whole no. 326).**

Beier, Ulli. 1960. "Oshogbo: Portrait of a Yoruba
town." Nigeria 1960, No. 66:94-102.

Bell, Evelyn M. 1963. "Polygons: A survey of the
African personnel of a Rhodesian factory, II--A
study of labour turnover." (Occasional Paper No. 3,
Department of African Studies) Salisbury, University
College of Rhodesia and Nyasaland.*

Bell, W. 1957. "Anomie, social isolation and the class
structure." Sociometry 20:105-116.**

Benedict, Burton. 1957. "Factionalism in Mauritian
villages." British Journal of Sociology 8:328-342.*

1958. "Education without opportunity: Education,
economics and communalism in Mauritius." Human
Relations 11:315-329.*

1962. "Stratification in plural societies." American
Anthropologist 64:1235-1246.**

Berelson, Bernard R., Paul F. Lazarsfeld, and William
N. McPhee. 1954. Voting: A study of opinion formation in a presidential campaign. Chicago, University
of Chicago Press.**

Berelson, Bernard, and Gary A. Steiner. 1964. Human

behavior: An inventory of scientific findings. New York, Harcourt, Brace & World.**

Berg, Elliot J. 1961. "Backward-sloping labor supply functions in dual economies--The Africa case." Quarterly Journal of Economics 75:469-492.

1963. "The external impact on trade unions in developing countries: The record in Africa." In Proceedings of the Sixteenth Annual Meeting of the Industrial Relations Research Association (IRRA Publication No. 32), pp. 89-101.

1964. "Major issues of wage policy in Africa." Paper read at the International Institute for Labour Studies Research Conference on Industrial Relations and Economic Development, Geneva, 24 August-4 September.

1965. "The economics of the migrant labor system." In Hilda Kuper, ed., Urbanization and migration in West Africa. Berkeley, University of California Press, pp. 160-181.

Berg, Elliot J., and Jeffrey Butler. 1964. "Trade unions." In James Smoot Coleman and Carl G. Rosberg, Jr., eds., Political parties and national integration in tropical Africa. Berkeley, University of California Press, pp. 340-381.

Berkun, M. M., H. M. Bialek, R. P. Kern, and K. Yogi. 1962. Experimental studies of psychological stress in man. Psychological Monographs 76 (whole no. 534).**

Berlyne, Daniel E. 1962. "New directions in motivation theory." In Thomas Gladwin and William E. Sturtevant, eds., Anthropology and human behavior. Washington, D.C., Anthropological Society of Washington, pp. 150-173.**

Bernard, Guy. 1968. Ville africaine, famille urbaine: Les enseignants de Kinshasa (African city, urban family: The teachers of Kinshasa). Paris, Mouton.

Bernus, Edmond. 1962. "Abidjan: Note sur l'agglomération d'Abidjan et sa population" ("Notes on Abidjan's
urban area and population"). Bulletin de l'Institut
Français d'Afrique Noire 24B (1-2):54-85.

Berry, Brian, J. L. 1962a. "Some relations of urbanization and basic patterns of economic development."
In Forrest R. Pitts, ed., Urban systems and economic
development: Papers and proceedings of a conference
on urban systems research in underdeveloped and
advanced economies. Eugene, University of Oregon
School of Business Administration, pp 1-15.**

1962b. "Urban growth and the economic development of
Ashanti." In Forrest R. Pitts, ed., Urban systems
and economic development: Papers and proceedings of
a conference on urban systems research in underdeveloped and advanced economies. Eugene, University
of Oregon School of Business Administration, pp.
53-64.

Bettelheim, Bruno, and Morris Janowitz. 1964. Social
change and prejudice. New York, Free Press of
Glencoe.**

Bettison, David G. 1958a. Cash wages and occupational
structure: Blantyre-Limbe, Nyasaland. Lusaka, Rhodes-
Livingstone Institute.

1958b. The demographic structure of seventeen villages: Blantyre-Limbe, Nyasaland. Lusaka, Rhodes-
Livingstone Institute.

1958c. "Migrancy and social structure in peri-urban
communities in Nyasaland." In Raymond J. Apthorpe,
ed., Present interrelations in central African rural
and urban life. Lusaka, Rhodes-Livingstone Institute,
pp. 24-39.

1959. Numerical data on African dwellers in Lusaka,
Northern Rhodesia. (Rhodes-Livingstone Communication
No. 16) Lusaka, Rhodes-Livingstone Institute.

1961. "Changes in the composition and status of kin

groups in Nyasaland and Northern Rhodesia." In
Aidan Southall, ed., Social change in modern Africa.
London, Oxford University Press, pp. 273-285.

Bharati, Agehananda. 1964a. "Political pressures and
reactions in the Asian minority in East Africa."
Paper read at the Annual Meeting of the African
Studies Association, Chicago, 22-24 October.

1964b. "Problems of the Asian minorities in East
Africa." Pakistan Horizon 17:342-349.

1965a. "Patterns of identification among the East
African Asians." Sociologus 15(2):128-142.

1965b. "A social survey." In Dharam P. Ghai, ed.,
Portrait of a minority: Asians in East Africa.
Nairobi, Oxford University Press, pp. 13-63.

Bicker, William, David Brown, Herbert Malakoff, and
William J. Gore. 1964. Comparative urban development: A bibliography. Chicago, American Society
for Public Administration.**

Biname, Andre, and Rene Eelens. 1958. Le rôle
social de la 'parcelle' au centre extra-coutumier
de Jadotville (The social role of the plot of
land in the non-traditional center of Jadotville).
Problèmes d'Afrique Centrale, No. 42:230-233.

Bird, Mary. 1963. "Urbanization, family and marriage
in Western Nigeria." In University of Edinburgh,
Centre of African Studies, Urbanization in African
social change: Proceedings of the Inaugral Seminar
held in the Centre, Edinburgh, 5-7 January, pp.
59-74.

Blair, T. L. V. 1965. Africa: A market profile. New
York, Frederick A. Praeger.

Blanksten, George I. 1963. "Transference of social
and political loyalties." In Bert F. Hoselitz and
Wilbert E. Moore, eds., Industrialization and
society. The Hague, Mouton, pp. 175-196.**

1964. "Local government in a rising technology:
Problems and prospects for Latin America." Paper read
at the Annual Meeting of the American Political
Science Association, Chicago, 9-12 September.**

Block, Clifford H. 1962. Interrelations of stress and
anxiety in determining problem-solving performance.
(Technical report 8) New Haven, Yale University,
Office of Naval Research, Department of Psychology
and Industrial Administration.**

Bloom, Leonard. 1964. "Some psychological concepts of
urban Africans." Ethnology 3(1):66-95.*

Boateng, E. A. 1955. "Recent changes in settlement in
South-East Gold Coast." In Institute of British
Geographers, Transactions and papers, No. 21:
157-169.

1959. "The growth and functions of Accra." Bulletin
of the Ghana Geographical Association 4(2):4-15.

Bogue, D. J. 1950. The structure of the metropolitan
community: A study of dominance and subdominance.
Ann Arbor, University of Michigan Press.**

Boguslaw, Robert. 1965. The new utopians: A study of
system design and social change. Englewood Cliffs,
N. J., Prentice-Hall.**

Boissevain, Jeremy. 1966. "Patronage in Sicily." Man:
Journal of the Royal Anthropological Institute 1:18-
33.**

Bollens, J. C. 1951. "Relating city areas to functions:
The California experience." Journal of the American
Institute of Planners 17:13-22.**

Bongolo, H. 1948. "A propos des 'coutumes indigènes'
dans la cité de Léopoldville" ("In reference to indigenous customs in the city of Leopoldville").
Voix du Congolais 4(22):16-19 and 4(23):55-60.

Bosa, G. R. 1967. "African business financing schemes

in Uganda." Paper read at the Makerere Institute of Social Research Conference, January.

Bott, Elizabeth. 1957. Family and social network. London, Tavistock Publications.**

Boulding, Kenneth E. 1962. Conflict and defense: A general theory. New York, Harper & Row.**

Bouvier, P. F. 1959. "Migrant labour in Africa south of the Sahara: Some aspects of labour migration in the Belgian Congo." Inter-African Labour Institute Bulletin 6(6):8-42 (even).

Brain, James Lewton. 1964. "The changing role of the European in East Africa." Paper read at the Annual Meeting of the African Studies Association, Chicago, 22-24 October.

Braithwaite, Lloyd. 1960. "Social stratification and cultural pluralism." Annals of the New York Academy of Sciences 83(Art.5):816-831.**

Brand, J. A. 1965. "The Mid-West state movement in Nigerian politics: A study of party formation." Political Studies 13:346-365.

Brassuer, J. P. 1948. "L'évolution des villes au Congo Belge" ("The evolution of cities in the Belgian Congo"). Bulletin de la Société Belge d'Etude d' Expansion, No. 129:39-43.

Braundi, Emile R., and Antonio Lettieri. 1964. "The general strike in Nigeria." International Socialist Journal 1(5-6):598-609.

Brausch, G. E. J. B. 1957. "Pluralisme ethnique et culturel au Congo Belge" ("Ethnic and cultural pluralism in the Belgian Congo"). In International Institute of Differing Civilizations, Ethnic and cultural pluralism in intertropical communities. Brussels, pp. 243-267.

Breese, Gerald. 1966. Urbanization in newly developing

<u>countries</u>. Englewood Cliffs, N. J., Prentice-Hall.✵✵

Breton, Raymond. 1966. "Ethnic factors in predicting the shape of stratification systems." Paper read at the Annual Meeting of the American Sociological Association, Miami, August.✵✵

Bretton, Henry L. 1966. "Political influence in southern Nigeria." In Herbert J. Spiro, ed., <u>Africa</u>: <u>The primacy</u> of <u>politics</u>. New York, Random House, pp. 49-84.

Brierly, T. G. 1966. "The evolution of local administration in French-speaking West Africa." Journal of Local Administration Overseas 5(1):56-71.

Brokensha, David. 1966. <u>Social change in Larteh, Ghana</u>. Oxford, Clarendon Press.

Broom, Leonard, and John I. Kitsuse. 1960. "The validation of acculturation: A condition of ethnic assimilation." In Kimball Young and Raymond W. Mack, eds., <u>Principles</u> of <u>sociology</u>: <u>A reader in theory and research</u>. New York, American Book Company, pp. 117-120.✵✵

Browne, G. St. J. Orde. 1933. <u>The African labourer</u>. London, Oxford University Press.

Browning, Clyde E. 1962. "Primate cities and related concepts." In Forrest R. Pitts, ed., <u>Urban systems and economic development</u>: <u>Papers and proceedings of a conference on urban systems research in underdeveloped and advanced economies</u>. Eugene, University of Oregon School of Business Administration, pp. 16-27.✵✵

Bruner, Edward M. 1961. "Urbanization and ethnic identit in North Sumatra." American Anthropologist 63:508-521.✵✵

Buitendag, F. W. C. 1951. "The emergence of the urban African." Race Relations Journal 18:205-211.

Bulmer-Thomas, Ivor. 1952. "The political aspect of migration from country to town--Nigeria." In International Institute of Differing Civilizations, The "pull" exerted by urban and industrial centres in countries in course of industrialization. Brussels, pp. 476-484.

1956. "Development of a middle class in tropical and sub-tropical countries." In International Institute of Differing Civilizations, Development of a middle class in tropical and sub-tropical countries. Brussels, pp. 356-364.**

Burke, Fred G. 1964a. "Local governance and nation-building in East Africa: A functional analysis." Paper read at the Annual Meeting of the American Political Science Association, Chicago, 9-12 September.

1964b. Local government and politics in Uganda. Syracuse, Syracuse University Press.

Busia, K. A. 1950. Sociology: Report on a social survey of Sekondi-Takoradi. London, Great Britain Colonial Office.

1953. "The impact of industrialization on West Africa." In West African Institute of Social and Economic Research, Annual conference proceedings.

1956. "Social survey of Sekondi-Takoradi." In International African Institute, Social implications of industrialization and urbanization in Africa south of the Sahara. Paris, UNESCO. pp. 74-86.

Bustin, Edouard. 1963. "The Congo." In Gwendolen U. Carter, ed., Five African states: Responses to adversity. Ithaca, N.Y., Cornell University Press, pp. 9-159.

Butcher, D. A. P. 1964. "The role of the Fulbe in the urban life and economy of Lunsar, Sierra Leone; being a study of the adaptation of an immigrant group." Unpublished doctoral dissertation, University of Edinburgh.

Byl, Adhemar. 1962. "Ghana: What role for unions?"
Africa Today 9(10):7-9.

1966. "The evolution of the labor market in French-
speaking West Africa." Weltwirtschaftliches Archiv:
Zeitschrift des Instituts für Weltwirtschaft an der
Universitat Kiel 97(1):163-212.

Byl, Adhemar, and Joseph White. 1966. "The end of
backward-sloping labor supply functions in dual
economics." Cahiers Economiques et Sociaux 4(1):
33-42.

Cahnman, Werner J. 1966. "The historical sociology of
cities: A critical review." Social Forces 45(2):
155-161.**

Caldwell, John C. 1967. "Population: General characteristics, populations change, migration and urbanization, and population prospects and policy." In
Walter Birmingham, I. Neustadt, and E. N. Omaboe,
eds., A study of contemporary Ghana, II. London:
Reinhardt.

1968. Population growth and family change in Africa:
The new urban elite in Ghana. Canberra, Australian
National University Press.

1969. African rural-urban migration: The movement to
Ghana's towns. Canberra, Australian National Universit
Press.

Callaway, Archibald C. n.d. "School leavers and the
developing economy in Nigeria." In Nigerian Institute
of Social and Economic Research, Conference proceedings. Ibadan, Caxton Press, pp. 60-72.

1963. "Unemployment among African school leavers."
Journal of Modern African Studies 1:351-371.

1964. "Nigeria's indigenous education: The apprenticeship system." Odu 1:1-18.

1965a. "Continuing education for Africa's school

leavers: The indigenous apprentice system." Inter-African Labour Institute Bulletin 12:61-73.

1965b. "From traditional crafts to modern industries." Odu 2:28-51.

1967a. "From traditional crafts to modern industries." In P. C. Lloyd, A. L. Mabogunje, and B. Awe, eds., The city of Ibadan: A symposium on its structure and development. London, Cambridge University Press, pp. 153-172.

1967b. "Education expansion and the rise of youth unemployment." In P. C. Lloyd, A. L. Mabogunje, and B. Awe, eds., The city of Ibadan: A symposium on its structure and development. London, Cambridge University Press, pp. 191-211.

(Cameroon) Cameroun, Direction des Affaires Economiques, Service de la Statistique Générale. 1956a. Résultats du recensement de la ville de Douala [1955-1956] (Results of the census of the city of Douala [1955-1956]). Yaounde.

1956b. Résultats du recensement de la ville de Douala [1955-1956]:Population autochtone (Results of the census of the city of Douala [1955-1956] : Aboriginal population. Yaounde.

(Cameroon) Cameroun, Ministère de l'Economie Nationale. 1963. Recensement de la ville de Yaoundé en 1962: Résultats principaux (Census of the city of Yaounde in 1962: Principal results). Yaoundé, Service de la Statistique et de la Mécanographie.

Campbell, Angus. 1958. "The political implications of community identification." In Roland Young, ed., Approaches to the study of politics. Evanston, Northwestern University Press, pp. 318-329.**

Campbell, J. J., and J. Wilson, eds. 1963. Report of the Conference on Problems of Urbanization in Northern Nigeria, 1962. Zaria, Ahmadu Bello University.

Campbell, M. J. 1963. Law and practice of local
government in Northern Nigeria. London, Sweet and
Maxwell.

Cantril, Hadley. 1966. The pattern of human concerns.
New Brunswick, N. J., Rutgers University Press.**

Capelle, Emmanuel. 1947. La cité indigène de Léopoldville (The indigenous city of Leopoldville). Elisabethville, Centre d'Etude des Problèmes Sociaux
Indigènes.

    1956. "The African town at Leopoldville." In
International African Institute, Social implications
of industrialization and urbanization in Africa
south of the Sahara. Paris, UNESCO, pp. 109-112.

Caprasse, Paul, and Guy Bernard. 1963. "Le mariage
chez les enseignants à Léopoldville" ("Marriage
among teachers in Leopoldville"). Cahiers Economiques et Sociaux 1(3):64-76.

    1964. "Analyse d'un mariage en milieu urbain
congolais" ("Analysis of a marriage in urban
Congo"). Cahiers Economiques et Sociaux 2(1):
75-90.

Caprasse, Pierre. 1959. Leaders africains en milieu
urbain [Elisabethville] (African leaders in an
urban milieu [Elisabethville]). (Collection de
l'École des Sciences Politiques et Sociales No.
162.) Brussels, Amibel.

Carleback, Julius. 1962. Juvenile prostitutes in
Nairobi. Kampala, East African Institute of Social
Research, Applied Research Unit.

Carson, D. H., and B. L. Driver. 1966. (Summary of)
"An ecological approach to environmental stress."
American Behavioral Scientist 10:8-11.**

Cartwright, Dorwin, and Alvin Zander. 1960. "Group
cohesiveness: Introduction." In Dorwin Cartwright
and Alvin Zander, eds., Group dynamics: Research

and theory. Evanston, Row, Peterson, pp. 69-94.
2nd edition.✶✶

(Central African Republic) Centrafricaine, Service
de la Statistique Generale. 1964. Enquête démographique en République Centrafricain 1959-1960
(Demographic inquiry in the Central African Republic 1959-1960). Paris, Ministère de la Coopération,
Service de Coopération.

Centre International de l'Enfance. 1959. Etude des
conditions de vie de l'enfant africain en milieu
urbain et de leur influence sur la délinquance
juvenile (Study of the living conditions of the
African child in urban milieu and their influence
on juvenile delinquency). Paris.

Chabot, Georges. 1948. Les villes (The cities). Paris,
Armand Colin.✶✶

(Chad) Tchad, Bureau de la Statistique. 1962. Recensement démographique de Fort-Lamy, Mars-Juillet
1962 (Demographic census of Fort Lamy, March-July,
1962). République Française, Ministère de la Coopération.

Champion, J. C. 1957. "Labour and managerial skills
in East African industrial development." East
African Economics Review 4:24-32.

Chance, Norman A. 1965. "Acculturation, self-identification, and personality adjustment." American
Anthropologist 67:373-393.✶✶

Chapelier, Alice. 1957. Elisabethville: Essai de
géographie urbaine (Elisabethville: Essay on urban
geography). Bruxelles, Académie Royale des Sciences
Coloniales.

Chapin, F. Stuart. 1940. "An experiment on the social
effects of good housing." American Sociological
Review 5:868-879.✶✶

Chapman, Audrey R. 1967. "Ethnic unions and the NCNC

232 *Urban Dynamics in Black Africa*

in Mbaise, Eastern Nigeria." Paper read at the
Tenth Annual Meeting of the African Studies Association, New York, 1-4 November.

Charles, Pierre. 1952. "Tribal society and labour
legislation." International Labour Review 65:426-
441.

Charles, V. 1955. "Familles ouvrières et évolution
sociale à Thysville" ("Workers' families and social
evolution in Thysville"). Zaire 9:731-739.

Charton, Albert. 1957. "Pluralisme ethnique et
culturel en Afrique Occidentale Française" ("Ethnic
and cultural pluralism in French West Africa"). In
International Institute of Differing Civilizations,
Ethnic and cultural pluralism in intertropical
communities. Brussels, pp. 136-160.

Chi, Nguyen H. 1965. "Political socialization and
political change." Unpublished doctoral dissertation, Michigan State University.**

Chin, Robert. 1962. "The utility of system models and
developmental models for practitioners." In W. G.
Bennis et al., eds., The planning of change. New
York, Holt, Rinehart and Winston, pp. 201-214.**

Chinn, W. H. 1963. "Social problems of rapid urbani-
zation with particular reference to British Africa."
In University of Edinburgh, Centre of African
Studies, Urbanization in African social change:
Proceedings of the Inaugural Seminar held in the
Centre, 5-7 January. Edinburgh, pp. 90-101.

Chodak, Szymon. 1966. "Social classes in sub-Saharan
Africa." Africana Bulletin (Warsaw), No. 4:7-48.

Church, R. J. Harrison. 1959. "West African urbanization: A geographical view." Sociological Review
7:15-28.

1967. "Urban problems and economic development in
West Africa." Journal of Modern African Studies

5:511-520.

Clark, John P. 1961. "Measuring alienation within a social system." American Sociological Review 26(5): 753-758.**

Clarkson, M. 1955. "The problem of begging and destitution in urban areas in the Gold Coast." In (Proceedings of the) Fourth Annual Conference of the West African Institute of Social and Economic Research. Ibadan, University College Ibadan, pp. 144-150.

Clausen, Lars. 1966. "On attitudes towards industrial conflict in Zambian industry." African Social Research, No. 2:117-138.

Clay, G. C. R. 1949. "African urban advisory councils in the Northern Rhodesia Copperbelt." Journal of African Administration 1:33-38.

Clelland, Donald A., and William H. Form. 1964. "Economic dominants and community power: A comparative analysis." American Journal of Sociology 69:511-521.**

Clement, Pierre. 1956. "Social patterns of urban life." In International African Institute, Social implications of industrialization and urbanization in Africa south of the Sahara. Paris, UNESCO, pp. 368-492.

Clignet, Remi. 1966. "Urbanization and family structure in the Ivory Coast." Comparative Studies in Society and History 8(4):385-401.

1967. "Urbanization, type of descent and child-rearing practices." In Horace Miner, ed., The city in modern Africa. New York, Frederick A. Praeger, pp. 257-296.

Clignet, Remi, and Philip Foster. 1966. The fortunate few: A study of secondary schools and students in the Ivory Coast. Evanston, Northwestern University

Press.

Clignet, Remi, and Joyce Sweene. 1967. "Accra and
Abidjan: A comparative analysis of the notion of
increase in scale." Paper read at the Tenth
Annual Meeting of the African Studies Association,
New York, 1-4 November.

1969. "Social change and type of marriage."
American Journal of Sociology 75:123-145.

Clinard, Marshall B. 1960. "A cross-cultural repli-
cation of the relation of urbanism to criminal behavior." American Sociological Review 25(2):253-
257.**

1966. Slums and community development: Experiments
in self-help. New York, Macmillan.**

Coatswith, R. 1954. Report of an inquiry to a
proposal to excise the Aba Urban District Council
from the Aba-Ngwa County. Enugu, Government Printer.

Cockin, George. 1944. "The land and education in the
Ibo country of south-east Nigeria." International
Review of Missions 33:274-279.

Cohen, Abner. 1965. "The social organization of
credit in a West African cattle market." Africa
35:8-20.

1966. "Politics of the Kola trade: Some processes
of tribal community formation among migrants in
West African towns." Africa 36(1):18-36.

1967. "The Hausa." In P. C. Lloyd, A. L. Mabogunje,
and B. Awe, eds., The city of Ibadan: A symposium
on its structure and development. London, Cambridge
University Press.

1969. Custom and politics in urban Africa: A study
of Hausa migrants of Yoruba towns. Berkeley,
University of California Press.

Cohen, Ronald. 1970. "Social stratification in Bornu."
In Arthur Tuden and Leonard Plotnicov, eds., Social
stratification in Africa. New York, Free Press of
Glencoe, pp. 225-268.

Cole, George Douglas Howard. 1954. Introduction to
trade unionism. New York, Macmillan.**

1955. Studies in class structure. London, Routledge
and Kegan Paul.**

Coleman, James Samuel. 1957. Community conflict.
Glencoe, Ill., Free Press.**

Coleman, James Smoot. 1952. "The role of tribal asso-
ciations in Nigeria." In (Proceedings of the) First
Annual Conference of the West African Institute of
Social and Economic Research. Ibadan, University
College Ibadan, pp. 61-66.

1955. "The problem of political integration in
emergent Africa." Western Political Quarterly 8:
44-57.

1958. Nigeria: Background to nationalism. Berkeley,
University of California Press.

1960. "The politics of sub-Saharan Africa." In
Gabriel A. Almond and James S. Coleman, eds., The
politics of the developing areas. Princeton,
Princeton University Press, pp. 247-368.

Coleman, James Smoot, and Carl G. Rosberg, Jr., eds.
1964. Political parties and national integration in
tropical Africa. Berkeley, University of California
Press.

Collins, G. R. 1952. "Movements of population from
rural to urban areas in Sierra Leone with special
reference to economic aspects, and to the Colony
rural areas." In International Institute of Differing Civilizations, The "pull" exerted by urban and
industrial centres in countries in course of
industrialization. Brussels, pp. 152-171.

Collins, John. 1969. Lusaka: The myth of the garden
    city. University of Zambia, Institute for Social
    Research.

Collomb, H. 1967. "La position du conflit et les
    structures familiales en voie de transformation"
    ("The position of conflict and family structures in
    transformation"). Canadian Psychiatric Association
    Journal 12(5)451-464.

Colson, Elizabeth. 1960. "Migration in Africa: Trends
    and possibilities." In Frank Lorimer and Mark Karp,
    eds., Population in Africa. Boston, Boston Univer-
    sity Press, pp. 60-88.

    1967. "Competence and incompetence in the context of
    independence." Current Anthropology 8 (1 and 2):
    92-111.

Comhaire, Jean L. L. n.d. "Leopoldville, Lagos and
    Port au Prince: Some points of comparison." In
    Nigerian Institute of Social and Economic Research,
    Conference proceedings. Ibadan, Caxton Press,
    pp. 73-83.

    1948. "Mélanges-mengelingen: Note sur les Musulmans
    de Léopoldville" ("Miscellaneous excerpts: Notes on
    the Muslims of Leopoldville"). Zaire 2:303-304.

    1949. "La délinquance dans les grandes villes
    d'Afrique Britannique" ("Delinquency in the large
    cities of British Africa"). Zaire 3:1101-1108.

    1950. "Urban segregation and racial legislation in
    Africa." American Sociological Review 15:392-397.

    1951a. "L'administration indigène à Nairobi" ("The
    indigenous administration in Nairobi"). Zaire 5:
    1067-1069.

    1951b. "Some African problems of today." Human
    Organization 10(2):15-18.

    1952. Urban conditions in Africa. London, Oxford

University Press.

1953a. "Aspects of urban administration in tropical and southern Africa." (n.s. No. 27) Cape Town, Communications from the School of African Studies, University of Cape Town.

1953b. "Vues générales sur le Cameroun" ("General observations on the Cameroon"). Zaire 5:55-64.

1956a. "Economic change and the extended family." Annals of the American Academy of Political and Social Science 305:46-52.

1956b. "Some aspects of urbanization in the Belgian Congo." American Journal of Sociology 62:8-13.

1959. "Rôle des villes dans la crise africaine" ("The role of cities in the African crisis"). Bulletin de la Société Belge d'Etude et d'Expansion, No. 186:348-351.

Comhaire-Sylvain, Suzanne. 1950a. "Associations on the basis of origin in Lagos, Nigeria." American Catholic Sociological Review 11:234-236.

1950b. "Food and leisure among the African youth of Leopoldville." (n.s. No. 25) Cape Town, Communications from the School of African Studies, University of Cape Town.

1956. "Food and leisure among the African youth of Leopoldville." In International African Institute, Social implications of industrialization and urbanization in Africa south of the Sahara. Paris, UNESCO, pp. 113-121.

Comhaire-Sylvain, Suzanne, and Jean L. L. Comhaire. 1960. "Problems relating to urbanization: Formation of African urban populations." In Frank Lorimer and Mark Karp, eds., Population in Africa. Boston, Boston University Press, pp. 41-59.

Commission for Technical Co-operation in Africa South

of the Sahara. 1956. <u>Nutrition</u>. Luanda.

Commission for Technical Co-operation in Africa South
of the Sahara, Inter-African Labour Institute.
1959a. "The housing of workers in urban living conditions in Africa." Inter-African Labour Institute
Bulletin 6(2):62-71 and 6(3):58-83.

1959b. "The housing of workers in urban living conditions in Africa--Some trends and experiments in
housing." Inter-African Labour Institute Bulletin
6(4):92-114 (even).

1959c. "Urban patterns of income, expenditure, and
consumption in Africa south of the Sahara." Inter-
African Labour Institute Bulletin 6(6):56-84 (even).

1961. <u>Migrant labour in Africa south of the Sahara</u>.
Abidjan.

1962. <u>Symposium on unemployed youth</u>. (Publication
No. 89) Dar es Salaam.

Commission for Technical Co-operation in Africa South
of the Sahara, Scientific Council for Africa South
of the Sahara. 1959a. <u>CSA meeting of specialists on
the basic psychology of African and Madagascan popu-
lations</u>. (No. 51) New York, International Publications
Service.

1959b. <u>Housing and urbanisation</u>. (Second session of
the Inter-African Conference at Nairobi) Nairobi.

1961a. <u>CSA meeting of specialists on urbanisation
and its social aspects: Abidjan, 23-31 August 1961</u>.
(Reports and recommendations, Publication No. 75)
Lagos.

1961b. <u>Study on migrations in West Africa</u>. Niamey.

1961c. <u>Symposium on hygiene and sanitation in relation to housing</u>. (No. 84) Niamey.

(Congo Brazzaville) Congo, Statistique Generale. 1958.

Recensement démographique de Pointe-Noire (Demographic census of Pointe-Noire). (Comp.: F. Ganon) Pointe-Noire.

Conyngham, L. D. 1951. "African towns in Northern Rhodesia." Journal of African Administration 3: 113-117.

Cook, Fred J. 1966. "Robin Hoods or real tough boys? Larry Gallo, Crazy Joe and Kid Blast." The New York Times Magazine, 23 October, pp. 37ff. **

Cook, Robert C., ed. 1960. "The world's great cities." Population Bulletin 16:109-131.**

Cooney, Timothy J., 1959. "How to make a slum." Nation 188:140-141.**

Coppens, n.f.n. 1947. "Une coopérative indigène à Léopoldville" ("An indigenous cooperative society in Leopoldville") Zaire 1:809-818.

Cornelius, Wayne A., Jr. 1971. "The political sociology of cityward migration in Latin America: Toward empirical theory." In Francine F. Rabinovitz and Felicity M. Trueblood, eds., Latin American urban research. Beverly Hills, Sage Publications, pp. 95-147.**

Coser, Lewis A. 1956. The functions of social conflict. Glencoe, Ill., Free Press.**

1966. "Some social functions of violence." Annals of the American Academy of Political and Social Science 364:8-18.**

Coumbassa, Firmin. 1963. "The worker and trade-unionism in Africa." International Federation of Christian Trade Unions 'Labor' 2(2):93-99.

Coursin, Leon. 1948. "Dakar: Port Atlantique" ("Dakar: Atlantic Port"). Cahiers d'Outre-Mer 1:275-285.

Cowan, L. Gray. 1958. Local government in West Africa. New York, Columbia University Press.

Crowder, Michael. 1962. Senegal: A study in French
assimilation policy. London, Oxford University Press.

Cutright, Phillips. 1963. "National political development: Measurement and analysis." American Sociological
Review 28:253-264.**

Dada, Paul O. A. 1966. "Evaluation of local government
courses in relation to careers of staff trained at
Zaria, 1954-1964." Journal of Administration Overseas 5(4):268-270.

Dahl, Robert A. 1961. Who governs? Democracy and
power in an American city. New Haven, Yale University Press.**

Dahomey, Ministère de la Coopération, Service de Coopération. 1964. Enquête démographique au Dahomey,
1961 (Demographic inquiry in Dahomey, 1961). Paris.

Dahrendorf, Ralf. 1959. Class and class conflict in
industrial society. Stanford, Stanford University
Press.**

Dahya, B. W. 1963a. "The 'evil eye' in an Asian community in East Africa." In East African Institute of
Social Research, January Conference Proceedings.

1963b. "Some characteristics of tribal associations
in Kampala." In East African Institute of Social
Research, January Conference Proceedings.

Daily Times (Lagos). 1963. "Scholarship awards." March 5

Daland, Robert T. 1966. "A strategy for research in
comparative urban administration." Paper read at the
Conference of the Comparative Administration Group,
American Society for Public Administration, University of Maryland, 16 April.**

Davidson, Basil. 1959. The lost cities of Africa.
Boston, Little, Brown and Company.

Davies, Ioan. 1966. African trade unions. Baltimore,

Penguin.

Davis, J. Merle, ed. 1956. "Modern industry and the African." In International African Institute, Social implications of industrialization and urbanization in Africa south of the Sahara. Paris, UNESCO, pp. 148-149

Davis, Kingsley. 1950. "Population and change in backward areas." Columbia Journal of International Affairs 4(2):43-49.**

1955. "Institutional patterns favoring high fertility in underdeveloped areas." Eugenics Quarterly 2(1): 33-39.**

Davis, Kingsley, and Hilda Hertz (Golden). 1951. "The world distribution of urbanization." Bulletin of the International Statistical Institute 33(Part 4): 227-242.**

1954-1955. "Urbanization and the development of pre-industrial area." Economic Development and Cultural Change 3:6-24.**

Davison, R. B. 1954. Migrant labour on the Gold Coast: A pilot survey. Achimota, University College of the Gold Coast.

Dawson, John. 1963. "Traditional values and work efficiency in a West African mine labour force." In University of Edinburgh, Centre of African Studies, Urbanization in African social change: Proceedings of the Inaugural Seminar held in the Centre, 5-7 January. Edinburgh, pp. 196-206.

1964. "Urbanization and mental health in a West African community." In Ari Kiev, ed., Magic, faith and healing: Studies in primitive psychiatry today. New York, Free Press of Glencoe, pp. 305-342.

1964-1965. "Race and inter-group relations in Sierra Leone." Race 6(Part 1):83-99 and 6(Part 2):217-231.

Dean, John P. 1949. "The myths of housing reform."

American Sociological Review 14:281-288.✲✲

De Blij, Harm J. 1963. Dar es Salaam. Evanston, Northwestern University Press.

1968. Mombasa--An African city. Evanston, Northwestern University Press.

De Briey, Pierre. 1952. "Introduction à l'étude des
migrations dans les pays en voie d'industrialisation"
("Introduction to the study of migrations in industrializing countries"). In International Institute
of Differing Civilizations, The "pull" exerted by
urban and industrial centres in countries in course
of industrialization. Brussels, pp. 56-59.✲✲

1955. "The productivity of African labour." International Labour Review 72(2-3):119-137.

1965a. "Town and country." Civilisations 15:290-305.✲

1965b. "Urbanisation and under-development." Civilisations 15:2-12.✲✲

1966. "Urban agglomerations and the modernisation of
the developing states." Civilisations 16:3-23 (odd).✲

1967. "Control of urbanisation." Civilisations 17:3-1

De Coppet, Marcel. 1952. "Aspects sociaux de 'attraction exercée par les centres urbains en voie
d'industrialisation de Dakar et de Thies, au Sénégal
et au Soudan" ("Social aspects of the attraction of
two industrializing urban areas:[Dakar, Senegal and
Thies, Sudan]). In International Institute of Differing Civilizations, The "pull" exerted by urban and
industrial centres in countries in course of industrialization. Brussels, pp. 297-303.

De Graft-Johnson, Kwaw Esiboa. 1957. "The mechanisms
of social control in a Gold Coast town." Unpublished
master's thesis, University of London.

De Laddersous, M. A.-J. Moeller. 1952. "Attraction
exercee par les centres urbains et industriels dans

le Congo Belge" ("The attraction of urban and industrial centers in the Belgian Congo"). In International
Institute of Differing Civilizations, The "pull"
exerted by urban and industrial centers in countries
in course of industrialization. Brussels, pp. 189-
196.

Delf, George. 1963. Asians in East Africa. London,
Oxford University Press.

Dellicour, F. 1952. "L'attraction exercée par les
centres urbains et industriels dans le Congo Belge:
Aspects politiques" ("The attraction of urban and
industrial centers in the Belgian Congo: Political
aspects"). In International Institute of Differing
Civilizations, The "pull" exerted by urban and industrial centres in countries in course of industrialization. Brussels, pp. 485-494.

Deniel, Raymond. 1967. De la savanne à la ville; Essai
sur la migration des mossi vers Abidjan et sa région.
Aix-en-Provence, Centre Africain des Sciences
Humaines Appliquées (From the savannah to the city;
essay on the migration of the Mossi peoples toward
the city of Abidjan and its near-by regions. Aix-en-
Provence, African Center of Applied Human Sciences).

Denis, Jacques. 1955. "Pointe-Noire." Cahiers d'Outre-
Mer 8:350-368.

1956a. "Elisabethville: Materiaux pour une étude de
la population africaine" ("Elisabethville: Materials
for a study of the African population"). Bulletin
du Centre d'Etude des Problèmes Sociaux Indigènes,
No. 34:137-195 and No. 35:1-48.

1956b. "Jadotville: Matériaux pour une étude de la
population africaine" ("Jadotville: Materials for
a study of the African population"). Bulletin du
Centre d'Etude des Problèmes Sociaux Indigènes,
No. 35:25-60.

1956c. "Léopoldville: Etude de géographie urbaine et
sociale" ("Leopoldville: Study of urban and social
geography"). Zaire 10:563-611.

1956-1957. "Coquilhatville: Eléments pour une étude de géographie sociale" ("Coquilhatville: Elements for a study of social geography"). Aequatoria (Coquilhatville), No. 4:137-148 and No. 1:1-4.

1958. Le phénomène urbain en Afrique centrale (The urban phenomenon in central Africa). (Mémoires, n.s., Vol. 19) Brussels, Académie Royale des Sciences Coloniales (now Académie Royale d'Outre-Mer).

1964. "Addis Ababa: Genèse d'une capitale impériale" ("Addis Ababa: Genesis of an imperial capital"). Revue Belge de Géographie, No. 3:283-314.*

1966. "The towns of tropical Africa." Civilisations 16(1)26-44.

De Roda, D. Rafael. 1952. "L'attraction des grands centres et la politique de l'industrialisation" ("The attraction of large centers and the politics of industrialization"). In International Institute of Differing Civilizations, The "pull" exerted by urban and industrial centres in countries in course of industrialization. Brussels, pp. 81-109.**

Desai, R. H. 1963. "Leadership in an Asian community." In East African Institute of Social Research, June Conference Proceedings.

1965. "The family and business enterprise among the Asians in East Africa." In East African Institute of Social Research, January Conference Proceedings.

1966. "Afro-Asian relationships in small towns." In East African Institute of Social and Cultural Affairs, Racial and communal tensions in East Africa. Nairobi, East African Publishing House, pp. 95-103.

De Schiervel, X. Lejeune. 1954. "Vers un urbanisme congolais" ("Towards Congolese town-planning"). France d'Outre Mer, Nos. 297-298:43-45.

Désiré-Vuillemin, G. 1963. Les capitales de l'Ouest-Africain: Villes modernes (The capitals of West

Africa: Modern cities), Nos. 4-5. Paris, Service
d'Etudes et de Recherches Pédagogiques pour les Pays
en Voie de développement.

De Thier, Franz M. 1956. Le centre extra-coutumier de
Coquilhatville (The non-traditional center of Coquil-
hatville). Bruxelles, Université Libre de Bruxelles,
Institut de Sociologie Solvay.

Deutsch, Karl W. 1953. Nationalism and social communication. New York, John Wiley & Sons.**

1961. "Social mobilization and political development."
American Political Science Review 55:493-515.**

1964. "Integration and the social system: Implications of functional analysis." In Philip E. Jacob
and James V. Toscano, eds., The integration of
political communities. Philadelphia, J. B. Lippincott
Company, pp. 179-208.**

Deutsch, Karl W., et al. 1957. Political community and
the North Atlantic area. Princeton, Princeton University Press.**

Deutsch, Morton. 1966. "Bargaining, threat, and com-
munication: Some experimental studies." In Kathleen
Archibald, ed., Strategic interaction and conflict.
Berkeley, University of California Press, pp. 19-41.**

Devauges, M. Roland. 1959. Le chômage à Brazzaville:
Etude sociologique (Unemployment in Brazzaville: A
sociological study). Paris, Office de la Recherche
Scientifique et Technique Outre-Mer.

1960. "Urban unemployment in Africa south of the
Sahara." Inter-African Labour Institute Bulletin
7(3):8-47.

Dewey, Richard. 1960. "The rural urban continuum:
Real but relatively unimportant." American Journal
of Sociology 66:60-66.**

Diakanua, A. 1966. "Réflexions sur la lutte des classes"

("Reflections on the class conflict"). Etudes Congolaises 9(1):80-85.

Diallo, Abdoulaye. 1949. "The African trade union movement." World Trade Union Movement, No. 6:5-6.

Dickson, K. B. 1965. "Evolution of seaports in Ghana: 1800-1928." Annals of the Association of American Geographers 55(1):98-111.

Diejomaoh, Victor P. 1965. Economic development in Nigeria: Its problems, challenges and prospects. Princeton, Princeton University, Industrial Relations Section.

Dihoff, Gretchen. 1970. Katsina: Profile of a Nigerian city. New York, Frederick A. Praeger.

Di Lucchesi, Riccardo Astuto. 1952. "Aspect politique (of urbanization): Rapport général" ("The political aspect of urbanization: General report"). In International Institute of Differing Civilizations, The "pull" exerted by urban and industrial centres in countries in course of industrialization. Brussels, pp. 438-457.**

Diop, Abdoulaye Bara. 1954. "Enquête sur la migration Toucouleur à Dakar" ("Inquiry on the migration of the Toucouleur peoples to Dakar"). Bulletin de l'Institut Français d'Afrique Noire 22B(3 & 4): 137-154.

1963. "Research methods in African sociology." In Nigerian Institute of Social and Economic Research, Conference Proceedings. Ibadan, pp. 174-178.

1965. Société toucouleur et migration (The Toucouleur society and migration). Dakar, Institut Français d'Afrique Noire.

Diziain, R. and A. Cambon. 1957. Etudes sur la population du quartier New-Bell à Douala (Studies of the population of the New-Bell quarter of Douala). Yaounde, Institut de Recherches Scientifiques du

Cameroun.

Djilas, Milovan. 1957. The new class: An analysis of the communist system. New York, Frederick A. Praeger.✸✸

Dodds, Fred W. 1920. "The Ibos and the Udi railway: Roads." West Africa 4(161):186 and 4(162):238.

Dodwell, C. B. 1955. "Iseyin: The town of weavers." Nigeria, No. 46:118-143.

Dollfuss, O. 1952. "Conakry en 1951-1952" ("Conakry in 1951-1952"). Etudes Guinéennes (Conakry), Nos. 10-11, 3-111.

Doob, Leonard W. 1960. "The psychological pressure upon modern Africans." Journal of Human Relations 8:465-472.

Dorjahn, V. R., and T. C. Hogg. 1966. "Job satisfaction, dissatisfaction and aspirations in the wage labor force in Magburaka, a Sierra Leone town." Journal of Asian and African Studies 1(14):261-278.

Dotson, Floyd. 1951. "Patterns of voluntary association among urban working-class families." American Sociological Review 16:687-693.✸✸

Doucy, A. 1954. "The unsettled attitude of Negro workers in the Belgian Congo." International Social Science Bulletin 6:442-451.

Doucy, A., and P. Feldheim. 1956. "Some effects of industrialization in two districts of Equatoria Province (Belgian Congo)." In International African Institute, Social implications of industrialization and urbanization in Africa south of the Sahara. Paris, UNESCO, pp. 670-692.

Doughty, Paul L. 1967. "The culture of regionalism and the acculturation of peasants into the urban life of Lima, Peru." Paper read at the American Anthropological Association, Washington, D.C.,

30 November-3 December.⁑

Douglas, Ann. 1957. "Peaceful settlement of industrial and intergroup disputes." Journal of Conflict Resolution 1:69-81.⁑

Drake, St. Clair. 1957. "Some observations on inter-ethnic conflict as one type of intergroup conflict." Journal of Conflict Resolution 1:155-178.⁑

Drake, St. Clair, and Leslie Alexander Lacy. 1966. "Government versus the unions; The Sekondi-Takoradi strike, 1961." In Gwendolen M. Carter, ed., Politics in Africa; 7 cases. New York, Harcourt, Brace & World, pp. 67-118.

Dresch, Jean. 1947. "Villes congolaises"("Congolese towns"). Acta Geographica 3:1-5.

    1948. "Villes congolaises: Etude de géographie urbaine et sociale" ("Congolese towns: A study of urban and social geography"). Revue de Géographie Humaine et d'Ethnologie 1(3):3-24.

    1950. "Villes d'Afrique Occidentale" ("Towns of West Africa"). Cahiers d'Outre-Mer 3:200-230.

Dryden, Stanley. 1967. "Local government in Tanzania." Journal of Administration Overseas 6(2):109-120.

Dubb, Allie A., ed. 1960. Myth in modern Africa. Lusaka, Rhodes-Livingstone Institute.

    1962. The multitribal society. Lusaka, Rhodes-Livingstone Institute.

Du Bois, Victor D. 1965. "Ahmadou's world--a case study of a Voltaic immigrant to the Ivory Coast." American Universities Field Staff Reports Service, West Africa Series 8(2):63-74.

Dubos, Rene. n.d. "Man meets his environment." In United States Organization for International Development, Health and Nutrition. (United States

papers prepared for the 1963 United Nations Conference on the Application of Science and Technology for the Benefit of the Less Developed Areas,
VI) Washington, D.C., pp. 1-11.**

Duchemin, G. J. 1948. "Urbanisme rural: Le village de
Camberene (Dakar)" ("Rural urbanism: The village of
Camberene [Dakar] "). Notes Africaines de l'Institut
Français d'Afrique Noire 39:17-18.

Duhl, Leonard J. 1963. "Introduction." In Leonard J.
Duhl, ed., The urban condition. New York, Basic
Cooks, pp. vii-xiii.**

Dupriez, Gerard. 1965. "Emploi et rémunérations à
Léopoldville" ("Employment and remuneration in
Leopoldville"). Cahiers Economiques et Sociaux
3(2):219-241.

Dupriez, Leon H. 1954. "Introduction: Factors of
economic progress." International Social Science
Bulletin 6:161-164.**

Durand, Oswald. 1957. "De l'influence du groupement
Haoussa dans le brassage des idées en Afrique occidentale" ("The influence of Hausa groups in the
intermingling of ideas in West Africa"). In International Institute of Differing Civilizations,
Ethnic and cultural pluralism in intertropical
communities. Brussels, pp. 173-180.

Durand, Oswald, and Jacques Durand. 1965. "The roles
and purposes of towns." (Summary) Civilisations
15:372-375.**

Durkheim, Emile. 1933. The division of labor in
society. New York, Free Press of Glencoe (1964).**

1952. Suicide: A study in sociology. London, Routledge and Kegan Paul.**

Dutillieux, G. 1950. "La femme detribalisée du centre
extra-coutumier" ("The detribalized woman in a
non-traditional urban center"). Bulletin du Centre

d'Etudes des Problèmes Sociaux Indigènes, No. 14: 106-114.

Eames, Edwin, and William Schwab. 1964. "Urban migration in India and Africa." Human Organization 23: 24-27.

East African Institute of Social and Cultural Affairs. 1966a. "Commentary from the East African Standard on Friday, November 20, 1964." In Racial and communal tensions. Nairobi, East African Publishing House, pp. 58-59.

    1966b. "Concluding statement and recommendations." In Racial and communal tensions in East Africa. Nairobi, East African Publishing House, pp. 128-133.

East Africa Royal Commission 1953-1955. 1955. Report. (Presented by the Secretary of State for the Colonies to Parliament by command of Her Majesty, June 1955) London, Her Majesty's Stationery Office.

Eastern Nigeria. 1955a. Report of the inquiry into the administration of the affairs of the Onitsha Urban District Council, February, 1955. (The O.P. Gunning Report) Enugu, Government Printer.

    1955b. Report of the inquiry into the allocation of market stalls at Aba. (The P. F. Grant Report) Enugu, Government Printer.

    1956a. Papers relating to the instrument establishing the Onitsha Urban District Council. (House of Assembly, Sessional papers no. 1 of 1956) Enugu, Government Printer.

    1956b. Policy for local government. Enugu, Government Printer.

    1957a. Report of the position, status and influence of chiefs and natural rulers in the Eastern Region of Nigeria. (The Jones Report) Enugu, Government Printer.

1957b. Report on the general election to the Eastern
House of Assembly 1957 including recommendations for
consideration in connection with the drafting of new
electoral regulations. (Sessional paper no. 1 of
1957) Enugu, Government Printer.

1958. Annual volume of the laws of Eastern Nigeria,
1958. Enugu, Government Printer.

Eastern Nigeria, Commission of Inquiry into the Work-
ing of the Port Harcourt Town Council. 1955. Report.
(The R. K. Floyer, D. O. Ibekwe, J. O. Njemanze
Report) Enugu, Government Printer.

Eastern Nigeria, House of Assembly. 1957. Report on
the general election, including recommendations for
consideration in connection with the drafting of new
electoral regulations. Enugu, Government Printer.

Eastern Nigeria, Ministry of Local Government. 1964.
Annual Report 1962-1963. Enugu, Government Printer.

Eastern States Express (Aba). 1964. "Beware of fraudulent 'employers.'" August 21:2.

Eburnea. 1967. "Stop to rural exodus." No. 1:7-9.
(Translated in Translations on Africa, No. 626:
42-46.)

Economist Intelligence Unit Limited. 1966. Quarterly
economic review, annual supplement: Former French
Tropical Africa and Liberia.

1967. Quarterly economic review, annual supplement:
Congo, Rwanda, Burundi. London.

Edel, May. 1965. "African tribalism: Some reflections
on Uganda." Political Science Quarterly 80: 357-372.

Edelman, Murray. 1964. The symbolic uses of politics.
Urbana, University of Illinois Press.**

Edgren, Gus. 1965a. "The employment problem in tropical
Africa." Inter-African Labour Institute Bulletin

12:174-190.

1965b. "Unemployment in tropical Africa." East Africa Journal 2(4):6-19.

Eichenberger, J. Y. 1954. "Aspects humains de l'industrialisation en Afrique noire" ("The human aspects of industrialization in Black Africa"). Revue de l'Industrie Minérale, No. 614:1149-1169.

Eisenstadt, Samuel Noah. 1952. "The place of elites and primary groups in the absorption of new immigrants in Israel." American Journal of Sociology 57:222-231.☆☆

1954. "Reference group behavior and social integration: An explorative study." American Sociological Review 19:175-185.☆☆

1957. "Sociological aspects of political development in underdeveloped countries." Economic Development and Cultural Change 5(4):289-307.☆☆

1963. The political systems of empires. London (New York), Free Press of Glencoe.☆☆

1964. Social change and modernization in African societies south of the Sahara. Jerusalem, The Hebrew University.

1965a. Essays on comparative institutions. New York, John Wiley & Sons.☆☆

1965b. "Processes of modernization and of urban and industrial transformation under conditions of structural duality." Social Sciences Information 4:40-50.☆☆

1965c. "Social change and modernization in African societies south of the Sahara." Cahiers d'Etudes Africaines 5:453-471.

1966. Modernization: Protest and change. Englewood Cliffs, N.J., Prentice-Hall.☆☆

Ekwensi, Cyprian. 1961. Jagua Nana. London, Hutchin-
& Company.

1963. Beautiful feathers. London, Hutchinson &
Company.

Eldridge, Hope Tisdale. 1956. "The process of urbanization." In J. J. Spengler and O. D. Duncan, eds.,
Demographic analysis. Glencoe, Ill., Free Press,
pp. 338-343.**

Elias, T. Olawale. 1953. Nigerian land law and
custom. London, Routledge and Kegan Paul.

Elkan, Susan. 1960-1961. "Primary school leavers in
Uganda." Comparative Education Review 4:102-109.

Elkan, Walter. 1956. An African labour force: Two
case studies in East African factory employment.
(East African Studies No. 7) Kampala, East African
Institute of Social Research.

1959a. "Migrant labor in Africa: An economist's
approach." American Economic Review 49:188-202.

1959b. "The persistence of migrant labour." Inter-
African Labour Institute Bulletin 6(5):36-42.

1960. Migrants and proletarians: Urban labour in
the economic development of Uganda. London, Oxford
University Press.

1961. The economic development of Uganda. London,
Oxford University Press.

1963. "Labour for industrial development in East
Africa." In University of Edinburgh, Centre of
African Studies, Urbanization in African social
change: Proceedings of the Inaugural Seminar held
in the Centre, 5-7 January. Edinburgh, pp. 181-185.

1964. "Some social policy implications of industrial
development in East Africa." International Social
Science Journal 15:390-399.

1967. "Central migration and the growth of towns ih East Africa." International Labour Review 96:581-589.

Elkan, Walter, and Lloyd A. Fallers. 1960. "The mobility of labor." In Wilbert E. Moore and Arnold S. Feldman, eds., Labor commitment and social change in developing areas. New York, Social Science Research Council, pp. 238-257.

El-Masri, F. H. 1967. "Islam." In P. C. Lloyd, A. L. Mabogunje, and B. Awe, eds., The city of Ibadan: A symposium on its structure and development. London, Cambridge University Press, pp. 249-257.

Emerson, Rupert. 1960. From empire to nation: The rise to self-assertion of Asian and African peoples. Cambridge, Harvard University Press.✹✹

Enahoro, Peter. 1966. How to be a Nigerian. Ibadan, Caxton Press.

Epstein, A. L. 1951a. "Some aspects of the conflict of law and urban courts in Norther Rhodesia." Rhodes-Livingstone Journal 12:28-40.

1951b. "Urban native courts on the Northern Rhodesian Copperbelt." Journal of African Administration 3:117-124.

1953. The administration of justice and the urban African. (Colonial Social Research Studies No. 7) London, His Majesty's Stationery Office.

1956. "An outline of the political structure of an African urban community on the Copperbelt of Northern Rhodesia." In International African Institute, Social implications of industrialization and urbanization in Africa south of the Sahara. Paris, UNESCO, pp. 711-724.

1957. "African townsmen." Rhodes-Livingstone Journal 22:67-70.

1958. Politics in an urban African community. Manchester, Manchester University Press.

1961. "The network and urban social organization." Rhodes-Livingstone Journal 29:29-62.

1964. "Urban communities in Africa." In Max Gluckman, ed., Closed systems and open minds: the limits of naivety in social anthropology. Chicago, Aldine Publishing Company, pp. 83-102.

1967. "Urbanization and social change in Africa." Current Anthropology 8:275-298.

1969a. "Gossip, norms and social network." In J. Clyde Mitchell, ed., Social networks in urban situations: Analyses of personal relationships in Central African towns. Manchester, Manchester University Press, pp. 117-127.

1969b. "The network and urban social organization." In J. Clyde Mitchell, ed., Social networks in urban situations: Analyses of personal relationships in Central African towns. Manchester, Manchester University Press, pp. 77-116.

Esman, Milton J., and Fred C. Bruhns. 1965. "Institution-building in national development: An approach to induced social change in transitional societies." Paper read at the Symposium on Comparative Theories of Social Change, Ann Arbor, Michigan, December.**

Etherington, D. M. 1965. "Projected changes in urban and rural population in Kenya and the implications for development policy." East African Economic Review 1(n.s.):65-83.

Etzioni, Amitai. 1965. Political unification: A comparative study of leaders and forces. New York, Holt, Rinehart and Winston.**

1966. Studies in social change. New York, Holt, Rinehart and Winston.**

Etzioni, Amitai, and Eva Etzioni, eds. 1964. Social
change: Sources, patterns and consequences. New
York, Basic Books.✷✷

Evans-Pritchard, E. E. 1950. The Nuer. Oxford,
Clarendon Press.

Fage, John D. 1965. "Some thoughts on migration and
urban settlement." In Hilda Kuper, ed., Urbanization and migration in West Africa. Berkeley,
University of California Press, pp. 39–49.

Fair, T. J. D. 1966. "Urban morphology and separate
development in South African cities." Paper read at
the Ninth Annual Meeting of the African Studies
Association, Bloomington, 26-29 October.✷

Fallers, L. A. 1955. "The predicament of the modern
African chief: An instance from Uganda." American
Anthropologist 57:290-305.

1961. "Are African cultivators to be called
'peasants'?" Current Anthropology 2:108-110.

Fanon, Frantz. 1963. The wretched of the earth. New
York, Grove Press.

Fashole-Luke, E. W. 1967. "Religion in Freetown."
Paper read at the Freetown Symposium, Institute of
African Studies, The University College of Sierra
Leone, Freetown.

Fava, Sylvia F. 1966. "Recent books in the urban
field--An essay review." Social Problems 14:93-
104.✷✷

Feldman, Arnold S., and Charles Tilly. 1960. "The
interaction of social and physical space."
American Sociological Review 25:877-884.✷✷

Fellin, Phillip, and Eugene Litwak. 1963. "Neighborhood cohesion under conditions of mobility."
American Sociological Review 28:364-376.✷✷

Fellows, Lawrence. 1967. "Kenya troubled by shanty towns." The New York Times, 23 April, p. 11.

Fenichel, Otto. 1945. The psychoanalytic theory of neurosis. New York, W. W. Norton & Company.**

Ferguson, Robert H. 1965. Unemployment: Its scope, measurement, and effect on poverty. Ithaca, Cornell University, New York State School of Industrial and Labor Relations.**

Ferman, Louis A. n.d. Sociological perspectives in unemployment research. (Reprint Series, No. 29) Ann Arbor and Detroit, University of Michigan--Wayne State University, Institute of Labor and Industrial Relations, pp. 504-514.**

Fernandez, James W. 1964. "Politics and prophecy: African religious movements." Practical Anthropology 12(2):71-75.

Festinger, Leon. 1957. A theory of cognitive dissonance. Evanston, Ill., Row, Peterson & Company.**

Festinger, Leon, Henry W. Riecher, and Stanley Schachter. 1956. When prophecy fails. Minneapolis, University of Minnesota.**

———. 1958. "When prophecy fails." In Eleanor E. Macoby, Theodore M. Newcomb, and Eugene L. Hartley, eds., Readings in social psychology, 3rd ed. New York, Holt, Rinehart and Winston, pp. 156-163.**

Fiawoo, D. K. 1959. "Urbanisation and religion in Eastern Ghana." Sociological Review 7:83-97.

Fichter, Joseph H. 1952. "Conceptualization of the urban parish." Social Forces 31:43-46.**

Field, Arthur J. 1967. Urbanization and work in modernizing societies. Detroit, Glengary Press.**

Field, J. O. 1945. "Sale of land in an Ibo community." Man: Journal of the Royal Anthropological Institute

45(47):70-71.

Firey, Walter. 1945. "Sentiment and symbolism as ecological variables." American Sociological Review 10:140-148.**

Firth, Raymond. 1957. "Factions in Indian and over-seas Indian societies: Introduction." British Journal of Sociology 8:291-295.**

Fischer, J. L. 1965. "Psychology and anthropology." In Bernard J. Siegel, ed., Biennial review of an-thropology 1965. Stanford, Stanford University Press, pp. 211-261.**

Fisher, Paul. 1961. "The economic role of unions in less-developed areas: Excerpt from address, April 5, 1961." Monthly Labor Review 84(9):951-956.**

Fitch, Lyle C. 1966. "Planning and administration in urban areas." In United Nations, Administration of national development planning. (ST/TAO/M/27) New York.**

Fleming, William G. 1964. "The District Commissioner and tribal administration in Uganda: A study of the relationship between African political systems and colonial policy achievement." Unpublished doctoral dissertation, Northwestern University.

_____ 1966. "Authority, efficiency, and role stress: Problems in the development of East African bureau-cracies." Administrative Science Quarterly 2(3): 386-404.

Floyd, T. D. 1960. Town planning in South Africa. Pietermaritzburg, Shuter and Shooter.*

Folson, B. D. G. 1964. "Coussey and local government structure in Ghana." Economic Bulletin of Ghana 8:3-17.

Foltz, William J. 1964. "Social structure and political behavior of Senegalese elites." Paper read at the

Annual Meeting of the American Political Science Association, Chicago, 9-12 September.

Foran, W. Robert. 1950. "Rise of Nairobi: From campsite to city." Crown Colonist 20:160-165.

Forde, Daryll. 1953. "The conditions of social develop-in West Africa: Retrospect and prospect." Civilisations 3:471-485.

1956. "Introductory survey." In International African Institute, Social implications of industrialization and urbanization in Africa south of the Sahara. Paris, UNESCO, pp. 11-50.

1963. "Methodology in the study of African urbanization." In University of Edinburgh, Centre of African Studies, Urbanization in African social change: Proceedings of the Inaugural Seminar held in the Centre, 5-7 January. Edinburgh, pp. 1-6.

Fordham, Paul. 1966. "Out-groups in East African society." In East African Institute of Social and Cultural Affairs, Racial and communal tensions in East Africa. Nairobi, East African Publishing House, pp. 84-94.

Form, William H., and William V. D'Antonio. 1959. "Integration and cleavage among community influentials in two border cities." American Sociological Review 24:804-814.**

Form, William H., and Warren L. Sauer. 1960a. Community influentials in a middle-sized city. (General Bulletin No. 5) East Lansing, Michigan State University, Labor and Industrial Relations Center.**

1960b. "Organized labor's image of community power structure." Social Forces 38:332-341.**

Form, William H., and Gregory P. Stone. 1957. "Urbanism, anonymity, and status symbolism." American Journal of Sociology 62:504-514.**

Forrester, Jay W. 1969. <u>Urban dynamics</u>. Cambridge,
M.I.T. Press.✻✻

Fortes, M., and D. Y. Mayer. 1966. "Psychoses and
social change among the Tallensi of Northern Ghana."
Cahiers d'Etudes Africaines 6(21):5-40.

Fortes, Steel, and Ady Fortes. 1956. "The Ashanti
survey." In International African Institute, <u>Social</u>
<u>implications</u> <u>of</u> <u>industrialization</u> <u>and</u> <u>urbanization</u>
<u>in</u> <u>Africa</u> <u>south</u> <u>of</u> <u>the</u> <u>Sahara</u>. Paris, UNESCO, pp.
91-96.

Foster, Philip. 1965. <u>Education</u> <u>and</u> <u>social</u> <u>change</u> <u>in</u>
<u>Ghana</u>. Chicago, University of Chicago Press.

1966. "Some remarks on education and unemployment
in Africa." Paper read at the African Research
Committee Conference on Unemployment in Africa,
Evanston, Ill., 6-7 May.

Fougeyrollas, Pierre. 1966. "Senegalese civil servants
and African socialism." Le Mois en Afrique, No. 11:
77-92. (Translated in Translations on Africa, No.
473:40-54.)

Fouraker, Lawrence E., and Sidney Siegel. 1963.
<u>Bargaining</u> <u>behavior</u>. New York, McGraw-Hill.✻✻

Fraenkel, Merran McCulloch. 1956a. <u>A</u> <u>social</u> <u>survey</u> <u>of</u>
<u>the</u> <u>African</u> <u>population</u> <u>of</u> <u>Livingstone</u>. (Rhodes-
Livingstone Papers No. 26) Manchester, Manchester
University Press for the Rhodes-Livingstone Insti-
tute.✻

1956b. "Survey of recent and current field studies
on the social effects of economic development in
inter-tropical Africa: Comparisons and conclusions."
In International African Institute, <u>Social</u> <u>implica-</u>
<u>tions</u> <u>of</u> <u>industrialization</u> <u>and</u> <u>urbanization</u> <u>in</u>
<u>Africa</u> <u>south</u> <u>of</u> <u>the</u> <u>Sahara</u>. Paris, UNESCO, pp. 209-
221.

1956c. "Survey of recent and current field studies on the social effects of economic development in inter-tropical Africa: Introduction." In International African Institute, <u>Social implications of industrialization</u> and <u>urbanization in Africa south of the Sahara</u>, Paris, UNESCO, pp. 53-71.

1964. <u>Tribe and class in Monrovia</u>. London, published for the International African Institute by the Oxford University Press.

Franck, Thomas M. 1962. "European communities in Africa: White settlers and independence movement." Journal of Negro Education 30:223-231.

Fraternite-Matin. 1966. "How the Ivorian industries train their African personnel." 2(464):7, June 22. (Translated in Translations on Africa, No. 419: 79-85.)

Frazier, E. Franklin. 1961. "Urbanization and its effects upon the task of nation-building in Africa south of the Sahara." Journal of Negro Education 30:214-222.

Free, Lloyd A. 1964. <u>The attitudes, hopes and fears of Nigerians</u>. Princeton, Institute for International Social Research.

Free Labour World. 1960. "African labour migration." No. 118:149-152.

1962. "Nigerian workers seek new wage structure." No. 141:88-90.

Frey, Roger. 1954. <u>Brazzaville, capitale de l'Afrique Equatoriale Française</u> (Brazzaville, <u>capital of French Equatorial Africa</u>). Paris, Encyclopédie Mensuelle d'Outre-Mer.

Freyre, Gilberto. 1957. "Ethnic and cultural pluralism in intertropical communities: Cultural aspect." In International Institute of Differing Civilizations, Ethnic and cultural pluralism in intertropical communities. Brussels, pp. 632-652 (even).**

Fried, Marc. 1967. "Functions of the working class community in modern urban society: Implications for forced relocation." Journal of the American Institute of Planners 33(2):90-103.**

Fried, Marc, and Peggy Gleicher. 1961. "Some sources of residential satisfaction in an urban slum." Journal of the American Institute of Planners 27(4): 305-315.**

Friedland, William H. 1959. "African trade unions: From bush to Copperbelt." Information (International Research Office of Social Implications of Technological Change, International Social Science Council), No. 22:1-6.

1960. "Some urban myths of East Africa." In Allie Dubb, ed., Myth in modern Africa. Lusaka, Rhodes-Livingstone Institute for Social Research, pp. 83-97.

1961. "The institutionalization of labor protest in Tanganyika and some resultant problems." Sociologus 11:132-146.

1963. Unions and industrial relations in underdeveloped countries. (Bulletin 47) Ithaca, Cornell University, New York School of Industrial and Labor Relations.**

1965. Unions, labor, and industrial relations in Africa. Ithaca, Center for International Studies of Cornell University.

Friedland, William H., and Dorothy Nelkin. 1967. "Migrant labor: A form of intermittent social organization." ILR Research 13(2):3-14.**

Friedman, G. 1952. "The social consequences of technical progress." International Social Science Bulletin 4:243-260.**

Friedmann, John. 1966. "Two concepts of urbanization: A comment." Urban Affairs Quarterly 1(4):78-84.**

Friedmann, John, and Tomas Lackington. 1967. "Hyper-urbanization and the national development in Chile: Some hypotheses." Urban Affairs Quarterly 2(4):3-29.**

Friendly, Alfred, Jr. 1967. "Ivory Coast seeks urban balance." The New York Times, 26 December, p. 12.

Froelich, Jean-Claude. 1954. "Ngaoundéré. La vie économique d'une cité peul" ("Ngaoundere. The economic life of a city of the Peul people"). Etudes Camerounaises (Douala), Nos. 43-44:3-66.

1966. "Muslim sects and Negro-African civilizations." Le Mois en Afrique 1(5):98-105. (Translated in Translations on Africa, No. 387:24-31).

Fromm, Erich. 1941. Escape from freedom. New York, Holt, Rinehart and Winston.**

Fyfe, Christopher. 1967. "The foundation of Freetown." Paper read at the Freetown Symposium, Institute of African Studies, the University of Sierra Leone, Freetown.

(Gabon) Gabon, Ministère de l'Economie Nationale, du Plan et des Mines, Commissariat au Plan, Service National de la Statistique, Commune de Libreville. 1965. Recensement de la population de la commune de Libreville, II, Octobre 1964. (Population census of the Libreville commune, II, October 1964). Libre-ville.

Galenson, Walter. 1959. Labor and economic development. New York, John Wiley & Sons.**

Gallais, Jean. 1954. "Dans la grande banlieue de Dakar: Les villages lèbous de la presqu'île du Cap Vert" ("In the large suburb of Dakar: The Lebous villages of the Cape Vert peninsula"). Les Cahiers d'Outre-Mer 7(26):137-158.

Gamble, David P. 1963a. "Family organization in new towns in Sierra Leone." In University of Edinburgh, Centre of African Studies, Urbanization in African social change: Proceedings of the Inaugural Seminar held in the Centre, January 5-7. Edinburgh, pp. 75-84.

1963b. "The Temne family in a modern town (Lunsar) in Sierra Leone." Africa 33(3):209-226.

1966. "Occupational prestige in an urban community (Lunsar) in Sierra Leone." Sierra Leone Studies 19: 98-108.

Gamson, William A. 1966. "Rancorous conflict in community politics." American Sociological Review 31: 71-81.**

Gann, L. H. 1961. "The white settler: A changing image." Race 2(2):28-40.

Gans, Herbert J. 1962. "Urbanism and suburbanism as ways of life: A re-evaluation of definition." In Arnold Rose, ed., Human behavior and social processes. Boston, Houghton Mifflin Company, pp. 625-648.**

Garbett, G. Kingsley. 1966. "The Rhodesian chief's dilemma: Government officer or tribal leader?" Race 8(2):113-128.*

Gardiner, R. K. A. 1956. "The new industrial communities in West Africa." In His Royal Highness the Duke of Edinburgh's study conference on the human problems of industrial communities within the Commonwealth and Empire, 9-27 July 1956, I--Report and proceedings. London, Oxford University Press, pp. 170-180.

Garigue, P. 1954. "Changing political leadership in West Africa." Africa 24(3):220-232.

Garlick, Peter C. [1961?] "African and Levantine trading firms in Ghana." In Nigerian Institute of Social and Economic Research, Conference proceedings, December 1960. Ibadan, Caxton Press, pp. 119-131.

Gatheru, R. Mugo. 1964. Child of two worlds: A Kikuyu's story. New York, Frederick A. Praeger.

Gaveh, D. 1961. "Tamale: A geographical study."
Bulletin of the Ghana Geographical Association 6(1):
12-29.

Gayet, Georges. 1952. "Le plus grand Dakar" ("Great
Dakar"). In International Institute of Differing
Civilizations, The "pull" exerted by urban and industrial centres in countries in course of industrialization. Burssels, pp. 400-405.

1957. "Les Libanais et les Syriens dans l'Ouest Africain" ("Lebanese and Syrians in West Africa"). In
International Institute of Differing Civilizations,
Ethnic and cultural pluralism in intertropical communities. Brussels, pp. 161-172.

Geertz, Clifford. 1963a. "The integrative revolution:
Primordial sentiments and civil politics in the new
states." In Clifford Geertz, ed., Old societies and
new states: The quest for modernity in Asia and
Africa. London, Free Press, pp. 105-157.**

1963b. Peddlers and princes: Social change and economic
modernization in two Indonesian towns. Chicago, University of Chicago Press.**

Gellar, Sheldon. 1967. "West African capital cities as
motors for development." Civilisations 17(3):254-262.

Georgulas, Nikos. 1963. "An approach to urban analysis
for East African towns with particular reference to
the African population." Unpublished paper prepared
for the Program of East African Studies, Fall.

1964. "An approach to urban analysis for East African towns with particular reference to the African
population." Ekistics 18(109):436-440.

Germani, Gino. 1963. "The strategy of fostering social
mobility." In Egbert de Vries and Jose Medina
Echavarria, eds., Social aspects of economic development in Latin America, I. Paris, UNESCO, pp. 211-230.**

Ghai, Dharam P. 1965. "An economic survey." In Dharam

P. Ghai, ed., Portrait of a minority: Asians in East
Africa. Nairobi, Oxford University Press, pp. 91-111.

Ghai, Dharam P., and Yash P. Ghai. 1965. "Asians in
East Africa: Problems and prospects." Journal of
Modern African Studies 3:35-51.

Ghai, Yash P. 1965. "The future prospects." In Dharam
P. Ghai, ed., Portrait of a minority: Asians in East
Africa. Nairobi, Oxford University Press, pp. 129-
154.

——— 1966. "Prospects for Asians in East Africa." In
East African Institute for Social and Cultural Af-
fairs, Racial and communal tensions in East Africa.
Nairobi, East African Publishing House, pp. 9-26.

Ghana, Census Office. 1962a. 1960 population census of
Ghana, I: The gazetteer alphabetical list of localities. Accra.

——— 1962b. 1960 population census of Ghana, II: Statistics of localities and enumeration areas. Accra.

——— 1964a. 1960 population census of Ghana, III: Demographic characteristics of local authorities,
regions and total country. Accra.

——— 1964b. 1960 population census of Ghana, IV: Economic
characteristics of local authorities, regions and
total country. Accra.

——— 1964c. 1960 population census of Ghana, V: General
report. Accra.

——— 1964d. 1960 population census of Ghana, special report 'A': Statistics of towns with 10,000 population
or more. Accra.

——— 1964e. 1960 population census of Ghana, special report 'E'. Accra.

(Ghana) Gold Coast, Office of the Government Statistician. 1956a. Kumasi survey of population and household

budgets, <u>1955</u>. (Statistical and economic papers, No. 5) Accra.

1956b. <u>Sekondi-Takoradi survey of population and household(s) budgets</u>, <u>1955</u>. (Statistical and economic papers, No. 4) Accra.

Ghosh, D. 1946. <u>Pressure of population and economic efficiency in India</u>. London, Oxford University Press.✻✻

Ghosh, Subratesh. 1960. <u>Trade unions in underdeveloped countries</u>. Calcutta, Bookland.✻✻

Gibbs, Jack P. 1966. "Measures of urbanization." Social Forces 45(2):170-177.✻✻

1968. "Further observations on 'Measures of urbanisation.'" Social Forces 46(3): 400-405.✻✻

Gibbs, Jack P., and Walter T. Martin. 1962. "Urbanization, technology, and the division of labor: International patterns." American Sociological Review 27:667-677.✻✻

Gilder, S. S. B. 1952. "Urbanization and social medicine." In International Institute of Differing Civilizations, <u>The "pull" exerted by urban and industrial centres in countries in course of industrialization</u>. Brussels, pp. 70-90.✻✻

Gillman, C. 1945. "Dar es Salaam, 1860-1940: A story of growth and change." Tanganyika Notes and Records, December, 1-23.

Gilmore, Horton. 1953. <u>Transportation and the growth of cities</u>. Glencoe, Ill., Free Press.✻✻

Ginsburg, Norton. 1965. "The international conference on 'the study of urbanization.'" Items 19:49-50.✻✻

Gist, Noel P., and Sylvia Fleis Fava. 1967. <u>Urban society</u>, 5th ed. New York, Thomas Y. Crowell Company.✻✻

Glass, Y. 1964. "Industrialization and urbanization in
   South Africa." In J. F. Holleman, Joan Knox, J. W.
   Mann, and K. A. Heard, eds., Problems of transition:
   Proceedings of the Social Sciences Research Confer-
   ence, 1962. Pietermaritzburg, Natal University Press,
   pp. 52-70.*

Glazer, Nathan, and D. P. Moynihan. 1963. Beyond the
   melting pot; The Negroes, Puerto Ricans, Jews,
   Italians, and Irish of New York City. Cambridge,
   M.I.T. Press.**

Glenn, Norval D., and J. L. Simmons. 1967. "Are regional cultural differences diminishing?" Public Opinion
   Quarterly 31(2):176-193.**

Glickman, Harvey. 1964. "Traditional pluralism and
   democratic process in Tanganyika." Paper read at the
   Annual Meeting of the American Political Science
   Association, Chicago, 9-12 September.

Gluckman, Max. 1943. Essays on Lozi land and royal
   property. Rhodes-Livingstone Paper, No. 10.*

   1956. Social anthropology in Central Africa. Rhodes-
   Livingstone Journal, No. 20:1-27.

   1958. Analysis of a social situation in modern Zulu-
   land. (Rhodes-Livingstone Papers, No. 28) Manchester,
   Manchester University Press.*

   1959. Custom and conflict in Africa. Glencoe, Ill.,
   Free Press.

   1960. "Tribalism in modern British Central Africa."
   Cahiers d'Etudes Africaines, No. 1:55-70.

   1961. "Anthropological problems arising from the
   African industrial revolution." In Aidan Southall,
   ed., Social change in modern Africa. London, Oxford
   University Press. pp. 67-82.

Goddard, S. 1965. "Town-farm relationships in Yoruba-
   land: A case study from Oyo." Africa 35:21-29.

Goldberg, Harvey. 1967. "Structure and attitudes in the study of change in an Israeli immigrant." Paper read at the 66th Annual Meeting of the American Anthropological Association, Washington, D.C., 30 November-3 December.**

Goldhamer, Herbert, and Andrew W. Marshall. 1953. Psychosis and civilization: Two studies in the frequency of mental disease. Glencoe, Ill., Free Press.**

Goldrich, Daniel. 1964. Sons of the establishment. Chicago, Rand McNally.**

Golds, J. M. 1961. "African urbanization in Kenya." Journal of African Administration 13:24-28.

Goldthorpe, J. E. 1958. Outlines of East African Society. Kampala, Makerere College, Department of Sociology.

Goodenough, Ward Hunt. 1963. Cooperation in change: An anthropological approach to community development. New York, Russell Sage Foundation.**

Gorvine, Albert. 1965. "The utilisation of local government for national development." Journal of Local Administration Overseas 4(4):225-231.**

Gosselin, M. 1953. "Bamako: Ville soudanaise moderne" ("Bamako: Modern Sudanese city"). L'Afrique et l'Asie, No. 21:31-37.

Gouellain, M. R. 1961. "Parenté et affinités ethniques dans l'écologie du 'Grand Quartier' de New-Bell, Douala" ("Parents and ethnic in-laws in the ecology of 'Grand Quartier' of New-Bell, Douala"). In Aidan Southall, ed., Social change in modern Africa. London, Oxford University Press, pp. 254-272.

Goyal, O. P. 1965. "Caste and politics: A conceptual framework." Asian Survey 5:522-525.**

Graves, Theodore D. 1966. "Alternative models for the study of urban migration." Human Organization 25(4):

295-299.**

Graves, Theodore D., and Minor Van Arsdale. 1966.
"Values, expectations and relocation: The Navaho
migrant to Denver." Human Organization 25:300-307.**

Greenberg, Joseph H. 1965. "Urbanism, migration, and
language." In Hilda Kuper, ed., Urbanization and
migration in West Africa. Berkeley, University of
California Press, pp. 50-59.

Greenfield, Sidney M. 1965. "Industrialization and the
family." In Neil J. Smelser, ed., Readings on economic sociology. Englewood Cliffs, N.J., Prentice-Hall,
pp. 85-96.**

Greenstone, J. David. 1966. "Corruption and self interest in Kampala and Nairobi: A comment on local
politics in East Africa." Comparative Studies in
Society and History 8:199-210.

Greer, Scott. 1956. "Urbanism reconsidered: A comparative study of local areas in a metropolis." American Sociological Review 21:19-25.**

1958. "Individual participation in mass society." In
Roland Young, ed., Approaches to the study of politics. Evanston, Northwestern University Press, pp.
329-342.**

1962. The emerging city. New York, Free Press of
Glencoe.**

Greer, Scott, and Ella Kube. 1951. "Urbanism and social
structure: A Los Angeles study." In Marvin Sussman,
ed., Community structure and analysis. New York,
Thomas Y. Crowell Company, pp. 93-112.**

Grevisse, F. 1951. Le centre extra-coutumier d'Elisabethville (The non-traditional center of Elisabethville). (Classe des Sciences morales et politiques,
Memoires, Volume 21) Brussels, Institut Royal Colonial Belge.

1956. "The African centre at Elisabethville." In International African Institute, Social implications of industrialization and urbanization in Africa south of the Sahara. Paris, UNESCO, pp. 161-166.

Griffin, D. W. 1965. "Urban redevelopment in Africa: The case of Lagos." Paper read at the Eighth Annual Meeting of the African Studies Association, 27-30 October.

Group of Kampala Students. 1960. "African labour migration." Free Labour World, No. 118:149-152.

Grove, David, and Huszar Laszlo. 1964. The towns of Ghana: The role of service centres in regional planning (Planning Research Studies 2). Accra, Ghana Universities Press.

Grundy, Kenneth W. 1964. "The 'class struggle' in Africa: An examination of conflicting theories." Journal of Modern African Studies 2(3):379-393.

1966. "Recent contributions to the study of African political thought." World Politics 18(4):674-689.

Guernier, Eugene. 1952. L'évolution politique de l'Afrique et les mouvements de population" ("The political development of Africa and population movements"). In International Institute of Differing Civilizations, The "pull" exerted by urban and industrial centres in countries in course of industrialization. Brussels, pp. 458-465.

Gugler, Josef. 1962. "The relationship urban dwellers maintain with their villages of origin in Eastern Nigeria." Paper read at the Fifth World Congress of Sociology, Washington, D.C., 2-8 September.

1965. "Life in a dual system." In East African Institute of Social Research, January Conference Proceedings.

Guilbot, Jaques. 1949. "Les conditions de vie indigènes de Douala" ("Living conditions of the indigenous population of Douala"). Etudes Camerounaises, Nos. 27-28:179-239.

1956. "Study of the labour force at Douala." In International African Institute, Social implications of industrialization and urbanization in Africa south of the Sahara. Paris, UNESCO, pp. 102-105.

Gulick, John, et al. 1962. "Newcomer enculturation in the city: Attitudes and participation." In F. Stuart Chapin, Jr. and Shirley Weiss, eds., Urban growth dynamics. New York, John Wiley & Sons, pp. 315-358.**

Gulliver, P. H. 1955. Labour migration in a rural economy: A study of the Ngoni and Ndendeuli of southern Tanganyika. Kampala, East African Institute of Social Research.

1957. Nyakyusa labour migration. Rhodes-Livingstone Journal, No. 21:32-63.

1960. "Incentives in labor migration." Human Organization 19:159-163.

1966. "The development of labour migration in Africa." Kroniek van Afrika 6(3):250-265.

Gussman, Boris. 1953. "Industrial efficiency and the urban African." Africa 23:135-144.

Gussow, Zachary. 1954. "The contribution of associations to evolutionary changes in cultures in four African societies." Unpublished doctoral dissertation, Columbia University.

Gutkind, Peter C. W. 1957. "Some African attitudes to multi-racialism from Uganda, British East Africa." In International Institute of Differing Civilizations, Ethnic and cultural pluralism in intertropical communities. Brussels, pp. 338-355.

1960a. "Congestion and overcrowding: An African urban problem." Human Organization 19:129-134.

1960b. "Notes on the Kibuga of Buganda." Uganda Journal 24:29-43.

1961a. "Some problems of African urban family life: An example from Kampala, Uganda, British East Africa." Zaire 15:59-74.

1961b. "Urban conditions in Africa." Town Planning Review 32:20-32.

1962a. "Accommodation and conflict in an African peri-urban area." Anthropologica 4:163-173.

1962b. "African urban family life: Comment on and analysis of some rural-urban differences." Cahiers d'Etudes Africaines, No. 10:149-217.

1962c. "The African urban milieu: A force in rapid change." Civilisations 12:167-191.

1962d. "Some problems of African urban family life: An example from Kampala, Uganda, British East Africa." Diogenes, Nos. 37-40:88-104.

1963a. "African urban marriage and family life: A note on some social and demographic characteristics from Kampala, Uganda." Bulletin de l'Institut Français d'Afrique Noire 25B(3-4):266-287.

1963b. The royal capital of Uganda: A study of internal conflict and external ambiguity. The Hague, Mouton.

1965a. "African urbanism, mobility and the social network." In Ralph Piddington, ed., Kinship and geographic mobility (Special issue of International Journal of Comparative Sociology). Leiden, E. J. Brill.

1965b. "Network analysis and urbanism in Africa: The use of micro and macro analysis." Canadian Review of Sociology and Anthropology 2:123-131.

1966a. "Urbanization and unemployment." Paper read

at the African Research Committee Conference on Unemployment in Africa, Evanston, Ill., 6-7 May.

1966b. "African urban chiefs: Agents of stability
or change in African urban life." Anthropologica 8
(2):249-268.

1966c. "African urban family life and the urban
system." Journal of Asian and African Studies 1(1):
35-42.

1967. "The pattern of migration in Madagascar and its
theoretical implications." Paper read at the Annual
Meeting of the African Studies Association, New York,
1-4 November.*

1968a. "African responses to urban wage employment."
International Labor Review 97:135-166.

1968b. "The poor in urban Africa: A prologue to
modernization, conflict, and the unfinished revolution." In Warner Bloomberg, Jr., and Henry J.
Schmandt, eds., Power, poverty, and urban policy.
Beverly Hills, Sage Publications, pp. 355-396.

Gutman, Robert. 1963. Urban sociology: A bibliography.
New Brunswick, N.J., Rutgers, The State University,
Urban Studies Center.**

Gutman, Robert, and Francine Rabinovitz. 1966. "The
relevance of domestic urban studies to international
urban research." Urban Affairs Quarterly 1(4): 45-
64.**

Hailey, Lord (William M.). 1938. An African survey: A
study of problems arising in Africa south of the
Sahara. London, Oxford University Press.

1950. Native administration in the British African
territories. Part I, East Africa: Uganda, Kenya,
Tanganyika. London, His Majesty's Stationery Office.

1951a. Native administration in the British African
territories. Part III, West Africa: Nigeria, Gold

Coast, <u>Sierra Leone</u>, <u>Gambia</u>. London, His Majesty's
Stationery Office.

1951b. <u>Native administration in the British African
territories</u>. <u>Part IV, General survey of the system
of native administration</u>. London, His Majesty's
Stationery Office.

Hair, P. E. H. 1953. "Enugu: An industrial and urban
community in East Nigeria, 1914-1953." In (Proceedings of the) <u>West African Institute of Social and
Economic Research</u>. Ibadan, University College Ibadan,
pp. 143-160.

1963. "Christianity at Freetown from 1792 as a field
for research." In University of Edinburgh, Centre of
African Studies, <u>Urbanization in African social
change</u>: <u>Proceedings of the Inaugural Seminar held in
the Centre, January 5-7</u>. Edinburgh, pp. 127-140.

Halliman, Dorothy M., and W. T. W. Morgan. 1967. "The
city of Nairobi." In W. T. W. Morgan, ed., <u>Nairobi,
city and region</u>. New York, Oxford University Press.

Hamdan, G. 1960. "The growth and functional structure
of Khartoum." Geographical Review 50:21-40.✶

1964. "Capitals of the New Africa." Economic Geography 40(3):239-253.

Hamilton, Ruth Simms. 1965. <u>Urbanization in West Africa</u>.
Evanston, Northwestern University Press.

1966. "Urban social differentiation and membership
recruitment among selected voluntary associations in
Accra, Ghana." Unpublished doctoral dissertation,
Northwestern University.

Hammond-Tooke, W. D. 1970. "Urbanization and the interpretation of misfortune: A quantitative analysis."
Africa 50(1):25-39.

Hance, William A. 1960. "Economic location and func-

tions of tropical African cities." Human Organization 19(3):135-136.

1964. The geography of modern Africa. New York,
Columbia University Press.

1966. "An overview of African urban development."
Paper read at the Ninth Annual Meeting of the African
Studies Association, Bloomington, Ind., 26-39 October.

1970. Population, migration, and urbanization
in Africa. New York, Columbia University Press.

Hance, William A., and Irene S. Van Dongen. 1956. "The
port of Lobito and the Benguela Railway." Geographical Review, No. 4:460-487.*

1957. "Beira, Mozambique: Gateway to central Africa."
Annals of the Association of American Geographers
47:307-335.*

Handlin, Oscar. 1959. The newcomers: Negroes and
Puerto Ricans in a changing metropolis. Cambridge,
Harvard University Press.**

1961. "Historical perspectives on the American ethnic group." Daedalus 90:220-232.**

Hanna, Marwan. 1958. "The Lebanese in West Africa:
How and when they came." West Africa, No. 2141:393.

Hanna, William John. 1962. "(Review of) Immanuel Wal-
lerstein, Africa: The politics of independence."
New York, Vintage Books, 1961. In American Political
Science Review 61:429-431.

1964a. "Introduction: The politics of freedom." In
William John Hanna, ed., Independent Black Africa:
The politics of freedom. Chicago, Rand McNally,
pp. 1-43.

1964b. "Students." In James Smoot Coleman and Carl
G. Rosberg, Jr., eds., Political parties and national

integration in tropical Africa. Berkeley, University
of California Press, pp. 413-443.

1965a. "Comments on urbanization, type of descent,
and child-rearing practices." Unpublished manuscript.

1965b. "The effect of international events upon
Soviet orthodoxy." Political Studies 13:241-246.**

1966a. "A point of departure: Labor union activity
and de-employment in Africa." Paper read at the African Research Committee Conference on Unemployment in
Africa, Evanston, Ill., 6-7 May.

1966b. "The study of urban Africa." Journal of Administration Overseas 5(2):124-127.

1968a. "Development administration and semi-urban
areas." Rural Africana 4:20-23.

1968b. "The relationship between legal authority and
sociopolitical influence in urban Africa. In The
government of African cities, pp. 89-06. Lincoln
University, Pennsylvania, Lincoln University.

1970. "Methodology, technology, and the study of
African elites." African Studies Review 13:95-103.

In press. "Labor union activity and dysemployment in
Africa." Manpower and Unemployment Newsletter 4(1),
1971.

Hanna, William John, and Judith Lynne Hanna. 1963a.
"University field notes." Unpublished manuscript.

1963b. "Urban field notes." Unpublished manuscript.

1965a. "Political elites and political integration
in East and West Africa." Paper read at the Michigan
State University African Studies Seminar, March.

1965b. "The political structure of urban-centered
African communities." In Horace Miner, ed., The city
in modern Africa. New York, Frederick A. Praeger,

pp. 151-184.

1966a. "Political integration and elite recruitment in Umuahia and Mbale." Paper read at the Annual Meeting of the African Studies Association, Bloomington, October.

1966b. "The problem of ethnicity and factionalism in African survey research." Public Opinion Quarterly 30:290-294.

1967a. "The integrative role of urban Africa's middleplaces and middlemen." Civilisations 17:12-27.

1967b. "Research report." African Urban Notes 2(4): 20-23.

1968. Polyethnicity and political integration in Umuahia and Mbale. CAG Occasional Paper. Washington, D.C., American Society for Public Administration.

1969a. "Influence and influentials in two urban-centered African communities." Comparative Politics 2:17-39.

1969b. "Polyethnicity and political integration in Umuahia and Mbale." In Robert T. Daland, ed., Comparative urban research. Beverly Hills, Sage Publications, pp. 163-202.

Hapgood, David. 1962. "Unions in search of their roles." Africa Today 9(5):7-8.

Harbison, Frederic. 1965. "Unemployment and development in Africa." Remarks prepared for the African Research Committee Conference on Unemployment in Africa. Evanston, Ill., 6-7 May.

Harlow, Vincent. 1955. "Tribalism in Africa." Journal of African Administration 7:17-20.

Harmsworth, J. 1963. "Peasant agricultural labour organisation in four selected areas of Eastern Uganda." Inter-African Labour Institute Bulletin

10:452-463.

Harrell, Roger H. 1966. "Governmental capacity in developing nations: A survey of urbanization in Tunisia." Maghreb Digest 4(9 and 10):5-36.*

Harries-Jones, Peter. 1964. "Marital disputes and the process of conciliation in a Copperbelt town." Rhodes-Livingstone Journal, No. 35:29-72.

1969. "'Home-boy' ties and political organization in a copperbelt township." In J. Clyde Mitchell, ed., Social networks in urban situations: Analyses of personal relationships in Central African towns. Manchester, Manchester University Press, pp. 297-347.

Harris, Chauncy D. 1943. "A functional classification of cities in the United States." Geographical Review 33:86-99.**

Harris, Marvin. 1959. "Labour emigration among the Mocambique Thonga: Cultural and political factors." Africa 29:50-64.*

Harsanyi, John C. 1956. "Approaches to the bargaining problem before and after the theory of games: A critical discussion of Zeuthen's, Hicks', and Nash's theories." Econometrica 24: 144-157.**

1962a. "Measurement of social power in n-person reciprocal power situations." Behavioral Science 7:81-91.**

1962b. "Measurement of social power, opportunity costs, and the theory of two-person bargaining games." Behavioral Science 7:67-80.**

1963. "A simplified bargaining model for the n-person cooperative game." International Economic Review 4: 194-220.**

1966. "A bargaining model for social status in informal groups and formal organizations." Behavioral Science 11 (5):357-369.**

Hart, Hornell. 1957. "The hypothesis of cultural lag: A present-day view." In Francis R. Allen, Hornell Hart, Delbert C. Miller, William F. Ogburn, and Meyer F. Nimkoff, eds., Technology and social change. New York, Appleton-Century-Crofts, pp. 417-434.**

Hart, J. F. et al. 1968. "Dying village and some notions about urban growth." Economic Geography 44: 343-349.

Hartshorne, K. B. 1950. "The background to education in the urban areas of South Africa." Overseas Education 22:26-30.*

Harvey, Milton. 1966. "Sierra Leone's largest provincial town." Sierra Leone Studies, No. 18:29-42.

Harvey, Milton, and John C. Dewdney. 1967. "Planning problems in Freetown." Paper read at the Freetown Symposium, Institute of African Studies, The University College of Sierra Leone, Freetown.

Hassinger, Edward. 1961. "Social relations between centralized and local social systems." Rural Sociology 26:354-364.**

Hatt, Paul. 1945. "Spatial patterns in a polyethnic area." American Sociological Review 10:352-356.**

Hauser, A. n.d. L'absentéisme et la mobilité des travailleurs des industries manufacturières de la région de Dakar (The absenteeism and worker mobility in the manufacturing industries of the Dakar region). Dakar, Université de Dakar, Institut Francais d'Afrique Noire.

———. 1954. "Les industries de transformation de la région de Dakar" ("Processing industries in the Dakar region"). In Centre IFAN, L'agglomération Dakaroise: quelques aspects sociologiques et démographiques (Urban Dakar: Some sociological and demographic aspects). (Etudes Sénégalaises No. 5) Saint Louis du Sénégal, pp. 69-83.

1956. "The mechanization of agriculture in tropical Africa." In International African Institute, <u>Social implications</u> of <u>industrialization</u> <u>and</u> <u>urbanization</u> <u>in Africa south of the Sahara</u>. Paris, UNESCO, pp. 546-556.

Hauser, M. A. 1963. "Quelques données factuelles et attitudinales sur un groupe de travailleurs en milieu urbain" ("Some factual and attitudinal data on a group of workers in the urban environment"). In University of Edinburgh, Centre of African Studies, <u>Urbanization in African social change:</u> <u>Proceedings of the Inaugural Seminar held in the Centre, January 5-7</u>. Edinburgh, pp. 186-195.

Hauser, Philip M. 1957. "World and Asian urbanization in relation to economic development and social change: Introduction to the seminar on urbanization in the Ecafe Region." In Philip M. Hauser, ed., <u>Urbanization in Asia and the Far East</u>. Calcutta, UNESCO, pp. 53-95.**

1958. "On the impact of urbanism on social organization, human nature and the political order." Confluence 7:57-69.**

1961. <u>On the impact of population and community changes on local government</u>. (Seventh Annual Wherrett Lecture on Local Government) Pittsburgh, Pa., University of Pittsburgh, Institute of Local Government.**

1963. "The social, economic, and technological problems of rapid urbanization." In Bert F. Hoselitz and Wilbert E. Moore, eds., <u>Industrialization and society</u>. The Hague, Mouton, pp. 199-217.**

1965. "Urbanization: An overview." In Philip M. Hauser and Leo F. Schnore, eds., <u>The study of urbanization</u>. New York, John Wiley & Sons, pp. 1-47.**

1966. <u>Handbook for social research in urban areas</u>. New York, UNESCO.**

Hawley, Amos H. 1964. "World urbanization: Trends and prospects." In Ronald Freedman, ed., Population: The vital revolution. New York, Doubleday and Company (Anchor Books), pp. 70-83.**

Heads, J. 1959. "Urbanization and economic progress." In Nigerian Institute of Social and Economic Research, Conference proceedings. Ibadan, pp. 65-73.

Heath, F. M. N. 1953. "The growth of African councils on the Copperbelt of Northern Rhodesia." Journal of African Administration 5(3):123-132.

Hellmann, Ellen P. 1949. "Urban areas." In Ellen Hellmann, ed., Handbook on race relations in South Africa. London, Oxford University Press, pp. 229-274.*

1950. "The native in the towns." In I. Schapera, ed., The Bantu-speaking tribes of South Africa. London, Routledge and Kegan Paul, pp. 405-434.*

1956. "The development of social groupings among urban Africans in the Union of South Africa." In International African Institute, Social implications of industrialization and urbanization in Africa south of the Sahara. Paris, UNESCO, pp. 724-743.

Hemphill, J. K. 1949. Situation factor in leadership. Columbus, Ohio State University Studies, Bureau of Research Monographs.**

Henderson, J. 1959. Africa, social change and mental health. New York, World Federation for Mental Health.

Henderson, Richard N. 1966. "Generalized cultures and evolutionary adaptability: A comparison of urban Efik and Ibo in Nigeria." Ethnology 5:365-391.

Hennin, Roger. 1965. "Les structures familiales en milieu urbain" ("Family structures in an urban environment"). Problemes Sociaux Congolais, No. 68:3-90.

Herrick, B. 1966. Urban migration and economic development in Chile. Cambridge, M.I.T. Press.**

Hershfield, Alan F. 1968. "Village leaders and the
modernization of agriculture: A study of leaders in
fifty-two Ibo villages." Unpublished doctoral dissertation, Indiana University.

Herskovits, Melville J. 1962. The human factor in changing Africa. New York, Alfred A. Knopf.

Herskovits, Melville J., and Mitchell Harwitz, eds.
1964. Economic transition in Africa. Evanston, Ill.,
Northwestern University Press.

Hicks, R. E. 1966. "Occupational prestige and its factors: A study of Zambian railway workers." African
Social Research, No. 1:41-58.

Hicks, Ursula K. 1961. Development from below: Local
government and finance in developing countries of
the commonwealth. Oxford, Clarendon Press.

Hill, Polly. 1960. "A survey of Tema." Economic Bulletin (Ghana) 4(7):13-14.

Himes, Joseph S. 1966. "The functions of racial conflict." Social Forces 45:1-10.**

Hodder, B. W. 1962-1963. "Badagri I: Slave port and
mission centre; II: One-hundred years of change."
Nigerian Geographical Journal 5(2):75-86 and 6(1):
17-30.

———— 1967. "The markets of Ibadan." In P.C. Lloyd, A.L.
Mabogunje, and B. Awe, eds., The city of Ibadan: A
symposium on its structure and development. London,
Cambridge University Press, pp. 173-190.

Hodge, Peter. 1959. "Community development in towns."
Community Development Bulletin 10(2):26-30.**

Hodgkin, Thomas. 1956. "The African middle class."
Corona 8(3):85-88.

1957a. "Letter to Biobaku." Odu, No. 4:42.

1957b. Nationalism in colonial Africa. New York,
New York University Press. (Extract reprinted as
"Africa's new towns," The Student 6 [11]:24-29,
1962.)

1964. "A note on the language of African national-
ism." In William John Hanna, ed., Independent Black
Africa: The politics of freedom. Chicago, Rand
McNally, pp. 235-252.

Hodgkin, Thomas, and Ruth Schachter Morgenthau. 1964.
"Mali." In James Smoot Coleman and Carl G. Rosberg,
Jr., eds., Political parties and national integra-
tion in tropical Africa. Berkeley, University of
California Press, pp. 216-258.

Hoffman, Martin L. 1951. "A study of some psycho-
dynamic determinants of compulsive conformity in a
task involving linear judgments. Unpublished doctoral dissertation, University of Michigan.**

Hoffmann-Burchardi, H. 1964. "Die Yoruba Städte in
Sudwest-Nigerien" ("The Yoruba State in Southwest
Nigeria"). Erdkunde 18:206-253.

Hogg, Thomas Clark. 1965. "Urban immigrants and associations in sub-Saharan Africa." Unpublished doctoral dissertation, University of Oregon.

Holden, David E. W. 1965. "Associations as reference
groups: An approach to the problem." Rural Sociology 30(4):63-74.**

Holden, Matthew, Jr. 1964. "The governance of the metropolis as a problem in diplomacy." Journal of
Politics 26:627-647.**

1966. "Ethnic accommodation in a historical case."
Comparative Studies in Society and History 8:

168-180.**

Holland, S. W. C. 1963. "Recent developments in local
government in Eastern Nigeria." Journal of Local
Administration Overseas 2:3-15.

Hollingsworth, L. W. 1960. The Asians of East Africa.
London, Macmillan & Co.

Holmes, H. 1950. "Urban schoolboys go to the country."
Rhodes-Livingstone Journal, No. 9:31-36.

Hopkins, Nicholas S. 1966. "Political integration and
elite recruitment in Kita." Paper read at the Ninth
Annual Meeting of the African Studies Association,
Bloomington, Ind., 26-29 October.

1967a. "Leadership and consensus in two Malian co-
operatives." In Local development in Africa: A
summary of a conference sponsored by The Foreign
Service Institute of the United States Department of
State, The Africa Subcommittee of the Foreign Area
Research Coordination Group, and The Agency for
International Development, Washington, D.C., 18-19
July, pp. 28-29.

1967b. "Government in Kita: Social institutions and
processes in a Malian town." Unpublished doctoral
dissertation, University of Chicago.

Horowitz, Irving Louis. 1967. "Electoral politics,
urbanization, and social development in Latin America." Urban Affairs 2(3):3-35.**

Horvath, Ronald J. 1966. "The impact of Addis Ababa
on its surroundings." Paper read at the Ninth Annual
Meeting of the African Studies Association, Bloomington, Ind., 26-29 October.*

Hoselitz, Bert F. 1952a. "Non-economic barriers to
economic development." Economic Development and
Cultural Change 1:8-21.**

1952b. The progress of underdeveloped areas. Chicago,

University of Chicago Press.✹✹

1953. "The role of cities in the economic growth of underdeveloped countries." Journal of Political Economy 61:195-208.✹✹

1954-1955. "Generative and parasitic cities." Economic Development and Cultural Change 3:278-294.✹✹

1955. "The city, the factory, and economic growth." Papers and proceedings of the American Economic Association 45:166-184.✹✹

1957. "Urbanization and economic growth in Asia." Economic Development and Cultural Change 6:42-54.✹✹

1960. Sociological aspects of economic growth. Glencoe, Ill., Free Press.✹✹

1962a. "The role of urbanization in economic development: Some international comparisons." In Roy Turner, ed., India's urban future. Berkeley, University of California Press, pp. 157-181.✹✹

1962b. "A survey of the literature on urbanization in India." In Roy Turner, ed., India's urban future. Berkeley, University of California Press, pp. 425-443.✹✹

1963. "Main concepts in the analysis of the social implications of technical change." In Bert F. Hoselitz and Wilbert E. Moore, eds., Industrialization and society. The Hague, Mouton, pp. 11-31.✹✹

Hoselitz, Bert F., and Wilbert E. Moore, eds. 1963. Industrialization and society. The Hague, Mouton.✹✹

Howton, F. William. 1967. "Cities, slums and acculturative process in the developing countries." Buffalo Studies 3:21-39.✹✹

Hoyle, B. S. 1963. "The economic expansion of Jinja, Uganda." Geographical Review 53:375-388.

Hoyt, Elizabeth E. 1956. "The impact of a money econ-
omey on consumption patterns." Annals of the American Academy of Political and Social Science 305:12-
22.**

Hsieh, C. 1952. "Underemployment in Asia." International Labour Review 65:703-725 and 66:30-39.**

Hsu, Francis L. K. 1943. "Incentives to work in primitive communities." American Sociological Review 8:
638-642.**

Hudson, R. S. 1957. "Urbanization--Problems and policies: Basic problems of urban administration in
Africa." In Town and Country Planning Summer School:
Report of proceedings. Oxford University, pp. 107-
110.

Hunter, Floyd. 1963. Community power structure: A study
of decision makers. Garden City, Anchor Books.**

Hyet, Edouard L. 1954. "Poto-Poto, le 'villate boueux',
se transforme en cité modèle" ("Poto-Poto, 'the
muddy village,' changes itself into a model city").
France d'Outre-Mer, No. 296:14-15, 17.

Ianni, Francis A. J. 1957. "Residential and occupational mobility as indices of the acculturation of
an ethnic group." Social Forces 36:65-72.**

Ibbotson, P. 1945. "The urban native problem." Nada
22:35-44.*

1946. "Urbanization in Southern Rhodesia." Africa
16:73-82.*

1956a. "Survey of juvenile delinquency in Southern
Rhodesia." In International African Institute,
Social implications of industrialization and urbanization in Africa south of the Sahara. Paris, UNESCO,
pp. 170-172.*

1956b. "Survey of urban African conditions in
Southern Rhodesia." In International African Insti-

288 *Urban Dynamics in Black Africa*

tute, <u>Social implications of industrialization and
urbanization in Africa south of the Sahara</u>. Paris,
UNESCO, pp. 166-169.*

Idenburg, P. J. 1957. "Ethnic and cultural pluralism
in intertropical communities: A social aspect." In
International Institute of Differing Civilizations,
<u>Ethnic and cultural pluralism in intertropical com-
munities</u>. Brussels, pp. 594-620 (even).**

Idowu, E. B. 1967. "Traditional religion and Christianity." In P. C. Lloyd, A. L. Mabogunje, and B. Awe,
eds., <u>The city of Ibadan: A symposium on its structure and development</u>. London, Cambridge University
Press, pp. 235-248.

Imoagene, Stephen Oshomha. 1966. "Problems and mechanisms of immigrant adjustment: Some socio-psycho-
logical aspects of urbanization." Unpublished
master's thesis, University of Ibadan.

1967. "Mechanisms of immigrant adjustment in a West
African urban community." Nigerian Journal of Economic and Social Studies 9(1):51-66.

Inkeles, Alex. 1970. "Exposure to urban life held aid
to psychic health." The New York Times, 26 May,
p. 22.**

Institut Français d'Afrique Noire. 1954. <u>L'agglomération dakaroise: Quelques aspects sociologiques et
démographiques</u> (Urban Dakar: <u>Some sociological and
demographic aspects</u>). Sénégal, Saint Louis du Sénégal.

International Institute of Differing Civilizations.
1952. <u>The "pull" exerted by urban and industrial
centres in countries in course of industrialization</u>.
(Record of the 27th Meeting held in Florence from
4-8 June) Brussels.**

1956. <u>Development of a middle class in tropical and
sub-tropical countries</u>. (Record of the 29th Session
held in London from 13-16 September) Brussels.**

1957. Ethnic and cultural pluralism in intertropical
communities. (Report of the 30th Meeting held in
Lisbon from 15-18 April) Brussells.**

International Labour Organisation. 1936. "Recruiting
policy in Nyasaland." International Labour Review
33:88-89.

1960a. Report of the Director-General. (First African Regional Conference, 1960, Report I) Geneva.

1960b. Why labor leaves the land, a comparative
study of the movement of labor out of agriculture.
(Studies and Reports, n.s., No. 59) Geneva.

1961. "Social security in Africa south of the Sahara."
International Labour Review 84:144-174.

Izzett, A. 1961. "Family life among the Yoruba, in
Lagos, Nigeria." In Aidan Southall, ed., Social
change in modern Africa. London, Oxford University
Press, pp. 305-315.

Jackson, I. C. 1956. Advance in Africa: A study in community development in East Nigeria. London, Oxford
University Press.

Jaco, E. Gartly. 1959. "Social stress and mental ill-
ness in the community." In Marvin B. Sussman, ed.,
Community structure and analysis. New York, Thomas
Y. Crowell Company, pp. 388-409.**

Jacob, Philip E. 1964. "The influence of values in
political integration." In Philip E. Jacob and James
V. Toscana, eds., The integration of political communities. Philadelphia, J. B. Lippincott Company,
pp. 209-246.**

Jacob, Philip E., James J. Flink, and Hedvah L. Schuch-
man. 1962. "Values and their function in decisionmaking." American Behavioral Scientist 5(9), Supplement.**

Jacob, Philip E., and Henry Teune. 1964. "The integra-

tive process: Guidelines for analysis of the bases
of political community." In Philip E. Jacob and
James V. Toscano, eds., The integration of political
communities. Philadelphia, J. B. Lippincott Company,
pp. 1-45.✲✲

Jacob, Philip E., and James V. Toscano, eds. 1964. The
integration of political communities. Philadelphia,
J. B. Lippincott Company.✲✲

Jacobs, B. L. 1965. "The state of the Uganda Civil Service two years after independence." In East African
Institute of Social Research, January Conference Proceedings.

Jacobson, David Ellis. 1967. "Social order among urban
Africans: A study of elite Africans in Mbale, Uganda."
Unpublished doctoral dissertation, University of
Rochester.

Jahoda, G. 1953. "Urban adolescents' views on social
changes in the Gold Coast." In (Proceedings of the)
Second Annual Conference of the West African Institute of Social and Economic Research. Ibadan, University College Ibadan, pp. 51-72.

Jakobson, Leo, and Ved Prakash. 1967. "Urbanization and
regional planning in India." Urban Affairs 2(3):36-
65.✲✲

Janis, Irving L. 1958. Psychological stress. New York,
John Wiley & Sons.✲✲

Janowitz, Morris, ed. 1961. Community political systems. Glencoe, Ill., Free Press.✲✲

Jarrett, H. Reginald. 1951. "Bathurst: Port of the
Gambia River." Geography 36:98-107.

1955. "The port and town of Freetown." Geography 40:
108-118.

1956. "Some aspects of the urban geography of Freetown, Sierra Leone." Geographical Review 46:334-354.

Jaulin, Robert. 1957. "Du pluralism d'ethnies aefien-
nes" ("On the ethnic pluralism of French Equatorial
Africans"). In International Institute of Differing
Civilizations, Ethnic and cultural pluralism in intertropical communities. Brussels, pp. 181-188.

Jenkins, George D. 1965a. "The career of Alhaji Ade-
goke Adelabu: Africa in transition." Paper read at
the Eighth Annual Meeting of the African Studies
Association, 27-30 October.

1965b. "Politics in Ibadan." Unpublished doctoral
dissertation, Northwestern University.

1967a. "Africa as it urbanizes: An overview of current research." Urban Affairs 2(3):66-80.

1967b. "An informal political economy." In Jeffrey
Butler and A. A. Castagno, eds., Boston University
Papers on Africa. New York, Frederick A. Praeger,
pp. 166-194.

1967c. "Government and politics in Ibadan." In P. C.
Lloyd, A. L. Mabogunje, and B. Awe, eds., The city
of Ibadan: A symposium on its structure and development. London, Cambridge University Press, pp. 213-
234.

1968. "Urban violence in Africa." American Behavioral Scientist 11:37-39.

Johnson, A. W. 1963. "Abeokuta." Nigerian Geographical
Journal 6(2):89-95.

Johnson, Lyndon B. 1966. Remarks of the President on
occasion of third anniversary of the Organization
of African Unity. Washington, D.C., Office of the
White House Press Secretary.

Johnson, R. W. M. 1967. "Disguised unemployment and
the village economy." African Social Research, No.
3:228-233.

Jones, Emrys. 1966. Towns and cities. London, Oxford

University Press.✲✲

Jones, J. D. Rheinallt. 1951. "Native housing in urban
areas with special consideration of its social aspects." Race Relations Journal 18:97-124.✲

1953. "Effects of urbanization in south and central
Africa." African Affairs 52:37-44.

Journal of African Administration. 1950. "Local government reform in the Eastern Province of Nigeria." 2:
44-53. ("Memorandum on local government policy in the
Eastern Provinces," adopted by the Eastern House of
Assembly on the 16 July, 1949. Printed by the Government Printer, Lagos, 1949.)

Kabonco, Illunga. 1967. "Pluralisme et intégration--
réflexions sur la dynamique politique en Afrique
noire post-coloniale" ("Pluralism and integration--
Reflections on the political dynamics in post-
colonial Black Africa"). Cahiers Economiques et
Sociaux 5(1):121-142.

Kagame, Alexis. 1957. "La pluralisme ethnique et culturel dans le Rwanda-Urundi" ("Ethnic and cultural
pluralism in Rwanda-Urundi"). In International Institute of Differing Civilisations, Ethnic and cultural
pluralism in intertropical communities. Brussels,
pp. 268-293.

Kahl, Joseph A. 1959. "Some social concomitants of industrialization and urbanization." Human Organization 18:53-74.

Kamarck, Andrew M. 1964. "The development of the economic infrastructure." In Melville J. Herskovits and
Mitchell Harwitz, eds., Economic transition in
Africa. Evanston, Northwestern University Press, pp.
263-276.

1967. The economics of African development. New York,
Frederick A. Praeger.

Kamau, J. 1965. "Problems of African business enter-

prise." In East African Institute of Social Research,
January Conference Proceedings.

Kamoga, F. K. 1965. "Future of primary school leavers
in Uganda." Inter-African Labour Institute Bulletin
12:5-18.

Kaplan, Morton. 1957. System and process in international politics. New York, John Wiley & Sons.**

Karmon, Yehuda. 1966. A geography of settlement in
Eastern Nigeria. Jerusalem, Magnes Press.

Katzin, Margaret. 1964. "The role of the small entre-
preneur." In M. J. Kerskovits and M. Harwitz, eds.,
Economic transition in Africa. Evanston, Northwestern
University Press, pp. 179-198.

Kay, George. 1960. A social and economic study of Fort
Roseberry: Part 1, The township; Part 2, The peri-
urban area. Lusaka, Rhodes-Livingstone Institute.

1967. Maps of the distribution and density of African
population in Zambia. Lusaka, University of Zambia,
Institute for Social Research.

Keita, Madeira. 1960. "The single party in Africa."
Présence Africaine 2(3):29-54.

Kelley, Harold H. 1965. "Experimental studies of threats
in interpersonal negotiations." Journal of Conflict
Resolution 9:79-105.**

Kendall, Henry. 1955. Town planning in Uganda. Entebbe,
Government Printer.

Kennedy, T. A. 1961. "The finances of urban local
government in Uganda." South African Journal of
Economics 29:103-116.

Kent, Raymond K. 1962. From Madagascar to the Malagasy
Republic. New York, Frederick A. Praeger.*

Kenya, Committee on African Wages. 1954. Report. (The

Carpenter Report) Nairobi, Government Printer.

Kenya, Ministry of Economic Planning and Development, Statistics Division. 1965. Kenya population census, 1962: II. Nairobi.

Kenya, Ministry of Finance and Economic Planning, Directorate of Economic Planning. 1964. Kenya population census, 1962: I. Nairobi.

Kenya, Ministry of Finance and Economic Planning, Economics and Statistics Division. 1964. Kenya population census, 1962. (Tables, advance report of Volumes I & II) Nairobi.

Kerr, Clark, John T. Dunlop, Frederick H. Harbison, and Charles A. Myers. 1960. Industrialism and industrial man. Cambridge, Harvard University Press.✵✵

Kerstiens, Thom. 1965. The new elite in Asia and Africa: A comparative study of Indonesia and Ghana. New York, Frederick A. Praeger.

Key, William. 1961. "Rural-urban differences and the family." Sociological Quarterly 2:49-56.✵✵

Khaldun, Ibn. 1958. The Muquddimah, I-III (trans. by Franz Rosenthal). New York, Pantheon Books.✵✵

Khuri, Fuad Ishac. 1964. "The influential men and the exercise of influence in Magburaka, Sierra Leone." Unpublished doctoral dissertation, University of Oregon.

1965. "Kinship, emigration, and trade partnership among the Lebanese of West Africa." Africa 35(4): 385-395.

Kiano, J. G. 1966. "Towards economic integration with special reference to racial tensions." In East African Institute of Social and Cultural Affairs, Racial and communal tensions in East Africa. Nairobi, East African Publishing House, pp. 27-35.

Kilson, Martin L., Jr. 1958. "Nationalism and social classes in British West Africa." Journal of Politics 20:368-387.

1964. "Grass-roots politics in Africa: Local government in Sierra Leone." Political Studies 12:47-66.

1966. Political change in a West African state; A study of the modernization forces in Sierra Leone. Cambridge, Harvard University Press.

1967. "The grass roots in African development: The Case of Ghana." In Local development in Africa: A summary of a conference sponsored by The Foreign Service Institute of the United States Department of State, The Africa Subcommittee of the Foreign Area Research Coordination Group, and The Agency for International Development, Washington, D.C., 18-19 July, pp. 16-23.

Kimble, George H. 1960. Tropical Africa. 2 vols. New York, Twentieth Century Fund.

Kirkwood, Kenneth. 1957. "Ethnic and cultural pluralism in British Central Africa." In International Institute of Differing Civilizations, Ethnic and cultural pluralism in intertropical communities. Brussels, pp. 293-324.

Ki-Zerbo, Joseph. 1962. "African personality and the new African society." In American Society of African Culture, Pan-Africanism reconsidered. Berkeley, University of California Press, pp. 267-282.

Kleiner, Robert J., and Seymour Parker. 1963. "Goal-striving, social status, and mental disorder: A research review." American Sociological Review 28: 189-203.**

Knoop, Henri. 1966. "Some demographic characteristics of a suburban squatting community of Leopoldville: A preliminary analysis." Cahiers Economiques et Sociaux 4(2):119-149.

296   *Urban Dynamics in Black Africa*

Knowles, William H. 1960. "Industrial conflict and unions." In Wilbert E. Moore and Arnold S. Feldman, eds., Labor commitment and social change in developing areas. New York, Social Science Research Council.

Kobrin, S. 1951. "The conflict of values in delinquency." American Sociological Review 16:653-661.**

Kolb, William L. 1954. "The social structure and functions of cities." Economic Development and Cultural Change 3:30-46.**

Komarovsky, Mirra. 1946. "The voluntary associations of urban dwellers." American Sociological Review 11: 686-698.**

Krapf-Askari, Eva. 1969. Yoruba towns and cities: An enquiry into the nature of urban social phenomena. Oxford, Clarendon Press.

Kuper, Hilda. 1965. Introduction. In Hilda Kuper, ed., Urbanization and migration in West Africa. Berkeley, University of California Press, pp. 1-22.

Kuper, Hilda, and Selma Kaplan. 1944. "Voluntary associations in an urban township: Western Native Township, Johannesburg." African Studies 3(4):178-186.*

Kuper, Leo. 1951. "Social science research and the planning of urban neighborhoods." Social Forces 29: 237-243.**

1967. "Structural discontinuities in African towns: Some aspects of racial pluralism." In Horace Miner, ed., The city in modern Africa. New York, Frederick A.Praeger, pp. 127-150.

Kuznets, Simon. 1954. "Towards a theory of economic growth." Paper read at the bicentenary celebration of Columbia University, New York.**

1963. "Consumption, industrialization, and urbanization." In Bert F. Hoselitz and Wilbert E. Moore, eds., Industrialization and society. The Hague, Mouton, pp. 99-115.**

Ky-Mamia. 1966. "The exportation of labor from Upper Volta." Tiers Monde 6(24):1043-1047. (Translated in Translations on Africa, No. 341:50-54.)

Labour Department Quarterly Review. 1946. "Labour and employment in Owerri Province." 4(14):24-25.

Lambo, T. Adeoye. 1956. "Neuropsychiatric observations in the Western Region of Nigeria." British Medical Journal, No. 5006:1338-1394.

1960. "Characteristic features of the psychology of the Nigerian." West African Medical Journal 9(3): 95-103.

1961. "Mental health in Africa." Medical World 95 (3):198-202.

1962. "Malignant anxiety: A syndrome associated with criminal conduct in Africans." Journal of Mental Science 108(454):256-263.

1964a. "Mental health in Nigeria." Nigerian Trade Journal 12(3):95-99.

1964b. "Socio-economic changes in Africa and their implications for mental health." Paper read at the Conference on Man and Africa, Addis Ababa.

Lamers, Ernest. 1967. "How fast will the gap close?" International Development 9(1):30-33.**

Lamine, Toure M. 1959. "Les ports de Guinée" ("Ports of Guinea"). Recherches Africaines, Nos. 1-4:63-69.

Lange, Charles H. 1965. "Cultural change." In Bernard J. Siegel, ed., Biennial Review of Anthropology 1965. Stanford, Stanford University Press, pp. 262-297.**

Langner, Thomas S., and Stanley T. Michael. 1963. Life stress and mental health. (Thomas A. C. Rennie series in social psychiatry, II.) New York, Free

Press of Glencoe.✲✲

Lantz, Herman R. 1958. The people of Coaltown. New
    York, Columbia University Press.✲✲

Lanzetta, John T. 1955. "Group behavior under stress."
    Human Relations 8:29-52.✲✲

LaPiere, Richard T. 1954. A theory of social control.
    New York, McGraw-Hill.✲✲

    1965. Social change. New York, McGraw-Hill.✲✲

Larimore, Ann Evans. 1958. The alien town: Patterns
    of settlement in Busoga, Uganda. (Department of
    Geography Research Paper No. 55) Chicago, University
    of Chicago Press.

Lasserre, Guy. 1956. "Le paysage urbain des Librevilles
    noires" ("The urban landscape of Libreville's black
    population"). Cahiers d'Outre-Mer (Bordeaux), No.
    36:363-388.

    1958. Libreville: La ville et sa région (Libreville:
    The city and its region). Paris, Librairie Armand
    Colin.

Lasswell, Harold D., and Abraham Kaplan. 1950. Power
    and society: A framework for political inquiry. New
    Haven, Yale University Press.✲✲

Laude, Norbert. 1956. La délinquance juvénile au Congo
    Belge et au Ruanda-Urundi (Juvenile delinquency in
    the Belgian Congo and Ruanda-Urundi). Bruxelles,
    Académie Royale des Sciences Coloniales.

Lazarsfeld, Paul F., Bernard Berelson, and Hazel Gaudet
    1944. The people's choice: How the voter makes up his
    mind in a presidential campaign. New York, Columbia
    University Press.✲✲

Lazarsfeld, Paul F., and Robert K. Merton. 1964. "Frien
    ship as social process: A substantive and methodologi
    al analysis." In Morroe Berger, Theodore Abel, and

Charles H. Page, eds., Freedom and control in modern
society. New York, Octagon Books, pp. 18-66.**

Lazarus, Richard S., James Deese, and Sonia F. Osler.
1952. "The effects of psychological stress upon performance." Psychological Bulletin 49(4) (Part I):
293-317.**

Lebeuf, J. P. 1953a. "Centres urbains d'Afrique Equatoriale Française" ("Urban centers in French Equatorial Africa"). Africa 23:285-297.

1953b. Ville africaine de Bangui (The African city
of Banqui). Encyclopédie Mensuelle d'Outre-Mer (Paris),
January, pp. 15-17.

1959. "An outline of survey methods for the study of
urbanisation in Africa south of the Sahara." In Scientific Council for Africa South of the Sahara, Housing and urbanisation. Nairobi, Commission for
Technical Co-operation in Africa South of the Sahara,
pp. 106-113.

Leduc, Gaston. 1957. "Racial and cultural pluralism in
tropical societies: Economic aspect." In International Institute of Differing Civilizations, Ethnic and
cultural pluralism in intertropical communities.
Brussels, pp. 550-580 (even).**

Lee, R. H. 1955. The city: Urbanism and urbanization
in major world regions. Philadelphia, J. P. Lippincott Company.**

Leichter, Hope Jensen, and William E. Mitchell. 1967.
Kinship and casework. New York, Russell Sage Foundation.**

Leighton, Alexander H. 1945. The governing of men.
Princeton, Princeton University Press.**

Leighton, Alexander H., T. Adeoye Lambo, Charles C.
Hughes, Dorothea C. Layton, Jane M. Murphy, and David
B. Macklin. 1963. Psychiatric disorder among the
Yoruba. Ithaca, Cornell University Press.

Leistner, G. M. E. 1964. "Patterns of urban Bantu
labour." South African Journal of Economics 32(4):
253-277.*

Lelong, R. M. 1955. "Yaounde: capitale du Cameroun"
("Yaounde: Capital of Cameroon"). A.O.F. Magazine,
No. 8:5-7.

Lemarchand, Rene. 1964. Political awakening in the Belgian Congo. Berkeley, University of California Press.

LeMoal, G. 1960. "Un aspect de l'émigration: La fixa-
tion des Voltaïques au Ghana" ("An aspect of emigration: The settling of Upper Voltans in Ghana").
Bulletin de l'IFAN 22(3-4):446-454.

Lenski, Gerhard E. 1954. "Status crystallization: A
non-vertical dimension of social status." American
Sociological Review 19:405-413.**

         1966. Power and privilege: A theory of social strati-
fication. New York, McGraw-Hill.**

Lerner, Daniel. 1958. The passing of traditional society: Modernizing the Middle East. Glencoe, Ill.,
Free Press.**

         1967. "Comparative analysis of processes of moderniza-
tion." In Horace Miner, ed., The city in modern Africa.
New York, Frederick A. Praeger, pp. 21-38.**

Leslie, J. A. K. 1963. A survey of Dar es Salaam. London
Oxford University Press.

Levine, Robert A. 1966. Dreams and deeds: Achievement
motivation in Nigeria. Chicago, University of Chicago Press.

Levine, Robert A., Nancy H. Klein, and Constance Rae
Owen. 1967. "Urban father-child relationships: An
exploration of Yoruba culture change." In Horace
Miner, ed., The city in modern Africa. New York,
Frederick A. Praeger, pp. 215-255.

LeVine, Victor T. 1964. The Cameroons: From mandate to independence. Berkeley, University of California Press.

Levy, Marion J., Jr. 1966. Modernization and the structure of societies: A setting for international affairs. 2 vols. Princeton, Princeton University Press.✶✶

Lewis, Oscar. "Urbanization without breakdown: A case study." Scientific Monthly 75:31-41.✶✶

Lewis, W. Arthur. 1967. "Random reflections on local development in Africa with special reference to West Africa." In Local development in Africa: A summary of a conference sponsored by The Foreign Service Institute of the United States Department of State, The Africa Subcommittee of the Foreign Area Research Coordination Group, and The Agency for International Development, Washington, D.C., 18-19 July, pp. 30-35.

Leys, Colin, and Malcolm Valentine. 1965. "The party after independence--The case of the UPC." In East African Institute of Social Research, January Conference Proceedings.

Lieberson, Stanley. 1963. Ethnic patterns in American cities. New York, Free Press of Glencoe.✶✶

1966. "The meaning of race riots." Race 7:371-378.✶✶

Linton, Ralph. 1952. "Cultural and personality factors affecting economic growth." In Berthold Frank Hoselitz, ed., The progress of underdeveloped areas. Chicago, University of Chicago Press, pp. 73-88.✶✶

Lippitt, Ronald, Norman Polansky, Fritz Redl, and Sidney Rosen. 1958. "The dynamics of power: A field study of social influence in groups of children." In Eleanor E. Maccoby, Theodore M. Newcomb, and Eugene L. Hartley, eds., Readings in social psychology. New York, Henry Holt and Company, 1958, pp. 251-264.✶✶

Lipset, Seymour Martin. 1959. Political man. New York, Doubleday & Company.✶✶

Litherland, S. 1966. "The Kampala-Mengo regional planning mission." East African Geographical Review, No. 4:57-62.

Little, Kenneth L. 1950. "The significance of the West African Creole for Africanist and Afro-American studies." African Affairs 49:308-319.

1951. The Mende of Sierra Leone: A West African people in transition. London, Routledge and Kegan Paul.

1953. "The study of 'social change' in British West Africa." Africa 23:274-283.

1957. "The role of voluntary associations in West African urbanization." American Anthropologist 59: 579-596.

1959a. "Introduction: Urbanism in West Africa." Sociological Review 7:5-13.

1959b. "The organisation of voluntary associations in West Africa." Civilisations 9:283-300.

1960a. "The West African town: Its social basis." Diogenes 29:16-31.

1960b. "West African urbanization as a social process." Cahiers d'Etudes Africaines 1:90-102.

1962a. "Some traditionally based forms of mutual aid in West African urbanization." Ethnology 1:197-211.

1962b. "The urban role of tribal associations in West Africa." African Studies 21:1-9.

1963. "Studies of urbanisation in Sierra Leone." In Nigerian Institute of Social and Economic Research, Conference proceedings. Ibadan, pp. 73-76.

1965. West African urbanization: A study of voluntary associations in social change. Cambridge, Cambridge University Press.

1966. Some contemporary trends in African urbanization. Evanston, Northwestern University Press.

Litwak, Eugene. 1960a. "Geographic mobility and extended family cohesion." American Sociological Review 25:385-394.✲✲

1960b. "Occupational mobility and extended family cohesion." American Sociological Review 25:9-21.✲✲

1960c. "Reference group theory, bureaucratic career, and neighborhood primary group cohesion." Sociometry 23:72-84.✲✲

1961. "Voluntary associations and neighborhood cohesion." American Sociological Review 26:258-271.✲✲

Lloyd, Barbara B. 1966. "Education and family life in the development of class identification among the Yoruba." In P. C. Lloyd, ed., The new elites of tropical Africa. London, Oxford University Press, pp. 163-181.

1967. "Indigenous Ibadan." In P. C. Lloyd, A. L. Mabogunje, and B. Awe, eds., The city of Ibadan: A symposium on its structure and development. London, Cambridge University Press, pp. 59-84.

Lloyd, Peter C. 1953a. "Craft organization in Yoruba towns." Africa 23:30-44.

1953b. "The integration of the new economic classes into local government in Western Nigeria." African Affairs 52:327-334.

1953c. "Some modern changes in the government of Yoruba towns." In (Proceedings of the) West African Institute of Social and Economic Research. Ibadan, University College Ibadan, pp. 7-20.

1956. "Tribalism in Warri." In West African Institute of Social and Economic Research, Annual conference proceedings. Ibadan, pp. 99-110.

1959. "The Yoruba town today." Sociological Review 7:45-63.

1962a. "Discussion." In A. A. Dubb, ed., The multi-tribal society. Lusaka, Rhodes-Livingstone Institute, pp. 81-82.

1962b. "Tribalism in Nigeria." In A. A. Dubb, ed., The multitribal society. Lusaka, Rhodes-Livingstone Institute, pp. 133-147.

1964. "Traditional rulers." In James S. Coleman and Carl G. Rosberg, Jr., eds., Political parties and national integration in tropical Africa. Berkeley, University of California Press, pp. 382-412.

1966a. "Class consciousness among the Yoruba." In P. C. Lloyd, ed., The new elites of tropical Africa. London, Oxford University Press, pp. 328-341.

1966b. "Introduction." In P. C. Lloyd, ed., The new elites of tropical Africa. London, Oxford University Press, pp. 1-85.

1966c. (Review of)"Kenneth Little, West African urbanization: A study of voluntary associations in social change." Africa 36(2):216-217.

1967a. Africa in social change. New York, Penguin Books.

1967b. "The elite." In P. C. Lloyd, A. L. Mabogunje, and B. Awe, eds., The city of Ibadan: A symposium on its structure and development. London, Cambridge University Press, pp. 129-150.

1967c. "Introduction." In P. C. Lloyd, A. L. Mabogunje, and B. Awe, eds., The city of Ibadan: A symposium on its structure and development. London, Cambridge University Press, pp. 3-10.

Lofchie, Michael F. 1967. "The theory of 'plural society' and the political scientist's study of Africa." Paper read at the Annual Meeting of the African Studies Association, New York, 1-4 November.

Lofchie, Michael F., and Carl G. Rosberg. 1966. "The political status of African trade unions." Maghreb Digest 4(5 & 6):27-39.

Lombard, J. 1953. Cotonou: Ville africaine (Cotonou: African city). Porto-Novo, Centre Institute Française d'Afrique Noire.

Long, Norton E. 1958. "The local community as an ecology of games." American Journal of Sociology 64:251-261.**

1967. "Political science and the city." In Leo F. Schnore and Henry Fagin, eds., Urban research and policy planning. (Urban Affairs Annual Reviews, 1) Beverly Hills, Sage Publications, pp. 243-262.**

Lorimer, Frank. 1964. "The population of Africa." In Ronald Freedman, ed., Population: The vital revolution. New York, Doubleday & Company (Anchor Books), pp. 206-214.

Lorimer, Frank, and Mark Karp. 1960. Population in Africa. Boston, Boston University Press.

Louchheim, Donald H. 1966a. "Brief self-rule finds Africa far from goal." Washington Post, 29 December, pp. 1, 14.

1966b. "Ibos avenge killings by rival tribe." Washington Post, 4 October, p. 1.

1966c. "300 Ibos slaughtered in Nigeria." Washington Post, 3 October, p. 1.

Low, Stephen. 1963. "The role of trade unions in the newly independent countries of Africa." In Everett M. Kassalow, ed., National labor movement in the postwar world. Evanston, Northwestern University

Press, pp. 205-222.

Lubove, Roy. 1967. "The urbanization process: An approach to historical research." Journal of the American Institute of Planners 33(1):33-39.✶✶

Luchins, Abraham S. 1942. "Mechanization in problem solving." Psychological Monographs 54 (whole no. 248).✶✶

Luttbeg, Norman R., and Harmon Zeigler. 1966. "Attitude consensus and conflict in an interest group: An assessment of cohesion." American Political Science Review 60(3):655-666.✶✶

Lux, André. 1958. "Migrations, accroissement et urbanisation de la population congolaise de Luluabourg" ("Migrations, growth and urbanization of the Congolese population of Luluabourg"). Zaire 8:675-724 and 819-877.

1963. "Agriculture as an alternative to wage employment in African economies." Cahiers Economiques et Sociaux, No. 4:32-37.

1966a. "Industrialisation et dynamiques des tensions raciales et sociales dans l'ancient Congo Belge" ("Industrialization and the dynamics of racial and social tensions in the former Belgian Congo"). Anthropologica 8(2):291-314.

1966b. "Unemployment and the changing patterns of urban labor supply in a developing economy." Paper read at the Ninth Annual Meeting of the African Studies Association, Bloomington, Ind., 26-29 October.

Lynch, Kevin. 1960. The image of the city. Cambridge, M.I.T. Press.✶✶

Lynch, Kevin, and Lloyd Rodwin. 1958. "A theory of urban form." Journal of the American Institute of Planners 24(4):201-214.✶✶

Maass, Arthur. 1959. <u>Area and power</u>. Glencoe, Ill., Free Press.**

Mabogunje, Akin L. 1961. "Lagos, a study in urban geography." Unpublished doctoral dissertation, University of London.

1962a. "The growth of residential districts in Ibadan." Geographical Review 52:56-77.

1962b. "The residential structure of Ibadan, Nigeria." Geographical Review 52:56-77.

1962c. <u>Yoruba towns</u>. Ibadan, Ibadan University Press.

1964. "The evolution and analysis of the retail structure of Lagos, Nigeria." Economic Geography 40:304-323.

1965a. "The economic implications of the pattern of urbanisation in Nigeria." Nigerian Journal of Economic and Social Studies 7(1):9-30.

1965b. "Urbanization in Nigeria--A constraint on economic development." Economic Development and Cultural Change 13(4) (Part 1):413-438.

1966. "Urbanization in West Africa." International Review of Missions 55 (219):298-306.

1967a. "A systems theory approach to rural-urban migration." Paper read at the Annual Meeting of the African Studies Association, New York, 1-4 November.

1967b. "The Ijebu." In P. C. Lloyd, A. L. Mabogunje, and B. Awe, eds., <u>The city of Ibadan</u>: <u>A symposium on its structure and development</u>. London, Cambridge University Press, pp. 85-97.

1967c. "The morphology of Ibadan." In P. C. Lloyd, A. L. Mabogunje, and B. Awe, eds., <u>The city of Ibadan</u>: <u>A symposium on its structure and development</u>. London, Cambridge University Press, pp. 35-36.

1967d. "The problems of a metropolis." In P. C. Lloyd, A. L. Mabogunje, and B. Awe, eds., The city of Ibadan: A symposium on its structure and development. London, Cambridge University Press, pp. 261-271.

1968. Urbanization in Nigeria. New York, Africana Publishing Corporation.

Mabogunje, Akin L., and M. O. Oyawoye. 1961. "The problems of the northern Yoruba towns: The example of Shaki." Nigerian Geographical Journal 4(2):2-10.

McCall, Daniel F. 1952. "Urban problems in West Africa" (Summary). In (Proceedings of the) West African Institute of Social and Economic Research. Ibadan, University College Ibadan, pp. 77-81.

1955. "Dynamics of urbanization in Africa." Annals of the American Academy of Political and Social Science 298:151-160.

1960. "Korforidua: A West African town." Journal of Human Relations 8(3-4):419-436.

McClosky, Herbert, and John H. Schaar. 1965. "Psychological dimensions of anomy." American Sociological Review 30:14-40.**

McCord, William. 1965. The springtime of freedom: Evolution of developing societies. New York, Oxford University Press.**

McCulloch, Merran. (See Fraenkel, Merran McCulloch.)

McDonell, Gavan. 1964. "The dynamics of geographic change: The case of Kano." Annals of the Association of American Geographers 54(3):235-271.

McElrath, Dennis C. 1962. "Social change and urban social differentiation: Accra, Ghana." Paper read at the Annual Meeting of the American Sociological Association, Los Angeles, August.

1965. "Migration status in Accra, Ghana." Paper read at the Social Science Research Council's Conference on Urbanization in Africa, Airlie House, Virginia, 1 May.

1968. "Societal scale and social differentiation: Accra, Ghana." In Scott Greer et al., eds., The new urbanization. New York, St. Martin's Press, pp. 33-52.

McEwan, Peter J. M. 1963. "The urban African population of Southern Rhodesia: A provisional analysis." Civilisations 13:267-290.*

McGairl, J. L. 1952. "Urban community development through adult literacy." Community Development Bulletin 4(4):71-77.

McKee, James B. 1958-1959. "Community power and strategies in race relations: Some critical observations." Social Problems 6:195-203.**

McKenzie, H. I. 1966. "The plural society debate: Some comments on a recent contribution." Social and Economic Studies 15:53-60.**

Mackenzie, W. J. M. 1956. "Local government elections in towns." Journal of African Administration 8(2): 61-68.

1960. "Some conclusions." In W. J. M. Mackenzie and Kenneth Robinson, eds., Five elections in Africa: A group of electoral studies. Oxford, Clarendon Press, pp. 462-488.

Mackintosh, John P. 1966. Nigerian government and politics: Prelude to the revolution. Evanston, Northwestern University Press.

McLoughlin, Peter F. M. 1963-1964. "The Sudan's three towns: A demographic and economic profile of an African urban complex." Economic Development and Cultural Change 12:7-85, 158-173, and 286-304.*

McMaster, David N. 1968. "The colonial district town in Uganda." In R. P. Beckindale and J. M. Houston, eds., Urbanization and its problems. New York, Barnes & Noble, pp. 304-329.

McNulty, Michael. 1966. "Urban centers and the spatial pattern of development in Ghana." Unpublished doctoral dissertation, Northwestern University.

McQueen, Albert. 1966a. "Economic deprivation, status frustration, and deviant patterns." Paper read at the Ninth Annual Meeting of the African Studies Association, Bloomington, Ind., 26-29 October.

1966b. "Youth unemployment and political socialization: A Nigerian study." Paper read at the Ninth Annual Meeting of the African Studies Association, Bloomington, Ind., 26-29 October.

Mafeje, Archie. 1963. "A chief visits town." Journal of Local Administration Overseas 2(2):88-99.*

Magid, Alvin. 1965. "District councillorship in an African society: A study in role and conflict resolution." Unpublished doctoral dissertation, Michigan State University.

Magnin, William. 1967. "Latin American squatter settlements: A problem and a solution." Latin American Research Review 2(3):65-98.**

Mahieu, A. 1912. "Les villes du Congo--Léopoldville: Son origine, ses développements" ("Cities of the Congo--Leopoldville: Its origin, its development"). Revue Congolaise 2:125-140, 218-251, and 382-387.

Mair, Lucy P. 1958. "Representative local government as a problem in social change." Journal of African Administration 10:11-24.

1963. New nations. Chicago, University of Chicago Press.**

Makulu, Henry F. 1960. "Patterns of rural-urban development in Africa." Research Group for European Migration Problems Bulletin 8(3):57-62.

Malawi (Nyasaland), Committee on Emigrant Labour. 1935. Report. (The Lacey Report) Zomba, Government Printer.

Malengreau, G. 1956. "Observations on the orientation of sociological researches in African urban centres, with reference to the situation in the Belgian Congo." In International African Institute, Social implications of industrialization and urbanization in Africa south of the Sahara. Paris, UNESCO, pp. 624-638.

Marco Surveys Limited. 1966. Comparative change in public opinion 1964-1966, Nairobi, Dar es Salaam, Kampala: Issues of national importance, No. 14. Marco Publishers Limited.

Marris, Peter. 1960-1961. "Social change and social class." International Journal of Comparative Sociology 1(1):119-124.

1961. Family and social change in an African city. London, Routledge and Kegan Paul.

1968. African city life. Nkanga, No.1. Kampala, Transition Books.

Marsh, Robert M. 1963. "Values, demand and social mobility." American Sociological Review 28:565-575.**

Marshall, Gloria A. 1965. "Yoruba market women in modern Nigeria." Paper read at the Eighth Annual Meeting of the African Studies Association, 27-30 October.

Martin, Roscoe C. 1957. Grass roots. University, Ala., University of Alabama Press.**

Martin, Walter T. 1953. The rural-urban fringe: A study of adjustment to residence location. Eugene, University of Oregon Press.**

Marwick, M. 1958. "The continuance of witch beliefs."
In P. Smith, ed., Africa in transition. Evanston,
Northwestern University Press.

Mason, Philip. 1957. "The plural society of Kenya." In
International Institute of Differing Civilizations,
Ethnic and cultural pluralism in intertropical com-
munities. Brussels, pp. 325-337.

Masse, L. 1954. "Contribution à l'étude de la nupital-
ité et de la fertilité dans l'agglomération Dakaroise" ("Contribution to the study of marriage and
fertility in urban Dakar"). In Centre de l'Institut
Français d'Afrique Noire, L'agglomération dakaroise:
Quelques aspects sociologiques et démographiques
(Urban Dakar: Some sociological and demographic aspects Etudes sénégalaises No. 5). Saint-Louis,
Senegal, pp. 41-67.

1956. "Preliminary results of demographic surveys in
the urban centres of Senegal." In International African Institute, Social implications of industrialization and urbanization in Africa south of the Sahara.
Paris, UNESCO, pp. 523-535.

Masser, F. I. 1964. "Changing patterns of African employment in Southern Rhodesia." In Robert W. Steel
and R. Mansell Prothero, eds., Geographers and the
tropics: Liverpool essays. London, Longmans, Green
& Company, pp. 215-234.*

Mathew, G. 1951. "Islamic merchant cities of East
Africa." The Times (London), 26 June, p. 5.

Mathieu, Marcel. 1959. "Le port de Matadi" ("The Port
of Matadi"). Bulletin de la Societe Royale Belge de
Geographie 83(1 and 2):41-65.

Matthews, David, and Raymond Apthorpe, eds. 1958.
Social relations in Central African industry: Pro-
ceedings of the 12th conference. Lusaka, Rhodes-
Livingstone Institute.

Mauldin, W. Parker. 1940. "Selective migration from

small towns." American Sociological Review 5:748-758.**

Mawhood, P. N. 1961. "Choosing the town councillor."
Journal of African Administration 13:131-138.

Mayer, Philip. 1961. Townsmen or tribesmen: Conserva-
tism and the process of urbanization in a South
African city. Cape Town, Oxford University Press.*

1962a. "Introduction: The study of multi-tribalism."
In A. A. Dubb, ed., The multitribal society. Lusaka,
Rhodes-Livingstone Institute, pp. v-x.

1962b. "Migrancy and the study of Africans in towns."
American Anthropologist 64(3)(Part 1):576-591.*

1963. "Some forms of religious organisation among
Africans in a South African city." In University of
Edinburgh, Centre of African Studies, Urbanization
in African social change: Proceedings of the Inaugural
Seminar held in the Centre, January 5-7. Edinburgh,
pp. 113-126.*

1964. "Labour migrancy and the social network." In
J. F. Holleman, Joan Knox, J. W. Mann, and K. A.
Heard, eds., Problems of transition: Proceedings of
the Social Sciences Research Conference, 1962.
Pietermaritzburg, Natal University Press, pp. 21-
34.*

Mayfield, Robert C. 1962. "An urban research study in
North India." In Forrest R. Pitts, ed., Urban systems and economic development: Papers and proceedings of a conference on urban systems research in
underdeveloped and advanced economies. Eugene,
University of Oregon, pp. 45-52.**

Mazrui, Ali A. 1969. "Violent contiguity and the
politics of retribalization in Africa." Journal of
International Affairs 23(1):89-105.

Mead, Margaret. 1950. "Culture change and character
structure." In Maurice R. Stein, Arthur J. Vidich,

and David Manning White, eds., Identity and anxiety. Glencoe, Free Press, pp. 88-98.✼✼

1955. Cultural patterns and technological change, ed. New York, New American Library.✼✼

Mehta, A. n.d. "The mediating role of the trade union in underdeveloped countries." Economic Development and Cultural Change 6(1):20-23.✼✼

Meillassoux, Claude. 1965. "The social structure of modern Bamako." Africa 35(2):125-142.

1968. Urbanization of an African community: Voluntary associations in Bamako. Seattle, University of Washington Press.

Meir, Richard L. 1966. (Summary of) "Some thoughts on conflict and violence in the urban setting." American Behavioral Scientist 10:11-12.✼✼

Melvin, Ernest E. 1961. "Native urbanism in West Africa." Journal of Geography 60:9-16.

Mendras, Henri. 1954. "Cities and countryside." Diogenes, No. 8:111-117.✼✼

Mercier, Paul. 1954a. "L'affaiblissement des processus d'intégration dans des sociétés en changement" ("The weakening of integration processes in societies undergoing change"). Bulletin de l'Institut Français d'Afrique Noire 16B(1-2):143-166.

1954b. "Aspects de la société africaine dans l'agglomération dakaroise: Groupes familiaux et unités de voisinage" ("Aspects of African society in urban Dakar: Family groups and neighborhood units"). In Centre de l'Institut Francais d'Afrique Noire, L'agglomération dakaroise: Quelques aspects sociologiques et démographiques (Urban Dakar: Some sociological and demographic aspects. [Etudes sénégalaises No. 5]) Saint-Louis, Senegal, pp. 11-40.

1954c. "Aspects des problèmes de stratification

sociale dans l'Ouest Africain" (Aspects of the problems of social stratification in West Africa"). Cahiers Internationaux de Sociologie 17:47-65.

1955. "Le groupement européen de Dakar: Orientation d'une enquête" ("The Europeans of Dakar: Orientation of an inquiry"). Cahiers Internationaux de Sociologie 19:130-146.

1956. "An experimental investigation into occupation and social categories in Dakar." In International African Institute, Social implications of industrialization and urbanization in Africa south of the Sahara. Paris, UNESCO, pp. 510-522.

1959. "La vie politique dans les centres urbains du Sénégal: Etude d'une période de transition" ("Political life in the urban centers of Senegal: Study of a period of transition"). Cahiers Internationaux de Sociologie 26:55-84. (Translated in Prod Translations 3:3-20, 1960)

1961. "Remarques sur la signification du 'tribalisme' actuel en Afrique noire" ("Remarks on the significance of 'tribalism' in Black Africa"). Cahiers Internationaux de Sociologie 31:61-80.

1964. "L'urbanisation au Sénégal" ("Urbanization in Senegal"). In W. Frohlich, ed., Afrika in seiner Gesellschaftsformen. Leiden, E. J. Brill, pp. 48-70.

1965. "Les classes sociales et les changements politiques récents en Afrique noire" ("Social classes and recent political changes in Black Africa"). Cahiers Internationaux de Sociologie 38:143-154.

Mersadier, Y. 1956. "An experimental investigation into urban African standards of living in Thies." In International African Institute, Social implications of industrialization and urbanization in Africa south of the Sahara. Paris, UNESCO, pp. 535-545.

1963. "Quelques aspects du chômage à Dakar" ("Some

aspects of unemployment in Dakar"). Notes Africaines,
No. 97:1-5.

Merton, Robert K. 1951. "The social psychology of housing." In Wayne Dennis, ed., Current trends in social
psychology. Pittsburgh, Pa., University of Pittsburgh
Press, pp. 163-217.**

1957. Social theory and social structure. Glencoe,
Ill., Free Press of Glencoe.**

Meyer, Julie. 1951. "The stranger and the city." American Journal of Sociology 56:476-483.**

Mezu, S. Okechukwu. 1966. "Communalism and local govern
ment." In Lincoln University, Institute of African
Government and Department of Political Science, Proceedings of the Conference on African Local Government Since Independence. Pennsylvania, Lincoln
University, pp. 144-150.

Middleton, Drew. 1966. "Two big problems facing Nigerians." The New York Times, 3 April, p. 10.

Millen, Bruce H. 1963. The political role of labor in
developing countries. Washington, D.C., Brookings
Institution.

Miller, Delbert C. 1957. "Theories of social change."
In Francis R. Allen, Hornell Hart, Delbert C. Miller,
William F. Ogburn, and Meyer F. Nimkoff, eds.,
Technology and social change. New York, Appleton-
Century-Crofts, pp. 72-103.**

Miller, Norman N. 1965. "Village leadership in Tanzania
A preliminary evaluation." In East African Institute
of Social Research, January Conference Proceedings.

1967. "The modern survival of African traditional
leaders: Political syncretism in Tanzania." Paper
read at the Annual Meeting of the African Studies
Association, New York, 1-4 November.

Mills, A. R. 1963. "Biological aspects of the African

family in Sierra Leone." In University of Edinburgh, Centre of African Studies, <u>Urbanization in African social change</u>: <u>Proceedings of the Inaugural Seminar held in the Centre, January 5-7</u>. Edinburgh, pp. 85-89.

Miner, Horace. 1952. "The folk-urban continuum." American Sociological Review 17:529-537.**

1965a. <u>The primitive city of Timbuctoo</u>, revised edition. New York, Doubleday & Company.

1965b. <u>Proposal for a conference on the methods and objectives of urban research in Africa</u>. Ann Arbor. Mimeographed.

1965c. "Urban influences on the rural Hausa." In Hilda Kuper, ed., <u>Urbanization and migration in West Africa</u>. Berkeley, University of California Press, pp. 110-130.

1967. <u>The city in modern Africa</u>, ed. New York, Frederick A. Praeger.

Mirams, A. E. 1930. <u>Reports on the town planning and development of Kampala, II</u>. Entebbe, Government Printer.

Mitchel, N. C. 1961. "Yoruba towns." In K. M. Barbour and R. M. Prothero, eds., <u>Essays on African population</u>. London, Routledge and Kegan Paul, pp. 279-301.

Mitchell, James Clyde. 1951. "A note on the urbanization of Africans on the Copperbelt." Rhodes-Livingstone Journal 12:20-27.

1954. <u>African urbanization in Ndola and Luanshya</u>. (Rhodes-Livingstone Communication No. 6) Lusaka, Rhodes-Livingstone Institute.

1956a. "The African middle classes in British Central Africa." In International Institute of Differing Civilizations, <u>Development of a middle class in tropical and sub-tropical countries</u>. Brussels, pp. 222-232.

1956b. "Africans in industrial towns in Northern Rhodesia." In His Royal Highness the Duke of Edinburgh's study conference on the human problems of industrial communities within the Commonwealth and Empire, 9-27 July 1956, Vol. 2. (Background Papers) London, Oxford University Press, pp. 1-9.

1956c. The Kalela dance. (Rhodes-Livingstone Paper No. 27) Manchester, Manchester University Press.

1956d. "Social survey of the Copper Belt towns." In International African Institute, Social implications of industrialization and urbanization in Africa south of the Sahara. Paris, UNESCO, pp. 159-161.

1956e. "Urbanization, detribalization and stabilization in Southern Africa: A problem of definition and measurement." In International African Institute, Social implications of industrialization and urbanization in Africa south of the Sahara. Paris, UNESCO, pp. 693-710.

1957. "Aspects of African marriage on the Copperbelt of Northern Rhodesia." Rhodes-Livingstone Journal, No. 22:1-30.

1958. "Factors motivating migration from rural areas." In Raymond J. Apthorpe, ed., Present interrelations in Central African rural and urban life. Lusaka, Rhodes-Livingstone Institute, pp. 12-23.

1959a. "The causes of labour migration." Inter-African Labour Institute Bulletin 6:12-46 (even).

1959b. "The study of African urban social structures." In Scientific Council for Africa South of the Sahara, Housing and urbanisation. Nairobi, Commission for Technical Cooperation in Africa South of the Sahara, pp. 99-101.

1960a. "The anthropological study of urban communities." African Studies 19:169-172.

1960b. Tribalism and the plural society. London,

Oxford University Press.

1961a. "The causes of labour migration." In Commission for Technical Co-operation in Africa South of the Sahara, Migrant labour in Africa south of the Sahara. (No. 79) Abidjan, pp. 259-280.

1961b. An outline of the sociological background to African Labour. Salisbury, Ensign Publishers.

1962a. "Social change and the new towns of Bantu Africa." In International Social Science Council, Social implications of technological change. Paris, pp. 117-130.

1962b. "Some aspects of tribal social distance." In A. A. Dubb, ed., The multitribal society. Lusaka, Rhodes-Livingstone Institute, pp. 1-38.

1962c. "Wage labour and African population movements in central Africa." In K. M. Barbour and R. M. Prothero, eds., Essays on African population. New York, Frederick A. Praeger, pp. 193-248.

1964a. "Occupational prestige and the social system: A problem in comparative sociology." International Journal of Comparative Sociology 5:78-90.

1964b. "Opening discussion: Labour migrancy and the social network." In J. F. Holleman, Joan Knox, J. W. Mann, and K. A. Heard, eds., Problems of transition: Proceedings of the Social Sciences Research Conference, 1962. Pietermaritzburg, Natal University Press, pp. 35-41.

1965a. "Differential fertility amongst urban Africans in Zambia." Rhodes-Livingstone Journal, No. 37:1-25.

1965b. "The meaning in misfortune for urban Africans." In M. Fortes and G. Dieterlen, eds., African systems of thought. London, Oxford University Press, pp. 192-203.

1966. "Theoretical orientations in African urban

studies." In Michael Banton, ed., The social anthropology of complex societies. New York, Frederick A.
Praeger, pp. 37-68.

1970. "Race, class, and status in South Central
Africa." In Arthur Tuden and Leonard Plotnicov, eds.,
Social stratification in Africa. New York, Free Press
of Glencoe, pp. 303-344.

Mitchell, James Clyde, and A. L. Epstein. 1959. "Occupational prestige and social status among urban Africans in Northern Rhodesia." Africa 29:22-39.

Mitchell, James Clyde, and S. H. Irvine. 1965. "Social
position and grading of occupations." Human Problems
in Central Africa 38:42-54.

Mitchell, James Clyde, and J. R. H. Shaul. 1965. "An
approach to the measurement of commitment to urban
residence." In George J. Snowball, ed., Science and
medicine in Central Africa. Oxford, Pergamon Press,
pp. 625-633.

Montague, Joel B., Jr., and Bernard Pustilnik. 1954.
"Prestige ranking of occupations in an American city
with reference to Hall's and Jones' study." British
Journal of Sociology 5:154-160.**

Moody, R. W. 1962. "Labour migration in Samia." In
East African Institute of Social Research, January
Conference Proceedings.

Moore, Wilbert E. 1952. "Social consequences of technical change from the sociological standpoint." International Social Science Bulletin 4:280-288.**

1963. "Industrialization and social change." In Bert
F. Hoselitz and Wilbert E. Moore, eds., Industrialization and society. The Hague, Mouton, pp. 299-370.**

1964. "The adaptation of African labor systems to
social change." In Melville J. Herskovits and Mitchel
Harwitz, eds., Economic transition in Africa. Evanston
Northwestern University Press, pp. 277-298.

1965. The impact of industry. Englewood Cliffs, N.J., Prentice-Hall.✼✼

Moore, Wilbert E., and Arnold S. Feldman, eds. 1960. Labor commitment and social change in developing areas. New York, Social Science Research Council.✼✼

Moreira, Adriano. 1957. "Ethnic and cultural pluralism in the intertropical societies: Legal and political aspects." In International Institute of Differing Civilizations, Ethnic and cultural pluralism in intertropical communities. Brussels, pp. 494-528 (even).✼✼

Moreno, J. L. 1941. "Foundations of sociometry." Sociometry 4:15-35.✼✼

Morgan, M. A. 1957. "The 'grassland towns' of the Eastern Region of Nigeria." In The Institute of British Geographers, Transactions and papers 1957. (Publication No. 23) London, George Philip and Son, pp. 213-224.

Morgan, W. T. W. 1965. "Kenya: White settlers under independence." New Society 6(163):11-13.

Morrill, Warren Thomas. 1961. "Two urban cultures of Calabar, Nigeria." Unpublished doctoral dissertation, University of Chicago.

1963. "Immigrants and associations: The Ibo in twentieth century Calabar." Comparative Studies in Society and History 5:428-448.

Morris, H. Stephen. 1956. "Indians in East Africa: A study in plural society." British Journal of Sociology 7:194-211.

1957a. "Communal rivalry among Indians in Uganda." British Journal of Sociology 8:295-306.

1957b. "The plural society." Man: Journal of the Royal Anthropological Institute 57:124-125.

Morrison, Denton E. 1966. "Relative deprivation and
    rural discontent in developing countries: A theoreti-
    cal proposal." Paper read at the Annual Meeting of
    the American Association for the Advancement of
    Science, Washington, D.C., 27 December.✳✳

Morse, Richard. 1965. "Urbanization in Latin America."
    Latin American Research Review 1:35-74.✳✳

Mottoulle, L. 1952. "Aspect social de l'attraction
    exercée par les centres urbains et industriels sur
    les populations Balubas du Congo Belge" ("Social
    aspects of the attraction of urban and industrial
    centers upon the Belgian Congo's Baluba population").
    In International Institute of Differing Civilizations,
    The "pull" exerted by urban and industrial centres
    in countries in course of industrialization. Brussels,
    pp. 304-311.

Mphahlele, Ezekiel. 1964. "African city people." East
    Africa Journal 1(3):3-10.

Munger, Edwin S. 1951. Relational patterns of Kampala,
    Uganda. (Research Papers No. 21) Chicago, University
    of Chicago, Department of Geography.

    1954. "Land use in Accra." Zaire 8:911-919.

Munson, Byron E. 1967. "Structural analysis of the com-
    munity." Paper read at the Annual Meeting of the
    Society for the Study of Social Problems, San Francis-
    co, August 28.✳✳

Murphy, Gardner. 1964. "The internalization of social
    controls." In Morroe Berger, Theodore Abel, and
    Charles H. Page, eds., Freedom and control in modern
    society. New York, Octagon Books, pp. 3-17.✳✳

Mustafa, Sophia. 1966. "Racial and communal tensions
    in East Africa." In East African Institute of Social
    and Cultural Affairs, Racial and communal tensions
    in East Africa. Nairobi, East African Publishing
    House, pp. 52-57.

Mwepu-Kyabutha, Gaspard. 1967. "Quelques aspects des conséquences sociales de l'industrialisation au Katanga" ("Some aspects on the social consequences of industrialization in Katanga"). Civilisations 17: 53-71.

Myrdal, Gunnar. 1944. An American dilemma: The Negro problem and modern democracy. New York, Harper & Brothers.**

1957. Economic theory and under-developed regions. London, Gerald Duckworth & Company.**

Nadel, S. F. 1942. A black Byzantium: The kingdom of Nupe in Nigeria. London, Oxford University Press.

1951. The foundations of social anthropology. Glencoe, Ill., Free Press.**

Namo, J. 1958. Contribution à l'étude démographique et sociologique d'une ville du Togo: Palime (Contribution to the demographic and sociological study of a Togolese town: Palime). (Documents and Statistiques, No. 22) Ministère de la France d'Outre-Mer, Service de Statistique.

Naroll, Raoul. 1964. "On ethnic unit classification." Current Anthropologist 5:283-312.**

Nash, Manning. 1960. "Kinship and voluntary association." In Wilbert E. Moore and Arnold S. Feldman, eds., Labor commitment and social change in developing areas. New York, Social Science Research Council, pp. 313-325.**

Nayak, P. R. 1960. "The challenge of urban growth to Indian local government." In Roy Turner, ed., India's urban future. Berkeley, University of California Press, pp. 361-381.**

Nelson, Joan M. 1969. Migrants, urban poverty, and instability in developing nations. Occasional Papers in International Affairs, No. 22. Harvard University, Center for International Affairs.**

1970. "The urban poor: Disruption or political integration in third world cities?" World Politics 22 (3):393-414.**

Nerfin, Marc. 1965. "Towards a housing policy." Journal of Modern African Studies 3(4):543-565.

Neuman, n.f.n. 1963. "Unemployment, full-employment, improvement of the standard of living, balanced economic development." Inter-African Labour Institute Bulletin 10:387-401.**

Neustadt, I., and E. N. Omaboe. 1959. Social and economic survey of Tema. Accra, Office of the Government Statistician.

Newcomb, Theodore M. 1964. "Motivation." In Julius Gould and William Kolb, eds., A dictionary of the social sciences. New York, Free Press of Glencoe, pp. 447-448.**

New York Times. 1966. "Life in Harlem: View from the back street." September 4, p. E5.**

Nicholas, Ralph W. 1965. "Factions: A comparative analysis." In Michael Banton, ed., Political systems and the distribution of power. New York, Frederick A. Praeger, pp. 21-61.**

Nicholls, E. G. L. 1947. "The local authority and its African citizen." Rhodes-Livingstone Journal, No. 5:56-59.

Nicholson, Marjorie. 1960. "Has trade unionism failed in West Africa?" West African Review, June, pp. 6-9.

Nicolai, H., and J. Jacques. 1954. La transformation des paysages congolais par le chemin de fer: L'exemple du B. C. K. (The transformation of the Congolese landscape by the railroad: The example of B. C. K.). Brussels, Institut Royal Colonial Belge.

Niculescu, Margaret. 1956. "Some aspects of the housing situation in Accra today." West African Institute of

Social and Economic Research 4:105-112.

Nie, Norman H., G. Bingham Powell, Jr., and Kenneth Prewitt. 1969. "Social structure and political participation: Developmental relationships, I." American Political Science Review 63(2):361-378.**

Niger. 1963. Etude démographique du Niger, II: Données individuelles (Demographic study of Niger, II: Individual data). Paris, Ministère de la Coopération, Service de Coopération.

Nigerian Opinion. 1965a. "The political class." 1(5):2.

1965b. "Trends in party politics since independence." 1(9):3-4.

Nisbet, Robert A. 1953. The quest for community: A study in the ethnics of order and freedom. New York, Oxford University Press.**

Njisane, Mlahleni. 1966. "Breaking the 'cake of custom.'" New African 5:15.

Noble, G. W. 1951. "African housing in the urban areas of Southern Rhodesia." Journal of African Administration 3(3):124-128.*

Noel, Donald L. 1964. "Group identification among Negroes: An empirical analysis." Journal of Social Issues 20(2):71-84.**

1966. "Minority group identification and social integration." Paper read at the Annual Meeting of the American Sociological Association, Miami Beach, August.**

Norbeck, Edward. 1962. "Common-interest associations in rural Japan." In Robert J. Smith and Richard K. Beardsley, eds., Japanese culture: Its development and characteristics. Chicago, Aldine Publishing Company, pp. 73-85.**

Northcott, C. H. 1956. "African labour efficiency sur-

vey." In International African Institute, Social Implications of industrialization and urbanization in
Africa south of the Sahara. Paris, UNESCO, pp. 131-
135.

Northern Nigeria, Committee on the Future Administration of Urban Areas. 1953. Report. Zaria, Gaskiya
Corporation.

Nsarkoh, J. K. 1964. Local government in Ghana. Accra,
Ghana Universities Press.

Nyarko, D. A. J. 1959. "The development of Kumasi."
Bulletin of the Ghana Geographical Association 4(1):
3-8.

Nyirenda, A. A. 1956. "African market vendors in
Lusaka: With a note on the recent boycott." Rhodes-
Livingstone Journal, No. 22:31-63.

Nzimiro, Ikenna. 1965. "A study of mobility among the
Ibos of Southern Nigeria." International Journal of
Comparative Sociology 6(1):117-130.

Ocitti, J. P. 1966. "Kitgum: An urban study." East
African Geographical Review, No. 4:37-48.

O'Connell, James. 1967. "The anatomy of a pogrom: An
outline model with special reference to the Ibo in
Northern Nigeria." Race 9(1):95-100.

O'Connor, A. M. 1965. Railways and development in
Uganda. Nairobi, Oxford University Press.

Offonry, H. Kanu. 1951. "The strength of Ibo clan
feeling." West Africa, May 26, p. 467 and June 2, pp.
489-490.

Ogba, Kalu K. 1958. "The development of local government in Eastern Nigeria." Unpublished bachelor's
thesis, Oxford University.

Ogbuagu, Bob. 1961. "Enugu--Coal town." Nigeria, No.
70:241-252.

Ogburn, W. F. 1946. "Inventions of local transportation and the patterns of cities." Social Forces 24:
373-379.**

Ogendo, Reuben B. 1967. "The significance of industrial
zoning to rural industrial development in Kenya."
Cahiers d'Etudes Africaines 7(27):444-484.

Ogundana, Babafemi. 1961. "Lagos: Nigeria's premier
port." Nigerian Geographical Journal 4(2):26-40.

O'Hagan, Desmond. 1949. "African's part in Nairobi
local government." Journal of African Administration
1:156-158.

Okediji, Francis Olu. 1966. (Review of Kenneth Little's)
"West African urbanization: A study of voluntary
associations in social change." (Cambridge, Cambridge
University Press, 1965). In Nigerian Journal of
Economic and Social Studies 8(3):500-508.

Okediji, O. O., and F. O. Okediji. 1966. "Marital
stability and social structure in an African city."
Nigerian Journal of Economic and Social Studies
8(1):151-163.

Okoko, Tunde. 1957. "Religion and politics in Nigeria."
West Africa, February 2, p. 103 and February 9,
p. 131.

Okonjo, C. 1967. "The Western Ibo." In P. C. Lloyd,
A. L. Mabogunje, and B. Awe, eds., The city of
Ibadan: A symposium on its structure and develop-
ment. London, Cambridge University Press, pp. 97-116.

Okot, P'Bitek. 1966. Song of Lawino. Nairobi, East
African Publishing House.

Olmsted, Donald W. 1954. "Organizational leadership
and social structure in a small city." American
Sociological Review 19:273-281.**

Oluwasanmi, H. A. 1967. "The agricultural environment."
In P. C. Lloyd, A. L. Mabogunje, and B. Awe, eds.,

The city of Ibadan: A symposium on its structure and development. London, Cambridge University Press, pp. 27-34.

Omari, Thompson Peter. 1956. "Of sacred things in a secular society--The changing African family system in the Gold Coast." Journal of Human Relations 4(4): 66-74.

1960. "The social services in Ghana." Journal of Human Relations 8(3-4):682-699.

Ominde, Simeon H. 1963. "Movement to towns from Nyanza Province, Kenya." In University of Edinburgh, Centre of African Studies, Urbanization in African social change: Proceedings of the Inaugural Seminar held in the Centre 5-7 January. Edinburgh, pp. 23-33.

1965. "Population movements to the main urban areas of Kenya." Cahiers d'Etudes Africaines 5(4):593-617.

Onwuegbuchu, C. 1963. "Plight of the jobless." Weekly News, June 20, p. 7.

Oppong, C. 1967. "Local migration in Northern Ghana." Ghana Journal of Sociology 3(1):1-16.

Oram, Nigel. 1965. Towns in Africa. London, Oxford University Press.

Ord, H. W. 1963. "Urban family budget studies in Middle Africa." In University of Edinburgh, Centre of African Studies, Urbanization in African social change: Proceedings of the Inaugural Seminar held in the Centre, 5-7 January. Edinburgh pp. 102-107.

Orleans, Peter. 1966. "Robert Park and social area analysis: A convergence of traditions in urban sociology." Urban Affairs Quarterly 1(4):5-19.**

Ortigues, M. C., et al. 1965. "La délinquance juvenile à Dakar" ("Juvenile delinquency in Dakar"). Psychopathologie Africaine 1(1):85-129.

Osgood, Charles E., George J. Suci, and Percy H. Tannenbaum. 1957. The measurement of meaning. Urbana, University of Illinois Press.**

Osman, Mohamed Scech. 1952. "Présuppositions politiques et aspects juridiques et sociaux des migrations et de l'urbanisme en Somalie" ("Political presuppositions and legal and social aspects of migration and urbanism in Somalia"). In International Institute of Differing Civilizations, The "pull" exerted by urban and industrial centres in countries in course of industrialization. Brussels, pp. 406-411.*

Ottenberg, Simon. 1953. "The development of village 'meetings' among the Afikpo people." In (Proceedings of the) West African Institute of Social and Economic Research. Ibadan, University College Ibadan, pp. 186-205.

1955. "Improvement associations among the Afikpo Ibo." Africa 25:1-28.

1956. "Comments on local government in Afikpo Division, South Eastern Nigeria." Journal of African Administration 8:3-10.

1958. "Ibo oracles and intergroup relations." Southwest Journal of Anthropology 14:295-317.

1962. "The development of local government in a Nigerian township." Anthropologica 4:122-161.

1966a. "Elite recruitment and political integration in Abakaliki Township." Paper read at the Annual Meeting of the African Studies Association. Bloomington, Ind., October.

1966b. "The social and administrative history of a Nigerian township." International Journal of Comparative Sociology 7(1):174-196.

1967. "Local government and the law in Southern Nigeria." Journal of Asian and African Studies 2(1-2):26-43.

330   *Urban Dynamics in Black Africa*

Ottenberg, Simon, and Phoebe Ottenberg. 1960. Intro-
duction. In Simon Ottenberg and Phoebe Ottenberg, eds.,
Cultures and societies in Africa. New York, Random
House, pp. 3-84.

Paci, S. B. 1954. "Pointe-Noire: Côte d'argent de
l'A.E.F." ("Pointe Noire: The silver coast of French
Equatorial Africa"). France d'Outre-Mer, No. 296:
18-19, 21, 23.

Paden, John. 1967. "Situational ethnicity in urban
Africa, with special reference to the Hausa." Paper
read at the Annual Meeting of the African Studies
Association. New York, 1-4 November.

Pahl, R. E. 1966. "The rural-urban continuum." Socio-
logia Ruralis 6(3-4):229-327.**

Panofsky, Hans E. 1960. "The significance of labour
migration for the economic welfare of Ghana and the
Voltaic Republic." Inter-African Labour Institute
Bulletin 7(4):30-45.

1961. A bibliography of labour migration in Africa
south of the Sahara. Evanston, Northwestern University, University Library.

Parenti, Michael. 1967. "Ethnic politics and the persistence of ethnic identification." The American
Political Science Review 61:717-726.**

Park, Robert E. 1928. "Human migration and the marginal
man." American Journal of Sociology 33:881-893.**

Parker, Mary. 1952. "Social and political development
in Kenya urban society." Problemes d'Afrique Centrale,
No. 15:12-20.

1956. "Political and social aspects of municipal
government in Kenya." In International African Institute, Social implications of industrialization and
urbanization in Africa south of the Sahara. Paris,
UNESCO, pp. 127-131.

1957. Political and social aspects of the development of municipal government in Kenya with special
reference to Nairobi. London, Oxford University Press.

Parker, Seymour, and Robert J. Kleiner. 1966. Mental
illness in the urban Negro community. New York, Free
Press of Glencoe.**

Parkin, David J. 1963a. "Some aspects of status and
role on a Kampala housing estate." In East African
Institute of Social Research, January Conference
Proceedings.

1963b. "Some ideas on the concept of neighborhood in
the town." In East African Institute of Social Research, June Conference Proceedings.

1965. "Social structure and social change in a
tribally heterogeneous East African city ward."
Unpublished doctoral dissertation, University of
London.

1966a. "Types of urban African marriage in Kampala."
Africa 36:269-285.

1966b. "Urban voluntary associations as institutions
of adaptation." Man: Journal of the Royal Anthropological Institute 1:90-95.

1969. Neighbours and nationals in an African city
ward. Berkeley, University of California Press.

Parrinder, G. 1953. Religion in an African city.
London and New York, Oxford University Press.

Parsons, Talcott, and Robert F. Bales, et al. 1955.
Family, socialization and interaction process.
Glencoe, Ill., Free Press.**

Parsons, Talcott, and Edward A. Shils, eds. 1954.
Toward a general theory of action. Cambridge, Harvard
University Press.**

Parsons, Talcott, and Neil J. Smelser. 1957. Economy

and society: A study in the integration of economic
and social theory. London, Routledge and Kegan Paul.**

Pauvert, Jean-Claude. 1962. Note sur quelques aspects
du 'développement communautaire''' ("A note on some
aspects of 'community development'''). In International
Social Science Council, Social implications of
technological change. Paris, pp. 143-152.**

1967. "Urbanisation et planification de l'éducation"
("Urbanization and the planning of education").
Civilisations 17:30-43.

Pauw, B. A. 1963. The second generation. Capetown,
Oxford University Press.*

Peil, Margaret. 1966. "Unemployment and labor mobility
in Ghana." Paper read at the Ninth Annual Meeting of
the African Studies Association, Bloomington, Ind.,
26-29 October.

1970. "The apprenticeship system in Accra." Africa
40(2):137-150.

Perilhou, J. 1955. "Présentation de Douala" ("Introduction to Douala"). A.O.F. Magazine, No. 8:9-11.

Peterec, Richard J. n.d. The port of Abidjan: An
important factor in the economic development of the
Ivory Coast. Lewisburg, Department of Geology and
Geography, Bucknell University.

1967. Dakar and West African economic development.
New York, Columbia University Press.

Phillips, Arthur. 1952. "Repercussions of migration
movements on the traditional institutions of private
law in East and Central Africa." In International
Institute of Differing Civilizations, The "pull"
exerted by urban and industrial centres in countries
in course of industrialization. Brussels, pp. 412-418.

1953. Survey of African marriage and family life.
Ed. New York, Oxford University Press.

Piault, M. P. 1961. "The migration of workers in West
Africa." Inter-African Labour Institute Bulletin
8:98-110.

Piddington, Ralph, ed. 1965. Kinship and geographical
mobility. Leiden, E. J. Brill.**

Pihlblad, C. T., and C. L. Gregory. 1954. "Selective
aspects of migration among Missouri high school
graduates." American Sociological Review 19:312-
324.**

1956. "Occupational selection and intelligence in
rural communities and small towns in Missouri."
American Sociological Review 21:63-71.**

1957. "Occupation and patterns of migration." Social
Forces 36:56-64.**

Plotnicov, Leonard. 1964a. "Individuals' responses to
problems of urbanization in Jos, Northern Nigeria."
Unpublished doctoral dissertation, Berkeley, University of California.

1964b. "'Nativism' in contemporary Nigeria." Anthropological Quarterly 37:121-137.

1965. "Going home again--Nigerians: The dream is un-
fulfilled." Trans-Action 3(1):18, 21, 22.

1967. Strangers to the city: Urban man in Jos, Nigeria.
Pittsburgh, University of Pittsburgh Press.

1970. "The modern African elite of Jos, Nigeria."
In Arthur Tuden and Leonard Plotnicov, eds., Social
stratification in Africa. New York, Free Press of
Glencoe, pp. 269-302.

Pocock, David F. 1957. "'Difference' In East Africa:
A study of caste and religion in modern Indian
society." Southwestern Journal of Anthropology 13:

289-300.

Pollack, N. C. 1968. "The development of urbanization in Southern Africa." In R. P. Beckindale and J. M. Houston, eds., Urbanization and its problems. New York, Barnes & Noble, pp. 333-351.

Pollak, Hansi P. 1955. The Baumanville community; A study of the first African family location in Durban. Durban, University of Natal, Institute for Social Research.*

1964. "Opening discussion: Industrialization and urbanization in South Africa." In J. F. Holleman, Joan Knox, J. W. Mann, and K. A. Heard, eds., Problems of transition: Proceedings of the Social Sciences Research Conference, 1962. Pietermaritzburg, Natal University Press, pp. 70-75.*

Polsby, Nelson W. 1963. Community power and political theory. New Haven, Yale University Press.**

Pomper, Gerald. 1966. "Ethnic and group voting in non-partisan municipal elections." Public Opinion Quarterly 30:79-97.**

Pons, Valdo G. 1956a. "The changing significance of ethnic affiliation and of Westernization in the African settlement patterns in Stanleyville (Belgian Congo)." In International African Institute, Social implications of industrialization and urbanization in Africa south of the Sahara. Paris, UNESCO, pp. 638-669.

1956b. "The growth of Stanleyville and the composition of its African population." In International African Institute, Social implications of industrialization and urbanization in Africa south of the Sahara. Paris, UNESCO, pp. 229-273.

1961. "Two small groups in Avenue 21: Some aspects of the system of social relations in a remote corner of Stanleyville, Belgian Congo." In Aidan Southall, ed., Social change in modern Africa. London, Oxford

University Press, pp. 205-216.

1969. Stanleyville: An African urban community under
Belgian administration. London, Oxford University
Press.

Popenoe, David. 1965. "On the meaning of 'urban' in
urban studies." Urban Affairs Quarterly 1:17-34.※※

Porter, Arthur T. 1953. "Religious affiliation in
Freetown, Sierra Leone." Africa 23:3-14.

1963. Creoledom: A study of the development of Freetown society. London, Oxford University Press.

Post, Kenneth, W. J. 1961. "Some pre-election public
opinion polls in Eastern Nigeria." In Nigerian Institute for Social and Economic Research, Conference
proceedings. Ibadan, pp. 186-208.

1963. The Nigerian federal election of 1959: Politics
and administration in a developing political system.
London, Oxford University Press.

1964. The new states of West Africa. Baltimore,
Penguin Books.

Poupart, P. 1960. Première esquisse de l'évolution du
syndicalisme au Congo (A preliminary outline of the
development of trade unionism in the Congo). Brussels,
Editions de l'Institut de Sociologie Solvay.

Powdermaker, Hortense. 1962. Copper town: Changing
Africa. New York, Harper & Row.

Powelson, John P., and Anatole A. Solow. 1965. "Urban
and rural development in Latin America." Annals of
the American Academy of Political and Social Science
360:48-62.※※

Prasad, Amba. 1963. "People of Indian origin in
Uganda." Africa Quarterly 2:240-250.

Pratt, S. A. J. 1967. "The government of Freetown."

Paper read at the Freetown Symposium, Institute of
African Studies, The University College of Sierra
Leone, Freetown.

Présence Africaine. 1965. "About the class struggle in
Negro Africa." 25(53):247-251.

Prest, A. R. 1965. "Population as a factor in African
development." Statistical and Economic Review
(United Africa Co.), No. 30:1-16.

Prothero, R. Mansell. 1958. Migrant labour from Sokoto
Province, Northern Region of Nigeria. Kudna, Government Printer.

1961. "Migrants and malaria." Inter-African Labour
Institute Bulletin 8:87-91.

1964a. "Continuity and change in African population
mobility." In Robert W. Steel and R. Mansell Prothero,
eds., Geographers and the tropics: Liverpool essays.
London, Longmans, Green and Company, pp. 189-214.

1964b. "Migrations and social change in Africa." In
W. Frohlich, ed., Afrika im seiner gesellschaftsformen. Leiden, E. J. Brill, pp. 14-34.

1965. "Socio-economic aspects of rural/urban migration
in Africa south of the Sahara." Scientia, No. 59:1-7.

Proudfoot, L. 1961. "Towards Muslim solidarity in Freetown." Africa 31:147-156.

Purcell, John F. H. 1969. "Cross-national comparisons
in the study of community power: Comparative implications from a case-study of Durban, South Africa."
Paper read at the annual meeting of the American
Political Science Association, New York, New York.*

Pye, Faye. 1965. "Aspects of the psychology of South
African women." Race 7:123-130.*

Pye, Lucian W. 1958a. "Administrators, agitators, and
brokers." Public Opinion Quarterly 22:342-348.**

1958b. "The non-Western political process." Journal
of Politics 20:468-486.**

1962. Politics, personality, and nation building:
Burma's search for identity. New Haven, Yale University Press.**

Quarterly Economic Review Annual Supplement. 1967.
"The Congo Republic." pp. 1-18.

Quinn, Brian. 1966. "Some problems of producing an industrial labor force in Africa." Unpublished doctoral
dissertation, Cornell University.

Rado, E. R. 1956a. "The pattern of town growth--Obser-
vations on the growth of Takoradi." West African
Institute of Social and Economic Research 4:113-119.

1956b. "A social and economic survey of Bentsir
Quarters, Cape Coast." In West African Institute of
Social and Economic Research, Third Annual Conference
Proceedings. Ibadan, pp. 37-45.

Rapson, R. N. 1959. Report of an inquiry by Mr. R. N.
Rapson, M.V.O., into alleged irregularities by the
Lagos Town Council in connection with the collection
of money and the issue of permits and the allocation
of market stalls in respect of proposed temporary
markets at Ereko and Oko-Awo. Lagos, Federal Government Printer.

Rattansi, Piyarally M., and M. Abdulla. 1965. "An
educational survey." In Dharam P. Ghai, ed., Portrait
of a minority: Asians in East Africa. Nairobi, Oxford
University Press, pp. 113-128.

Raulin, Henri. 1957. Mission d'étude des groupements
immigrés en Côte d'Ivoire (A study mission on immigrant groups in the Ivory Coast). Paris, Office de
la Recherche Scientifique et Technique Outre-Mer.

Raymaekers, Paul. 1963a. L'organisation des zones de
squatting: Elément de résorption du chômage structural dans les milieux urbains des pays en voies de

développement, application au milieu urbain de Léopoldville (République du Congo) (The organization, of squatting areas: Principals of reabsorbing the structurally unemployed in countries whose urban centers are in the process of development--An application to the urban environment of Leopoldville). (Université Catholique de Louvain, Faculté des Sciences Economique et Sociales, Collection de l'Ecole des Sciences Economiques, No. 88) Belgique, Gembloux.

1963b. "Pre-delinquency and juvenile delinquency in Leopoldville." Inter-African Labour Institute Bulletin 10:329-357.

Read, Margaret. 1942. "Migrant labour in Africa and its effects on tribal life." International Labour Review 45:605-631.

Reader, D. H. 1966. "Tribalism in South Africa." Scientific South Africa 3(4):15-18.*

Redfield, Robert, and Milton B. Singer. 1954. "The cultural role of cities." Economic Development and Cultural Change 3:53-73.**

Reiner, Janet S., and Thomas A. Reiner. 1965. "Urban poverty." Journal of the American Institute of Planners 31(3):261-266.**

Reissman, Leonard. 1964. The urban process: Cities in industrial societies. New York, Free Press of Glencoe.

Reporter. 1966. "Housing." January 14, pp. 21, 23-24.

1967. "African businesses: Probe into why so many fail." September 8, pp. 28-29.

Revista de Angola. 1967. "Aspects of Angolan rural worker emigration discussed." 7(146, 147, 148):no pagination. (Translated in Translations on Africa, No. 628:10-16.)*

Rex, John. 1959. "The plural society in sociological theory." British Journal of Sociology 10:114-124.**

Rhodesia and Nyasaland. 1962. Preliminary results of federal censuses of population and of employees: (1) Industrial and racial distribution of employees. Salisbury, Central Statistical Office.

(Rhodesia) Southern Rhodesia, Bulawayo. 1964. City of Bulawayo: Some facts about the municipal government of Bulawayo, 11th (revised) edition.*

Richards, Audrey I. 1954a. "The assimilation of the immigrants." In A. I. Richards, ed., Economic Development and tribal change: A study of immigrant labour in Buganda. Cambridge, W. Heffer and Sons, pp. 161-193.

1954b. Economic development and tribal change: A study of immigrant labour in Buganda, Ed. Cambridge, W. Heffer and Sons.

1958. "Problems of urbanization and community development in changing societies." In Town and Country Planning Summer School: Report of proceedings. Bangor, pp. 127-136.

1963. "Multi-tribalism in African urban areas." In University of Edinburgh, Centre of African Studies, Urbanization in African social change: Proceedings of the Inaugural Seminar held in the Centre, 5-7 January. Edinburgh, pp. 43-51.

1966. "Multi-tribalism in African urban areas." Civilisations 16(3):354-364.

Richelle, Marc. 1960. Aspects psychologiques de l'acculturation: Recherche sur les motivations de la stabilisation urbaine au Katanga (Psychological aspects of acculturation: Research on the motivations of urban stabilization in Katanga). Elisabethville, n.p.

Richmond, Anthony H. 1961. The colour problem: Revised edition. Harmondsworth, Penguin Books.

Riddell, John. 1962. "Trade unionism in Africa as a

factor in nation-building." Civilisations 12(1):27-
40.

1965. "The housing needs of developing countries:
Some recent trade union initiatives." Civilisations
15(1):31-44.

Riemer, Svend. 1959. "Urban personality--reconsidered."
In Marvin B. Sussman, ed., Community structure and
analysis. New York, Thomas Y. Crowell, pp. 433-444.✲✲

Riesman, David, Nathan Glazer, and Reuel Denney. 1950.
The lonely crowd. New Haven, Yale University Press.✲✲

Riezler, Kurt. 1950. "The social psychology of fear."
In Maurice R. Stein, Arthur J. Vidich, and David
Manning White, eds., Identity and anxiety. Glencoe,
Ill., Free Press, pp. 144-157.✲✲

Riggs, Fred W. 1964. Administration in developing
countries: The theory of prismatic society. Boston,
Houghton Mifflin Company. ✲✲

1966. Thailand: The modernization of a bureaucratic
polity. Honolulu, East-West Center Press. ✲✲

Riley, Bernard W. 1967. "Toward a 'space concept'
theory of migration." Paper read at the Annual Meeting of the African Studies Association, New York,
1-4 November.

Rivkin, Malcolm D. 1967. "Urbanization and national
development: Some approaches to the dilemma (in
the underdeveloped states)." Socio-Economic Planning Sciences 1:117-142.

Robin, Jean. 1954. "L'électrification de Bamako "
("The electrification of Bamako"). France d'Outre-
Mer,No. 292:39-40.

Robinson, R. E. 1949. "The relationship of major and
minor local government authorities." Journal of African Administration 1(1):30-33.

Rokeach, Milton. 1960. The open and closed mind. New York, Basic Books.✲✲

Rokeach, Milton, Hans H. Toch, and Theodore Rottman. 1960. "The effect of threat on the dogmatization of Catholicism." In Milton Rokeach, The open and closed mind. New York, Basic Books, pp. 376-388.✲✲

Roman, Paul M., and Harrison M. Trice. 1966. "Schizophrenia and the poor." ILR Research 11:3-9.✲✲

Rose, Arnold M., and Leon Warshay. 1957. "The adjustment of migrants to cities." Social Forces 36:72-76.✲✲

Rose, Gordon. 1966. "Anomie and deviation: A conceptual framework for empirical studies." British Journal of Sociology 17:29-45.✲✲

Rosow, Irving. 1961. "The social effects of the physical environment." Journal of the American Institute of Planners 27(2):127-133.✲✲

Ross, H. Laurence. 1962. "The local community: A survey approach." American Sociological Review 27: 75-84.✲✲

Ross, Marc. 1968. "Politics and urbanization: Two communities in Nairobi." Unpublished doctoral dissertation, Northwestern University.

Rossi, Peter H. 1960a. "Power and community structure." Midwest Journal of Political Science 4(4):390-401.✲✲

1960b. "Theory, research, and practice in community organization." In Charles R. Adrian, ed., Social science and community action. East Lansing, Michigan State University, Institute for Community Development and Services, pp. 9-24.✲✲

Rostow, W. W. 1960. The stages of economic growth. London, Cambridge University Press.✲✲

Rotberg, Robert I. 1965. The rise of nationalism in central Africa: The making of Malawi and Zambia,

1873-1964. Cambridge, Harvard University Press.

Roth, H. Ling. 1903. Great Benin: Its customs, art and horrors. England, F. King and Sons.

Rottenberg, Simon. 1952. "Income and leisure in an underdeveloped economy." Journal of Political Economy 60:95-101.**

Rouch, Jean. 1956. "Migrations au Ghana" (Gold Coast) ("Migrations to Ghana"). Journal de la Société des Africanistes 26(1-2):33-196.

1961. "Second generation migrants in Ghana and the Ivory Coast." In Aidan Southall, ed., Social change in modern Africa. London, Oxford University Press, pp. 300-304.

Rougerie, G. 1950. "Le port d'Abidjan" ("The Port of Abidjan"). Bulletin de l'Institut Français d'Afrique Noire 12:751-837.

Russell, A. H. 1959. "Urban housing for the unskilled labourer in Uganda." Inter-African Labour Institute Bulletin 6:48-57.

Russell, A. H., and J. R. Hather. 1957. "Urbanization—Problems and policies: Aspects of development within the urban area of greater Kampala." In Town and Country Planning Summer School: Report of Proceedings. Oxford University, pp. 110-125.

Russett, Bruce M., Hayward R. Alker, Jr., Karl W. Deutsch, and Harold D. Lasswell, eds. 1964. World handbook of political and social indicators. New Haven, Yale University Press.**

Rustow, Dankwart. 1956. Politics and Westernization in the Near East. Princeton, Center of International Studies.**

Ryan, Edward. 1963. "Personal identity in an urban slum." In Leonard Duhl, ed., The urban condition. New York, Basic Books, pp. 135-150.**

Sanders, Irwin T. 1958. The community: An introduction to a social system. New York, Ronald Press Company.✲✲

Santigan, Massis Marty. 1965. "Educational activities of tribal unions in Nigeria." Unpublished doctoral dissertation, University of California (Los Angeles).

Sartori, Giovanni. 1966. "Opposition and control prob-lems and prospects." Government and Opposition 1(2): 149-154.✲✲

Sautter, Gilles. 1951. "Aperçu sur les villes 'Afri-caines' du moyen Congo" ("Insight into the 'African' towns of the Middle Congo"). L'Afrique et l'Asie, No. 14:34-53.

Sauvy, Alfred. 1952. Théorie générale de la population (A general theory of population). Paris, Presses Universitaires de France.✲✲

Savvonet, Georges. 1955a. "Les villages de la banlieue thiessoise" ("Suburban villages of Thies"). Bulletin de l'Institut Francais d'Afrique Noire 17B(3-4): 371-387.

1955b. La ville de Thies: Etude de geographie ur-baine (The city of Thies: A study of urban geography). (Etudes senegalises No. 6) Saint-Louis, Senegal, Centre de l'Institut Français d'Afrique Noire.

1956. "Une ville neuve du Sénégal: Thies" ("A new city in Senegal: Thies"). Cahiers d'Outre-Mer 9: 70-93.

Scaff, Alvin H. n.d. "Impact of urbanization on the labor force and economic development: The Kampala case." Unpublished manuscript.

1965. "Urbanization and development in Uganda: Growth, structure, and change." Paper read at the Annual Meeting of the American Sociological Associ-ation, Chicago, 1 September.

Schachter, Stanley. 1951. "Deviation, rejection, and

communication." Journal of Abnormal and Social Psychology 46:190-207.✶✶

Schapera, I. 1947. Migrant labour and tribal life: A
study of conditions in Bechuanaland Protectorate.
London, Oxford University Press.

1956. "Migrant labour and tribal life in Bechuanaland." In International African Institute, Social
implications of industrialization and urbanization
in Africa south of the Sahara. Paris, UNESCO, pp.
205-208.

Schattschneider, E. D., and Victor Jones. 1962. Local
political surveys. New York, Holt, Rinehart and
Winston.✶✶

Schildkrout, Enid. 1969. "Ethnicity, Kinship and politics among Mossi immigrants in Kumasi." Unpublished
doctoral dissertation, Cambridge University.

Schermerhorn, Richard A. 1967. "Polarity in the approach to comparative research in ethnic relations."
Sociology and Social Research 51:235-240.✶✶

Schnore, Leo F. 1965. The urban scene: Human ecology
and demography. New York, Free Press of Glencoe.✶✶

Schnore, Leo F., and Eric E. Lampard. 1967. "Social
science and the city; A survey of research needs."
In Leo F. Schnore and Henry Fagin, eds., Urban research and policy planning (Urban Affairs Annual
Reviews, I) Beverly Hills, Sage Publications, pp.
21-47.✶✶

Schuetz, Alfred. 1944. "The stranger: An essay in
social psychology." American Journal of Sociology
49:499-507.✶✶

Schwab, William B. 1952. "The political and social organization of an urban African community." Unpublished doctoral dissertation, University of Pennsylvania.

1961. "Social stratification in Gwelo." In Aidan

Southall, ed., Social change in modern Africa.
London, Oxford University Press, pp. 126-144.*

1965. "Oshogbo--An urban community?" In Hilda Kuper,
ed., Urbanization and migration in West Africa.
Berkeley, University of California Press, pp. 85-109.

Schwab, William B., and Edwin Eames. 1964. "Urban
migration in India and Africa." Human Organization
23(1):24-27.

Scotch, Norman A. 1960. "A preliminary report on the
relation of socio-cultural factors to hypertension
among the Zulu." Annals of the New York Academy of
Sciences 84:1000-1009.*

Scott, R. D. 1965. "The determination of statutory
minimum wages in East Africa: A case study in the
politics of resource allocation." In East African
Institute of Social Research, January Conference
Proceedings.

Seashore, Stanley E. 1954. Group cohesiveness in the
industrial work group. Ann Arbor, University of
Michigan Press.**

Seck, Assane. 1961. "Dakar." Cahiers d'Outre-Mer 14:
372-392.

Seeley, John R. 1959. "The slum: Its nature, use, and
users." Journal of the American Institute of Planners 25:7-14.**

Seeman, Melvin. 1959. "On the meaning of alienation."
American Sociological Review 24(6):783-791.**

1966. "Antidote to alienation--Learning to belong."
Trans-Action 3(4):35-39.**

Segal, Aaron. 1965. "The problem of urban unemployed."
Africa Report 10(4):17-21.

1966. "What price survival?" In East African Institute of Social and Cultural Affairs, Racial and

communal tensions in East Africa. Nairobi, East African Publishing House, pp. 62-69.

Segal, Ronald. 1966. "Editorial foreword: African trade
unions." In Ioan Davies, ed., African trade unions.
Baltimore, Penguin Books, pp. 7-9.

Seligman, Lester G. 1964. "Elite recruitment and
political development." Journal of Politics 26:612-
626.**

Senegal, Ministère du Plan et du Développement et de
la Coopération Technique, Service de la Statistique
et de la Mécanographie. 1962. Recensement démographique de Dakar (1955): Résultats définitifs, II
(Demographic census of Dakar (1955): Final results,
II). Paris.

Senegal, Ministère du Plan et du Développement, Service de la Statistique. 1964. Résultats de l'enquête
démographique 1960/1961: Données régionales (Results
of a demographic 1960/1961 inquiry: Regional data).
Dakar.

Sesay, S. M. 1966. "Drivers in the transport industry:
A case study of road transport in Sierra Leone."
Sierra Leone Studies 19:86-97.

Sesay, S. M., and P. K. Mitchell. 1967. "The port of
Freetown." Paper read at the Freetown Symposium,
Institute of African Studies, The University College
of Sierra Leone, Freetown.

Seytane, Samba. 1966. "Les classes sociales et les
dirigeants politiques de l'Ouest-Africain" ("West
Africa's social classes and political leaders").
Partisans, Nos. 29-30:44-69.

Shannon, Lyle W. 1957. "Social factors in economic
growth." Current Sociology 6:173-186.**

Shannon, Lyle W., and Elaine Krass. 1963. "The urban
adjustment of immigrants: The relationship of education to occupation and total family income." Pacific

Sociological Review 6(1):37-42.**

Shannon, Lyle W., and Magdaline Shannon. 1967. "The
assimilation of migrants to cities: Anthropological
and sociological contributions." In Leo F. Schnore
and Henry Fagin, eds., Urban research and policy
planning (Urban Affairs Annual Reviews, I) Beverly
Hills, Sage Publications, pp. 49-75.**

Shaw, Max. 1963. "Free men and free unions." Africa
Today 10(6):6-9.

Shepperson, G. A. 1963. "Religion and the city in Afri-
ca: A historian's observations." In University of
Edinburgh, Centre of African Studies, Urbanization in
African social change: Proceedings of the Inaugural
Seminar held in the Centre, 5-7 January. Edinburgh,
pp. 141-150.

Sherif, Muzafer. 1936. The psychology of social norms.
New York, Harper & Row.**

Sherif, Muzafer, and Carolyn W. Sherif. 1953. Groups
in harmony and tension. New York, Harper & Row.**

Shibutani, Tamotsu, and Kian M. Kwan. 1965. Ethnic
stratification: A comparative analysis. New York,
Macmillan.**

Shils, Edward. 1957. "Primordial, personal, sacred and
civil ties." British Journal of Sociology 8:130-145.**

1958. "The concentration and dispersion of charisma:
Their bearing on economic policy in underdeveloped
countries." World Politics 11:1-19. **

1960. "Political development in the new states."
Comparative Studies in Society and History 2:265-
292 and 379-411.**

1961. "Centre and periphery." In The logic of personal knowledge; Essays presented to Michael Polanyi
on his 70th birthday, 11 March 1961. Glencoe, Ill.,
Free Press.**

1966. "Opposition in the new states of Asia and Africa." Government and Opposition 1(2):175-204.**

Shuval, Judith T. 1965. Immigrants on the threshold. New York, Atherton Press.**

Siddel, D. J. 1968. "War towns in Sierra Leone: A study in social change." Africa 38(1):47-56.

Siegel, Bernard F. 1957. "The role of perception in urban-rural change in a Brazilian case study." Economic Development and Cultural Change 5(3):7-13.**

Sierra Leone, Central Statistics Office. 1965a. 1963 population census of Sierra Leone, I: Number of inhabitants. Freetown.

1965b. 1963 population census of Sierra Leone, II: Social characteristics. Freetown

1965c. 1963 population census of Sierra Leone, III: Economic characteristics. Freetown.

Sierra Leone, Commission of Inquiry into the Strike and Riots in Freetown, Sierra Leone During February 1955. 1955. Report. (The Shaw Report) (Sessional Paper No. 1) Freetown, Government Printing Department.

Sierra Leone, Makeni Township. 1957. Report of the Medical Officer. Makeni.

Sigel, Roberta S., and H. Paul Friesema. 1963. "Urban community leaders' knowledge of public opinion." Paper read at the Annual Meeting of the American Political Science Association, New York, New York, September.**

Silberman, L. 1950. "The social survey of the old town of Mombasa." Journal of African Administration 2: 14-21.

1952. "Civic survey of Mombasa old town." Zaire 6: 699-718.

1954. "The urban social survey in the colonies." Zaire, 8:279-299.

1956. "Social survey of Mombasa old town." In International African Institute, Social implications of industrialization and urbanization in Africa south of the Sahara. Paris, UNESCO, pp. 136-139.

Silberman, L., L. W. White, and P. R. Anderson. 1948. Nairobi: Master plan for a colonial capital. London, His Majesty's Stationery Office.

Simmel, Georg. 1955. "Conflict." In Georg Simmel, ed., Conflict--The web of group-affiliations. Glencoe, Ill., Free Press.**

Simms, Ruth P. See Ruth Simms Hamilton.

Simon, William, and John H. Gagnon. 1967. "The decline and fall of the small town." Trans-Action 4(5):52-51.**

Simpson, Dick W. 1968. "The political evolution of two African towns." Unpublished doctoral dissertation, Indiana University.

Simpson, Richard L. 1965. "Sociology of the community: Current status and prospects." Rural Sociology 30(4): 127-149.**

Singer, H. W. 1964. "Demographic factors in subsaharan economic development." In Melville J. Herskovits and Mitchell Harwitz, eds., Economic transition in Africa. Evanston, Northwestern University Press, pp. 241-262.

Singer, Marshall R. 1964. The emerging elite: A study of political leadership in Ceylon. Cambridge, M.I.T. Press.**

Singh, Tarlok. 1960. "Problems of integrating rural, industrial, and urban development." In Roy Turner, ed., India's urban future. Berkeley, University of

California Press, pp. 327-334.**

1965. "The historical background." In Dharam P. Ghai, ed., Portrait of a minority: Asians in East Africa. Nairobi, Oxford University Press, pp. 1-11.

Sjoberg, Gideon. 1960a. "Contradictory functional requirements and social systems." Conflict Resolution 4:198-208.**

1960b. The preindustrial city: Past and present. Glencoe, Ill., Free Press.**

1966. "Rural-urban balance and models of economic development." In Neil J. Smelser and Seymour Martin Lipset, eds., Social structure and mobility in economic development. Chicago, Aldine Publishing Company, pp. 235-261.**

Skalnikova, O. 1964. "Ethnographical research into the present changes in the mode of life of urban population in Africa." In Lalage Bown and Michael Crowder, eds., The proceedings of the First International Congress of Africanists. Evanston, Northwestern University Press, pp. 286-297.

Skapa, Barbara A. 1967. "A select, preliminary bibliography on urbanism in Eastern Africa." Paper from the Publications Program of Eastern African Studies, Syracuse University.

Skinner, B. F. 1966. "Contingencies of reinforcement in the design of a culture." Behavioral Science 11:159-166.**

Skinner, Elliott P. 1960. "Labour migration and its relationship to socio-cultural change in Mossi society." Africa 30:375-401.

1963. "Strangers in West African societies." Africa 33:307-320.

1965. "Labor migration among the Mossi of the Upper Volta." In Hilda Kuper, ed., Urbanization and migra-

tion in West Africa. Berkeley, University of California Press. pp. 60-84.

Sklar, Richard L. 1960. "The contribution of tribalism
to nationalism in Western Nigeria." Journal of Human
Relations 8(3 & 4):407-418.

1962. "A note on the study of community power in
Nigeria." Paper read at the Annual Meeting of the
African Studies Association, Washington, D.C., 13
October.

1963. Nigerian political parties: Power in an emergent
African nation. Princeton, Princeton University Press.

1967. "Political science and national integration--A
radical approach." Journal of Modern African Studies
5(1):1-11.

Slater, Sherwood B. 1967. "The function of the urban
kinship network under normal and crisis conditions."
Paper read at the Annual Meeting of the American
Sociological Association, San Francisco, August.**

Smelser, Neil J. 1959. Social change in the industrial
revolution. Chicago, University of Chicago Press.**

1963. "Mechanisms of change and adjustment to change."
In Bert F. Hoselitz and Wilbert E. Moore, eds., Industrialization and society. The Hague, Mouton, pp.
32-54.**

Smith, Brian C. 1967. "The evolution of local government in Northern Nigeria." Journal of Administration
Overseas 6:28-42.

Smith, Michael Garfield. 1955. The economy of Hausa
communities of Zaria. London, Stationery Office for
the Colonial Office.

1960a. Government in Zazau: 1800-1950. London, Oxford University Press.

1960b. "Social and cultural pluralism." Annals of the

New York Academy of Sciences 83:762-777.☆☆

1965. The plural society in the British West Indies. Berkeley and Los Angeles, University of California Press.☆☆

Smith, R. T. 1961. (Review of) "Social and cultural pluralism in the Caribbean." American Anthropologist 63(1):155-157.☆☆

Smith, T. Lynn. 1942. "The role of the village in American rural society." Rural Sociology 7:10-21.☆☆

Smith, Willie. 1966. "The concept of the African worker." Kroniek van Afrika 6(2):169-181.

Smythe, Hugh H. 1960. "Urbanization in Nigeria." Anthropological Quarterly 33(3):143-148.

Smythe, Hugh H., and Mabel M. Smythe. 1960. The new Nigerian elite. Stanford, Stanford University Press.

Soares, Flaucio. 1964. "The political sociology of uneven development in Brazil." In Irving L. Horowitz, ed., Revolution in Brazil. New York, E.P. Dutton & Co., pp. 164-195.☆☆

Sofer, Cyril. 1954. "Working groups in a plural society." Industrial and Labour Relations Review 8: 68-78.

1956. "Urban African social structure and working group behaviour in Jinja (Uganda)." In International African Institute, Social implications of industrialization and urbanization in Africa south of the Sahara. Paris, UNESCO, pp. 590-612.

Sofer, Cyril, and Rhona Sofer. 1951. "Some characteristics of an East African European population." British Journal of Sociology 2:315-327.

1955. Jinja transformed: A social survey of a multiracial township. Kampala, East African Institute of Social Research.

Sofer, Rhona. 1956. "Adaptation problems of Africans
in an early phase of industrialization at Jinja."
In International African Institute, Social implications of industrialization and urbanization in
Africa south of the Sahara. Paris, UNESCO, pp. 613-
623.

Solus, Henry, and Valere Gelders. 1952. "Aspects juri-
dique (of urbanization): Rapport general." ("Legal
aspects of urbanization: General report"). In International Institute of Differing Civilizations,
The "pull" exerted by urban and industrial centres
in countries in course of industrialization. Brussels, pp. 386-399.**

Song, Mallam Muhammadu. 1960. "Nigerian local government in transition." Journal of African Administration 12:74-76.

Southall, Aidan William. 1953. Alur society: A study
in processes and types of domination. Cambridge,
England, W. Heffer & Sons.

1954. "Alur migrants." In A. I. Richards, ed.,
Economic development and tribal change: A study of
immigrant labour in Buganda. Cambridge, England,
W. Heffer & Sons, pp. 141-160.

1956a. "Determinants of the social structure of
African urban populations, with special reference
to Kampala (Uganda)." In International African
Institute, Social implications of industrialization
and urbanization in Africa south of the Sahara.
Paris, UNESCO, pp. 557-578.

1956b. "Some problems of statistical analysis in
community studies, illustrated from Kampala (Uganda)."
In International African Institute, Social implications of industrialization and urbanization in
Africa south of the Sahara. Paris, UNESCO, pp. 578-
590.

1961a. "Kinship, friendship, and the network of
relations in Kisenyi, Kampala." In Aidan Southall,

ed., Social change in modern Africa. London, Oxford University Press, pp. 217-229.

1961b. Social change in modern Africa, Ed. London, Oxford University Press.

1963. "Race and class in an African town." Sociological Journal 1:24-36.

1965a. "Patterns of urban growth or the growth of urban society in East Africa." Unpublished manuscript.

1965b. "Traditional structure and the formation of elites in East Africa." Unpublished manuscript.

1966a. "The concept of elites and their formation in Uganda." In P. C. Lloyd, ed., The new elites of tropical Africa. London, Oxford University Press, pp. 342-366.

1966b. "Determinants of the social structure of African urban populations." In Immanuel Wallerstein, ed., Social change: The colonial situation. New York, Wiley, pp. 321-339.

1966c. "The growth of urban society." In Stanley Diamond and Fred G. Burke, eds., The transformation of East Africa. New York, Basic Books, pp. 463-493.

1967. "Kampala-Mengo." In Horace Miner, ed., The city in modern Africa. New York, Frederick A. Praeger, pp. 297-332.

Southall, Aidan William, and Peter C. W. Gutkind. 1967. Townsmen in the making: Kampala and its suburbs. Kampala, East African Institute of Social Research.

Sovani, N. V. 1961. "Urban social situation in India." Artha Vijnana (Journal of the Gokhale Institute of Politics and Economics, Poona, India) 3(3):85-105 and 195-222.**

1964. "The analysis of 'over-urbanization.'" Economic Development and Cultural Change 12:113-122.**

Spearpoint, F. 1937. "The African native and the

Rhodesian copper mines." Supplement to the Journal of the Royal African Society 37(144):1-60.

Speck, Samuel W. 1966. "African local government in transition." In Lincoln University, Institute of African Government and Department of Political Science, Proceedings of the Conference on African local government since independence. Lincoln University, pp. 3-10.

Spengler, J. J. 1951. "The population obstacle to economic betterment." American Economic Review 41: 343-354.☆☆

Spiro, Herbert J. 1966. "The primacy of political development." In Herbert J. Spiro, ed., Africa: The primacy of politics. New York, Random House, pp. 150-169.

Spitaels, G. 1960. "Considérations sur le chômage à Léopoldville" ("Thoughts on unemployment in Leopoldville"). Revue de l'Institut de Sociologie 33(1): 55-72.

Splansky, Joel Bruce. 1966. "The concentric zone theory of city structure as applied to an African city: Ibadan, Nigeria." Association of Pacific Coast Geographers Yearbook 28:135-146.

Steel, Robert W. 1952a. "Economic aspects (of urbanization): General report." In International Institute of Differing Civilizations, The "pull" exerted by urban and industrial centres in countries in course of industrialization. Brussels, pp. 112-123.☆☆

1952b. "The towns of Ashanti: A geographical study." In Union Géographique Internationale, Comptes rendus de congrès international de géographie, Lisbonne, 1949. Lisbon, pp. 81-93.

1962. "The towns of tropical Africa." In K. M. Barbour and R. M. Prothero, eds., Essays on African population. New York, Frederick A. Praeger, pp. 249-278.

1963. "African urbanization: A geographer's viewpoint." In University of Edinburgh, Centre of African Studies, Urbanization in African social change:
Proceedings of the Inaugural Seminar held in the
Centre, January 5-7. Edinburgh, pp. 7-13.

Steel, Robert W., and R. Mansell Prothero. 1964.
Geographers and the tropics: Liverpool essays.
London, Longmans, Green & Company.

Stevens, R. A. 1949. "The application of English local
government principles in Africa." Journal of African Administration 1:68-73.

1953. "Progress in local government in the Eastern
Region of Nigeria." Journal of African Administration 5:15-21.

Stewart, I. G. 1963. "Economic analysis, urbanization
and African studies." In University of Edinburgh
Centre of African Studies, Urbanization in African
social change: Proceedings of the Inaugural Seminar
held in the Centre, January 5-7. Edinburgh, pp. 14-
17.

Stone, Gregory P. 1954. "City shoppers and urban identification: Observations on the social psychology of
city life." American Journal of Sociology 60:36-45.**

Stone, I. T. 1964. "An approach to the comparative
study of social integration." American Anthropologist
66(4) (Part 1):805-821.**

Strauss, Anselm L. 1961. Images of the American city.
Glencoe, Ill., Free Press.**

1967. "Strategies for discovering urban theory."
In Leo F. Schnore and Henry Fagin, eds., Urban research and policy planning (Urban Affairs Annual
Reviews, I) Beverly Hills, Sage Publications, pp.
79-98. **

Suffrin, Sidney C. 1964. Unions in emerging societies:
Frustration and politics. Syracuse, Syracuse Univer-

sity Press.✲✲

Sumner, William G. 1906. Folkways. Boston, Ginn & Company.✲✲

Sutherland, Alasdair C. 1956a. "Housing and town planning as instrument of social control in Africa." In West African Institute of Social and Economic Research, Annual conference proceedings. Ibadan, pp. 67-74.

1956b. "Private enterprise housing in the urban area of Kumasi." In (Proceedings of the) West African Institute of Social and Economic Research. Ibadan, University College Ibadan, pp. 120-127.

1958. "Planning law and practice in Ghana." Town Planning Institute Journal 44(6):137-139.

Suttles, Gerald D. 1968. The social order of the slum: Ethnicity and territory in the inner city. Chicago, University of Chicago Press.✲✲

Suzuki, P. 1964. "Encounters with Istanbul: Urban peasants and village peasants." International Journal of Comparative Sociology 5:208-216.✲✲

Swanson, Bert E. 1966. "The concern for community in the metropolis." Urban Affairs Quarterly 1(4):33-44.✲✲

Swift, D. F. 1965. "A critique of the concepts of community organization and community development." International Journal of Comparative Sociology 6(2): 241-255.✲✲

Tandon, Yash. 1965. "A political survey." In Dharam P. Ghai, ed., Portrait of a minority: Asians in East Africa. Nairobi, Oxford University Press, pp. 65-89.

Tangri, Shanti. 1962. "Urbanization, political stability, and economic growth." In Roy Turner, ed., India's urban future. Berkeley, University of California Press, pp. 192-212.✲✲

Tanner, R. E. S. 1964. "Conflict within small European communities in Tanganyika." Human Organization 24: 319-327.

1966a. "Crime and the East Africa child." Kenya Education Journal 2(7):13-15.

1966b. "European leadership in small communities in Tanganyika prior to independence: A study of conflicting social and political interracial roles." Race 7:289-302.

(Tanzania) Tanganyika, Commission to Enquire into Disturbances which Occurred in the Port of Tanga, August 1939. 1940. Report. (The Scupham Report) Dar es Salaam, Government Printer.

(Tanzania) Tanganyika, East African Statistical Department. 1958a. Analysis of total population: Certain analyses by race and sex, geographical area, age, religion and nationality. (Nairobi?).

1958b. General African census, August 1957: Tribal analysis (Part I). Nairobi.

Tardits, Claude. 1958. Porto-Novo: Les nouvelles générations africaines entre leurs traditions et l'occident (Porto Novo: The new African generations between their traditions and those of the West). Paris, Mouton and Company.

Taylor, Councill, ed. 1965. Voluntary associations in the new Africa: African systems after kinship. New York, Selected Academic Readings.

Taylor, G. Brooke. 1961. "The social effect of dispersal." Town and Country Planning 29:36-39.**

Taylor, P. L. 1966. "Local government training in Zambia." Journal of Local Administration Overseas 5(1):11-18.

Temple, P. H. 1963. "Kampala: Influences upon its growth and development." In East African Institute of Social Research, June Conference Proceedings.

Templeton, Frederic. 1966. "Alienation and political participation: Some research findings." Public Opinion Quarterly 30(2):249-261.✢✢

Teune, Henry. 1964a. "The learning of integrative habits." In Philip E. Jacob and James V. Toscano, eds., The integration of political communities. Philadelphia, J. B. Lippincott Company, pp. 247-282.✢✢

1964b. "Models in the study of political integration." In Philip E. Jacob and James V. Toscano, eds., The integration of political communities. Philadelphia, J. B. Lippincott Company, pp. 283-303.✢✢

Theodorson, George A. 1953. "Acceptance of industrialization and its attendant consequences for social patterns of non-western societies." American Sociological Review 18:477-484.✢✢

Thomas, Benjamin E. 1965. "The location and nature of West African cities." In Hilda Kuper, ed., Urbanization and migration in West Africa. Berkeley, University of California Press, pp. 23-38.

1970. "On the growth of African cities." African Studies Review 13(1):1-8.

Thomas, Louis V. 1965. "Les populations africaines" ("African populations"). Revue de Psychologies des Peuples 20(4):363-406.

Thompson, Wilbur R. 1967. "Toward an urban economics." In Leo F. Schnore and Henry Fagin, eds., Urban research and policy planning (Urban Affairs Annual Reviews, I) Beverly Hills, Sage Publications, pp. 135-159.✢✢

Thorsen, Thomas W. 1966. "African local government in transition." In Lincoln University, Institute of African Government and Department of Political Science, Proceedings of the Conference on African local government since independence. Lincoln University, pp. 11-14.

Thorsrud, Einar. 1952. "The social consequences of technical change from the psychological standpoint." International Social Science Bulletin 4:300-319.**

Tietze, C., P. Lemkau, and M. C. Cooper. 1942. "Personality disorders and spatial mobility." American Journal of Sociology 48:29-39.**

Tiger, Lionel. 1966. "Bureaucracy and charisma in Ghana." Journal of Asian and African Studies 1(1): 13-26.

Tilly, Charles, and James Rule. 1965. Measuring political upheaval. (Research Monograph No. 19) Princeton, Center of International Studies, Princeton University.**

Tisdale, Hope. 1941-1942. "The process of urbanization." Social Forces 20:311-316.**

Toffler, Alvin. 1970. "New York faces future shock." New York 3(30):20-29.**

Tooth, G. 1956. "Survey of juvenile delinquency in the Gold Coast." In International African Institute, Social implications of industrialization and urbanization in Africa south of the Sahara. Paris, UNESCO, pp. 86-91.

Tordoff, William. 1965. "Regional administration in Tanzania." Journal of Modern African Studies 3:63-89.

Trachtman, Lester. 1962. "The labor movement of Ghana: A study in political unionism." Economic Development and Cultural Change 10(2):183-200.

Translations on Africa. 1966. "Minorities in Africa." No. 335:34-39.*

Tregar, P. S. 1963. "The primary school leaver in

Africa." Nada, No. 40:17-26.

Trist, E. L., and K. W. Bamforth. 1951. "Some social
and psychological consequences of the Longwall method
of coal-getting." Human Relations 4:3-38.**

Trouwborst, Albert. 1965. "Kinship and geographical
mobility in Burundi (East Central Africa)." In
Ralph Piddington, ed., Kinship and geographic mobility. (Special issue of the International Journal of
Comparative Sociology) Leiden, E. J. Brill.

Tryon, Robert C. 1955. Identification of social areas
by cluster analysis. Berkeley, University of California Press.**

Tuden, Arthur, and Leonard Plotnicov. 1970. "Introduc-
tion." In Arthur Tuden and Leonard Plotnicov, eds.,
Social stratification in Africa. New York, Free
Press of Glencoe, pp. 1-30.

Tugbiyele, E. A. 1962. "Local government in Nigeria."
Journal of Local Administration Overseas 1:225-230.

1963. "Problems of local government in Nigeria."
In Nigerian Institute of Social and Economic Research, Conference proceedings. Ibadan, pp. 54-64.

Tumin, Melvin M. 1962. Caste in a peasant society: A
case study in the dynamics of caste. Princeton,
Princeton University Press.**

Udo, R. K. 1963. "Patterns of population distribution
and settlement in Eastern Nigeria." Nigerian Geographical Journal 6(2):73-88.

1964. "The migrant tenant farmer of Eastern Nigeria."
Africa 34:326-339.

Udoh, O. W. 1964. "Tribal unions in politics." Nigerian Outlook, November 24, p. 2.

Uganda Argus. 1964. "Jobless crowd heckle Kenya minister." July 14, p. 1.

Uganda, Commission of Inquiry into the Affairs of the
  Bugisu Co-operative Union Limited. 1958. Report.
  (Sessional Paper No. 14) Entebbe, Government Printer.

Uganda Commission of Inquiry into the Affairs of the
  Bugisu District Council. 1960. Report. Entebbe, Government Printer.

Uganda, Commission of Inquiry into the Coffee Industry. 1958. Report. Entebbe, Government Printer.

Uganda, Commission of Inquiry into the Cotton-Ginning
  Industry of Uganda. 1962. Report. Entebbe, Government Printer.

Uganda, Commission of Inquiry into Disturbances in the
  Eastern Province. 1960. Report. Entebbe, Government
  Printer.

Uganda, Commission of Inquiry into the Recent Disturbances Amongst the Baamba and Bakonjo People of Toro.
  1962. Report. Entebbe, Government Printer.

Uganda, Committee on Unalienated Crown Land in Towns.
  1957. Report. Entebbe, Government Printer.

Uganda, East African Statistical Department. 1957.
  The patterns of income, expenditure and consumption
  of African unskilled workers in Kampala, February,
  1957. Entebbe, Government Printer.

  1960a. The patterns of income, expenditure and consumption of African unskilled workers in Fort Portal,
  February, 1960. Entebbe, Government Printer.

  1960b. Uganda census 1959: Non-African population.
  Nairobi.

  1960c. Uganda General African census 1959 II(3):
  Tribal analysis for Eastern Province districts--
  Counties and divisions. (Nairobi?).

Uganda, Ministry of Economic Affairs, Statistics
  Branch. 1962. 1962 statistical abstract. Entebbe,

Government Printer.

Uganda, Ministry of Economic Development, Statistics Branch. 1961. The patterns of income, expenditure and consumption of African unskilled workers in Gulu, February, 1961. Entebbe, Government Printer.

Uganda, Ministry of Planning and Community Development, Statistics Branch. 1966. The patterns of income, expenditure and consumption of African unskilled workers in Jinja, June, 1965. Entebbe, Government Printer.

Uganda, Ministry of Planning and Community Development, Statistics Division. n.d. 1965 statistical abstract. Entebbe, Government Printer.

Uganda, Relationships Commission. 1961. Report. (The Munster Report) Entebbe.

United Kingdom Colonial Office. 1950. Report, November 1949. (Colonial No. 256) London, His Majesty's Stationery Office.

_____ 1958. Nigeria: Report of the commission appointed to enquire into the fears of minorities and the means of allaying them. London, Her Majesty's Stationery Office.

United Nations. 1963. Compendium of social statistics: 1963. New York.**

_____ 1965a. Report of the interregional seminar on social aspects of industrialization. (ST/TAO/Ser.C/.74) New York.**

_____ 1965b. World housing conditions and estimated housing requirements. New York.**

United Nations, Committee on Information from Non-Self-Governing Territories. 1955. Report. (Official Records of the General Assembly, 10th Session, Supplement No. 16 [A/2908]) New York.**

_____ 1958. Report. (Official Records of the General As-

sembly, 13th Session, Supplement No. 15 [A/3837])
New York.**

United Nations, Department of Economic and Social
Affairs. 1955. Processes and problems of industrialization in underdeveloped countries. New York.**

1958. World housing conditions and estimated housing
requirements. (ST/SOA/58) New York.**

1963. 1963 report on the world social situation. New
York.**

1968. "Urbanization: Development policies and planning." International Social Development Review No.
1. New York.**

United Nations, Department of Economic and Social Affairs, Statistical Office of the United Nations.
1964. Demographic yearbook, 1963. (Fifteenth Issue.
Special topic: Population census statistics II) New
York.**

1966a. Demographic yearbook, 1965. New York. **

1966b. Statistical yearbook, 1965. New York.**

1969. Demographic yearbook, 1968. New York.**

United Nations, Economic and Social Council. 1957.
"Urbanization in Africa south of the Sahara." In
Report on the world social situation. (E/CN.5/324/
Rev. 1) New York, pp. 144-169.

1962a. Population distribution, internal migration
and urbanization in Africa. (E/CN.14/ASPP/L.3) New
York.

1962b. Report of the workshop on urbanization in
Africa. (E/CN.14/170) (ST/TAO/Ser.C/57) (ST/SOA/
Ser.T/4) Addis Ababa, Economic Commission for
Africa.

1965. World survey of urban and rural population

growth. (E/CN.9/187) New York.✻✻

United Nations, Economic and Social Council, African
Seminar on Central Services to Local Authorities.
1964. Report of the Seminar. (E/CN.14/UAP/37) New
York.

United Nations, Economic Commission for Africa. 1961.
"Leopoldville and Lagos: Comparative study of urban
conditions in 1960." Economic Bulletin for Africa
1(2):50-65.

1964. Patterns of social welfare organization and
administration in Africa. (No. 2) (E/CN.14/SWSA/2)
New York.

1965a. Annual report, 3 March 1964 to 23 February
1965. (Supplement No. 10) (E/4004 [E/CN.14/343/Rev.
1]) New York.

1965b. "Recent demographic levels and trends in Africa." Economic Bulletin for Africa 5:30-79.

United Nations Educational, Scientific and Cultural
Organization. 1958. Social, economic and technological change: A theoretical approach. Paris.✻✻

United Nations Educational, Scientific and Cultural
Organization, Research Center on the Social Implications of Industrialization in Southern Asia. 1957.
Urbanization in Asia and the Far East. (Proceedings
of the Joint UN/UNESCO Seminar, Bangkok, 8-18 August
1956) Calcutta.✻✻

United Nations, General Assembly, Committee on Information from Non-Self-Governing Territories. 1955.
Contributions of the social sciences to the study of
social conditions in the African non-self-governing
territories. (Prepared by UNESCO) (A/AC.35/L.194)
New York.

1961. Social aspects of urban development. (Prepared
by the Secretariat, 12th Session) (A/AC.35/L.335)
New York.✻✻

United Nations, Secretariat. 1959. Approaches to community development in urban areas. (ST/SOA/Ser.0/32)
(ST/TAO/Ser.D/32) New York.**

1960. "Quelques considérations sur la prévention de
la délinquance juvenile dans les pays africains
subissant des changements sociaux rapides" ("Some
thoughts on the prevention of juvenile delinquence
in African countries undergoing rapid social changes."
International Review of Criminal Policy, No. 16:33-
46.**

United Nations, Secretary-General. 1958. Special study
of social conditions in non-self-governing territories. (ST/TRI/Ser.A) New York.**

United States, National Advisory Commission on Civil
Disorders. 1968. Report. New York, E. P. Dutton & Co.

United States Information Agency. 1961. Basic attitudes
and general communication habits in four West African
capitals. Washington, D.C.

University of Edinburgh, Centre of African Studies.
1963. "Discussion." Urbanization in African social
change: Proceedings of the Inaugural Seminar held in
the Centre, 5-7 January. Edinburgh, pp. 18-22, 52-
58, 108-112, 174-180.

University of Natal, Institute of Social Research.
1959. Baumanville: A study of an urban African community. (Natal Regional Survey, Report No. 6) Cape
Town, Oxford University Press for the University of
Natal.*

(Upper Volta) Haute-Volta, Service de Statistique.
1961. La situation démographique en Haute-Volta:
Résultats partiels de l'enquête démographique 1960-
1961 (The demographic situation in Upper Volta:
Partial results of the demographic 1960-1961 inquiry).
République Française, Ministère de la Coopération,
Service de Coopération.

Useem, John, Ruth Useem, and John Donoghue. 1963. "Men

in the middle of the third culture: The roles of
American and non-Western people in cross-cultural
administration." Human Organization 22(3):169-179.✶✶

Uzoma, R. I. 1952. "Universal schooling in Ngwa Clan
of Aba Division, Nigeria." Overseas Education 23(2):
234-236.

van Cauwenbergh, A. 1956. "Le développement du commerce et de l'artisanat indigènes à Léopoldville"
("The development of indigenous commerce and artis-
anship in Leopoldville"). Zaire 10:637-663.

van der Berghe, Pierre. 1964. "Toward a sociology of
Africa." Social Forces 43:11-18.

1965. Africa: Social problems of change and conflict. Ed. San Francisco, Chandler Publishing Co.

1967. Race and racism: A comparative perspective.
New York, Wiley.

van der Horst, Sheila. 1964. African workers in town:
A study of labour in Cape Town. Cape Town, Oxford
University Press.✶

van der Kolff, G. H. 1952. "Social aspects (of urbanization): General report." In International Institute
of Differing Civilizations, The "pull" exerted by
urban and industrial centres in countries in course
of industrialization. Brussels, pp. 264-284.✶✶

van de Walle, Etienne. 1960. "Chômage dans une petite
ville d'Afrique: Usumbura" ("Unemployment in a small
African town: Usumbura"). Zaire 14:341-359.

1961. "Facteurs et indices de stabilisation et
d'urbanisation à Usumbura [Ruanda-Urundi]" ("Factors
and indices of stabilization and urbanization in
Usumbura [Ruanda-Urundi]"). Recherches Economiques
de Louvain 27:97-121.

van Hoey, Leo. 1968. "The coercive process of urbanization: The case of Niger." In Scott Greer, Dennis

368 _Urban Dynamics in Black Africa_

McElrath, David Minar, and Peter Orleans, eds.,
The new urbanization. New York, St. Martin's Press,
pp. 15-32.

Vanhove, M. J. 1952. "Aspects culturels de la detribalisation dans une grande ville congolaise: Leopoldville" ("The cultural aspects of detribalization in
a large Congolese city: Leopoldville"). In International Institute of Differing Civilizations, The
"pull" exerted by urban and industrial centres in
countries in course of industrialization. Brussels,
pp. 542-560.

Vansina, Jan. 1956. "Migrations dans la province du
Kasai: Une hypothèse" ("Migrations in Kasai province:
An hypothesis"). Zaire 10:69-85.

van Velsen, J. 1961. "Labour migration as a positive
factor in the continuity of Tonga tribal society."
In Aidan Southall, ed., Social change in modern Africa
London, Oxford University Press, pp. 230-241.

1963. "Some methodological problems of the study of
labour migration." In University of Edinburgh, Centre
of African Studies, Urbanization in African social
change: Proceedings of the Inaugural Seminar held in
the Centre, January 5-7. Edinburgh, pp. 34-42.

Vennetier, Pierre. 1957. "Banlieue noire de Brazzaville:
La vie rurale et les rapports entre la ville et la
campagne à Bacongo" ("The black suburb of Brazzaville:
Rural life and the relationship between city and
Bakongo countryside"). Cahiers d'Outre-Mer 10:131-
157.

1963. "L'urbanisation et ses conséquences au Congo
[Brazzaville]" ("Urbanization and its consequences
to the Congo [Brazzaville]"). Cahiers d'Outre-Mer
16(63):263-280.

Venter, Herman J. 1962. "Urbanization and industriali-
zation as criminogenic factors in the Republic of
South Africa." International Review of Criminal
Policy 20:59-67.*

Verhaegen, Benoit, and Maurice Lovens. 1964. "La fonc-
tion politique des villes au Congo" ("The political
function of cities in the Congo"). Cahiers Economiques et Sociaux 2(3):271-279.

Verhaegen, P. 1962. L'urbanisation de l'Afrique noire:
Son cadre, ses causes et ses conséquences économique,
sociale et culturelle (The urbanization of Black
Africa: Its framework and its economic, social, and
cultural causes and effects). Brussels, Centre de
Documentation Economique et Sociale Africaine.

Vidich, Arthur J., and Joseph Bensman. 1958. Small
town in mass society: Class, power and religion in a
rural community. Princeton, Princeton University
Press.**

Villien-Rossi, Marie-Louise. 1966. "Bamako, capital de
Mali" ("Bamako, capital of Mali"). Bulletin IFAN 28B
(1 & 2):249-380.

Wallace, Anthony F. C. 1952. Housing and social structure. Philadelphia, Philadelphia Housing Authority.**

Wallerstein, Immanuel. 1960. "Ethnicity and national
integration in West Africa." Cahiers d'Etudes Africaines 3:129-139.

1961. Africa: The politics of independence. New York,
Vintage Books.

1964a. "Class, tribe, and party in West African
politics." Transactions of Fifth World Congress of
Sociology 3:203-216.

1964b. "Voluntary associations." In James S. Coleman
and Carl G. Rosberg, Jr., eds., Political parties
and national integration in tropical Africa. Berkeley,
University of California Press, pp. 318-339.

1965. "Migration in West Africa: The political perspective." In Hilda Kuper, ed., Urbanization and
migration in West Africa. Berkeley, University of
California Press, pp. 148-159.

1966a. "The decline of the part in single-party African states." In Joseph LaPalombara and Myron Weiner, eds., <u>Political parties</u> and <u>political development</u>. Princeton, Princeton University Press, pp. 201-214.

1966b. <u>Social change: The colonial situation</u>, Ed. New York, John Wiley & Sons.✲✲

Wallis, C. A. G. 1958. "The administration of towns in the Belgian Congo." Journal of African Administration 10(2):95-100.

Wallis, H. R. 1920. <u>The handbook of Uganda</u>, 2nd ed. London, Crown Agents for the Colonies.

Ward, Robert E., and Dankwart A. Rustow. 1964. "Conclusion." In Robert E. Ward and Dankwart A. Rustow, eds., <u>Political modernization in Japan and Turkey</u>. Princeton, Princeton University Press, pp. 434-468.✲✲

Warren, Roland L. 1963. <u>The community in America</u>. Chicago, Rand McNally.✲✲

1966. <u>Studying your community</u>. New York, Free Press of Glencoe.✲✲

Warren, W. M. 1966. "Urban real wages and the Nigerian trade union movement, 1939-1960." Economic Development and Cultural Change 15(1):21-36.

<u>Washington Post</u>. 1966. "The second Watts." March 17, p. A20.✲✲

Wassermann, Ursula. 1966. "West Africa's drug-takers." West Africa, No. 2567:915-916.

Watson, William. 1958. <u>Tribal cohesion in a money economy</u>. Manchester, Manchester University Press for the Rhodes-Livingstone Institute.

1959. "Migrant labour and detribalisation." Inter-African Labour Institute Bulletin 6(2):8-33.

1967. "Migrant labor in Africa: A consideration of its various forms and their relation to traditional and bureaucratic socio-economic systems." Paper read at the Annual Meeting of the African Studies Association, New York, New York, 1-4 November.

Weber, Max. 1958. The city. Glencoe, Ill., Free Press.✵✵

Weinberg, Leonard. 1964. "Party politics in West Africa." Genève-Afrique 3(2):180-242.

Weinberg, S. Kirson. n.d. "Urbanization and delinquency in West Africa." Estudios de Sociología 9:139-154.

1964. "Juvenile delinquency in Ghana: A comparative analysis of delinquents and non-delinquents." Journal of Criminal Law, Criminology and Police Science 55:471-481.

1965. "Urbanization and male delinquency in Ghana." Journal of Research in Crime and Delinquency 2(2): 85-94.

Weiner, Myron. 1967. "Urbanization and political protest." Civilisations 17:44-52.✵✵

Weiss, Herbert F. 1967. Political protest in the Congo: The Parti Solidaire Africain during the independence struggle. Princeton, Princeton University Press.

Weissleder, Wolfgang. 1964. "The socio-political character of an historical Ethiopian capital." In East African Institute of Social Research, January Conference Proceedings.✵

Weissmann, Ernest. 1965. "The urban crisis in the world." Urban Affairs Quarterly 1:65-81.✵✵

Welch, Claude E. 1965. "The growth of political consciousness among the Ewe." Paper read at the Annual Meeting of the American Anthropological Association, Denver.

Welldon, R. M. C. 1957. "The human geography of a Yoruba township in Southwestern Nigeria, I & II." Unpublished bachelor's thesis, Oxford University.

Werlin, Herbert Holland. 1963. "Profile of Nairobi in the time of Uhuru." Africa Today 10(10):7-10.

_____. 1964. "The politics of Nairobi." In East African Institute of Social Research, January Conference Proceedings.

_____. 1966a. "The Nairobi City Council: The problems of cooperation in African local politics." Unpublished doctoral dissertation, University of California, Berkeley.

_____. 1966b. "The Nairobi City Council: A study in comparative local government." Comparative Studies in Society and History 8:181-198.

West Africa. 1966a. "Finecountry done come-o." No. 2581:1331.

_____. 1966b. "Nigeria on the move." No. 2544:265.

_____. 1966c. "People under pressure." No. 2562:763.

Wheaton, William L. C. 1964. "Integration at the urban level: Political influence and the decision process." In Philip E. Jacob and James V. Toscano, eds., The integration of political communities. Philadelphia, J. B. Lippincott Company, pp. 120-142.**

_____. 1967. "Moving from plan to reality." In Leo F. Schnore and Henry Fagin, eds., Urban research and policy planning (Urban Affairs Annual Reviews, I) Beverly Hills, Sage Publications, pp. 521-547.**

Wheelis, Allen. 1958. The quest for identity. New York, W. W. Norton & Company.**

Whitaker, C. S., Jr. 1967. "A dysrhythmic process of political change." World Politics 19(2):190-217.

White, C. M. N. 1964. "The changing scope of urban native courts in Northern Rhodesia." Journal of African Law 8(1):29-33.

Whiteley, Wilfred. 1954. "Modern local government among the Makua." Africa 24:349-358.

Whitten, Norman E., Jr. 1965. Class, kinship, and power in an Ecuadorian town: The Negroes of San Lorenzo. Stanford, Stanford University Press.**

Whittlesey, Derwent. 1937. "Kano, a Sudanese metropolis." Geographical Review 27:177-199.

1941. "Dakar and the other Cape Verde settlements." Geographical Review 31:609-638.

Williams, Babatunde A., and Annmarie Hauck Walsh. In press. Urban government for metropolitan Lagos. New York, Frederick A. Praeger.

Williams, Oliver P., and Charles R. Adrian. 1963. Four cities: A study in comparative policy making. Philadelphia, University of Pennsylvania Press.**

Williams, P. Morton. 1956. "A discussion of the theory of elites in a West African (Yoruba) context." In (Proceedings of the) West African Institute of Social and Economic Research. Ibadan, University College of Ibadan, pp. 25-32.

Williams, Robin M., Jr. 1947. "The reduction of intergroup tensions: A survey of research on problems of ethnic, racial, and religious group relations." Social Science Research Council Bulletin 57:514-515.**

1951. American society: A sociological interpretation. New York, Alfred A. Knopf.**

1957. "Unity and diversity in modern America." Social Forces 36:1-8.**

Williams, Robin M., Jr., et al. 1964. Strangers next

door. Englewood Cliffs, N.J., Prentice-Hall.✻✻

Wilner, Daniel M., and Rosabelle Price Walkley. 1963. "Effects of housing on health and performance." In Leonard J. Duhl, ed., The urban condition. New York, Basic Books, pp. 215-228.✻✻

Wilson, Elizabeth. 1963. "Lusaka: A city of tropical Africa." Geography 25(221):411-414.

Wilson, Godfrey. 1936. "An African morality." Africa 9:75-98.

1941-1942. An essay on the economics of detribaliza-tion in Northern Rhodesia. Rhodes-Livingstone Insti-tute, Papers 5 and 6.

Wilson, Godfrey, and Monica Wilson. 1945. The analysis of social change. Cambridge, Cambridge University Press.✻✻

Wilson, Gordon. 1961. "Mombasa--A modern colonial municipality." In Aidan Southall, ed., Social change in modern Africa. London, Oxford University Press, pp. 98-112.

Wilson, Monica, and Archie Majefe. 1963. Langa: A study of social groups in an African township. Cape Town, Oxford University Press.✻

Winch, R. F., and S. A. Greer. 1968. "Urbanism, ethnicity and extended familism." Journal of Mar-riage and Family 30:40-45.✻✻

Winder, R. Bayly. 1962. "The Lebanese in West Africa." Comparative Studies in Society and History 4:296-333.

Wingo, Lowdon, Jr. 1967. "Recent patterns of urbaniza-tion among Latin American countries." Urban Affairs 2(3):81-109.✻✻

Winter, E. H. 1953. Bwanba economy. Kampala, East African Institute of Social Research.

Wipper, Audrey. 1964. "A comparative study of nascent unionism in French West Africa and the Philippines." Economic Development and Cultural Change 13(1):20-55.

Wirth, Louis. 1938. "Urbanism as a way of life." American Journal of Sociology 44:1-24.**

1964. On cities and social life: Selected papers. Albert J. Reiss, Jr., ed. Chicago, University of Chicago Press.**

Woddis, J. 1962. "Role of the African working class in the national liberation movement." World Marxist Review 5(7):44-50.

Wolf, Eleanor P., and Charles N. Lebeaux. 1967a. "Class and race in the changing city; Searching for new approaches to old problems." In Leo F. Schnore and Henry Fagin, eds., Urban research and policy planning (Urban Affairs Annual Reviews, I) Beverly Hills, Sage Publications, pp. 99-129.**

1967b. "On the destruction of poor neighborhoods by urban renewal." Social Problems 15(1):3-8.**

Wolf, Eric R. 1966. "Kinship, friendship, and patron-client relations in complex societies." In Michael Banton, ed., The social anthropology of complex societies. New York, Frederick A. Praeger, pp. 1-22.**

Wolff, Kurt H. 1964. "Social control." In Julius Gould and William L. Kolb, eds., A dictionary of the social sciences. London, Tavistock Publications.**

Wolfinger, Raymond. 1965. "The development and persistence of ethnic voting." American Political Science Review 59:896-908.**

Wolpe, Howard. 1965. "Local government for what?" Nigerian Opinion 1(7):10-12.

1966. "Port Harcourt--A community of strangers: The politics of urban development in Eastern Nigeria."

Unpublished doctoral dissertation, M.I.T.

Wood, Eric. 1968. "The implications of migrant labour for urban social systems in Africa." Cahiers d'Etudes Africaines 8(1):5-31.

Wood, James R., and Omer R. Galle. 1965. "Urbanization, industrialization, and modernization: The South American experience." Unpublished manuscript, Vanderbilt University.**

Woodhouse, Charles E., and Henry J. Tobias. 1966. "Primordial ties and political process in pre-revolutionary Russia: The case of the Jewish bund." Comparative Studies in Society and History 8:331-360.**

Woodroffe, I. 1957. "The relationship between central and local government in Africa." Journal of African Administration 9:3-15.

Worsley, Peter. 1964. The third world. Chicago, University of Chicago Press.**

Wraith, Ronald E. 1959. East African citizen. London, Oxford University Press.

        1964. Local government in West Africa. New York, Frederick A. Praeger.

        1965. "Institutional training in Africa." Journal of Local Administration Overseas 4:27-37 and 79-87.

Wraith, Ronald, and Edgar Simpkins. 1963. Corruption in developing countries. New York, W. W. Norton & Company.

Wright, A. C. A. 1945. "Notes on the Iteso social organization." Uganda Journal 9(2):57.

Wrigley, C. C. 1956. "The development of a middle class in British East Africa." In International Institute of Differing Civilizations, Development of a middle class in tropical and sub-tropical countries. Brussels, pp. 213-221.

Wrong, Dennis, H. 1961. "The oversocialized conception
of man in modern sociology." American Sociological
Review 26(2):183-193.**

Wurster, Catherine Bauer. 1960. "Urban living condi-
tions, overhead costs, and the development pattern."
In Roy Turner, ed., India's urban future. Berkeley,
University of California Press, pp. 277-298.**

Xydias, Nelly. 1956. "Labor: Conditions, aptitudes,
training." In International African Institute,
Social implications of industrialization and urbanization in Africa south of the Sahara. Paris, UNESCO,
pp. 275-367.

Yesofu, T. M. 1962. An introduction to industrial relations in Nigeria. London, Oxford University Press.

Young, Michael, and Peter Willmott. 1957. Family and
kinship in East London. New York, Free Press of
Glencoe.**

Zack, Arnold. 1964. Labor training in developing
countries: A challenge in responsible democracy.
New York, Frederick A. Praeger.**

Zahan, D. 1956. "Immigrant communities of the Office
of Niger." In International African Institute,
Social implications of industrialization and urbanization in Africa south of the Sahara. Paris, UNESCO,
pp. 99-101.

Zaire. 1951. "L'administration indigène à Nairobi"
("Indigenous administration in Nairobi"). 5:1067-
1069.

Zambia, 1964. Second report of the May/June, 1963
census of Africans. Lusaka, Ministry of Finance.

(Zambia) Northern Rhodesia. 1958. African affairs
annual report for the year 1957. Lusaka, Government
Printer.

(Zambia) Northern Rhodesia, Commission of Inquiry into

Unrest on the Copperbelt. 1963. Report, July-August, 1963. Lusaka, Government Printer.

(Zambia) Northern Rhodesia, Ministry of Local Government and Social Welfare. 1959. Report on the preliminary investigations into the complaints as to the conduct and management of the affairs of the Municipal Council of Luanshya. Lusaka, Government Printer.

Zolberg, Aristide R. 1964. One-party government in the Ivory Coast. Princeton, Princeton University Press.

1966a. Creating political order: The party-states of West Africa. Chicago, Rand McNally.

1966b. "Political problems of African unemployment." Paper read at the African Research Committee Conference on Unemployment in Africa, Evanston, 6-7 May.

1967. "Political development in tropical Africa: Center and periphery." In Local development in Africa: A summary of a conference sponsored by the Foreign Service Institute of the United States Department of State, The Africa Subcommittee of the Foreign Area Research Coordination Group, and The Agency for International Development, Washington, D.C., 18-19 July, pp. 14-15.

Zollschan, George K., and Walter Hirsch, eds. 1964. Explorations in social change. Boston, Houghton Mifflin Company.**

Index

379

Urban Dynamics in Black Africa